Treasurer's and Controller's Financial Acccounting Desk Book

Treasurer's and Controller's Financial Accounting Desk Book

Martin F. Towles, CPA

Prentice-Hall, Inc., Englewood Cliffs, N.J.

Prentice-Hall International, Inc., *London*
Prentice-Hall of Australia, Pty. Ltd., *Sydney*
Prentice-Hall of Canada, Ltd., *Toronto*
Prentice-Hall of India Private Ltd., *New Delhi*
Prentice-Hall of Japan, Inc., *Tokyo*
Prentice-Hall of Southeast Asia Pte. Ltd., *Singapore*
Whitehall Books, Ltd., *Wellington, New Zealand*

Library of Congress Cataloging in Publication Data

Towles, Martin F
    Treasurer's and controller's financial accounting
desk book.

    Includes bibliographical references and index.
    1. Accounting—Problems, exercises, etc.
I. Title.
HF5635.T673   657'.48   79-26864
ISBN 0-13-930453-3

Printed in the United States of America

ABOUT THE AUTHOR

Martin F. Towles is a CPA and has a degree in accounting from Johns Hopkins University. Presently a manager with the firm of Wooden and Benson, Baltimore, Maryland, Mr. Towles has more than 25 years of practical experience with national, regional, and local accounting firms. He has supervised and conducted audits of banks, savings and loan associations, investment bankers, insurance companies, hospitals, charitable organizations, radio broadcasting companies, construction contractors, real estate firms, government agencies, housing developers as well as a wide range of companies engaged in manufacturing, and wholesale and retail enterprises.

Mr. Towles is a contributor to national accounting periodicals; a member of the American Institute of Certified Public Accountants, the American Accounting Association, and the Maryland Association of Certified Public Accountants; and the author of *Practical Accounting Systems and Procedures*, published by Prentice-Hall, Inc. in 1978.

ACKNOWLEDGMENT

The author wishes to express gratitude to his daughter, Louise T. Bindseil, for her work in editing and correcting the text of the manuscript for this book. Also, acknowledgment is made to the American Institute of Certified Public Accountants and the Financial Accounting Standards Board for permission to use excerpts from their Institute publications.

A Word from the Author

Here are specific techniques for practical solutions to perplexing financial accounting problems that arise in implementing the vast array of complex and highly technical directives now being issued by authoritative accounting bodies. This book will provide tools which enable the reader to contend successfully with the new accounting requirements by establishing short-cut, time-and-money-saving accounting systems and procedures.

Thus, the overriding objective of the book is to demonstrate explicit techniques for the practical solution of problems encountered in the application of the provisions of a series of official accounting directives, and to illustrate appropriate procedures for recording the financial accounting effects of such solutions. To that end, the author has prepared eleven chapters comprehending the significant and highly essential areas of financial accounting concerned with income tax allocation; earnings per share; non-monetary transactions; capital, sales-type, direct financing, and leveraged leases; marketable equity securities; capital changes; allocation of the cost of depreciable assets; reporting changes in financial position; and accounting for Subchapter S operations. In each chapter he has formulated examples of genuine accounting problems which exhibit the essential characteristics of problems encountered in the important areas of financial accounting selected for exposition. Every chapter in the book contains case studies constructed for the purpose of fixing these complex problems within a realistic framework of accounting processes, and includes tables, schedules, mathematical formulas, algorithms of electronic calculator keystroke sequences, journal entries, and fully developed financial statements to illustrate examples of, and to demonstrate quick, step-by-step, how-to-do-it solutions to, the complex problems involved in the studies, such as:

Allocation of Income Taxes

Comprehensive schedules showing origination and reversal of timing differences created by such events as accelerated depreciation, installment sales, warranty expense, lease obligations, deferred pension expense, purchased subsidiaries, investee accounting, and interim reporting are used to illustrate pretax accounting income; adjustments for, and accumulation and amortization of timing differences; the effect on pretax accounting income; and both current and deferred income tax expense. Complex timing differences created by loss carryforwards where deferred taxes already exist are displayed in similar schedules, which also are designed to reflect extraordinary credits and provisions in lieu of income taxes. These schedules are presented in tabular form, and cover the entire period of amortization, thus rendering the total effect of the creation and amortization of deferred income taxes readily comprehensible.

Accounting for Leases

Computational techniques for present values of lease obligation are graphically demonstrated by illustrations of algebraic, logarithmic, tabular, and electronic calculator methods of solution. Algorithms of electronic calculator keystroke sequences demonstrate almost instantaneous computation of compound interest, present value of an amount at compound interest, amount of an annuity, and the present value of an annuity. The chapter displays detailed schedules which reflect analyses of lease provisions, classification data, application of lease classification criteria, and determination of appropriate accounting treatment. In connection with capitalized leases, schedules were prepared to show liquidation of the lease obligation and depreciation of the leased asset. Comprehensive and exhaustive schedules have been prepared for leveraged lease operations and include separate schedules for analysis of the lease agreement and financing arrangement, loan amortization, depreciation, taxable income derived from the lease, annual cash flow, allocation of annual cash flow to investment income, components of income, and entries required to record the leveraged lease transaction.

Marketable Securities

Particularized schedules have been prepared for both single and consolidated enterprises which illustrate transactions in marketable securities occurring in both current and noncurrent portfolios. Each schedule reflects cost, market, excess of cost over market, purchase, sale, transfer between portfolios, realized gain, and unrealized gain or loss for every individual security in the portfolios. Separate schedules were prepared to provide examples of security transactions by entities within an industry having specialized accounting practices with respect to marketable securities. A set of financial statements has been prepared to illustrate the reporting requirements for marketable securities, including required disclosure in notes to the statements, and examples of the negative stockholders' equity account representing unrealized loss on marketable securities.

Depreciation Accounting

Comprehensive schedules have been prepared which tabularize the interaction of cost, rate of allocation, periodic depreciation, accumulated depreciation, net book value and, where applicable, imputed interest and income tax timing differences. The schedules cover examples of both single and multiple asset accounts, and illustrate the following methods of cost allocation: straight-line, declining-balance, sum-of-the-digits, units-of-production, hours-of-production, depletion-oriented, sinking-fund, and annuity.

Algebraic equations are used to demonstrate techniques for computing values required in the use of the declining-balance, sum-of-the-digits, sinking-fund, and annuity methods of depreciation, and for changing from declining balance to straight-line allocation. An illustration of instantaneous computation of the involved formula for determining a constant rate for the declining-balance method is provided by an algorithm for a short series of keystrokes on an electronic calculator.

Reporting Changes in Financial Position

Worksheets have been prepared which demonstrate computation of the values to be assigned to the elements of the funds statement under the cash funds, working capital, and all financial resources concepts. A series of funds statements have been prepared from the worksheets to illustrate reporting formats for all three concepts referred to above, and the series includes illustrations of funds statements for entities that have a classified balance sheet as well as those which do not classify balance sheet components.

Subchapter S Corporations

The chapter on Subchapter S corporations was designed to provide comprehensive procedures for the special accounting requirements of Subchapter S corporations and, to that end, extensive schedules have been prepared which summarize income and dividends paid and analyze the attendant changes that occur in stockholders' equity with respect to specific accounts representing current earnings and profits, undistributed taxable income, previously taxed income, accumulated earnings and profits, and paid-in capital for tax purposes. The schedules illustrate accounting for Subchapter S corporations in the separate circumstances where operations are generally normal; capital gains and preference taxes arise; excess depreciation occurs from using the straight line methods for financial accounting and accelerated depreciation for tax purposes; allocating dividends under the special election provided by IRS regulations section 1.1575-4(c); and the election and termination of tax option status.

In addition to providing explicit solutions to practical problems exemplified in case studies, the text takes a unique approach to certain theoretical concepts set forth in the accounting directives that is not generally found in other accounting literature, for example:

Algorithms of Keystroke Sequences for Electronic Calculators

Throughout the book computational techniques are oriented to the use of algebraic equations, rather than the use of voluminous published value tables, and the book contains a series of keystroke sequences that demonstrate almost instantaneous solution to these equations.

Earnings per Share

The chapter on earnings per share is designed for entities having a simple capital structure and, accordingly, the intricate, complicated, and highly technical rules concerned with the dilution concept are omitted, and the text of the chapter goes directly to the earnings per share problems of corporations that do not issue dilutive rights nor potentially dilutive convertible securities. Illustrations contained in the chapter with reference to earnings per share for corporations with incomplex capital structures include computation of the weighted average of shares outstanding based on daily, monthly, and quarterly changes; computation of weighted averages for business combinations accounted for as poolings of interest; computation of earnings per share; adjustment to net income to compute earnings per share; claims of senior securities; net income resulting in loss per share; and the two-class method of computing earnings per share for participating securities.

Capital Changes

The available official guidelines for accounting for capital changes are obscurely embodied in an irregular series of official publications that date from 1934 to the present. The chapter on capital changes assembles and presents these directives in logical and continuous order, identifies each specific directive, sets forth its provisions, and illustrates accounting procedures designed to comply with its requirements.

The author believes that the preformulated accounting problems set forth in this volume will parallel those encountered in actual practice by the reader and, further, that the algorithmic-oriented method of solution of such problems demonstrated in the book will provide the reader with quick, time-saving accounting processes that will improve the character and quality of his work, and the profitability of his occupation.

Martin F. Towles

Table of Contents

7. **Marketable Securities—Valuation Standards, Accounting Procedures and Reporting Requirements** **184**

8. **Capital Changes—Accounting for Nonrevenue Adjustments in Stockholders' Equity Accounts** **211**

10. Reporting Changes in Financial Position—Concepts, Formats, and Elements of Disclosure 284

1

Interperiod Allocation of Income Taxes—
Computational Techniques and
Accounting Procedures

The process of allocating income taxes requires accounting procedures that permit income tax expense to be appropriately associated with the income that generates the tax obligation. The circumstances that require allocation develop from the fact that, in some instances, income tax regulations impose a tax on an indicated gain prior to the time it is realized for financial accounting purposes and, in other instances, the regulations permit taxpayers to take tax deductions in advance of the time the corresponding expenses are recognized for financial reporting.

When transactions have tax effects in accounting periods different from the periods in which they enter into the determination of financial accounting income, such differences are generally referred to as "timing differences," and these differences create the conditions that require interperiod tax allocation.

After World War II it became apparent to accountants that income taxes are an expense of business enterprise, not a division of earnings, and they began to recognize the need for sophisticated procedures for tax allocation to account for tax effects of transactions which involve timing differences. However, divergent interpretations of the nature of timing differences resulted in the formulation of a variety of allocation concepts and the adoption of many different methods of applying allocation procedures.

The American Institute of Certified Public Accountants was aware of the almost chaotic conditions surrounding accountants' practical application of tax allocation methods and finally, in December 1967, after an enormous amount of controversy among accountants, its Accounting Principles Board (APB) published Opinion No. 11 which was designed to require uniform accounting for income taxes. The primary objective of the Opinion was to standardize accounting for income taxes by announcing a precise allocation concept, specifying an acceptable allocation procedure, providing criteria for the measurement of deferred income taxes, and formulating guidelines for applying the tax allocation method.

This chapter explains the provisions of the Opinion, demonstrates computational techniques for measuring deferred income taxes, and illustrates appropriate accounting procedures for recording and reporting income tax expense.

PRINCIPLES OF INCOME TAX ALLOCATION

THE PROBLEMS SURROUNDING TAX ALLOCATION

As indicated in a preceding paragraph, the federal tax structure is such that some income tax regulations create conditions wherein certain transactions have tax effects in accounting periods other than the accounting period in which the transactions enter into the determination of financial accounting income. Thus, income taxes determined to be payable for a period do not necessarily represent the appropriate income tax expense for that period. Such discrepancies between income taxes payable and income tax expense generally require appropriate allocation of income taxes between accounting periods. In its efforts to outline specific allocation procedures, the Accounting Principles Board encountered major problems in the areas of reconciling the principles of the matching concept to those of the realization concept, determining proper intraperiod allocation of tax expense to classified components of the income statement, and providing for adequate and informative disclosure in financial statements.

The Matching Concept

Matching is a fundamental concept of income determination, and the principles of the matching concept require that costs be associated with specific revenue, and that such costs and revenue be identified with the accounting period in which the resulting net income is realized, or net loss recognized. Revenue and costs identified with future periods are required to be deferred or accrued, and costs that cannot be identified with either current or future revenues are required to be recognized as an expense of the current period. The matching of income tax expense of a particular accounting period with the income of that period is not, in itself, a complicated problem if the revenue and expenses of the period have been previously accrued, deferred, and properly matched, and are reasonably identifiable for analysis purposes. However, a major problem arises in matching the tax benefits of loss carrybacks and carryforwards with the income of the periods to which they are carried, and the problem increases in complexity when there has been deferral or accrual of income tax expenses in prior accounting periods.

The Realization Concept

A second fundamental concept of income determination is that of realization, and one of the principles of the realization concept requires that the benefits from accrued income entering into the determination of current income be assured beyond a reasonable doubt. Theoretically, the tax benefits of loss carryforwards to future accounting periods should be allocated to the year in which the loss is sustained. However, a serious problem in tax allocation is developed by the fact that the tax benefits of loss carryforwards can be realized only if the tax-paying enterprise in the seven years following the loss has taxable income sufficient to absorb the benefits of the loss carryover. The problem is further complicated where there have been previous deferrals of income tax expense in the loss carryback years, and realization of the tax benefits of such deferrals is currently in doubt.

Intraperiod Tax Allocation Problems

Problems of intraperiod income tax allocation are encountered in cases where the components of the income statement are classified as to operating income and expenses, nonrecurring items, extraordinary items, prior period adjustments, and direct entries to stockholders' equity accounts. The problems of intraperiod allocation are further complicated where operating income and expenses result in a net loss before consideration of attendant nonrecurring items, extraordinary items, etc.

Problems of Disclosure

Both interperiod and intraperiod allocation of income tax expense pose the important problem of appropriate and adequate disclosure in the financial statements. The problems of disclosure of intraperiod allocation involve computational techniques and classification policies, and the problems encountered in interperiod allocation revolve around informative disclosure of the results of applying the principles of the matching concept and of the realization concept, and an explanation of the allocation method applied in situations where the principles of the two separate concepts are in conflict.

SPECIFIC PRINCIPLES OF INCOME TAX ALLOCATION

In stating its conclusions on the problems described in the preceding paragraphs the Board, in effect, announced a set of five specific principles of income tax allocation. Paragraph 19 of the Opinion sets forth in five subparagraphs the conclusions reached by the Board. These conclusions are indicated below by their subparagraph designation, and are quoted verbatim:[1]

   a. Interperiod tax allocation is an integral part of the determination of income tax expense, and income tax expense should include the tax effects of revenue and expense transactions included in the determination of pretax accounting income.
   b. Interperiod tax allocation procedures should follow the deferred method both in the manner in which tax effects are initially recognized and in the manner in which deferred taxes are amortized in future periods.
   c. The tax effects of operating loss carrybacks should be allocated to the loss periods. The tax effects of operating loss carryforwards usually should not be recognized until the periods of realization.
   d. Tax allocation within a period should be applied to obtain fair presentation of the various components of results of operations.
   e. Financial statements presentations of income tax expense and related deferred taxes should disclose (1) the composition of income tax expense as between amounts currently payable and amounts representing tax effects allocable to the period and (2) the classification of deferred taxes into a net current amount and a net noncurrent amount.

DIFFERENCES BETWEEN TAXABLE AND ACCOUNTING INCOME

Two distinct types of differences between taxable income and financial accounting income can occur within an accounting period. These differences are referred to in the Opinion as "permanent differences" and "timing differences."

PRETAX ACCOUNTING INCOME

The Opinion defines "pretax accounting income" as income or loss for a period, exclusive of the related income tax expense.

PERMANENT DIFFERENCES

Permanent differences are differences between taxable income and pretax accounting income which develop in circumstances where an enterprise has nontaxable in-

---

[1]*Accounting for Income Taxes,* Opinion of the Accounting Principles Board No. 11. (New York, NY: Copyright 1967 by the American Institute of Certified Public Accountants.)

come, unallowable deductions, or is entitled to specific tax credits. Examples of such items are: interest from municipal bonds, premiums paid on officers' life insurance, and deductions for dividends received. Permanent differences affect only the accounting period in which they occur and the tax effects of such differences are not susceptible of interperiod allocation.

TIMING DIFFERENCES

Timing differences are differences between the periods in which transactions affect taxable income and the periods in which they enter into determination of pretax accounting income. Timing differences are created in circumstances where the differential between taxes payable and taxes computed on pretax accounting income for a particular accounting period is temporary and will be reversed subsequent to the period in which it occurred. Since the timing differences created by such differentials will reduce or increase income taxes that would otherwise be payable in either the current period or in one or more subsequent periods, income tax expense should be allocated to the affected accounting period in relation to the pretax accounting income of each respective period without regard to the income taxes to be paid in that period.

The following types of transactions give rise to timing differences that originate in one accounting period and reverse in one or more subsequent periods:

    a. Revenues and gains that are taxed subsequent to accrual for accounting purposes,
    b. Expenses or losses deducted for tax purposes subsequent to accrual for accounting purposes,
    c. Revenues and gains taxed prior to accrual for accounting purposes, and
    d. Expenses or losses deducted for tax purposes prior to accrual for accounting purposes.

THE ALLOCATION CONCEPT AND METHOD OF APPLICATION

In forming its design for standard income tax accounting procedures, the Board elected to direct accountants to adhere to the "comprehensive" allocation concept and to follow the "deferred" method of applying conceptual principles.

COMPREHENSIVE ALLOCATION

The comprehensive concept of income tax allocation requires that income tax expense include the tax effects of revenue and expense transactions included in the determination of pretax accounting income.

DEFERRED METHOD

The deferred method of interperiod tax allocation is a procedure whereby the tax effects of current timing differences are deferred currently and allocated to income tax expense of future periods when the timing differences reverse.

ELEMENTS OF THE BOARD'S OPINIONS

Accounting Principles Board Opinion No. 11 comprehends five segments dealing separately with income tax allocation, operating losses, tax allocation within a period, other unused credits and deductions, and financial reporting. The following recapitulation sets forth the essential elements of each segment of the Opinion:

OPINION ON TAX ALLOCATION

1. The comprehensive concept should be used.
2. The deferred method should be used.
3. The effects of timing differences should be measured by the differential between income taxes computed with and without including the transactions creating the difference between taxable income and pretax accounting income.
4. Timing differences may be considered individually or similar timing differences may be grouped.
5. The net change in deferred taxes for a period for a group of similar timing differences may be determined on the basis of either:
   (a) The net tax effects of timing differences originating at current rates less reversals of timing differences originating in prior periods at the rates as of the beginning of the period, or
   (b) The tax effects of the net change in the cumulative timing difference where timing differences are recorded on a cumulative basis.

OPINION ON OPERATING LOSSES

1. The tax effects of realized loss carrybacks should be recognized in the loss year.
2. Appropriate adjustment of existing net deferred tax credits should be made in the loss period, if necessary.
3. Tax effects of loss carryforwards generally should not be recognized until actually realized.
4. Where loss carryforwards are realized in subsequent periods, the tax benefits should be reported in those periods as extraordinary items.
5. When, at the time loss carryforwards arise, realization of the tax benefits therefrom is assured beyond any reasonable doubt, the potential benefits should be recognized in the loss period.

   (a) The benefits should be computed at the rates expected to be in effect at the time of realization.
   (b) If the tax rate used in the computation changes, the effect of the change should be accounted for in the period of the change as an adjustment of the asset account and of income tax expense.
   (c) There should be no adjustment of deferred tax credits existing when the carryforward benefits are recognized in the loss period and they should be amortized by the normal deferred method.
   (d) Realization of the tax benefits of loss carryforwards would appear to be assured beyond any reasonable doubt when both of the following conditions exist:
       (1) the loss results from an identifiable, isolated, and nonrecurring cause and the company has been continuously profitable over a long period, and
       (2) future taxable income is virtually certain to be sufficient to offset the loss carryforward during the permitted loss carryforward period.
6. *Net deferred tax credits existing at the time a loss carryforward arises:*
   (a) Net deferred tax credits should be eliminated to the extent of the lower of:
       (1) the tax effect of the loss carryforward, or
       (2) the amortization that would otherwise have occurred during the loss carryforward period.
   (b) Where loss carryforwards are realized in whole or in part in periods subsequent to the loss period eliminated deferred tax credits should be restored at the then current tax rates on a cumulative basis to the extent the loss carryforward is realized.
7. The tax effects of loss carryforwards of purchased subsidiaries should be recognized as assets at date of purchase *only* if realization is assured beyond any reasonable doubt. When such benefits are actually realized they should be recorded as retroactive adjustments of the purchase transaction.

8. Tax effects of loss carryforwards arising prior to a quasi-reorganization should be recorded as assets at the date of the quasi-reorganization *only* if realization is assured beyond a reasonable doubt. If subsequently the benefits are actually realized, the tax effects should be added to contributed capital.

OPINION ON TAX ALLOCATION WITHIN A PERIOD

1. Tax allocation within a period should be applied to obtain an appropriate relationship between income tax expense and:
   (a) income before extraordinary items,
   (b) extraordinary items,
   (c) prior period adjustments, and
   (d) direct entries to stockholders' equity accounts.
2. The income tax expense attributable to each of the above items is determined by the tax consequences of transactions involving those items.
3. If an operating loss exists before extraordinary items, the tax consequences of such loss should be associated with the loss.

OPINION ON OTHER UNUSED DEDUCTIONS AND CREDITS

The conclusions of the Opinion on operating losses also apply to other unused deductions and credits that may be carried backward or forward in determining taxable income.

OPINION ON FINANCIAL REPORTING

1. *Balance Sheet*
   (a) Deferred income tax debits and deferred income tax credits should be classified into net current amounts and net noncurrent amounts.
   (b) Receivables representing refunds due for loss carrybacks or carryforwards should be classified either as current or noncurrent.
2. *Income Statement*
   (a) The components of income tax expense for a period should be described.
   (b) The expense should be allocated to income before extraordinary items and to extraordinary items.
   (c) Realization of the benefits of a loss carryforward should be reported as an extraordinary item.
   (d) Tax effects attributable to prior period adjustments and direct entries to stockholders' equity accounts should be presented as adjustments of such items with disclosure of the amounts of the tax effects.
3. *General*
   The following disclosures should be made in notes to the financial statements:
   (a) Amounts of unused operating loss carryforwards together with expiration dates,
   (b) Amounts of any other unused deductions or credits together with expiration dates,
   (c) Reasons for variations in the customary relationship between income tax expense and pretax accounting income, and
   (d) Nature of the difference between pretax accounting income and taxable income.
4. *"Net of Tax" Presentation*
   The tax effects of timing differences should be reported in the income statement as elements of income tax expense and the "net of tax" form of presentation should not be used for such tax effects. The tax effects of timing differences should be reported on the balance sheet as deferred taxes and not as elements of valuation of assets or liabilities.

COMPUTATIONAL TECHNIQUES

Computations for the measurement of deferred income taxes can be very intricate, but they are not necessarily complicated unless the realization of loss carrybacks and carryforwards, and the attendant elimination and restoration of existing deferred tax debits and credits, become factors in the calculations.

This section demonstrates computational techniques for measuring deferred income taxes for all of the situations covered in the Opinion, and illustrates appropriate accounting procedures for recording income tax expense in each case.

COMPUTATION OF DEFERRED TAXES

The Opinion states that the effect of a timing difference should be measured by the differential between income taxes computed with and without inclusion of the transactions that create the difference between taxable income and pretax accounting income. In practice, however, the same effect is achieved by simply applying the current rate to the amount of the timing difference. Caution must be exercised to determine that the timing difference, itself, does not cause a change in rates; for example, change taxable income from a normal tax bracket to a surtax bracket.

TAX RATES USED TO DEMONSTRATE COMPUTATIONAL TECHNIQUES

For simplicity of presentation all computations made in this chapter are based on an assumed tax rate of 50%. This rate is used arbitrarily and is not meant to indicate a rate that should be used in actual practice.

ORIGINATION AND AMORTIZATION OF DEFERRED TAXES

The model cases demonstrated in this section of the chapter illustrate the tax effects of the origination and amortization of timing differences, and appropriate accounting procedures for recording deferred income taxes and income tax expense resulting from such effects.

NONRECURRING TIMING DIFFERENCES

Model Case 1 is an example of the tax effects generated by simple, uncomplicated, nonrecurring timing differences, and of the accounting entries necessary to record the origination and amortization of the deferred income taxes created by the timing differences.

MODEL CASE NO. 1

In 19x1 Realty Bankers, Inc. recorded initial service fee income of $25,000 in connection with a $500,000 mortgage loan which was to be repaid in equal annual installments over five years. Income tax regulations required that the total $25,000 be included in taxable income in the year received. For financial accounting purposes Realty Bankers was required to recognize income from the initial service fee ratably over the term of the mortgage. Annual differences between taxable income and pretax accounting income resulting from dissimilar treatments for tax purposes and for accounting purposes are shown in Schedule 1

TIMING DIFFERENCES—INITIAL SERVICE FEE INCOME

Year	Initial Service Fee Income		Excess (Deficiency) of Accounting Income Over Taxable Income
	Accounting	Taxable	
19x1	5,000	25,000	(20,000)
19x2	5,000	—	5,000
19x3	5,000	—	5,000
19x4	5,000	—	5,000
19x5	5,000	—	5,000
	25,000	25,000	-0-

SCHEDULE 1

Also, in 19x1, Realty Bankers, Inc. purchased an electronic computer for $375,000. The expected useful life of the computer was estimated to be five years, and the company decided to depreciate it over that period by the straight-line method for accounting purposes and by the sum-of-the-digits method for tax purposes. Annual differences resulting from using straight-line depreciation for accounting purposes and accelerated depreciation for tax purposes are shown in Schedule 2.

TIMING DIFFERENCES—ACCELERATED DEPRECIATION

Year	Depreciation Expense		Excess (Deficiency) of Accounting Income Over Taxable Income
	Accounting	Taxable	
19x1	75,000	125,000	50,000
19x2	75,000	100,000	25,000
19x3	75,000	75,000	—
19x4	75,000	50,000	(25,000)
19x5	75,000	25,000	(50,000)
	375,000	375,000	-0-

SCHEDULE 2

In 19x1 taxable income was increased by $20,000 over accounting income as a result of the timing difference created by the initial service fee transactions, as indicated in Schedule 1. At a tax rate of 50% the effect of the timing difference created a deferred tax debit of $10,000.

In the same year taxable income was decreased by $50,000 in relation to accounting income due to the timing difference generated by accelerated depreciation for tax purposes, as indicated in Schedule 2. At a 50% tax rate the effect of the timing difference for depreciation originated a deferred tax credit of $25,000.

In 19x1 the company realized pretax accounting income of $120,000. However, due to the decrease in taxable income of $50,000 and the increase in taxable income of $20,000 arising from depreciation and service fee timing differences, respectively, the taxable income shown on the company's tax return for that year was $90,000, and resulted in a tax currently payable of $45,000.[2] Since income tax on pretax accounting income was computed to be $60,000, deferred income tax debits and credits were created, and income tax expense was properly allocated by the following entries made by the company at December 31, 19x1:

	Debit	Credit
Income Tax Expense	45,000	
Income Taxes Payable		45,000
To record tax liability for 19x1.		
Deferred Income Tax Debits	10,000	
Income Tax Expense		10,000
To set up deferred income tax debits required to allocate tax expense on initial service fee income over five years.		
Income Tax Expense	25,000	
Deferred Income Tax Credits		25,000
To set up income tax credits required to allocate income tax benefits from depreciation expense over five years.		

In 19x2 the company had pretax accounting income of $130,000 and, at a tax rate of 50%, the applicable income tax expense amounted to $65,000. However, due to a reversal of $5,000 in the initial service fee timing difference, as shown on Schedule 1, and an increase of $25,000 in the timing difference resulting from accelerated depreciation, as indicated in Schedule 2, taxable income for the year was $100,000 and the tax currently payable was therefore $50,000. To record amortization of deferred income tax debits, origination of additional deferred income tax credits, and properly allocate income tax expense, the company made the following entries as of December 31, 19x2:

	Debit	Credit
Income Tax Expense	50,000	
Income Taxes Payable		50,000
To record income tax liability for 19x2.		
Income Tax Expense	15,000	
Deferred Income Tax Debits		2,500
Deferred Income Tax Credits		12,500
To amortize deferred tax debits, originate deferred tax credits, and allocate income taxes at December 31, 19x2.		

---

[2] For simplicity of presentation, investment credits are not considered in the computations made in this chapter for the purpose of illustrating the tax effect of timing differences arising from the use of straight-line and accelerated depreciation.

Similar entries for the allocation of income tax expense and amortization of deferred tax debits and credits were made over the next three years by Realty Bankers. Schedule 3 reveals the effects of the timing differences over the five-year period, and Schedule 4 discloses the appropriate income statement presentation for income before taxes, provision for income taxes, and net income for the same period.

TAX EFFECTS OF TIMING DIFFERENCES

Year	Pretax Accounting Income	Adjustment for Timing Differences — Add to (Deduct from) Pretax Accounting Income — Depreciation	Service Fees	Net Addition (Deduction from) Pretax Accounting Income	Taxable Income	Income Tax Expense — Tax on Taxable Income Currently Payable	Adjustment for Timing Differences	Accounting Income Tax Expense
19x1	120,000	(50,000)	20,000	(30,000)	90,000	45,000	15,000	60,000
19x2	130,000	(25,000)	(5,000)	(30,000)	100,000	50,000	15,000	65,000
19x3	145,000	—	(5,000)	(5,000)	140,000	70,000	2,500	72,500
19x4	150,000	25,000	(5,000)	20,000	170,000	85,000	(10,000)	75,000
19x5	160,000	50,000	(5,000)	45,000	205,000	102,500	(22,500)	80,000
	705,000	-0-	-0-	-0-	705,000	352,500	-0-	352,500

SCHEDULE 3

INCOME STATEMENT PRESENTATION

	19x1	19x2	19x3	19x4	19x5
Income before Income Taxes	120,000	130,000	145,000	150,000	160,000
Provision for Income Taxes					
Currently Payable	45,000	50,000	70,000	85,000	102,500
Deferred	15,000	15,000	2,500	(10,000)	(22,500)
	60,000	65,000	72,500	75,000	80,000
Net Income	60,000	65,000	72,500	75,000	80,000

SCHEDULE 4

COMPLEX TIMING DIFFERENCES

Model Cases 2 and 3 demonstrate the tax effects of complex and complicated timing differences, and appropriate accounting procedures for recording the resulting deferred income tax debits and credits.

Model Case 2 is an example of complex timing differences resulting from different accounting and tax treatment of warranty expense and installment sales. In this case, the increase or decrease in deferred tax debits and in deferred tax credits is determined by a single computation for each respective classification, made by applying the assumed current tax rate of 50% to the net change in the cumulative timing differences during each year.

Model Case 3 illustrates the effects of timing differences created by dissimilar treatment of a capitalized lease for accounting purposes and for the tax return. Changes in deferred income taxes are computed on a specific identification basis by applying the assumed current tax rate of 50% to the timing differences originating or reversing, as the case may be, in each accounting period. The complexity of the timing differences in Model Case 3 arises from the complicated accounting entries that must be made to record the tax effects of such differences.

MODEL CASE NO. 2

Carey, Inc. manufactures small pleasure boats and sells them direct to individual customers on an installment plan which permits the purchasers to make payments thereon over a period of 36 months. Carey also gives customers a warranty which covers specified defects discovered in the product within an 18-month period following the date of purchase. The accounting policy of the company is to recognize gross profit on installment sales at the time the sales are made, and, simultaneously, to accrue estimated warranty expense in connection with each sale and amortize the expense over the period of the warranty agreement. For tax purposes, however, Carey realizes gross profit on installment sales when payments are received, based on the ratio of the cash received to the total sales price applied to the total gross profit ultimately to be realized; and recognizes warranty expense when actually paid in cash.

The origination and reversal of timing differences resulting from installment sales over a five-year period are shown in Schedule 5.

ORIGINATION AND REVERSAL OF TIMING DIFFERENCES RESULTING FROM INSTALLMENT SALES

| | Gross Profit on Installment Sales | | | | Deferred Income Tax Credits | | Effect on Income Tax Expense | | |
| | Profit Realized | | Timing Differences | | | | | | |
Year	Per Books	Per Tax Return	Increase (Decrease)	Cumulative	Annual	Cumulative	Currently Payable	Origination or Amortization	Total Tax Expense
Balance 12/31/x1				200,000		100,000			
19x2	100,000	50,000	50,000	250,000	25,000	125,000	25,000	25,000	50,000
19x3	75,000	100,000	(25,000)	225,000	(12,500)	112,500	50,000	(12,500)	37,500
19x4	150,000	100,000	50,000	275,000	25,000	137,500	50,000	25,000	75,000
19x5	80,000	180,000	(100,000)	175,000	(50,000)	87,500	90,000	(50,000)	40,000
19x6	120,000	100,000	20,000	195,000	10,000	97,500	50,000	10,000	60,000

SCHEDULE 5

In 19x2 gross profit on sales for accounting purposes exceeded the gross profit shown on the tax return by $50,000. The increase of $25,000 in deferred income tax debits was computed by applying the assumed tax rate of 50% to the $50,000 net increase in timing differences. The gross profit on sales recognized for accounting purposes in 19x3 was $25,000 less than the gross profit reflected on the tax return. Therefore, deferred income tax debits were reduced by $12,500 computed as 50% of the net decrease in timing differences during the year.

The origination and reversal of timing differences resulting from the different treatments of warranty expense for accounting and tax purposes over the same five-year period are shown on Schedule 6.

ORIGINATION AND REVERSAL OF TIMING DIFFERENCES RESULTING FROM WARRANTY EXPENSE

	Warranty Expense				Deferred Income Tax Debits		Effect on Income Tax Expense		
	Expense Recognized		Timing Differences						
Year	Per Books	Per Tax Return	Increase (Decrease)	Cumulative	Annual	Cumulative	Currently Payable	Origination or Amortization	Total Tax Expense
Balance 12/31/x1				10,000		5,000			
19x2	5,000	2,500	2,500	12,500	1,250	6,250	(1,250)	(1,250)	(2,500)
19x3	4,000	5,000	(1,000)	11,500	(500)	5,750	(2,500)	500	(2,000)
19x4	7,500	6,000	1,500	13,000	750	6,500	(3,000)	(750)	(3,750)
19x5	4,000	9,000	(5,000)	8,000	(2,500)	4,000	(4,500)	2,500	(2,000)
19x6	5,000	2,000	3,000	11,000	1,500	5,500	(1,000)	(1,500)	(2,500)

SCHEDULE 6

COMBINED EFFECTS OF NET CHANGES IN TIMING DIFFERENCES
RESULTING FROM INSTALLMENT SALES AND WARRANTY EXPENSE

	Excess (Deficiency) of Accounting Pretax Income Over Taxable Income Due to Origination and Reversal of Timing Differences				Taxable Income	Income Tax Expense		
		Timing Differences						
Year	Pretax Accounting Income	Installment Sales (Tax Credits)	Warranty Expense (Tax Debits)	Net Excess (Deficiency) Over Taxable Income	Taxable Income Per Tax Return	Currently Payable	Tax Effect of Timing Differences	Accounting Tax Expense
19x2	80,000	50,000	(2,500)	47,500	32,500	16,250	23,750	40,000
19x3	60,000	(25,000)	1,000	(24,000)	84,000	42,000	(12,000)	30,000
19x4	120,000	50,000	(1,500)	48,500	71,500	35,750	24,250	60,000
19x5	64,000	(100,000)	5,000	(95,000)	159,000	79,500	(47,500)	32,000
19x6	96,000	20,000	(3,000)	17,000	79,000	39,500	8,500	48,000
	420,000	(5,000)	(1,000)	(6,000)	426,000	213,000	(3,000)	210,000

SCHEDULE 7

In 19x2 the amortization of estimated warranty expense exceeded the cash payments made on warranty claims by $2,500. Since amortized expense was recognized for accounting purposes and actual cash payments for tax purposes, deferred income tax debits were increased by $1,250, computed by applying the assumed tax rate of 50% to the net increase in timing differences. In 19x3 there was a net decrease of $1,000 in the cumulative timing differences and a corresponding decrease of $500 was made in the deferred income tax debits account.

The combined effects of the net changes in timing differences over the five-year period referred to above are shown in Schedule 7.

In 19x2 the tax return indicated a tax liability of $16,250, but income tax expense computed on pretax accounting income amounted to $40,000. The $23,750 difference was the tax effect of the net change of $47,500 in timing differences during the year. Tax currently payable at the end of 19x3 exceeded tax expense computed on pretax accounting income by $12,000. This difference also was the tax effect resulting from the net change in timing differences during the year.

The entries made by Carey in 19x2 and 19x3 to record the tax liability, income tax expense, and allocation of income taxes were as follows:

	19x2		19x3	
	Debit	Credit	Debit	Credit
Income Tax Expense	16,250		42,000	
Income Taxes Payable		16,250		42,000
To record income tax liability.				
Deferred Income Tax Debits	1,250			500
Deferred Income Tax Credits		25,000	12,500	
Income Tax Expense	23,750			12,000
To record allocation of income taxes.				

Similar entries were made by Carey each year to record the tax currently payable, income tax expense, and the allocation of deferred income taxes.

MODEL CASE NO. 3

Effective January 1, 19x1 Baker Company leased an electronic computer component for six years at an annual rental of $10,000. The asset had a useful life of only six years and Baker therefore decided to capitalize the lease, and depreciate the asset over the period of the lease by the sum-of-the-digits method. Using the current interest rate of 8.75% Baker computed the present value of the six annual payments to be $49,150 and made the following entry to record the capitalization of the lease:

	Debit	Credit
Computer Component	49,150	
Deferred Interest Expense	10,850	
Liability Under Lease		60,000

For tax purposes Baker Company decided to disregard capitalization of the lease and report the $10,000 annual payments as rent expense on its tax returns for the years covered by the lease.

In this case the difference between rent expense reported annually on the income tax return and the interest and depreciation expenses recorded for accounting purposes originated and reversed timing differences during the period of the lease payments. The development of these timing differences is shown in Schedule 8.

TIMING DIFFERENCES AND TAX EFFECTS

RESULTING FROM DIFFERENT ACCOUNTING AND TAX TREATMENT OF LEASE OBLIGATION

		Financial Accounting Treatment				Tax Treatment	Excess (Deficiency) of	Deferred Income Tax Debits	
Year	Total Payment	Applied to Principal of Notes Payable	Applied to Interest Expense	Depreciation of Asset Purchased	Total Accounting Expense	Rent Expense Deduction for Tax Purposes	Book Expense Over Tax Expense Deduction	Annual	Cumulative
19x1	10,000	10,000	—	14,046	14,046	10,000	4,046	2,023	2,023
19x2	10,000	6,574	3,426	11,700	15,126	10,000	5,126	2,563	4,586
19x3	10,000	7,150	2,850	9,364	12,214	10,000	2,214	1,107	5,693
19x4	10,000	7,775	2,225	7,020	9,245	10,000	(755)	(378)	5,315
19x5	10,000	8,456	1,544	4,680	6,224	10,000	(3,776)	(1,888)	3,427
19x6	10,000	9,195	805	2,340	3,145	10,000	(6,855)	(3,427)	—
	60,000	49,150	10,850	49,150	60,000	60,000	-0-	-0-	—

SCHEDULE 8

Each year during the term of the lease Baker Company made appropriate entries to record the income tax liability, amortization of deferred interest expense, payment on the lease, and allocation of interperiod income taxes.

The entries made for the second and last years of the least period are outlined as follows:

	19x2		19x6	
	Debit	Credit	Debit	Credit
Liability Under Lease Obligation	10,000		10,000	
Interest Expense	3,426		805	
Depreciation Expense	11,700		2,340	
Deferred Interest Expense		3,426		805
Accumulated Depreciation		11,700		2,340
Income Tax Expense		2,563	3,427	
Deferred Income Tax Debits	2,563			3,427
Cash		10,000		10,000
	27,689	27,689	16,572	16,572

OPERATING LOSSES

Accountants are sometimes confronted by intricate problems of income tax allocation in situations where operating losses give rise to income tax carryback adjustments and carryforward benefits. Generally, in such circumstances, the allocation of income taxes and benefits involve a conflict between the matching concept and the principles of realization, and a decision must be made as to what method of allocation should be applied. The model cases in this section of the chapter illustrate problems of allocation encountered in situations where operating losses have been sustained by business entities operating on a going-concern basis.

CARRYBACK WHERE DEFERRED CREDITS EXIST

If the carryback benefits arising from an operating loss are fully realized by a carryback adjustment, the operating loss will have no effect on existing deferred credits, and no adjustment to such credits need be made.

Model Case 4 illustrates the type of situation referred to above.

MODEL CASE NO. 4

In 19x1 James Company purchased a machine for $144,000, having an estimated useful life of eight years. The company decided to depreciate the machine for accounting purposes by the straight-line method and use the sum-of-the-digits method for tax purposes. Prospective accounting and tax depreciation, origination and amortization of timing differences, and allocation of income taxes during the expected life of the asset are shown in Schedule 9.

SCHEDULE OF TIMING DIFFERENCES
RESULTING FROM ACCELERATED DEPRECIATION FOR TAX PURPOSES

| Year | Depreciation | | Timing Difference | Deferred Income Tax Credits | |
	Books (Straight-Line)	Tax Return (Sum-of-the-Digits)	Excess (Deficiency) of Book Income Over Taxable Income	Current	Cumulative
19x1	18,000	32,000	14,000	7,000	7,000
19x2	18,000	28,000	10,000	5,000	12,000
19x3	18,000	24,000	6,000	3,000	15,000
19x4	18,000	20,000	2,000	1,000	16,000
19x5	18,000	16,000	(2,000)	(1,000)	15,000
19x6	18,000	12,000	(6,000)	(3,000)	12,000
19x7	18,000	8,000	(10,000)	(5,000)	7,000
19x8	18,000	4,000	(14,000)	(7,000)	—
	144,000	144,000	—	—	—

SCHEDULE 9

The company had taxable income for each of the years 19x1 through 19x4, depreciation expense was reported on the tax return, and resulting deferred income tax credits were recorded on the books as shown on Schedule 9. However, in 19x5 the company sustained an accounting loss of $340,000 and a tax loss of $338,000. The difference between the accounting loss and the tax loss resulted from a reversal of $2,000 in timing differences caused by accelerated depreciation for tax purposes, as indicated on Schedule 9.

Since the aggregate of both pretax accounting income and taxable income for the three years preceding the operating loss exceeded the amount of the accounting loss and the taxable loss, respectively, the carryback benefit of $170,000 for accounting purposes was realized in full, and the tax benefit was also realized in full by the restitution of $169,000. Therefore no adjustment of existing deferred tax credits was necessary, and there was no disruption in the program of prospective reversal of timing differences as shown on Schedule 9.

A summary of accounting and taxable income and the effect of accelerated depreciation for tax purposes is shown in Schedule 10 for the first five years of the estimated life of the asset.

SUMMARY OF INCOME, INCOME TAX EXPENSE, AND INCOME TAX ALLOCATION

	Income Before Income Taxes		Income Tax Expense			Deferred Income Tax Credits	
Year	Accounting	Taxable	Currently Payable	Deferred	Total Expense	Current	Cumulative
19x1	110,000	96,000	48,000	7,000	55,000	7,000	7,000
19x2	120,000	110,000	55,000	5,000	60,000	5,000	12,000
19x3	130,000	124,000	62,000	3,000	65,000	3,000	15,000
19x4	140,000	138,000	69,000	1,000	70,000	1,000	16,000
19x5	(340,000)	(338,000)	(169,000)	(1,000)	(170,000)	(1,000)	15,000
	160,000	130,000	65,000	15,000	80,000	15,000	

SCHEDULE 10

The entry made at December 31, 19x5 by James Company to record the income tax benefits of the loss carryback and the reversal of deferred income tax credits was as follows:

	Debit	Credit
Refundable Income Taxes	169,000	
Deferred Income Tax Credits	1,000	
Income Tax Expense (Benefits)		170,000

A summary of the allocation of income taxes by James Company for the full eight years of the life of the asset that caused the timing difference is set forth in Schedule 11.

CARRYFORWARD BENEFIT REALIZED IN LOSS YEAR

When realization of the tax benefits of a loss carryforward is assured beyond any reasonable doubt, the potential benefits should be recognized in the loss year. Model Case 4A illustrates accounting procedures that provide for recognition in the loss year of potential tax benefits from a loss carryforward.

MODEL CASE NO. 4A

In 19x7 Johnson Company suffered a casualty loss from a fire that destroyed an old warehouse. The warehouse had not been used for some time and was not properly insured. However, recognition of the loss on the books resulted in an accounting and taxable operating loss of $675,000 for the year 19x7. The aggregate income of the

SUMMARY OF INTERPERIOD ALLOCATION OF INCOME TAXES

Year	Income Before Income Taxes		Income Tax Expense			Deferred Income Tax Credits	
	Accounting	Taxable	Currently Payable	Deferred	Total Expense	Current	Cumulative
19x1	110,000	96,000	48,000	7,000	55,000	7,000	7,000
19x2	120,000	110,000	55,000	5,000	60,000	5,000	12,000
19x3	130,000	124,000	62,000	3,000	65,000	3,000	15,000
19x4	140,000	138,000	69,000	1,000	70,000	1,000	16,000
19x5	(340,000)	(338,000)	(169,000)	(1,000)	(170,000)	(1,000)	15,000
19x6	110,000	116,000	58,000	(3,000)	55,000	(3,000)	12,000
19x7	120,000	130,000	65,000	(5,000)	60,000	(5,000)	7,000
19x8	130,000	144,000	72,000	(7,000)	65,000	(7,000)	—
	520,000	520,000	260,000	—	260,000	—	—

SCHEDULE 11

three years preceding the loss year was not sufficient to permit Johnson to realize the total tax benefits of the loss from a loss carryback adjustment. However, the company decided to recognize currently the potential tax benefits of the loss carryforward because it considered the benefits to be assured beyond any reasonable doubt. The decision was based on the fact that the company had a long earnings history, and that the loss of the warehouse would not curtail operations but would, in fact, increase future operating income by relieving it of depreciation expense for a warehouse that was not fully utilized.

The tax benefits from the loss carryback and carryforward were computed by the following method:

Net Operating Loss		675,000
Taxable Income in the Loss Carryback Years		
19x4	140,000	
19x5	145,000	
19x6	150,000	435,000
Loss Carryforward to be Recognized in Loss Year		240,000
Tax Benefits of Operating Loss at 50% Tax Rate		
Carryback (Loss—435,000)		217,500
Carryforward (Loss—240,000)		120,000
		337,300

The entry made by Johnson Company to record the tax benefits was as follows:

	Debit	Credit
Refundable Income Taxes	217,500	
Income Taxes Receivable	120,000	
Income Tax Expense		337,500

Classification of income taxes receivable on the balance sheet at December 31, 19x7 was determined as follows:

Current

Refundable Income Taxes	217,500
(Amount due from carryback adjustment)	
Income Taxes Receivable	70,000
(Amount of realization within one year of carryback benefits based on estimated taxable income of 140,000 in 19x8)	
	287,500

Noncurrent

Income Taxes Receivable	50,000

(Realization of carryforward benefits subsequent to 19x8, based on 240,000 loss carryover less 140,000 to be realized in 19x8)

CARRYFORWARD WHERE DEFERRED CREDITS EXIST

Generally, where operating loss carryforwards arise from a loss that cannot be completely carried back, an adjustment must be made to the deferred income tax credits that exist on the books at that time. This adjustment is necessary because the actual tax refund is based on *taxable* income for each carryback year affected and *not* on pretax accounting income. For example, if, in a loss carryback year, a company had pretax accounting income of $125,000 and taxable income of $116,000 due to a timing difference of $9,000, the tax refund from a carryback adjustment would be based on the taxable income of $116,000. Therefore, the potential decrease in *accounting* income tax expense from the amount of taxes currently payable in future years provided for by the deferred tax credits might not occur simply because the company might not have sufficient taxable income in future years to absorb the deferred income tax credits. Therefore, the Opinion provides for including in the loss year the benefits of the deferred tax credits set up during the loss carryback years and prohibits setting up deferred tax credits that would otherwise originate in the loss year. However, the Opinion also provides for restoring the eliminated tax credits and recording the omitted loss-year tax credit to the extent that the tax benefits of the loss carryforward are realized in actual tax refunds during the loss carryforward years.

Model Case 5 illustrates a situation where deferred income tax credits existed at the time a potential loss carryforward developed.

MODEL CASE NO. 5

In December 19x0 Landover Company purchased a machine for $180,000. Management estimated the useful life of the asset to be 15 years and decided to measure depreciation expense over that period by the straight-line method for financial accounting purposes and by the sum-of-the-digits method for income tax reporting.

Based on an estimated annual tax rate of 50%, the projected tax effects of this accelerated depreciation for tax purposes on the financial reports of the company over the life of the asset are shown in Schedule 12.

<u>SCHEDULE OF TIMING DIFFERENCES</u>

<u>RESULTING FROM ACCELERATED DEPRECIATION FOR TAX PURPOSES</u>

	Depreciation		Timing Difference	Deferred Income Tax Credits	
Year	Books (Straight-Line)	Tax Return (Sum-of-the-Digits)	Excess (Deficiency) of Book Income Over Taxable Income	Current	Cumulative
19x1	12,000	22,500	10,500	5,250	5,250
19x2	12,000	21,000	9,000	4,500	9,750
19x3	12,000	19,500	7,500	3,750	13,500
19x4	12,000	18,000	6,000	3,000	16,500
19x5	12,000	16,500	4,500	2,250	18,750
19x6	12,000	15,000	3,000	1,500	20,250
19x7	12,000	13,500	1,500	750	21,000
19x8	12,000	12,000	—	—	21,000
19x9	12,000	10,500	(1,500)	(750)	20,250
19y0	12,000	9,000	(3,000)	(1,500)	18,750
19y1	12,000	7,500	(4,500)	(2,250)	16,500
19y2	12,000	6,000	(6,000)	(3,000)	13,500
19y3	12,000	4,500	(7,500)	(3,750)	9,750
19y4	12,000	3,000	(9,000)	(4,500)	5,250
19y5	12,000	1,500	(10,500)	(5,250)	—
	180,000	180,000	—	—	—

SCHEDULE 12

For the years 19x1 through 19x4 the company had both pretax accounting income and taxable income. Accordingly, at the end of each year income tax expense was charged with the tax effect of the timing difference applicable to the respective year, and the deferred income tax account was credited concurrently with a like amount.

However, in 19x5 the company encountered a problem in its attempt to determine the proper interperiod tax allocation because it had sustained an accounting loss of $730,000 and a tax loss of $734,500, which would require both a carryback adjustment and the carryforward of a portion of the loss.

In its approach to resolving the problem the company first made an analysis of the effect of the accelerated depreciation over the prior four years. The analysis is summarized in Schedule 13.

ANALYSIS OF INCOME TAX EXPENSE AND DEFERRED INCOME TAX CREDITS

Year	Income Before Income Taxes		Income Tax Expense			Deferred Income Tax Credits	
	Accounting	Taxable	Currently Payable	Deferred	Total Expense	Current	Cumulative
19x1	110,000	99,500	49,750	5,250	55,000	5,250	5,250
19x2	125,000	116,000	58,000	4,500	62,500	4,500	9,750
19x3	135,000	127,500	63,750	3,750	67,500	3,750	13,500
19x4	140,000	134,000	67,000	3,000	70,000	3,000	16,500
	510,000	477,000	238,500	16,500	255,000	16,500	

SCHEDULE 13

In recording the tax effects of the operating loss it was necessary to make an adjustment to the deferred income tax credits account in an amount sufficient to eliminate the credits accumulated for the loss carryback years, as follows:

Deferred Tax Credits

19x2	$4,500
19x3	3,750
19x4	3,000
	$11,250

Since annual deferred income tax credits were being determined by the specific identification method, the company determined from the projected deferred income tax credits shown on Schedule 12 that during the five-year carryover period from December 31, 19x5 to December 31, 19y0 the timing difference would be exactly equal to the reverse timing differences. Therefore, no part of the $5,250 allocation made in 19x1 could be used to adjust the deferred tax credits at December 31, 19x5.

Furthermore, the deferred tax credit of $2,250 applicable to 19x5 could not be set up because, while it increased the total amount of the tax carryback adjustment, that portion of the carryback was not included in the tax refund due at December 31, 19x5, and therefore the credit of $2,250 became, in fact, a carryover.

Therefore, at December 31, 19x5 the company made the following entry to record the net amount of the tax refund receivable, the required adjustment to deferred income tax credits, and income tax expense for the year:

	Debit	Credit
Refundable Income Taxes	188,750	
Deferred Income Tax Credit	11,250	
Income Tax Expense		200,000

After the above entry was recorded, the analysis summarized in Schedule 13 was brought up to date and is shown on Schedule 14.

ANALYSIS OF INCOME TAX EXPENSE AND DEFERRED INCOME TAX CREDITS

Year	Income Before Income Taxes		Income Tax Expense			Deferred Income Tax Credits	
	Accounting	Taxable	Currently Payable	Deferred	Total Expense	Current	Cumulative
19x1	110,000	99,500	49,750	5,250	55,000	5,250	5,250
19x2	125,000	116,000	58,000	4,500	62,500	4,500	9,750
19x3	135,000	127,500	63,750	3,750	67,500	3,750	13,500
19x4	140,000	134,000	67,000	3,000	70,000	3,000	16,500
19x5	(730,000)	(734,500)	(188,750)	(11,250)	(200,000)	(11,250)	5,250
	(220,000)	(257,500)	49,750	5,250	55,000	5,250	

SCHEDULE 14

At the end of 19x5 the balance in the deferred income tax credits account was $5,250. According to the schedule of timing differences, Schedule 12, the balance in the account should have been $18,750. The deficiency of $13,500 in the account was made up of the following:

Deferred income tax credits eliminated
  for loss carryback years:

19x2	4,500	
19x3	3,750	
19x4	3,000	11,250

Deferred income tax credits not
  recorded for loss year—19x5

	2,250
	13,500

In subsequent years computation of the adjustments to the deferred income tax credits account had to be made on two bases:

1. Adjustments had to be made on the basis of the timing difference, or reverse timing difference, that occurred in each respective year, as shown in Schedule 12.
2. Deferred income tax credits in the amount of $11,250 had to be restored to replace the credits eliminated for the carryback years 19x2, 19x3, and 19x4, and a pick-up had to be made of the unrecorded deferred income tax credit of $2,250 for 19x5. In each year these deferred credits were to be restored to the extent of the realization of the loss carryforward by crediting the account with an amount equal to the tax that would have been currently payable had the net operating loss deduction not existed.

Accordingly, when in 19x6 Landover Company realized pretax accounting income of $15,000 and taxable income of $12,000 before applying the net operating loss deduction, the addition to the deferred income tax credits account was computed as follows:

Addition to the account in accordance with the schedule of timing differences (Schedule 12)		1,500
Restoration of a portion of deferred income tax credits eliminated for carryback years to the extent of realization of the loss carryforward in 19x6		
Taxable income before net operating loss deduction	12,000	
Tax that would have been paid on taxable income (12,000 × 50%)		6,000
Total addition to the deferred income tax credits account for 19x6		7,500

In 19x7 the company reported pretax accounting income in the amount of $28,000 and taxable income of $26,500 before application of the net operating loss deduction. The adjustment to the deferred income tax credits account for 19x7 was computed as follows:

Addition to the account in accordance with the schedule of timing differences (Schedule 12)		750
Restoration of the remaining deferred income tax credits eliminated in carryback years, and the pick-up of the unrecorded deferred income tax credit of $2,250 for 19x5:		
Taxable income before net operating loss deduction	26,500	
Tax that would have been paid on taxable income (26,500 × 50%)	13,250	
Deferred income tax credits to be restored:		
Total credits eliminated in 19x5	11,250	
Less: Deferred credits restored in 19x6	6,000	
	5,250	
Deferred credits for 19x5 not previously recorded	2,250	
Total credits to be restored		7,500
Total addition to the deferred income tax credits account in 19x7		8,250

Since the income tax that would have been payable, except for the net operating loss carryover, exceeded the amount of the required adjustment, the total amount was credited to the deferred income tax credits account.

In 19x7 it was also necessary to record the amount of realization of the accounting net operating loss carryforward that was in excess of the amount credited to the deferred income tax account. The realization was computed as follows:

Accounting pretax income	28,000

Tax expense based on pretax accounting income (28,000 × 50%)	14,000
Less: Amount credited to deferred income tax credits account	8,250
Extraordinary credit representing provision in lieu of income tax	5,750

The entries required to record income tax expense for the year 19x6 and 19x7 were as follows:

	19x6		19x7	
	Debit	Credit	Debit	Credit
Income Tax Expense	7,500		14,000	
Deferred Income Tax Credits		7,500		8,250
Extraordinary Credits				5,750

The income statement for the years 19x7 and 19x6 reported income, provision for income taxes, extraordinary credit, and net income in the following manner:

	19x7	19x6
Income before income taxes and extraordinary credit	28,000	15,000
Provision for income taxes		
Provision in lieu of income taxes	5,750	
Deferred	8,250	7,500
	14,000	
Income before extraordinary credit	14,000	
Extraordinary credit		
Tax benefits derived from realization of operating loss carryforward	5,750	
Net Income	19,750	7,500

At December 31, 19x7 an analysis was again made of the tax effects of the accelerated depreciation timing differences in relation to the net operating loss carrybacks and carryforwards and Schedule 14 was brought up to date, as shown in Schedule 15.

ANALYSIS OF INCOME TAX EXPENSE AND DEFERRED INCOME TAX CREDITS

	Income Before Income Taxes		Income Tax Expense				Extra-Ordinary	Deferred Income Tax Credits	
Year	Accounting	Taxable	Currently Payable	Provision in Lieu	Deferred	Total Expense	Credits	Current	Cumulative
19x1	110,000	99,500	49,750	—	5,250	55,000	—	5,250	5,250
19x2	125,000	116,000	58,000	—	4,500	62,500	—	4,500	9,750
19x3	135,000	127,500	63,750	—	3,750	67,500	—	3,750	13,500
19x4	140,000	134,000	67,000	—	3,000	70,000	—	3,000	16,500
19x5	(730,000)	(734,500)	(188,750)	—	(11,250)	(200,000)	—	(11,250)	5,250
19x6	15,000	12,000	—	—	7,500	7,500	—	7,500	12,750
19x7	28,000	26,500	—	5,750	8,250	14,000	5,750	8,250	21,000
	(177,000)	(219,000)	49,750	5,750	21,000	76,500	5,750	21,000	

SCHEDULE 15

At the end of 19x7 the balance of $21,000 in the deferred income tax credits account agreed with the balance indicated in Schedule 12. The remaining net operating loss carryovers at that date were as follows:

	Accounting		Income Tax	
Net Operating Loss—19x5		730,000		734,500
Less: Carrybacks to:				
19x2	125,000		116,000	
19x3	135,000		127,500	
19x4	140,000	400,000	134,000	377,500
		330,000		357,000
Less: Carryovers to:				
19x6	15,000		12,000	
19x7	28,000	43,000	26,500	38,500
Available Net Operating Loss Carryforwards		287,000		318,500

In the three remaining years of the loss carryforward period the company reported the following income:

	Accounting Pretax Income	Taxable Income— Before Operating Loss Deduction
Year ended December 31, 19x8	60,000	60,000
19x9	130,000	131,500
19y0	133,000	136,000
	323,000	327,500

Both taxable and pretax accounting income during the remaining loss carryover years exceeded the balance to be carried over and, consequently, the full amount of the net operating loss carryover was ultimately realized. Also, the net operating loss carryover realized in 19x6 and 19x7 permitted the restoration in those years of all the deferred income tax credits eliminated or unrecorded in 19x5. Therefore, the reverse timing difference that would occur during the remaining years of accelerated depreciation would be the amounts indicated on Schedule 12 for the respective years.

A summary of timing differences and income tax paid and deferred for the full 15-year period is shown in Schedule 16.

Schedule 16 indicates that the net income expense reported over the 15-year period was $669,000, and that the net amount of income tax payments and refunds amounted to only $504,000. The difference of $165,000 represents the aggregate income tax benefits derived from realization of the operating loss carryforwards. Each year it was required that the tax benefits realized on pretax accounting income be reported simultaneously as a provision in lieu of income tax and an extraordinary credit. The aggregate extraordinary credits were developed as follows:

SUMMARY OF TIMING DIFFERENCES AND INCOME TAXES PAID AND DEFERRED

Year	Income Before Income Taxes		Income Tax Expense				Extra-Ordinary Credits	Deferred Income Tax Credits	
	Accounting	Taxable	Currently Payable	Provision in Lieu	Deferred	Total Expense		Current	Cumulative
19x1	110,000	99,500	49,750	—	5,250	55,000	—	5,250	5,250
19x2	125,000	116,000	58,000	—	4,500	62,500	—	4,500	9,750
19x3	135,000	127,500	63,750	—	3,750	67,500	—	3,750	13,500
19x4	140,000	134,000	67,000	—	3,000	70,000	—	3,000	16,500
19x5	(730,000)	(734,500)	(188,750)	—	(11,250)	(200,000)	—	(11,250)	5,250
19x6	15,000	12,000	—	—	7,500	7,500	—	7,500	12,750
19x7	28,000	26,500	—	5,750	8,250	14,000	5,750	8,250	21,000
19x8	60,000	60,000	—	30,000	—	30,000	30,000	—	21,000
19x9	130,000	131,500	—	65,750	(750)	65,000	65,750	(750)	20,250
19y0	133,000	136,000	4,500	63,500	(1,500)	66,500	63,500	(1,500)	18,750
19y1	146,000	150,500	75,250	—	(2,250)	73,000	—	(2,250)	16,500
19y2	160,000	166,000	83,000	—	(3,000)	80,000	—	(3,000)	13,500
19y3	168,000	175,500	87,750	—	(3,750)	84,000	—	(3,750)	9,750
19y4	185,000	194,000	97,000	—	(4,500)	92,500	—	(4,500)	5,250
19y5	203,000	213,500	106,750	—	(5,250)	101,500	—	(5,250)	—
	1,008,000	1,008,000	504,000	165,000	—	669,000	165,000	—	

SCHEDULE 16

Pretax Accounting operating loss in 19x5		730,000
Tax benefits to be realized (730,000 × 50%)		365,000
Tax benefits realized from carrybacks to the years indicated below, and reported as a credit to income tax expense in 19x5:		
19x2	62,500	
19x3	67,500	
19x4	70,000	200,000
Tax benefits realized in years 19x6 to 19y0, and reported as extraordinary credits		165,000

CARRYFORWARD WHEN DEFERRED TAX DEBITS EXIST

Where operating loss carryforwards arise from a loss that cannot be completely carried back, the deferred income tax debits that were originated or amortized during the loss carryback period should be eliminated. This elimination will, in effect, adjust the loss year *accounting* income tax benefits resulting from the loss to an amount equivalent to the tax recorded on *accounting* income during the loss carryback period.

Where, in such cases, a balance remains in the deferred income tax debits account and the benefits of the loss carryforward are not assured beyond any reasonable doubt, a determination should be made as to whether or not to continue to carry the deferred income tax debits. The Opinion provides no specific instructions for this situation, and it appears to be up to the business enterprise to evaluate the realizability of such deferred debits, and to decide on the propriety of continuing to carry them on the books.

Model Case 6 illustrates a situation where deferred income tax debits existed at a time when a net operating loss carryforward developed.

MODEL CASE NO. 6

In 19x1 an employee of Larkin Company was retired after 45 years of service. Because of his age the employee had not been eligible to participate in a pension plan that had been set up by the company two years previously. However, the Board of Directors of the Company adopted a resolution to pay the employee a direct pension benefit of $60,000, payable in annual installments of $10,000 each over a period of six years.

The pension cost of $60,000 was charged to current operations in 19x1 for accounting purposes, but tax deductions for the pension expense were taken in the year the cash payments were made to the employee. The timing differences developed from the different treatments for accounting purposes and tax purposes are shown in Schedule 17.

TIMING DIFFERENCES — PENSION EXPENSE

Year	Pension Expense		Timing Difference Excess (Deficiency) of Book Income	Deferred Income Tax Debits	
	Books	Tax Return	Over Taxable Income	Current	Cumulative
19x1	60,000	10,000	(50,000)	25,000	25,000
19x2	—	10,000	10,000	(5,000)	20,000
19x3	—	10,000	10,000	(5,000)	15,000
19x4	—	10,000	10,000	(5,000)	10,000
19x5	—	10,000	10,000	(5,000)	5,000
19x6	—	10,000	10,000	(5,000)	—
	60,000	60,000	—	—	

SCHEDULE 17

Larkin had taxable income from 19x1 to 19x4, but in 19x5 it sustained an acounting loss of $450,000 and a taxable loss of $460,000. The loss could not be completely carried back because the aggregate income of the prior three years was not sufficient to absorb the total loss. Larkin Company eliminated the amortization of timing differences that had been recorded in the loss carryback years and in so doing developed a balance of $25,000 in the deferred income tax debit account, which was equivalent to the amount originated in the year 19x1. The income tax benefits of the loss carryforward were not assured beyond any reasonable doubt, so Larkin did not take up the potential benefits of the carryforward in the loss year. However, the company felt reasonably certain that pretax accounting income in the following year would be sufficient to eliminate the deferred charge, even though it might not be sufficient to realize the full benefits of the loss carryforward. Therefore Larkin carried the deferred income tax debits in its accounts at the end of 19x5, the loss year. In 19x6 the Company had pretax accounting income of $150,000 and taxable income of $140,000, which was sufficient to permit realization of the full benefits of the loss carryforward and full amortization of the deferred income tax debits. The effects of the timing differences and the operating loss carryback and carryforward are shown for the full six-year period in Schedule 18.

SUMMARY OF INTERPERIOD ALLOCATION OF INCOME TAXES

Year	Income Before Income Taxes Accounting	Income Before Income Taxes Taxable	Income Tax Expense Currently Payable	Income Tax Expense Provision in Lieu	Income Tax Expense Deferred	Income Tax Expense Total Expense	Extra-Ordinary Credit	Deferred Income Tax Debits Current	Deferred Income Tax Debits Cumulative
19x1	100,000	150,000	75,000		(25,000)	50,000		25,000	25,000
19x2	110,000	100,000	50,000		5,000	55,000		(5,000)	20,000
19x3	120,000	110,000	55,000		5,000	60,000		(5,000)	15,000
19x4	130,000	120,000	60,000		5,000	65,000		(5,000)	10,000
19x5	(450,000)	(460,000)	(165,000)		(15,000)	(180,000)		15,000	25,000
19x6	150,000	140,000	5,000	45,000	25,000)	75,000	45,000	(25,000)	—
	160,000	160,000	80,000	45,000	—	125,000	45,000	—	

SCHEDULE 18

INVESTMENT CREDIT CARRYBACK AND CARRYFORWARD

The application of unused investment credits should be accounted for by the same method as that used to account for the tax benefits of operating loss carrybacks and carryforwards. The benefits of the carryback of an investment credit should be recognized in the period in which the investment credit is created, and the benefits of a carryforward should be recognized when the benefits are actually realized. When the benefits of investment credit carryforwards are realized in periods subsequent to that in which the investment credit originated, the income statement for those periods should reflect the benefits as a reduction in income tax expense, and not as an extraordinary credit.

Model Case 7 illustrates a situation where an investment credit carryback and potential carryforward occurred at a time when deferred income tax credits were being originated.

MODEL CASE NO. 7

In 19x1 Milton, Inc. purchased a series of billboards in suburban areas for $240,000. The expected useful life of the assets was estimated to be 15 years, and Milton determined to depreciate them over that period by the straight-line method for accounting purposes and by the sum-of-the-digits for tax purposes. The billboards were not Section 38 property, and therefore did not entitle the Company to an investment credit. The timing differences resulting from the different methods of recording depreciation are summarized for the first eight years of the life of the asset in Schedule 19.

SCHEDULE OF TIMING DIFFERENCES

RESULTING FROM ACCELERATED DEPRECIATION FOR TAX PURPOSES

	Depreciation		Timing Difference	Deferred Income	
	Books	Tax Return	Excess (Deficiency)	Tax Credits	
	(Straight-	Sum-of-the-	of Book Income		
Year	Line)	Digits)	Over Taxable Income	Current	Cumulative
19x1	16,000	30,000	14,000	7,000	7,000
19x2	16,000	28,000	12,000	6,000	13,000
19x3	16,000	26,000	10,000	5,000	18,000
19x4	16,000	24,000	8,000	4,000	22,000
19x5	16,000	22,000	6,000	3,000	25,000
19x6	16,000	20,000	4,000	2,000	27,000
19x7	16,000	18,000	2,000	1,000	28,000
19x8	16,000	16,000	—	—	28,000
	128,000	184,000	56,000	28,000	

SCHEDULE 19

In 19x1 Milton was entitled to an investment credit of $1,000 for other tangible property purchased in that year, and the benefit therefrom was realized currently.

In 19x5 Milton purchased a printing press at a cost of $560,000, and the company decided to depreciate it by the straight-line method for both accounting and tax purposes. Milton was entitled to an investment credit of $56,000 arising from the purchase of the press. However, the aggregate taxable income for the current year and the preceding three carryback years was not sufficient to allow the company to completely realize the benefits of the investment credit, and it was necessary to carry forward the unused portion. Taxable income during the following two years, however, permitted complete realization of the investment credit carryover.

Schedule 20 details the effects of the investment credit and the timing differences for the years from 19x1 to 19x7.

SUMMARY OF INTERPERIOD ALLOCATION OF INCOME TAXES

| | Income Before | | Investment | Income Tax Expense | | | Cumulative Deferred |
| | Income Taxes | | | Currently | | Total | Income Tax |
Year	Accounting	Taxable	Credit	Payable	Deferred	Expense	Credits
19x1	24,000	10,000	1,000	4,000	7,000	11,000	7,000
19x2	25,000	13,000		6,500	6,000	12,500	13,000
19x3	26,000	16,000		8,000	5,000	13,000	18,000
19x4	27,000	19,000		9,500	4,000	13,500	22,000
19x5	28,000	22,000	56,000	(24,000)	(15,000)	(39,000)	7,000
19x6	32,000	28,000		—	14,000	14,000	21,000
19x7	92,000	90,000		38,000	7,000	45,000	28,000
	254,000	198,000	57,000	42,000	28,000	70,000	

SCHEDULE 20

A review of Schedule 20 indicates that the investment credits had the following effect on income taxes currently payable in the years indicated:

1. The investment credit of $1,000 in 19x1 reduced taxes currently payable and income taxes both by that amount.
2. The investment credit of $56,000 in 19x5 was applied to income taxes currently payable for the years indicated as follows:

Investment Credit	56,000
Applied to 19x5 taxable income (22,000 × 50%)	11,000
	45,000
Applied to income taxes paid in carryback years to obtain tax refund:	
19x2 6,500	
19x3 8,000	
19x4 9,500	24,000
	21,000
Applied to 19x6 taxable income (28,000 × 50%)	14,000
	7,000
Applied to 19x7 taxable income (remaining balance)	7,000
Carryover after 19x7	-0-
19x7 indicated income tax (90,000 × 50%)	45,000
Less: Application of investment credit carryover	7,000
Taxes currently payable—19x7	38,000

3. The carryback and carryforward of the investment credit of $56,000 in 19x5 affected income tax expense and deferred income tax credits for the years indicated as follows:
   (a) Deferred income tax credits originating in 19x2, 19x3, and 19x4 were eliminated in 19x5 as a result of the investment credit carryback reducing taxable income to zero for each of the three years.
   (b) In 19x6, $2,000 deferred credits were originated for the $4,000 timing difference occurring in that year. In addition, $10,000 deferred credits were set up to restore those eliminated in 19x5 so that the increase in deferred income tax credits in 19x6 would be equal to the tax that would have been currently payable had it not been for the investment credit carryforward—taxable income of $28,000 at the 50% tax rate.
   (c) In 19x7 deferred credits of $1,000 were originated for the $2,000 timing difference occuring in that year. In addition, pretax accounting income was sufficient to restore the remaining $5,000 deferred credits eliminated in 19x5, and not reinstated in 19x6.
   (d) The totals of the columns at the end of 19x7 indicate that the taxes paid over the seven-year period were equivalent to the aggregate taxable income for that period at the tax rate of 50%, less the total of the investment credits. ($198,000 at 50%—$99,000 less $57,000 = $42,000.)
   (e) The difference between the tax on aggregate pretax accounting income and taxes actually paid for the seven-year period was equivalent to the cumulative deferred income tax credits of $28,000 at the end of 19x7, as indicated on Schedule 20.

LOSS CARRYFORWARDS OF PURCHASED SUBSIDIARIES

The tax benefits of loss carryforwards of purchased subsidiaries should be recognized as assets at the date of purchase *only* if realization is assured beyond a reasonable doubt. If realization is not thus assured, they should be recognized only when actually realized in subsequent periods. When realization occurs, the tax benefits of the carryforwards existing at the time of purchase should be treated as an adjustment of the purchase price.

Model Case 8 illustrates the accounting treatment for tax benefits of purchased loss carryforwards realized subsequent to the date of purchase.

MODEL CASE NO. 8

In 19x5 Able Company purchased all the stock of Baker Company and operated the enterprise as a subsidiary. The purchase price was $700,000, and the fair value of the net assets of Baker Company at that time was as follows:

Cash	50,000
Accounts Receivable	100,000
Plant and Equipment (net)	550,000
Total Assets	700,000
Less: Accounts Payable	40,000
Net Assets	660,000

The difference of $40,000 between the purchase price and the fair value of the net assets acquired was recorded as goodwill by Able Company. At the date of purchase Baker Company was entitled to a net operating loss carryover of $30,000, but because realization was not assured Able Company did not record the potential tax benefits receivable as an asset. However, in 19x6 the subsidiary had taxable income of $50,000, which was sufficient to permit the benefits of the carryforward to be realized completely.

The tax effects of the subsidiary's earnings were as follows:

Tax on pretax accounting income (50,000 × 50%)	25,000
Less: Operating Loss carryforward (30,000 × 50%)	15,000
Taxes currently payable	10,000

Able Company decided to reduce goodwill by the amount of the tax benefits of the loss carryover existing at the time of purchase, and therefore recorded the tax effects of the subsidiary's earnings in 19x6 as follows:

	Debit	Credit
Provision in lieu of income taxes	15,000	
Income tax expense	10,000	
Income taxes payable		10,000
Goodwill		15,000

LOSS CARRYFORWARDS EXISTING PRIOR TO QUASI-REORGANIZATION

The tax benefits of loss carryforwards existing at the time of quasi-reorganization should not be recorded as assets unless realization is assured beyond any reasonable doubt. If such tax benefits are realized subsequent to the date of the quasi-reorganization, they should be added to capital in excess of par, since they would be benefits attributable to loss periods prior to the quasi-reorganization.

Model Case 9 illustrates the accounting method required to record subsequent realization of the tax effects of loss carryforwards existing at the time of a quasi-reorganization.

MODEL CASE NO. 9

In 19x5 Liston Company decided to write down the carrying value of its assets in accordance with a quasi-reorganization plan that had been approved by the stockholders. At that time the retained earnings of the company had a deficit balance due to a series of losses over the years. Sales were expected to increase substantially in subsequent years however, and the company wanted its future financial statements to more clearly reflect the company's financial progress. The balance sheet of Liston Company at December 31, 19x5 is shown in Schedule 21.

LISTON COMPANY

Balance Sheet—December 31, 19x5

Assets		Liabilities and Stockholders' Equity	
Cash	2,000	Accounts Payable	8,000
Accounts Receivable—net	10,000	Stockholders' Equity	
Plant and Equipment—net	600,000	Capital Stock	1,000,000
Other Assets	8,000	Capital in excess of par	50,000
		Retained Earnings	(438,000)
	620,000		620,000

SCHEDULE 21

In accordance with the plan of quasi-reorganization Liston made the following entries on January 1, 19x6 to adjust the book values:

	Debit	Credit
1. Capital Stock	600,000	
Capital in excess of par		600,000
To reduce book value of capital stock.		
2. Retained Earnings	200,000	
Plant and Equipment		200,000
To reduce carrying value of fixed assets.		
3. Capital in excess of par	638,000	
Retained Earnings		638,000
To eliminate deficit in retained earnings.		

The effect on the book values of the balance sheet items of Liston Company resulting from posting the above entries is shown in Schedule 22.

LISTON COMPANY

WORKSHEET FOR QUASI-REORGANIZATION—JANUARY 1, 19x6

| | Trial Balance Before Adjustment | | Adjustments | | | | Trial Balance After Adjustment | |
	Dr.	(Cr.)	Debit		Credit		Dr.	(Cr.)
Cash	2,000						2,000	
Accounts Receivable	10,000						10,000	
Plant and Equipment	600,000				(2)	200,000	400,000	
Other Assets	8,000						8,000	
Accounts Payable		(8,000)						(8,000)
Capital Stock		(1,000,000)	(1)	600,000				(400,000)
Capital in excess of par		(50,000)	(3)	638,000	(1)	600,000		(12,000)
Retained Earnings	438,000		(2)	200,000	(3)	638,000		-0-
		-0-		1,438,000		1,438,000		-0-

SCHEDULE 22

The company substained a loss of $30,000 in 19x5, and it had at that time a loss carryforward of $20,000 from 19x4. The tax benefits of the carryforwards were not set up as assets at the time of the quasi-reorganization because realization of the benefits was not assured beyond any reasonable doubt.

In 19x6, the year following the quasi-reorganization, the company had a taxable loss of $20,000, but in 19x7 it had taxable income of $80,000. The history of the income and losses for years 19x4 through 19x7 was as follows:

Year	Taxable Income (Loss)
19x4	(20,000)
19x5	(30,000)
19x6	(20,000)
19x7	80,000

In 19x7 the company used the net operating loss carryforward of $70,000 as a net operating loss deduction and, consequently, paid taxes on only $10,000. The tax benefits of the carryforward from 19x4 and 19x5 were credited to capital in excess of par, and the benefits of the carryforward from 19x6 were reported as an extraordinary credit. The entries made by Liston Company to record tax expense and the tax effects of the loss carryforwards at a tax rate of 50% were as follows:

	Credit	Debit
Income Tax Expense	5,000	
Provision in lieu of income taxes	35,000	
Capital in excess of par		25,000
Extraordinary Credits		10,000
Income Taxes Payable		5,000

Income taxes were presented on the income statement for 19x7 in the following manner:

Income before income taxes		80,000
Income Taxes		
Currently Payable	5,000	
Provision in lieu of income taxes— (substituted for utilization of loss carryforward providing credit to capital in excess of par (25,000) and extraordinary credit (10,000))	35,000	40,000
Income before extraordinary item		40,000
Extraordinary item—utilization of loss carryforward to the extent indicated in the provision for income taxes		10,000
Net Income		50,000

TAX ALLOCATION WITHIN A PERIOD

APB Opinion No. 11 directs that tax allocation within a period should be applied to obtain an appropriate relationship between tax expense and

(a) income before extraordinary items,
(b) extraordinary items,
(c) adjustment of prior periods,
(d) direct entries to other stockholders' equity accounts.

The computations required to determine intraperiod allocation of income taxes usually are not complicated. Generally, they simply require computing the tax effect of a particular item included in the list above that occurs during the period, and presenting that item net of tax. Thus, items representing income or increases in other stockholders' equity accounts would be decreased by an amount equivalent to the increase in income taxes currently payable, resulting from their respective inclusion in the tax return for the current period. Similarly, items representing expenses or charges to other stockholders' equity accounts would be decreased by an amount equivalent to the decrease in income taxes currently payable, arising from their respective inclusion in the current period tax return. Model Case 10 illustrates the presentation of extraordinary items arising from a net operating loss carryover and from a negotiated settlement of long-term debt.

MODEL CASE NO. 10

During 19x5 Frey & Company negotiated an early settlement of long-term debt that resulted in an extraordinary gain of $30,000. At the end of the year the company had an operating income of $70,000, exclusive of the extraordinary credit. The company also was entitled to a net operating loss carryforward of $20,000 from 19x4.

The tax effects of transactions in 19x5 are summarized below, using a tax rate of 50%.

Tax on Pretax Accounting Income	Amount of Income	Tax Effect
Income from Operations	70,000	35,000
Extraordinary Gain	30,000	15,000
	100,000	50,000
Taxes Currently Payable		
Taxable Income	100,000	50,000
Less: Application of loss carryforward	20,000	10,000
	80,000	40,000

Presentation on the income statement of operating income, extraordinary items, and income tax expense for 19x5 was as follows:

Income from Operations before income taxes and extraordinary items		70,000
Income Taxes		
Current	25,000	
Provision in lieu of income taxes	10,000	35,000
Income before extraordinary items		35,000
Extraordinary items		
Gain from negotiated settlement of long term debt (less applicable income taxes of 15,000)	15,000	
Realization of tax benefits of loss carryforward equal to provision in lieu of income taxes	10,000	25,000
Net Income		60,000

FINANCIAL REPORTING

The requirements for financial reporting are listed earlier in the chapter under the caption "Opinion on Financial Reporting," and the structure of the financial statements with respect to income tax reporting has been displayed in the model cases included in the chapter.

SPECIAL AREAS AND INTERIM REPORTS

APB Opinion No. 11 is the basic official directive on accounting for income taxes. However, the Board did not include preparation of interim financial statements nor certain special areas of tax allocation in the Opinion. These special areas and the presentation of income tax expense in interim statements were covered by later Opinions of the Accounting Principles Board and Statements and Interpretations of the Financial Accounting Standards Board. Therefore, accounting for income taxes in these special areas and for interim reporting purposes is explained and illustrated in the next chapter.

2

Allocation of Income Taxes—
Special Areas and Interim Reports

Accounting Principles Board Opinion No. 11 sets forth the fundamental principles of accounting for income taxes, and develops the basic concept of interperiod tax allocation. However, in the Opinion, the Board deferred any conclusions on certain areas of income tax allocation, including interim statements and certain transactions peculiar to particular industries. Subsequent publications of Opinions by the Accounting Principles Board and Statements and Interpretations by the Financial Accounting Standards Board have been issued for the purpose of settling some of the unresolved areas by explaining and clarifying the application of, or granting specific exemption from, the provisions of APB Opinion No. 11. In every subsequent directive the procedures, principles, and concepts of APB Opinion No. 11 have been reaffirmed, and they continue to be the essential principles of accounting for income taxes.

Chapter 1 analyzed APB Opinion No. 11 and explained and illustrated the provisions with respect to the allocation concept, the allocation method, allocation procedures, and measurement techniques.

This chapter continues the explanations and illustrations contained in Chapter 1 to encompass the provisions of the official directives on income taxes published subsequent to the issuance, and based on the principles, of APB Opinion No. 11.

"SPECIAL AREAS" OF ACCOUNTING FOR INCOME TAXES

The "special areas" of income tax accounting omitted from consideration in APB Opinion No. 11 are listed below under the caption of the subsequently published explanatory directive for each respective area.

Accounting Principles Board Opinion No. 23[1]
    Undistributed Earnings of Subsidiaries
    Investments in Corporate Joint Ventures
    "Bad Debt Reserves" of Savings and Loan Associations
    "Policyholders' Surplus" of Stock Life Insurance Companies
Accounting Principles Board Opinion No. 24[2]

---

[1]*Accounting for Income Taxes—Special Areas,* Opinion of the Accounting Principles Board No. 23. (New York, NY: Copyright 1972 by The American Institute of Certified Public Accountants.)
[2]*Accounting for Income Taxes—Investments in Common Stock Accounted for by the Equity Method (Other Than Subsidiaries and Corporate Joint Ventures),* Opinion of the Accounting Principles Board No. 24. (New York, NY: Copyright 1972 by the American Institute of Certified Public Accountants.)

Investments in Common Stock Accounted for by the Equity Method
(Other than Subsidiaries and Corporate Joint Ventures)
Financial Accounting Standards Board Statement No. 19[3]
Intangible Development Costs in the Gas and Oil Industry
Accounting Principles Board Opinion No. 28[4]
Financial Accounting Standards Board Interpretation No. 18[5]
Accounting for Income Taxes in Interim Periods

PRINCIPLES OF INCOME TAX ALLOCATION

The principles of income tax allocation are fully described in Chapter 1, "Interperiod Allocation of Income Taxes," including the comprehensive concept, the deferred method, pretax accounting income, permanent differences, and timing differences. The principles and definitions outlined in Chapter 1 apply, without any modification whatever, to the allocation of income taxes in the special areas covered in this chapter.

INDEFINITE REVERSAL CONCEPT

APB Opinion No. 23 develops the concept of "indefinite reversal" which infers that in certain circumstances a difference between taxable income and pretax accounting income may not reverse until indefinite future periods, or may never reverse. Such inference exists in situations where the taxpaying entity controls the events that create the tax consequence, and the entity is required to take specific action before the initial differences reverse. Examples of transactions to which the principles of the indefinite reversal concept may be applied are:

(a) Accounting for the undistributed earnings and losses of subsidiaries where the parent company has specific plans for the reinvestment of undistributed earnings of the subsidiary, which provide that remittance of the earnings will be postponed indefinitely; and

(b) Additions to bad debt reserves of savings and loan associations and stockholders' surplus of stock life insurance companies, both of which require deliberate action of the taxpayer to subsequently reduce the reserves and surplus, and thus create taxable income.

Differences subject to indefinite reversal are in the nature of permanent differences and, accordingly, no allocation of income taxes is recorded for such differences.

ESTIMATED EFFECTIVE TAX RATE FOR UNDISTRIBUTED EARNINGS AND INTERIM STATEMENTS

The estimated effective tax rate used to measure the tax effects of undistributed earnings of subsidiaries, and the estimated *annual* effective tax rate applied to periodic

---

[3]*Financial Accounting and Reporting by Oil and Gas Producing Companies*—Statement of the Financial Accounting Standards Board No. 19. (Stamford, Connecticut, Financial Accounting Standards Board, 1977. Reprinted with permission. Copies of the complete document are available from the FASB.)
[4]*Interim Financial Reporting*, Opinion of the Accounting Principles Board No. 28. (New York, NY: Copyright May, 1973, by the American Institute of Certified Public Accountants.)
[5]*Accounting for Income Taxes in Interim Periods—an Interpretation of APB Opinion No. 28*, Interpretation of the Financial Accounting Standards Board No. 18. (Stamford, Connecticut, Financial Accounting Standards Board, 1977. Reprinted with permission. Copies of the complete document are available from the FASB.)

carnings for interim reporting both should reflect all allowable tax credits and deductions, anticipated investment credits, foreign tax rates, and all other applicable tax planning alternatives.

TAX RATES USED TO DEMONSTRATE COMPUTATIONAL TECHNIQUES

For simplicity of presentation all computations made in this chapter are based on an assumed tax rate of 50%. This rate is used arbitrarily and is not meant to indicate a rate that should be used in actual practice.

ELEMENTS OF THE BOARD'S OPINIONS

Accounting Principles Board Opinions Nos. 23 and 24 consist of five separate Opinions dealing, respectively, with accounting for the tax effects of undistributed carnings of subsidiaries, investees, and corporate joint ventures, and with disclosing the potential tax consequences inherent in the current practice of accounting for the bad debt reserves of savings and loan associations and the policyholders' surplus of stock life insurance companies. The following recapitulation sets forth the essential elements contained in the separate Opinions on undistributed earnings. Analyses of the Opinions on bad debt reserves and stockholders' surplus are made later in the chapter, following the section on computational techniques.

UNDISTRIBUTED EARNINGS OF SUBSIDIARIES (APB OPINION NO. 23)

1. Generally, the undistributed earnings of a subsidiary included in income of the parent company should be accounted for as a timing difference, and the income taxes attributable to such timing difference should be accounted for in accordance with the provisions of APB Opinion No. 11.
2. However, the undistributed earnings of a subsidiary do not create a timing difference where earnings will be remitted in a tax-free liquidation or where the parent company has specific plans for reinvesting undistributed earnings of a subsidiary which provide that remittance of the earnings will be postponed indefinitely.
3. The tax effects of a difference between taxable income and pretax accounting income attributable to losses of a subsidiary should be accounted for in accordance with the net operating loss provisions of APB Opinion No. 11.
4. *Change of circumstances with respect to the presumption of distribution or non-distribution of earnings of a subsidiary*
   (a) Income taxes on undistributed earnings which have not been accrued should be set up by the parent company, and treated as an adjustment to income tax expense of the current period when it becomes apparent that some or all of such earnings will be distributed in the foreseeable future.
   (b) The income taxes on undistributed earnings which have been accrued by the parent company should be eliminated as a credit to income tax expense of the current period when it becomes apparent that such earnings will not be remitted in the foreseeable future.
   (c) The adjustments in (a) and (b) should not be accounted for as an extraordinary item.
5. *Change in status of investment—subsidiary becomes an investee accounted for by the equity method*
   (a) The investor should recognize income taxes on its share of current earnings of the investee company in accordance with APB Opinion No. 24.
   (b) Where a parent company did not recognize income taxes on its equity in undistributed earnings of a subsidiary because of the indefinite reversal concept, it

should accrue, as a current period expense, income taxes on undistributed earnings in the period that it becomes apparent that any of those undistributed earnings (prior to the change in status) will be remitted; the accrual of those income taxes should not be accounted for as an extraordinary item. However, the change in the status of an investment should not in itself indicate that remittance of those undistributed earnings should be considered apparent.

    (c) In cases where the parent company recognized income taxes on its equity in undistributed earnings of a subsidiary, such accrued income taxes should be considered in accounting for a disposition through sale or other transaction which reduces the investment.

6. *Disclosure*

Information concerning undistributed earnings of a subsidiary for which income taxes have not been accrued that should be disclosed in notes to the financial statements includes:

    (a) A declaration of an intention to reinvest undistributed earnings of a subsidiary to support the conclusion that remittance of those earnings has been indefinitely postponed, or a declaration that the undistributed earnings will be remitted in the form of a tax-free liquidation.

    (b) The cumulative amount of undistributed earnings on which the parent company has not recognized income taxes.

UNDISTRIBUTED EARNINGS OF CORPORATE JOINT VENTURES

1. The principles applicable to undistributed earnings of subsidiaries, set forth above, also apply to tax effects of differences between taxable income and pretax accounting income attributable to earnings of corporate joint ventures that are essentially permanent in duration, and accounted for by the equity method.

2. *Disclosure*

Information concerning the undistributed earnings of a corporate joint venture accounted for by the equity method for which income taxes have not been accrued should be disclosed in notes to the financial statements in the same manner as that required for undistributed earnings of subsidiaries, as described in a preceding paragraph.

INVESTMENTS IN COMMON STOCK ACCOUNTED FOR BY THE EQUITY METHOD (OTHER THAN SUBSIDIARIES AND JOINT VENTURES)

1. The undistributed earnings of an investee accounted for by the equity method included in the income of the investor should be accounted for as a timing difference, and the income taxes attributable to such timing difference should be accounted for in accordance with APB Opinion No. 11.

2. The tax effects of a difference between taxable income and pretax accounting income attributable to losses of an investee accounted for by the equity method should be accounted for in accordance with the net operating loss provisions of APB Opinion No. 11.

3. *Change in status of investment*

The method of accounting for the tax effects of undistributed earnings of an investee accounted for by the equity method should be modified to accommodate changes in the status of the investment, as outlined below.

    (a) *Investee becomes a subsidiary*

Where an investor acquires additional stock in an investee so that it becomes a subsidiary, the income taxes previously accrued by the investor should be included in the income of the parent only as dividends from the subsidiary are received in amounts that exceed the parent company's share of the earnings of the subsidiary subsequent to the date it became a subsidiary. (MODEL CASE NO. 6)

(b) *Equity method discontinued for investee*

Where an investment in the investee falls below the level of ownership necessary to enable the investee to follow the equity method of accounting, the deferred income taxes previously accrued by the investor should be included in the income of the former investor only as dividends from the former investee are received in amounts which exceed the former investor's allocable share of earnings of the former investee subsequent to the date it ceased to qualify as an investee. (MODEL CASE NO. 7)

(c) The amount of deferred income taxes of the investor attributable to its share of the equity in earnings of the investee company should be considered in accounting for a disposition through sale or other transactions that reduce the investment.

COMPUTATIONAL TECHNIQUES

The computational techniques demonstrated in this section are designed to illustrate all the situations covered in the Opinions with respect to undistributed earnings of subsidiaries and investees. These computational examples also serve the concomitant purpose of reducing the complex rhetoric of the Opinions to graphic illustration.

COMPUTATION OF THE TAX EFFECTS OF UNDISTRIBUTED EARNINGS

Computation of the tax effects of undistributed earnings of investees must be based on the status of the investment and on the tax rate appropriate in the circumstances. Varying degrees of percentage of ownership of an investee require differing treatments of income for tax purposes, and the tax benefits of capital gains, dividend deductions, etc. result in divergent effective income tax rates.

EFFECTIVE TAX RATES ON EARNINGS OF SUBSIDIARIES

The effective federal income tax rate to be applied to unremitted earnings of subsidiaries depends upon the percentage of ownership of the investor.

Percentage of Ownership 80% or More

Federal income tax regulations permit 80% or more owned corporations to file consolidated tax returns, and thus eliminate all intercompany dividends. Also, 80% or more owned companies constitute a controlled group and are entitled to a 100% dividend deduction for intercompany dividends.

Therefore, the effective federal income tax rate to be applied to undistributed earnings of 80% or more owned subsidiaries is zero, and income taxes on such earnings should not be accrued by the parent company.

Percentage of Ownership Less Than 80%

The effective tax rate to be applied to unremitted earnings of less than 80% owned subsidiaries should be based on the assumption that unremitted earnings were distributed in the current period and that the parent company received the benefit of all available tax planning alternatives and available tax credits and deductions. The major tax credit with respect to unremitted subsidiary earnings is the 85% dividend deduction allowed for tax purposes.

EFFECTIVE TAX RATES ON EARNINGS OF INVESTEES

The effective federal income tax rate to be applied to undistributed earnings of investees depends upon the percentage of ownership and the intention of the investor.

Percentage of Ownership Less Than 20%

An investment of less than 20% of the voting stock of the investee generally cannot be accounted for by the equity method and therefore income taxes should not be accrued on such investment.

Percentage of Ownership 20% to 50%

As in the case of less than 80% owned subsidiaries, the effective tax rate to be applied to investments comprehending 20% to 50% ownership of the investee should be based on the assumption that unremitted earnings were distributed in the current period and that the parent company received the benefit of all available tax planning alternatives and available tax credits and deductions. The major tax credit is, of course, the 85% dividend deduction.

Investments Subject to Ultimate Disposition

Where an investor's equity in undistributed earnings of a 20% to 50% owned investee will be realized by ultimate disposition of the investment, the investor should accrue income taxes attributable to the timing differences at capital gains or other appropriate rates, recognizing all available deductions and credits.

DEFERRED TAXES ON UNDISTRIBUTED EARNINGS AND LOSSES OF SUBSIDIARY

Generally there is a presumption that all undistributed earnings of a subsidiary will be transferred to the parent company. This presumption may be overcome if the earnings ultimately will be remitted in a tax-free liquidation, *or* if the parent company has specific plans for reinvestment of undistributed earnings of the subsidiary which provides that remittance of such earnings will be postponed indefinitely.

In the absence of conditions indicating a tax-free liquidation or indefinite postponement of remittance of earnings, the parent company should account for the undistributed earnings of a subsidiary as a timing difference, and income taxes at current rates should be accrued on all such undistributed earnings included in consolidated income, or in the parent company's income.

Where a parent company follows the practice of accruing income taxes on undistributed earnings of a subsidiary, the parent should adjust its deferred income tax credits for any losses sustained by the subsidiary. However, the parent should recognize the *tax benefits* of subsidiary losses only when realization *by the subsidiary* of such benefits is assured beyond any reasonable doubt. For example, subsidiary losses that can be carried back by the subsidiary result in a tax benefit that may be recognized in the loss year, and the operating loss of the subsidiary would be reduced by the amount of the refundable income taxes. In such a situation, the parent would reduce its deferred income tax credits in an amount computed by applying the current tax rate to the net loss of the subsidiary. However, if the operating loss of the subsidiary *cannot* be carried back, and results in a carryforward, the tax benefits of the carryforward normally should not be recognized by the parent company, and it should adjust its deferred income tax credits in an amount equivalent to that determined by applying the current tax rate to the operating loss of the subsidiary.

Model Case No. 1 is an example of a parent company accruing income taxes on the undistributed earnings of a subsidiary, and also an example of the reduction of the parent's deferred income tax credits resulting from an operating loss that can be carried back by the subsidiary.

MODEL CASE NO. 1

In 19x2 Conlon, Inc. purchased 60% of the outstanding shares of common stock of Warner Company. At the time of the purchase Conlon had no specific plans for re-investment of the undistributed earnings of the subsidiary, nor was there any indication that remittance of such earnings would be postponed indefinitely. Consequently, Conlon, Inc. determined that undistributed earnings of Warner Company included in consolidated income would be accounted for as a timing difference.

The operations of the subsidiary in 19x2 and 19x3 were profitable and resulted in earnings, but in 19x4 the subsidiary sustained a loss. In each of the years, however, the subsidiary paid a cash dividend of $100,000. Warner Company's earnings, loss, and payments of dividends for the three-year period are summarized below:

	Income (Loss) Before Income Taxes	Cash Dividends Paid
19x2	500,000	100,000
19x3	600,000	100,000
19x4	(300,000)	100,000

Conlon, Inc. computed the tax effect of the timing differences resulting from the changes in undistributed earnings of the subsidiary as shown in Schedule 1.

COMPUTATION OF THE TAX EFFECTS OF TIMING DIFFERENCES

	19x2	19x3	19x4
Subsidiary income (loss) before income taxes	500,000	600,000	(300,000)
Income taxes to be paid by (refunded to) subsidiary	250,000	300,000	(150,000)
Subsidiary net income (loss)	250,000	300,000	(150,000)
Cash dividends paid by subsidiary	100,000	100,000	100,000
Net increase (decrease) in stockholders' equity in subsidiary	150,000	200,000	(250,000)
Parent's percentage of ownership	60%	60%	60%
Parent's share of earnings (loss)	90,000	120,000	(150,000)
Parent's dividend deduction—85%	76,500	102,000	(127,500)
Taxable increase (decrease in parent's share of undistributed earnings of subsidiary	13,500	18,000	(22,500)
Tax rate	50%	50%	50%
Increase (decrease) in deferred income tax credits on undistributed earnings of subsidiary	6,750	9,000	(11,250)

SCHEDULE 1

The following summary indicates the entry made by Conlon, Inc. at the end of each respective year to account for the deferred income tax credits related to the changes in timing differences as shown in Schedule 1.

	19x2 Dr. (Cr.)	19x3 Dr. (Cr.)	19x4 Dr. (Cr.)
Income Tax Expense	6,750	9,000	(11,250)
Deferred income tax credits	(6,750)	(9,000)	11,250

At the end of 19x4 the balance in the deferred income tax credits' account on Conlon's books was $4,500. This amount represented the tax effect at 7.50% on the $60,000 increase in equity in the subsidiary since date of purchase that had been included in consolidated income.

EFFECT OF SALE OF SUBSIDIARY STOCK ON ACCUMULATED DEFERRED INCOME TAX CREDITS

Where a parent company follows the practice of accruing income taxes on the undistributed earnings of a subsidiary, the related accumulated deferred income tax credits should be considered in accounting for disposition of stock in the subsidiary through sale or other transaction which reduces the percentage of the parent's ownership.

Model Case No. 2 demonstrates the required computation and the appropriate procedures to account for deferred income tax credits where the parent company reduces its percentage of ownership in a subsidiary by selling a portion of its investment in the subsidiary.

MODEL CASE NO. 2

In Model Case No. 1 it was demonstrated that at December 31, 19x4 Conlon, Inc. had a credit balance in its deferred income tax credits' account in the amount of $4,500, representing the tax effects of the timing differences resulting from the undistributed earnings of its subsidiary, Warner Company.

At that time Conlon, Inc. owned 60% of the outstanding common stock of the subsidiary. However, on January 2, 19x5 Conlon sold 8-$1/3$% of the stock it held in the subsidiary and, consequently, after the sale it owned only 55% of the outstanding stock of Warner Company. Since the sale of the subsidiary stock resulted in an 8-$1/3$% reduction in the equity in undistributed earnings of Warner, it was necessary for the parent company to adjust the deferred income tax credits' account. Accordingly, on January 2, 19x5 Conlon, Inc. made the following entry to accomplish the required adjustment, and to record the adjustment as an element of income in the current period:

	Debit	Credit
Deferred income tax credits	375	
Income from elimination of deferred income tax credits		375

To reduce deferred income taxes credit balance of $4,500 by 8-$1/3$% due to sale of 8-$1/3$% of common stock of subsidiary.

Warner Company operations in 19x5 resulted in a net income of $175,000, and during the year it paid cash dividends of $100,000. Conlon, Inc. computed the tax effect of the timing difference due to the undistributed 19x5 earnings of the subsidiary included in consolidated income as follows:

Subsidiary net income	175,000
Cash dividends paid by subsidiary	100,000
Increase in stockholders' equity in subsidiary	75,000
Parent's percentage of ownership	55%
Parent's share of earnings	41,250
Parent's dividend deduction—85%	35,063
Taxable increase in parent's share of undistributed earnings of subsidiary	6,187
Tax rate	50%
Increase in deferred income tax credits on undistributed earnings of subsidiary	3,094

The balance in the deferred income tax credits' account at December 31, 19x5 was $7,219, and the changes in the account during the year are summarized as follows:

Balance—January 1, 19x5	4,500
Deduct—Adjustment for sale of stock	375
	4,125
Add—Tax effect of origination of timing differences in 19x5 due to increase in undistributed earnings of subsidiary	3,094
Balance—December 31, 19x5	7,219

CHANGES IN CONDITIONS AFFECTING ACCRUAL OF INCOME TAXES ON UNDISTRIBUTED EARNINGS OF A SUBSIDIARY

A parent company is either required to accrue income taxes on the timing difference resulting from the undistributed earnings of a subsidiary under the presumption that all the earnings will be ultimately remitted, or it is exempt from such requirement under the indefinite reversal concept. Changes can occur in the circumstances that determine a particular company's policy in connection with accruing income taxes on undistributed earnings, and when a company changes its policy, it should make appropriate adjustments to its deferred income taxes, if any, to accommodate the change in conditions.

Model Cases Nos. 3 and 4 illustrate situations where, because of a change in circumstances, parent companies were compelled to change their accounting policies with respect to accrual of income taxes on undistributed earnings of subsidiaries.

TERMINATION OF PRACTICE OF ACCRUING INCOME TAXES

When it becomes apparent that some or all of the undistributed earnings of a subsidiary on which income taxes have been accrued will not be remitted in the foreseeable future, the parent company should make an appropriate adjustment to income tax expense of the current period.

Model Case No. 3 illustrates the computation and accounting procedures required for the elimination of deferred income tax credits where circumstances change so that undistributed earnings of a subsidiary will not be distributed in the foreseeable future.

MODEL CASE NO. 3

At December 31, 19x5 Conlon, Inc. owned 55% of the outstanding stock of Warner Company, and at that time it had a balance of $7,219 in its deferred income tax credits account, representing the tax effects of the timing differences resulting from undistributed earnings of the subsidiary.

During the year 19x6 the Board of Directors of Conlon, Inc. authorized the purchase of an additional 20% of the total outstanding stock of Warner Company from its minority stockholders and at the same time adopted a long-term investment plan in connection with the subsidiary that provided for reinvestment of undistributed earnings of the subsidiary and an indefinite postponement of remittance of such earnings. The changed fiscal plans required that the deferred income tax credits be eliminated from the books of the parent company and, accordingly, at December 31, 19x6 Conlon, Inc. made the following entry to eliminate the accumulated deferred income tax credits and to record income from the elimination in the current period:

	Debit	Credit
Deferred income tax credits	7,219	
Income from elimination of deferred income tax credits		7,219
To eliminate the balance of deferred income tax credits and		
to take up an equivalent amount in current income.		

A history of the tax effect of the changes in cumulative timing differences from the date of the purchase of the subsidiary to the time of adoption of the indefinite reversal policy is shown in Schedule 2. These changes are set forth in Model Cases Nos. 1, 2, and 3.

SUMMARY OF CHANGES IN CUMULATIVE TIMING DIFFERENCES

Tax effect of origination of timing differences resulting from an increase in undistributed earnings of subsidiary:	
19x2	6,750
19x3	9,000
19x5	3,094
Tax effect of a reduction in timing differences resulting from a decrease in undistributed earnings of subsidiary due to net operating loss sustained in 19x4	(11,250)
Tax effect of a reduction in timing differences resulting from a decrease in equity in the subsidiary due to a sale of subsidiary stock in 19x5	(375)
Balance in deferred income tax credits account at December 31, 19x5	7,219
Elimination of tax effects on cumulative timing differences due to adoption of a policy of indefinite reversal in 19x6	7,219
Balance in deferred income tax credits account at December 31, 19x6	None

---

SCHEDULE 2

INITIATING THE PRACTICE OF ACCRUING INCOME TAXES

Where it becomes apparent that some or all of the undistributed earnings of a subsidiary will be remitted in the foreseeable future, and accrued income taxes have not been set up by the parent company, the parent company should accrue, as an expense of the current period, income taxes attributable to that remittance.

Model Case No. 4 demonstrates the required computations and accounting procedures to create deferred income tax credits where circumstances change so that undistributed earnings of a subsidiary will be remitted in the foreseeable future.

MODEL CASE NO. 4

Arnold, Inc. purchased 75% of the authorized and outstanding stock of Kerr & Company in 19x1. At the time of the purchase the Board of Directors of Arnold, Inc. approved long-term fiscal plans that provided for a program of expansion for the subsidiary through reinvestment of the subsidiary's undistributed earnings and, accordingly, adopted a resolution that remittance of earnings from the subsidiary would be postponed indefinitely. Under the circumstances, it was determined by Arnold, Inc. that earnings of the subsidiary included in the consolidated income would constitute differences that would not reverse until indefinite future periods, and, therefore, income taxes were not required to be accrued for the tax effects of the timing differences.

In the first three years the operations of the subsidiary were profitable and the resulting net income of the subsidiary was included in consolidated income without any provision being made for deferred income taxes on the undistributed earnings of the subsidiary. However, by the end of 19x4 the plans for expansion of the operations of Kerr & Company had been abandoned, and it became apparent that most or all of the undistributed earnings of the subsidiary would be remitted to the parent company in the foreseeable future. In the changed circumstances it was determined that Kerr & Company would pay a substantial cash dividend in 19x4 and at the end of the year Arnold, Inc. would accrue deferred income tax credits for the tax effects of the timing differences resulting from the undistributed earnings of Kerr & Company that had been, and would be in the current year, included in the consolidated income of the parent company. Kerr & Company's earnings and payment of dividends for the four-year period are summarized below:

	Net Income	Cash Dividends Paid
19x1	150,000	—
19x2	200,000	—
19x3	250,000	—
19x4	300,000	300,000
	900,000	300,000

Schedule 3 discloses the method used by Arnold, Inc. to compute the deferred income tax credits originating from the tax effects of including undistributed earnings of the subsidiary in the consolidated income of the parent over the four-year period.

COMPUTATION OF THE TAX EFFECTS OF TIMING DIFFERENCES

From Foregoing Summary

Subsidiary net income for four years	900,000
Less: Cash dividends paid	300,000
Net increase in stockholders' equity in subsidiary over four years	600,000
Parent's percentage of ownership	75%
Parent's share of earnings	450,000
Parent's dividend deduction—85%	382,500
Taxable increase in parent's share of undistributed earnings of subsidiary	67,500
Tax rate	50%
Deferred income tax credits required to be accrued in 19x4	33,750

SCHEDULE 3

Income taxes on its share of the $300,000 dividend from the subsidiary in 19x4 were paid currently by Arnold, Inc., and Arnold made the following entry to accrue deferred income taxes on the undistributed earnings of the subsidiary over the four-year period and to record an equivalent amount as an expense of the current period:

	Debit	Credit
Loss from creating deferred income tax credits	33,750	
Deferred income tax credits		33,750

CHANGES IN STATUS OF INVESTMENT AFFECTING ACCRUAL OF INCOME TAXES ON UNDISTRIBUTED EARNINGS OF SUBSIDIARY

A change in percentage of ownership of an investment accounted for by the equity method can affect the investor's income tax accrual policy. The paragraph that follows, and Model Case No. 5, illustrate the effects on accounting policy caused by a change in percentage of stock held in a subsidiary.

INVESTMENT LOSES STATUS AS A SUBSIDIARY

Where the investment in common stock of a subsidiary changes so that it no longer is a subsidiary, and the remaining investment in common stock is accounted for by the equity method, the investor should recognize income taxes on its share of current earnings of the investee company in accordance with the provisions of APB Opinion No. 24, which are described in a following section of this chapter, and illustrated in Model Case No. 1.

Where the parent company had been accruing income taxes on the undistributed earnings of the subsidiary prior to the change in percentage of ownership, it is necessary for the investor to adjust its deferred income tax credits to conform to the changed conditions as demonstrated in Model Case No. 2, which illustrates the required computations and accounting procedures necessary to develop and record the required adjustments.

In a case where a parent company did not recognize income taxes on its equity in undistributed earnings of the subsidiary because of application of the principles of the indefinite reversal concept, and the investment ceases to be a subsidiary, it should accrue as a current period expense income taxes on undistributed earnings in the period that it becomes apparent that any of these undistributed earnings accumulated prior to the change in status will be remitted.

Model Case No. 5 illustrates the computations and accounting procedures required in a situation where an investment loses its status as a subsidiary and it is subsequently determined that a portion of the pre-change earnings on which no income taxes were accrued will be remitted to the investor.

MODEL CASE NO. 5

In 19x1 The Cole Corporation purchased 60% of the outstanding shares of common stock of Lucas Bros. Cole made the investment in Lucas Bros. in accordance with a long-term fiscal plan that called for reinvestment of undistributed earnings of the subsidiary and indefinite postponement of remittance of such earnings. Therefore, it did not accrue income taxes on the undistributed earnings of Lucas Bros. for the years 19x1, 19x2, and 19x3.

In 19x4 Cole sold one-third of its stock holdings in Lucas Bros. The sale reduced Cole's percentage of ownership of Lucas Bros. from 60% to 40%, and resulted in a change of status of the investment from that of a subsidiary to that of an investee company. Consequently, Cole was required to account for its investment in Lucas Bros. by the equity method, and it was further required to accrue income taxes at normal tax rates on its share of the undistributed earnings of the investee which were earned subsequent to the date of the change of status of the investment.

A history of the earnings and cash dividends paid by Lucas Bros. in the years from 19x1 to 19x6 is summarized below:

	Net Income	Cash Dividends Paid
As a Subsidiary		
19x1	150,000	None
19x2	200,000	None
19x3	250,000	None
	600,000	None
As an Investee Company		
19x4	250,000	100,000
19x5	300,000	200,000
19x6	350,000	150,000
	900,000	450,000

The Cole Corporation computed the tax effects of the differences between its taxable income and pretax accounting income attributable to its share of earnings of Lucas Bros. and accrued deferred income tax credits for such tax effects as shown in Schedule 4.

COMPUTATION OF TAX EFFECTS OF DIFFERENCES BETWEEN TAXABLE INCOME AND PRETAX
ACCOUNTING INCOME ATTRIBUTABLE TO EARNINGS OF INVESTEE COMPANY

	19x4	19x5	19x6
Investee net income	250,000	300,000	350,000
Less: Cash dividends paid by investee	100,000	200,000	150,000
Net increase in stockholders' equity in investee	150,000	100,000	200,000
Percentage of investor's ownership	40%	40%	40%
Investor's share of earnings	60,000	40,000	80,000
Investor's dividend deduction—85%	51,000	34,000	68,000
Taxable increase in investor's share of undistributed earnings of investee	9,000	6,000	12,000
Tax rate	50%	50%	50%
Increase in deferred income tax credits on undistributed earnings of investee	4,500	3,000	6,000

SCHEDULE 4

The following is a summary of the entries made by The Cole Corporation to ac-crue income taxes on the increase in its equity in Lucas Bros. for each respective year:

	19x4 Dr.(Cr.)	19x5 Dr.(Cr.)	19x6 Dr.(Cr.)
Income tax expense	4,500	3,000	6,000
Deferred income tax credits	(4,500)	(3,000)	(6,000)

In 19x6 it became apparent that the new management of Lucas Bros. had aban-doned the fiscal plan that required reinvestment of undistributed earnings and The Cole Corporation was persuaded that all, or almost all, of the undistributed earnings of Lucas Bros. would be remitted in the foreseeable future. Consequently, Cole decid-ed to accrue income taxes on its share of the earnings of Lucas Bros. that had accumu-lated prior to the change in status from subsidiary to investee company.

In making the computation for deferred income taxes on undistributed earnings applicable to the period in which Lucas Bros. was a subsidiary, Cole took into consid-eration that had the parent company accrued income taxes on such earnings, one-third of such accrued taxes would have been eliminiated at the time Cole sold the stock in Lucas Bros. that reduced its percentage of ownership to 40%. Therefore, Cole used 40% of the $600,000 aggregate net income of Lucas Bros. for the years 19x6 to 19x3, shown in the foregoing summary of the history of earnings of the subsidiary, and com-puted deferred income taxes on those earnings as follows:

Net income of Lucas Bros.—19x1 to 19x3	600,000
Investor's percentage of ownership at December 31, 19x6	40%
Increase in equity in Lucas Bros. over cost of investment applicable to years 19x1 to 19x3	240,000
Investor's dividend deduction—85%	204,000
Taxable increase in investor's share of undistributed earnings of Lucas Bros.	36,000
Tax rate	50%
Aggregate deferred income tax credits to be created for years 19x1, 19x2, and 19x3	18,000

At December 31, 19x6 The Cole Corporation made the following entry to record the deferred income tax credits applicable to the years 19x1 to 19x3, and to charge the adjustment to expense in the current period:

	Debit	Credit
Provision for accrual of deferred income tax credits	18,000	
Deferred income tax credits		18,000

DEFERRED INCOME TAX CREDITS ON UNDISTRIBUTED EARNINGS AND LOSSES OF CORPORATE JOINT VENTURES

APB Opinion No. 18[6] requires that all corporate joint ventures be accounted for by the equity method. Accordingly, income taxes on undistributed earnings of corporate joint ventures generally should be accrued at the time the earnings or losses are included in the investor's income. APB Opinion No. 23 differentiates between corporate joint ventures of permanent duration and those having a limited life; and the Opinion sets forth the principles of interperiod tax allocation applicable to each respective type.

Permanent Corporate Joint Ventures

The principles applicable to tax allocation or undistributed earnings of subsidiaries also apply to undistributed earnings of corporate joint ventures that are essentially permanent in duration. Therefore, the computational techniques and the accounting procedures described and demonstrated in the foregoing Model Cases Nos. 1 to 5 apply to investments in corporate joint ventures of permanent duration, as well as to investments in subsidiaries.

Limited-Life Corporate Joint Ventures

APB Opinion No. 23 states that there is a presumption that a part or all of the undistributed earnings of a corporate joint venture of limited duration will be transferred to the investor in a taxable distribution, and that deferred taxes should be recorded in accordance with the concepts of APB Opinion No. 11 at the time the earnings or losses are included in the investor's income. Chapter 1 explained and illustrated the concepts and principles of interperiod income tax allocation contained in APB Opinion No. 11. Model Case No. 1 in this chapter illustrates the method of computing and accounting for deferred income taxes applicable to earnings and losses of a corporate joint venture having a limited life.

UNDISTRIBUTED EARNINGS OF INVESTEES OTHER THAN SUBSIDIARIES AND CORPORATE JOINT VENTURES

Deferred income taxes on the earnings and losses of investees accounted for by the equity method other than subsidiaries and corporate joint ventures should be recorded in accordance with the concepts of APB Opinion No. 11 at the time such earnings and losses are included in the investor's income. As stated in the preceding paragraph, Chapter 1 of this volume contained detailed explanations and illustrations of the principles and concepts of interperiod income tax allocation contained in APB Opinion No. 11. Model Case No. 1 in this chapter demonstrates the computations and accounting procedures necessary to properly record the deferred income taxes on undistributed earnings of investees in accordance with the provisions of APB Opinion No. 11.

---

[6]*The Equity Method of Accounting for Investments in Common Stock,* Opinion of the Accounting Principles Board No. 18. (New York, NY: Copyright 1967 by the American Institute of Certified Public Accountants.)

INDEFINITE REVERSAL CONCEPT NOT APPLICABLE TO EARNINGS OF INVESTEES OTHER THAN SUBSIDIARIES AND CORPORATE JOINT VENTURES

APB Opinion No. 24 states that the ability of an investor to exercise significant influence over an investee differs significantly from the ability of a parent company to control investment policies of a subsidiary and that only control can justify the conclusion that undistributed earnings may be invested for indefinite periods.

CHANGE IN STATUS OF INVESTMENT AFFECTING ACCRUAL OF INCOME TAXES ON UNDISTRIBUTED EARNINGS OF AN INVESTEE ACCOUNTED FOR BY THE EQUITY METHOD

As previously indicated, a change in percentage of ownership of an investment accounted for by the equity method can affect the investor's income tax accrual policy. Model Cases Nos. 6 and 7 illustrate the effects on accounting policy caused by a change in percentage of stock held in an investee other than a subsidiary or corporate joint venture.

INVESTEE BECOMES A SUBSIDIARY

Where the percentage of ownership of an investee is increased so that the investee becomes a subsidiary the deferred income taxes previously accrued by the investor should be included in the income of the parent company only as dividends from the subsidiary are received in amounts which exceed the parent company's share of the earnings of the subsidiary subsequent to the date it became a subsidiary.

Model Case No. 6 illustrates the required computations and accounting procedures in a situation where an investee becomes a subsidiary and subsequent dividends from the subsidiary exceed the parent company's share of the earnings of the subsidiary.

MODEL CASE NO. 6

In 19x1 Oakland Corp. purchased 30% of the outstanding shares of common stock of Maxwell Bros., and accounted for the investment by the equity method. In 19x4 Oakland purchased an additional 30% of the outstanding stock of Maxwell Bros., thereby changing the status of Maxwell Bros. from that of an investee to a 60% owned subsidiary.

At December 31, 19x3 the net undistributed earnings of Maxwell Bros. included in the income of Oakland Corp. over the three-year term of the investment amounted to $150,000, and Oakland Corp. had to create deferred income tax credits of $11,250 on such earnings. In 19x4 and 19x5 the dividends received from the subsidiary did not exceed the parent's share of the aggregate earnings of the subsidiary for those two years. However, the dividend received in 19x6 from the subsidiary caused the aggregate dividends received over the three years during which Maxwell was a subsidiary to exceed Oakland's share of the subsidiary's earnings over the same period. Consequently, it became necessary for Oakland to adjust the deferred income tax credits created for the years prior to the year Maxwell became a subsidiary, and to take an amount equivalent to such adjustment into current income.

The subsidiary's earnings and cash dividend payments over the three-year period are summarized below:

	Net Income	Dividends Paid	Increase (Decrease) in Stockholders' Equity
19x4	200,000	100,000	100,000
19x5	250,000	200,000	50,000
19x6	300,000	500,000	(200,000)
	750,000	800,000	(50,000)

The tax effects of the origination and reduction in timing differences that occurred in 19x4 and 19x5 are shown in Schedule 5.

COMPUTATION OF TAX EFFECTS IN ORIGINATION AND REDUCTION OF TIMING DIFFERENCES

	19x4	19x5
Subsidiary net income	200,000	250,000
Cash dividends paid by subsidiary	100,000	200,000
Net increase in stockholders' equity in subsidiary	100,000	50,000
Parent's percentage of ownership	60%	60%
Parent's share of earnings (loss)	60,000	30,000
Parent's dividend deduction—85%	51,000	25,500
Taxable increase (decrease) in parent's share of undistributed earnings of subsidiary	9,000	4,500
Tax rate	50%	50%
Increase in deferred income tax credits on undistributed earnings of subsidiary	4,500	2,250

SCHEDULE 5

The entries made by Oakland Corp. to record the changes in deferred income tax credits for the two years were as follows:

	19x4 Dr. (Cr.)	19x5 Dr. (Cr.)
Income tax expense	4,500	2,250
Deferred income tax credits	(4,500)	(2,250)

The foregoing summary of the subsidiary's earnings and dividend distribution indicates that the 19x6 dividend of $500,000 decreased the stockholders' equity for the year by $200,000 and caused the aggregate dividends paid to exceed the subsidiary's aggregate earnings by $50,000 over the three-year period. Therefore, the tax effects of the parent's share of $50,000 of the $200,00 decrease in equity was taken into current income as an adjustment of deferred taxes accrued for the years prior to the year Maxwell became a subsidiary. The tax effects of the parent's share of the remaining $150,000 decrease in equity were applied to reduce deferred income taxes set up in 19x4 and 19x5. Schedule 6 shows the method of computation for the required adjustment to deferred income taxes.

COMPUTATION OF ADJUSTMENT TO DEFERRED INCOME TAX CREDITS
CREATED PRIOR TO CHANGE IN INVESTMENT

	Tax Effect of Decrease in Timing Difference (Credit to Current Income Tax Expense)	Tax Effect of Excess of Dividends Paid Over Earnings (Credit to Current Income)
Net (decrease) in stockholders' equity in subsidiary	(150,000)	(50,000)
Parent's percentage of ownership	60%	60%
Parent's share of (decrease) in stockholders' equity in subsidiary	(90,000)	(30,000)
Parent's dividend deduction—85%	76,500	25,500
Taxable (decrease) in parent's share of undistributed earnings of subsidiary	(13,500)	(4,500)
Tax rate	50%	50%
(Decrease) in deferred income tax credits	(6,750)	(2,250)

SCHEDULE 6

At December 31, 19x6 Oakland Corp. made the following entry to record the adjustment in deferred income tax credits:

	Debit	Credit
Deferred income tax credits	9,000	
Income tax expense		6,750
Income from elimination of deferred income tax credits		2,250

TERMINATION OF THE EQUITY METHOD OF ACCOUNTING FOR AN INVESTEE

Where the investment in an investee falls below the level of ownership necessary to enable the investor to follow the equity method of accounting, the deferred income taxes previously accrued by the investor should be included in the income of the former investor. This should be done only as dividends from the former investee are received in amounts which exceed the former investor's allocable share of earnings of the former investee, subsequent to the date it ceased to qualify as an investee.

Model Case No. 7 illustrates procedures to be followed in situations where the equity method of accounting is discontinued, and subsequent dividends from the former investee exceed the former investor's allocable share of earnings.

MODEL CASE NO. 7

In 19x1 Cumberland Corp. purchased 30% of the outstanding common stock of Ingram, Inc. and accounted for the investment by the equity method. From 19x1 to 19x3 the undistributed earnings of the investee company included in Cumberland's income amounted to $240,000, and during that time Cumberland had set up deferred income tax credits aggregating $18,000.

In 19x4 Cumberland sold two-thirds of its stock in Ingram, Inc., thereby reducing its percentage of ownership to 10%. Consequently, Cumberland was required to change its method of accounting for the investment in Ingram, Inc. from the equity method to the cost method.

At the time of the sale of Ingram, Inc. stock Cumberland eliminated two-thirds of the deferred income tax credits by making the following entry:

	Debit	Credit
Deferred income tax credits	12,000	
Income from eliminating deferred income tax credits		12,000

In the three years from 19x4 to 19x6 the aggregate dividends received from Ingram, Inc. exceeded Cumberland's aggregate share of the earnings of the former investee. Therefore, Cumberland was required to adjust the deferred income tax credits accrued by Cumberland for the years prior to the year in which Ingram ceased to be an investee, and to take an amount equivalent to such adjustment into current income.

Ingram's income and dividend distributions from 19x4 to 19x6 are summarized below:

	Net Income	Cash Dividends Paid	Increase (Decrease) in Stockholders' Equity
19x4	200,000	100,000	100,000
19x5	250,000	200,000	50,000
19x6	300,000	600,000	(300,000)
	750,000	900,000	(150,000)

The entries made by Cumberland at the end of 19x4 and 19x5 to record its share of the dividends paid by Ingram, Inc. in each respective year were as follows:

	19x4		19x5	
	Debit	Credit	Debit	Credit
Cash	10,000		20,000	
Dividend income		10,000		20,000

In 19x6 Cumberland again recorded its dividend income in the same manner as above, but it was also necessary at that time to eliminate a portion of the deferred income tax credits it had accrued prior to the time Ingram, Inc. ceased to qualify as an investee. Cumberland computed the required adjustment as follows:

Excess of dividends received over net income earned for the years
    subsequent to the time Ingram, Inc. ceased to qualify as an investee

accounted for by the equity method	150,000
Cumberland's percentage of stock ownership	10%
Cumberland's share of decrease in stockholders' equity in Ingram, Inc.	15,000
Cumberland's dividend deduction—85%	12,750
Taxable portion of Cumberland's share in decrease in stockholders' equity in Ingram, Inc.	2,250
Tax rate	50%
Deferred tax credits to be eliminated	1,125

Cumberland therefore made the following entries to record its dividend income and to take into current income an amount equivalent to the eliminated deferred income tax credits:

	Debit	Credit
Cash	60,000	
Dividend income		60,000
Deferred income tax credits	1,125	
Income from eliminating deferred income tax credits		1,125

SAVINGS AND LOAN ASSOCIATIONS AND STOCK LIFE INSURANCE COMPANIES

The particular transactions of savings and loan associations and of stock life insurance companies, respectively described in the following paragraphs, are subject to the principles of the indefinite reversal concept and, accordingly, are exempt from the requirements for accrual of income taxes on the differences between taxable income and pretax accounting income created by such transactions.

"BAD DEBT RESERVES" OF SAVINGS AND LOAN ASSOCATIONS

A savings and loan association should not provide income taxes on the differences between taxable income and pretax accounting income attributable to a bad debt reserve that is accounted for as a part of the general reserves and undivided profits of the association.

DISCLOSURE

Information that should be disclosed in notes to financial statements of a savings and loan association concerning bad debt reserves that are accounted for as a part of the general reserves and undivided profits includes:

(a) The purposes for which the reserves are provided under the applicable rules and regulations and the fact that income taxes may be payable if the reserves are used for other purposes, and

(b) The accumulated amount of the reserves for which income taxes have not been accrued.

"POLICYHOLDERS' SURPLUS" OF STOCK LIFE INSURANCE COMPANIES

A stock life insurance company should not accrue income taxes on the difference between taxable income and pretax accounting income attributable to amounts designated as policyholders' surplus.

DISCLOSURE

Information concerning amounts designated as policyholders' surplus of a stock life insurance company that should be disclosed in notes to financial statements includes:

(a) The treatment of policyholders' surplus under the United States Internal Revenue Code and the fact that income taxes may be payable if the company takes certain specified actions, which should be appropriately described, and

(b) The accumulated amount of the policyholders' surplus for which income taxes have not been accrued.

INTANGIBLE DEVELOPMENT COSTS AND STATUTORY DEPLETION IN THE OIL AND GAS INDUSTRY

In APB Opinion No. 11 the Board deferred any conclusion on the problems of income tax allocation in the oil and gas producing industry with respect to intangible development costs or the interaction of statutory depletion and cost depletion. In December 1977, after enormous controversy, the Financial Accounting Standards Board (FASB) published Statement No. 19, "Financial Accounting and Reporting by Oil and Gas Producing Companies," which contains guidelines for the allocation of income taxes by such companies.

The provisions of FASB Statement No. 19 in connection with allocation of income taxes by oil and gas producing companies are as follows:

1. Comprehensive interperiod income tax allocation by the deferred method, as described in APB Opinion No. 11, shall be followed by oil and gas producing companies for intangible drilling and development costs and other costs incurred that enter into the determination of taxable income and pretax accounting income in different periods.

2. The excess of statutory depletion over cost depletion for tax purposes shall be accounted for as a permanent difference in the period in which the excess is deducted from income tax purposes.

TAX ALLOCATION FOR INTERIM FINANCIAL REPORTS

The Accounting Principles Board published Opinion No. 28 in May 1973 for the purpose of clarifying the application of accounting and reporting principles to interim financial information, including interim financial statements. Paragraphs 19 and 20 of the Opinion state that income taxes provisions for interim financial statements should be determined under the procedures set forth in APB Opinions Nos. 11, 23, and 24, and further provided that the tax or benefits related to ordinary income or loss should be computed at an estimated annual effective tax rate and the tax or benefit related to all other items be individually computed and recognized when the items occur.

TAX EFFECTS OF LOSSES IN INTERIM PERIODS

With respect to recognizing the tax effects of losses in interim statements, APB Opinion No. 28 provides the following guidelines:

1. The tax effects of losses that arise in the early portion of a fiscal year (in the event carryback of such losses is not possible) should be recognized only when realization is assured beyond any reasonable doubt.

2. An established seasonal pattern of loss in early periods offset by income in later interim periods should constitute evidence that realization is assured beyond reasonable doubt.

3. The tax effects of losses incurred in early interim periods may be recognized in a later interim period of a fiscal year if their realization, although initially uncertain, later becomes assured beyond reasonable doubt.
4. When the tax effects of losses that arise in the early portions of a fiscal year are not recognized in that interim period, no tax provision should be made for income that arises in later interim periods until the tax effects of the previous interim losses are utilized.
5. The tax benefits of interim losses accounted for in this manner should not be reported as extraordinary items in the results of operations of the interim periods.

EFFECTS OF NEW TAX LEGISLATION

Changes resulting from new tax legislation should be reflected after the effective dates prescribed in the statutes.

FASB INTERPRETATION NO. 18

In March 1977 the Financial Accounting Standards Board published Interpretation No. 18 for the purpose of explaining the provisions of APB Opinion No. 28 with respect to accounting for income taxes in interim periods. The Interpretation did not change the basic concept of APB Opinion No. 28 and thus income tax accounting for interim statements should continue under the procedures described in APB Opinion Nos. 11, 23, and 24.

EXAMPLES OF INCOME TAX PROCEDURES FOR INTERIM STATEMENTS

Chapter 1 of this volume explains the provisions of APB Opinion No. 11 and the computations, and procedures comprehended in APB Opinions Nos. 23 and 24 have been fully demonstrated and illustrated in preceding paragraphs of this chapter. In addition to the examples indicated above, an illustration of the reversal of net deferred income tax credits in interim statements is set forth in Model Case No. 8.

REVERSAL OF NET INCOME TAX CREDITS FOR INTERIM STATEMENTS

Where an enterprise anticipates a loss for the fiscal year or has a year-to-date loss in excess of the anticipated loss for the fiscal year and all or part of the tax benefit of the loss will not be realized (or its realization is not assured beyond any reasonable doubt), existing deferred tax credits arising from timing differences should be adjusted. The amount of the adjustment should not exceed the lower of:

(a) the otherwise unrecognized tax benefit of the loss, or
(b) the amount of the net deferred tax credits that would otherwise be amortized during the carryforward period attributable to the loss.

If the adjustment relates to an estimated loss for the fiscal year, the amount of the adjustment shall be considered an additional current year tax benefit in the determination of the estimated annual effective tax rate.

Model Case No. 8 illustrates the computation of the estimated annual effective tax rate where a company anticipates a loss that cannot be carried back, and, at the same time, is amortizing net deferred income tax credits.

MODEL CASE NO. 8

At the end of 19x1 the management of Lloyds, Inc. forecast that the company would sustain a $250,000 operating loss for the ensuing year. The loss could not be carried back for tax purposes, and management was not assured beyond any reasonable doubt that future profits would permit full realization of the tax benefits of the loss carryforward. However, Lloyds had deferred income tax credits on its book that would reverse in the amount of $75,000 during the carryforward period. Therefore, Lloyds computed the estimated annual effective tax rate to be used in interim statements as follows:

Estimated loss for year		250,000
(a) Tax effect of loss carryforward at 50% tax rate	125,000	
(b) Deferred income tax credits that would amortize during the loss carryforward period	75,000	

Estimated annual effective rate based on lesser of
 (a) and (b) above—75,000 ÷ 250,000 = 30%

In 19x2 the quarterly and year-to-date ordinary (losses) of Lloyds, Inc. were as follows:

	Quarterly (Loss)	Year-To-Date (Loss)
First quarter	(20,000)	(20,000)
Second quarter	(40,000)	(60,000)
Third quarter	(80,000)	(140,000)
Fourth quarter	(110,000)	(250,000)

The income tax section of Lloyds' quarterly and annual income statements reported the operating losses, and the income tax benefits derived from reversal of timing differences, as follows:

	Quarter Ended				Year Ended
	March 31, 19x2	June 30, 19x2	September 30, 19x2	December 31, 19x2	December 31, 19x2
(Loss) before income taxes	(20,000)	(40,000)	(80,000)	(110,000)	(250,000)
Income tax (benefits)					
Deferred	(6,000)	(12,000)	(24,000)	(33,000)	(75,000)
Net (loss)	(14,000)	(28,000)	(56,000)	(77,000)	(175,000)

DISCLOSURE

Disclosure should be made of the reasons for significant variations in the customary relationship between income tax expense and pretax accounting income, if they are not apparent from the financial statements or from the nature of the entity's business.

3

Earnings Per Share—
Reporting for Incomplex Capital Structures

In 1969 the Accounting Principles Board of the American Institute of Certified Public Accountants published Opinion No. 15 with the objective of providing guidelines to be applied uniformly in computing earnings per share data for presentation in financial statements.[1] The rules set forth in the Opinion and the computational methods prescribed to implement them are intricate, complicated, and highly technical. The major complications that arise in computing earnings per share are derived from dealing with elements of the dilution concept. This dilution concept was designed to clarify the financial impact of various transactions on the complex stockholders' equity structure of large corporations. However, allusion to the dilution concept is so pervasive throughout the text of the Opinion and throughout the exposition in its unofficial accounting interpretation, that an accountant who seeks computational methods for a corporation with an incomplex capital structure is practically compelled to absorb the whole theory of dilution before he can find the provisions of the Opinion that are applicable in his circumstances.

This chapter is designed to go directly to the earnings per share problems of corporations that do not issue dilutive rights or potentially dilutive convertible securities. Therefore, elements of dilution are not contained in the chapter's illustrations and, except for relevant definitions and an overview paragraph, the dilution concept is not discussed in its text. Thus, the chapter is developed to give an explanation of the provisions of the Opinion that apply specifically to corporations with simple capital structures and to provide computational methods that will accurately determine earnings per share for such corporations.

THE REQUIREMENT TO REPORT EARNINGS PER SHARE

Originally, APB Opinion No. 15 required all corporations, except those specifically exempt in the Opinion, to report earnings or loss per share in financial statements, or summaries of financial statements, that presented results of operations in conformity with generally accepted accounting principles. However, in April, 1978 the Financial Accounting Standards Board issued Statement No. 21 which suspended the application of APB Opinion No. 15 to financial statements of nonpublic enterprises and, accordingly, provided that the information specified by the Opinion would no longer

---

[1] *Earnings Per Share*, Opinion of the Accounting Principles Board No. 15. (New York, N.Y.: American Institute of Certified Public Accountants) 1969.

be required in such statements. The Board apparently felt that many nonpublic entities would, nevertheless, continue to report earnings per share and it declared in the Statement that, although the presentation of earnings per share would not be required in the financial statements of nonpublic enterprises, any such information presented should be consistent with the requirements of APB Opinion No. 15. Thus, the provisions of APB Opinion No. 15 explained and illustrated in this chapter continue to apply to nonpublic corporations which voluntarily report earnings per share in their financial statements.

CORPORATE CAPITAL STRUCTURES

The Opinion stresses a dichotomy in corporate capital structures, dividing them into two mutually exclusive groups: simple capital structures and complex capital structures.

1. *Simple Capital Structure*
   A corporation has a simple capital structure if it does not issue convertible securities, options, warrants, or other rights that upon conversion or exercise could dilute earnings per common share.
2. *Complex Capital Structure*
   Capital structures other than those described in the preceding subparagraph are classified as complex capital structures.

The nature of the capital structure of a corporation determines what methods can be used to compute its earnings per common share. Computational methods used for complex capital structures must consider all elements of the dilution concept to determine the dilutive effect of the securities that create the complexity in the capital structure. On the other hand, simple capital structures, by definition, do not have potentially dilutive securities, and the computation of earnings per share is based solely on securities that are or have been actually issued.

As stated previously, the exposition in this chapter will be limited to the computation of earnings per share for corporations having a simple, or incomplex, capital structure.

EARNINGS PER SHARE—HISTORICAL BASE

The original concept of earnings per share contemplated a historical computational base and the computation was made simply by dividing the number of shares outstanding at the end of the year into the net income for the year, as demonstrated in the following example.

The capital structure of Dublin, Inc. contained only one class of common stock. There were 19,000 shares outstanding at December 31, 19x1, and Dublin's income statement for the year ended on that date reported a net income of $48,640. Dublin computed its earnings per share of common stock to be $2.56 simply by dividing the number of shares outstanding into the net income reported:

$$\$48,640 \div 19,000 = \$2.56$$

EARNINGS PER SHARE—EMPLOYMENT OF CAPITAL BASE

In Opinion No. 15 the Board reaffirmed its earlier position that computation of earnings per share data should be based on the weighted average number of shares outstanding during each period presented. The use of the weighted average number of shares as a base for computations is required under the assumption that earnings are affected by variations in available capital, and thus earnings per share data should be related to the actual employment of capital during the periods comprehended in the financial statements.

WEIGHTED AVERAGE NUMBER OF SHARES OUTSTANDING

The Opinion states that the weighted average number of shares outstanding during a period is the number of shares determined by relating

(a) the portion of time within a reporting period that a particular number of shares has been outstanding

to

(b) the total time in that period.

The Opinion gives an example by stating that if 100 shares of a certain security were outstanding during the first quarter of a fiscal year and 300 shares were outstanding during the balance of the year, the weighted average number of shares outstanding would be 250.

ASSUMPTIONS IN COMPUTING THE WEIGHTED AVERAGE

The following assumptions must be made and taken into consideration in computing the weighted average of the number of shares outstanding during an accounting period.

1. Shares issued to stockholders for a consideration should be included from date of issue.
2. Retired shares should be excluded from date of reacquisition.
3. The shares distributed in stock dividends or stock splits should be recognized retroactively for all periods presented.
4. The reduction of shares in a reverse split should be recognized retroactively for all periods presented.
5. The effects of stock dividends, stock splits, and reverse splits occurring after the end of the period for which the computation is being made, but before statements are issued, should be given retroactive recognition for all periods presented.

COMPUTATIONAL METHODS FOR COMPUTING THE WEIGHTED AVERAGE

The weighted average contemplated by the Opinion is essentially the arithmetic mean of shares outstanding during an accounting period. The most precise average would be the sum of the shares outstanding each day, divided by the number of days in the period. The example given in the Opinion illustrates a computation on a *quarterly* basis. This method is satisfactory if it produces reasonable results. However, in actual practice, the computation generally is refined to the extent of at least using months and half months as the basis for computing the sum of the shares outstanding, and dividing the result by the number of months in the period for which the computation is made. In many instances actual *days* are used in computing the sum of outstanding shares, and the sum is then divided by the number of days in the period.

COMPUTING ANNUAL WEIGHTED AVERAGE—BASED ON MONTHLY SUM OF SHARES OUTSTANDING

In computing the sum of the shares outstanding during an annual accounting period, the computation can be made on the *total* shares outstanding after each issuance or reacquisition; or it can be based on the increment or reduction that occurs. Both methods produce the same results. Model Case No. 1 demonstrates computations by both the methods, using months as the basis for computing the sum of the shares outstanding during the year.

MODEL CASE NO. 1

The capital structure of Liberty, Inc. contained only one class of common stock. At January 1, 19x1 Liberty had 100,000 shares outstanding and Schedule 1 sets forth the changes in the number of shares of common stock outstanding that occurred during the year 19x1.

CHANGES IN NUMBER OF SHARES OUTSTANDING

March 1, 19x1 — Sold 6,000 shares
April 30, 19x1 — Reacquired 30,000 shares
May 15, 19x1 — Sold 18,000 shares
August 1, 19x1 — Sold 30,000 shares
November 15, 19x1 — Sold 36,000 shares

SCHEDULE 1

To determine the weighted average number of shares outstanding during the year, Liberty's bookkeeper made the computation set forth in Schedule 2, based on the total number of shares outstanding after giving effect to each acquisition and retirement.

COMPUTATION OF WEIGHTED AVERAGE BY TOTAL SHARES METHOD

		Total Number of Shares Outstanding		Number of Months Total Number of Shares Were Outstanding		Sum of Shares Outstanding
January 1		100,000	x	2	=	200,000
March 1	— add	6,000				
		106,000	x	2	=	212,000
April 30	— deduct	(30,000)				
		76,000	x	.5	=	38,000
May 15	— add	18,000				
		94,000	x	2.5	=	235,000
August 1	— add	30,000				
		124,000	x	3.5	=	434,000
November 15	— add	36,000				
		160,000	x	1.5	=	240,000
				12.0		1,359,000

SCHEDULE 2

The weighted average number of shares outstanding was computed to be 113,250, arrived at by dividing the number of months into the sum of the shares outstanding (1,359,000 ÷ 12 = 113,250).

Liberty's independent accountants verified the weighted average number of shares determined by the bookkeeper by basing their computation on the increment or reduction that occurred with each sale or reacquisition of common stock. Their computation is shown in Schedule 3.

COMPUTATION OF WEIGHTED AVERAGE BY INCREMENT METHOD

	Balance at Beginning of Year and Number of Shares Sold or (Reacquired)		Number of Months Beginning Balance and Sales and Reacquisitions Were in Effect		Sum of Shares Outstanding
January 1	100,000	X	12	=	1,200,000
March 1	6,000	X	10	=	60,000
April 30	(30,000)	X	8	=	(240,000)
May 15	18,000	X	7.5	=	135,000
August 1	30,000	X	5	=	150,000
November 15	36,000	X	1.5	=	54,000
	160,000				1,359,000

SCHEDULE 3

The sum of the shares outstanding indicated by the accountants' schedule was 1,359,000, which was the same as the sum computed by the bookkeeper. The accountants then determined the weighted average shares outstanding by dividing 1,359,000 by 12, and arrived at 113,250, which was equivalent to the average computed by the bookkeeper. Thus, both computational methods provided precisely the same results.

COMPUTING QUARTERLY WEIGHTED AVERAGES—BASED ON MONTHLY SUM OF SHARES OUTSTANDING

Computations of quarterly earnings per share are made in precisely the same manner as annual earnings per share, and can be based on either the total-shares method or the incremental method. Model Case 2 illustrates quarterly computations of weighted average shares outstanding by each respective method referred to above, using months as the basis for computing the sum of shares outstanding during each quarter.

MODEL CASE NO. 2

At the end of 19x1 Liberty, Inc., in connection with the formulation of certain fiscal plans, instructed its bookkeeper to prepare quarterly income statements for the year 19x1, and simultaneously arranged for its independent accountants to verify the computation of earnings per share made by the bookkeeper.

The bookkeeper prepared computations based on changes in the capital stock account shown in Schedule 1 of Model Case No. 1, using the total-shares method to determine the sum of shares outstanding during each quarter. The independent accountants made their own computations, using the incremental method, and also based on the change in the stock account shown in Schedule 1 of Model Case No. 1. Schedule 4 sets forth the computations made by the bookkeeper and independent accountants, respectively.

COMPUTATION OF QUARTERLY WEIGHTED AVERAGES

	TOTAL-SHARES METHOD			INCREMENTAL METHOD		
	Beginning Balance and Sales and Reacquisition Number of Shares	Number of Months Shares Were Outstanding	Sum of Shares Outstanding	Beginning Balance and Sales and Reacquisition Number of Shares	Number of Months Increment (Reduction) Was In Effect	Sum of Shares Outstanding
FIRST QUARTER						
Jan. 1—Balance	100,000 ×	2	= 200,000	100,000 ×	3	= 300,000
Mar. 1—Add	6,000			6,000 ×	1	= 6,000
	106,000 ×	1	= 106,000			
		3	306,000	106,000		306,000
	Weighted Average: 306,000 ÷ 3 = 102,000					
SECOND QUARTER						
Apr. 1—Balance	106,000 ×	1	= 106,000	106,000 ×	3	= 318,000
Apr. 30—Deduct	(30,000)			(30,000) ×	2	= (60,000)
	76,000 ×	.5	= 38,000			
May 15—Add	18,000			18,000 ×	1.5	= 27,000
	94,000 ×	1.5	= 141,000			
		3	285,000	94,000		285,000
	Weighted Average: 285,000 ÷ 3 = 95,000					
THIRD QUARTER						
July 1—Balance	94,000 ×	1	= 94,000	94,000 ×	3	= 282,000
Aug. 1—Add	30,000			30,000 ×	2	= 60,000
	124,000 ×	2	= 248,000			
		3	342,000	124,000		342,000
	Weighted Average: 342,000 ÷ 3 = 114,000					
FOURTH QUARTER						
Oct. 1—Balance	124,000 ×	1.5	= 186,000	124,000 ×	3	= 372,000
Nov. 15—Add	36,000			36,000 ×	1.5	= 54,000
	160,000 ×	1.5	= 240,000			
		3	426,000	160,000		426,000
	Weighted Average: 426,000 ÷ 3 = 142,000					

SCHEDULE 4

COMPUTING ANNUAL WEIGHTED AVERAGE—BASED ON DAILY SUM OF SHARES OUTSTANDING

As stated previously, the most precise method of computing an annual weighted average is to divide the summation of the number of shares outstanding each day by the number of days in the year.

Model Case No. 3 demonstrates the computation of the annual weighted average by both the total shares method and the incremental method, based on a summation of the daily shares outstanding during the year. Model Case No. 3 also demonstrates recognition of a stock dividend and a stock split, which were recognized retroactive to the beginning of the year.

MODEL CASE NO. 3

The Belle Company, Inc. has a simple capital structure, consisting of only one class of common stock. At January 1, 19x5 Belle had 100,000 shares issued and outstanding. Schedule 5 reflects the changes that occurred in Belle's capital stock during the year 19x5 with respect to the *number* of shares involved in each transaction.

CHANGES IN NUMBER OF SHARES OUTSTANDING

January 30, 19x4 — 10% stock dividend distributed
April 15, 19x5 — Sold 20,000 shares
July 31, 19x5 — Sold 15,000 shares
October 15, 19x5 — Reacquired 30,000 shares
December 15, 19x5 — Sold 40,000 shares
December 30, 19x5 — Distributed 2 for 1 stock split

SCHEDULE 5

Belle's accounting department computed the weighted average number of shares outstanding using the total-shares method and based on the sum of shares outstanding each day during the year. The computation made by the accounting department is shown in Schedule 6.

The public accountant engaged to examine Belle's financial statements verified the accounting department's computation of the weighted average shares outstanding during the year by making their own independent computations using the incremental method based on the sum of the daily number of shares outstanding, as shown in Schedule 7.

COMPUTATION OF WEIGHTED AVERAGE—BUSINESS COMBINATIONS

Two separate methods are required for computing the weighted average number of shares outstanding for companies involved in business combinations: one method for the acquiring company in a combination accounted for as a purchase, and a different method for the surviving company in a combination determined to be a pooling of interests. The difference in treatment is because of the fact that in a purchase the results of operations of the acquired business are included in income only from the date of acquisition, while the results of operations in a pooling of interests are combined for the full accounting period.

COMPUTATION OF WEIGHTED AVERAGE—TOTAL-SHARES METHOD
BASED ON SUM OF NUMBER OF SHARES OUTSTANDING EACH DAY

	Beginning Balance and Number of Shares Sold, Purchased, and Distributed as a Stock Dividend	Multiplied by 2 to Give Effect to Stock Split		Number of Shares Out- standing Recognizing Stock Split		Number of Days Out- standing	Sum of Shares Outstanding
Jan. 1—Balance	100,000						
Jan. 30—Dividend	10,000						
	110,000	× 2	=	220,000	×	104	= 22,880,000
Apr. 15—Add	20,000						
	130,000	× 2	=	260,000	×	107	= 27,820,000
July 31—Add	15,000						
	145,000	× 2	=	290,000	×	76	= 22,040,000
Oct. 15—Deduct	(30,000)						
	115,000	× 2	=	230,000	×	61	= 14,030,000
Dec. 15—Add	40,000						
	155,000	× 2	=	310,000	×	17	= 5,270,000
						365	92,040,000

Weighted Average: 92,040,000 ÷ 365 = 252,164

SCHEDULE 6

COMPUTATION OF WEIGHTED AVERAGE—INCREMENTAL METHOD
BASED ON SUM OF NUMBER OF SHARES OUTSTANDING EACH DAY

	Beginning Balance and Number of Shares Sold, Purchased, and Distributed as a Stock Dividend	Multiplied by 2 to Give Effect to Stock Split		Number of Shares Out- standing Recognizing Stock Split		Number of Days Increment (Reduction) Was in Effect	Sum of Shares Outstanding
Jan. 1—Balance	100,000	× 2	=	200,000	×	365	= 73,000,000
Jan. 30—Dividend	10,000	× 2	=	20,000	×	365	= 7,300,000
Apr. 15—Add	20,000	× 2	=	40,000	×	261	= 10,440,000
July 31—Add	15,000	× 2	=	30,000	×	154	= 4,620,000
Oct. 15—Deduct	(30,000)	× 2	=	(60,000)	×	78	= (4,680,000)
Dec. 15—Add	40,000	× 2	=	80,000	×	17	= 1,360,000
	155,000	× 2	=	310,000			92,040,000

Weighted Average: 92,040,000 ÷ 365 = 252,164

SCHEDULE 7

COMBINATION ACCOUNTED FOR AS A PURCHASE

When shares are issued to acquire a business in a combination accounted for as a purchase, the computation of the weighted average should give recognition to the existence of the new shares only from the date the acquisition took place. Model Case No. 4 illustrates the computation of the weighted average number of shares outstanding for the acquiring corporation in a business combination accounted for as a purchase.

MODEL CASE NO. 4

Evans Company has a simple capital structure and issues only one class of common stock. On July 1, 19x1 Evans entered into an agreement to purchase Witt & Company in a business combination that was required to be accounted for as a purchase. The purchase plan provided that the acquirer would exchange 30,000 shares of its common stock for the total outstanding common stock of the acquired company. The issuance of 30,000 shares under the purchase agreement was the only transaction in its common stock made by Evans Company during the year.

At December 31, 19x1 Evans had 130,000 common shares outstanding, comprised of 100,000 shares that were outstanding at the beginning of the year and 30,000 shares issued on July 1 under the purchase agreement. Net income for 19x1 included income from the purchased company only from date of acquisition and, accordingly, Evans computed the weighted average number of shares outstanding during the year by giving effect to the 30,000 shares only as of the date of issuance (July 1). Thus, the weighted average number of shares outstanding during the year was computed as follows:

$$
\begin{array}{ll}
\text{100,000 shares for six months} = 6 \times 100,000 = & 600,000 \\
\text{130,000 shares for six months} = 6 \times 130,000 = & \underline{780,000} \\
& 1,380,000
\end{array}
$$

Weighted Average: $1,380,000 \div 12 = 115,000$

COMBINATION DETERMINED TO BE A POOLING OF INTERESTS

When a business combination is determined to be a pooling of interests, computation of the weighted average number of shares outstanding should be based on the aggregate outstanding shares of the constituent businesses, adjusted to equivalent shares of the surviving company for the full accounting period. Model Case No. 5 demonstrates the computational methods for computing the weighted average number of shares outstanding for a business combination accounted for as a pooling of interests.

MODEL CASE NO. 5

Federal Corporation, Ruby, Inc., and Stagg Bros. were unrelated closely held corporations engaged in analogous enterprises. At special meetings called in July, 19x5 the Board of Directors of the respective companies adopted identical resolutions to effect a pooling of interest of the three companies, and directed that the pooling be consummated on September 30, 19x5. The combination plan provided that Federal Corporation would issue its one-class common stock for all of the voting common stock interests of the other two companies on the basis of one share of Federal Corporation, respectively, for 1.20 shares of Ruby, Inc. and .96 shares of Stagg Bros.

The transactions in the capital stock accounts of the constituent companies during 19x5 with respect to the *number* of shares are shown in Schedule 8.

CHANGES IN OUTSTANDING STOCK OF CONSTITUENT COMPANIES

	Federal Corporation	Ruby, Inc.	Stagg Bros.
January 1, 19x5 Balance	200,000	150,000	132,000
June 30, 19x5—Shares issued	50,000	—	60,000
September 30, 19x5—Balance	250,000	150,000	192,000
September 30, 19x5—Shares issued and (retired) in business combination			
Ruby, Inc. —150,000 ÷ 1.20	125,000	(150,000)	
Stagg Bros.—192,000 ÷ .96	200,000		(192,000)
December 31, 19x5 —Balance	575,000	—0—	—0—

SCHEDULE 8

Net income for the year 19x5 included the combined results of operations of all three companies for the full year. Therefore, Federal Corporation computed the weighted average based on the number of shares of the constituent companies outstanding during the year adjusted to equivalent shares of the surviving company, as shown in Schedule 9.

COMPUTATION OF WEIGHTED AVERAGE SHARES OF CONSTITUENT COMPANIES ADJUSTED TO EQUIVALENT SHARES OF SURVIVING COMPANY

	Total Number of Shares		Number of Months		Sum of Shares Outstanding		Exchange Ratio		Adjusted Sum of Shares Outstanding
Ruby, Inc.									
	150,000	×	12	=	1,800,000	÷	1.20	=	1,500,000
Stagg Bros.									
	132,000	×	6	=	792,000	÷	.96	=	825,000
	192,000	×	6	=	1,152,000	÷	.96	=	1,200,000
Federal Corporation									
	200,000	×	6	=	1,200,000	÷	1.00	=	1,200,000
	250,000	×	6	=	1,500,000	÷	1.00	=	1,500,000
									6,225,000

Weighted Average: 6,225,000 ÷12 =518,750

SCHEDULE 9

COMPUTING EARNINGS PER SHARE

Computing earnings per share (EPS) for a corporation with only one class of stock is a very simple operation. In such cases EPS is determined by dividing net income by either the actual number of shares outstanding at the end of the period or the weighted average number of shares outstanding during the period, whichever is appropriate. If there has been no change in the number of shares, net income should be divided by the actual number of shares outstanding; if stock has been issued, retired, or reacquired, net income should be divided by the weighted average number of shares outstanding during the period.

ADJUSTMENTS TO NET INCOME FOR EARNINGS PER SHARE

Generally, earnings per share are based on net income for the period without consideration of the amount of dividends declared or paid on common stock. However, in cases where the corporation issues preferred stock or more than one class of common stock, adjustments to net income may be necessary for the purpose of computing earnings per share because of claims on such income by senior securities.

Claims of Senior Securities

Senior securities are defined as securities having preferential rights and which are not common stock. The claims of such securities on earnings should be deducted from net income for the purpose of computing earnings per share. The Opinion sets forth the following rules with respect to adjusting net income for the purpose of computing earnings per share:

1. Dividends on cumulative preferred senior securities, whether or not earned, should be deducted from net income.
2. If there is a net loss, the amount of the loss should be increased by any cumulative dividends on preferred stocks for the period.
3. If interest or preferred dividends are cumulative only if earned, no adjustment of this type is required, except to the extent of income available therefor.
4. If interest or preferred dividends are noncumulative, only the interests accruable or dividends declared should be deducted.

It is important to note that the adjustments described above do not affect the net income or net loss reported in the financial statements. Such adjustments are made solely for the computation of earnings per share, and have no effect on financial position or results of operations.

ADJUSTMENTS TO NET INCOME RESULTING IN EARNINGS PER SHARE

Model Case No. 6 illustrates the adjustments to be made to net income for the purpose of computing earnings per share for a corporation that issues preferential securities and has net income for the year in excess of the claims of the senior securities.

MODEL CASE NO. 6

Amos & Company issues two classes of preferred and one class of common stock. Class A preferred dividends are cumulative, whether or not earned, and Class B dividends are noncumulative. There was no change in the number of shares outstanding of either preferred or common stock during the year 19x5, and at the end of the year the capital structure of Amos & Company was as follows:

Preferred Stock
 Class A—Cumulative—4.20%— Par $100
   Issued: 1,000 shares   100,000
 Class B—Noncumulative—2.80%—Par $100
   Issued: 1,000 shares   100,000
 Common Stock — Par $30 —Issued: 10,000 shares   300,000
                   500,000

On December 15, 19x5 the Board of Directors declared a regular dividend on preferred stock and a dividend of $10 per share on common stock. Amos & Company realized a net income of $50,000 for the year 19x5 and made the following adjustment to net income for the purpose of computing earnings per common share:

Net Income		50,000
Less: Dividends Declared on		
Preferred Stock		
Class A—$100,000 × 4.20%	4,200	
Class B—$100,000 × 2.80%	2,800	7,000
Income applicable to earnings		
per common share		43,000

Earnings per common share: 43,000 ÷ 10,000 = $4.30

ADJUSTMENTS TO NET INCOME RESULTING IN LOSS PER SHARE

Dividends on cumulative preferred senior securities must be deducted from net income for the purpose of computing earnings per share, even though net income is less than the aggregate cumulative dividends on the preferential securities. In some cases such adjustments to net income for the purpose of computing earnings per share can result in reporting a *loss* per share on financial statements that report *net income* from operations. Model Case No. 7 illustrates the adjustments to be made to net income for the purpose of determining earnings per share for a corporation in which the claim of its senior securities is in excess of its net income.

MODEL CASE NO. 7

At December 31, 19x8 the outstanding stock of Young Company comprehended the securities listed in the following summary. Dividends on Class A preferred stock were cumulative whether or not earned, and dividends on Class B stock were noncumulative.

Preferred Stock
 Class A—Cumulative—6.00%—Par $100
   Issued: 10,000 shares   1,000,000
 Class B—Noncumulative—6.80%—Par $100
   Issued: 10,000 shares   1,000,000
 Common Stock—Par $100—Issued: 10,000 shares   1,000,000
                  3,000,000

Young's net income for the year 19x8 amounted to only $40,000, and consequently the Board of Directors did not declare dividends on any class of the company's stock. In computing earnings per common share for 19x8, Young took into consideration the fact that the dividend on the preferential Class A stock was cumulative and would have to be paid before any distribution could be made to the common shareholders. Therefore, the cumulative dividend of $60,000 had to be deducted from net income of $40,000 for the purpose of computing earnings per common share. Since the dividend on Class B stock was noncumulative, and no dividend had been declared, no adjustment was made to net income with respect to the unpaid Class B dividend.

Earnings (loss) per common share for the year ended December 31, 19x8 were computed as follows:

Net Income	40,000
Less: Cumulative Dividend on Class A Stock— (1,000,000 × 6.00%)	60,000
Net (loss) for purpose of computing earnings (loss) per common share	(20,000)

Loss per common share: 20,000 ÷ 10,000 = $2.00

ADJUSTMENTS TO NET LOSS RESULTING IN LOSS PER SHARE

Dividends on cumulative preferential securities must be added to the net loss of a corporation for the purpose of computing loss per common share. However, such adjustment need not be made if the preferred stock is cumulative only if earned. If preferred dividends are noncumulative, net income or net loss should be adjusted only to the extent that such dividends are *declared.* Model Case No. 8 demonstrates the adjustments that must be made to the *net loss* of a corporation for the purpose of computing loss per share where dividends are declared only on noncumulative preferred stock.

MODEL CASE NO. 8

The capital structure of Scott & Company was made up of two classes of preferential securities and one class of common stock. The dividends on Class A preferred stock were cumulative only if earned, and Class B preferred dividends were noncumulative. Although Scott sustained a net loss of $100,000 for the year 19x7, the Board of Directors nevertheless declared a regular dividend on the Class B preferred stock. There was no change during the year in the number of shares outstanding in any of the various classes of stock, and at December 31, 19x7 the issued stock of the company was as follows:

Preferred Stock

Class A—Cumulative—6.20%—Par $100	
Issued: 5,000 shares	500,000
Class B—Noncumulative—2.80%—Par $100	
Issued: 5,000 shares	500,000
Common Stock—Par $10—Issued: 100,000 shares	1,000,000
	2,000,000

Scott adjusted its net loss for the purpose of computing loss per share by adding the amount of the noncumulative Class B dividend declared by the Board of Directors. However, since dividends on Class A stock were cumulative only if earned, and no dividend on that class of stock was declared, Scott was not required to adjust its net loss for dividends on its Class A preferred stock. Computation of loss per common share was made as follows:

Net Loss	100,000
Add: Dividends declared on Class B Preferred Stock	14,000
Net loss applicable to loss per common share	114,000

Loss per common share: 114,000 ÷ 100,000 = $1.14

PARTICIPATING SECURITIES

A corporation may issue participating preferred stock or more than one class of common stock. Where participation by a preferred stock is limited to a specified dividend from current earnings, and the specified dividend is noncumulative, the preferred stock is simply a noncumulative senior security and only the dividend declared for the period need be deducted from net income to determine earnings per common share. Similarly, where a class of common stock is guaranteed a noncumulative dividend from current earnings prior to any distribution to ordinary common shareholders, and its participation is limited to such dividend, that class of common stock is equivalent to a noncumulative preferred stock, and only the dividends declared for the accounting period should be used to adjust net income for the purpose of computing earnings per "ordinary" common share.

TWO-CLASS METHOD

If a corporation issues participation securities that are not limited to participation in *current* dividends with common stock, it must use the two-class method of computing earnings per common share. In such cases the participating securities have participation rights in undistributed earnings and the two-class method is an earnings allocation formula which determines earnings per share for the participating securities according to the dividends paid and the residual claims on undistributed earnings by the participating securities.

Participating securities issued by corporations comprehend an enormous variety of conditions and stipulations, and it is not feasible to cover all of them in this chapter. However, the two types of securities described below demonstrate the general character of unlimited participation securities:

(a) Preferred stock with a noncumulative guaranteed rate of return before distribution can be made to common stockholders, and a right to participate in further dividends after a specified distribution has been made on common stock; and

(b) A class of common stock with a noncumulative guaranteed rate of return before distribution can be made to holders of "ordinary" common stock along with a right to participate in further dividends after the required distribution has been made on "ordinary" common stock.

In applying the two-class method, net income is first reduced by dividends paid or declared on each class of stock. The remaining undistributed income is then allocated to common stock and participating securities in accordance with the claims of each respective security. The total allocated to each security is determined by adding the actual dividend declared or paid and the amount determined to be the participating claim on undistributed income. The total allocated to each security is then divided by the number of its outstanding shares. The earnings per share of the "ordinary" common stock is the amount that is required to be reported in the financial statements.

Model Case No. 9 illustrates the two-class method of computing earnings per common share for a corporation that issues participating preferred stock and two classes of common stock.

MODEL CASE NO. 9

Tyler, Inc. issues a noncumulative participating preferred stock and two classes of common stock. The dividend preferences and participation rights of the respective securities are as follows:

Preferred Stock—Par $100—Noncumulative Participating
Entitled to $6.20 before dividends are paid to either class of common stock. Participates on an equal per share basis in dividends paid after required dividends have been paid on both classes of common.

Common Stock
  Class A—Par $100—Nonvoting
  Entitled to a noncumulative dividend of $5.00 after preferred dividend is paid and before any dividend to Class B common stockholders. Participates on an equal per share basis in dividends paid after required dividends have been paid on Class B common.

  Class B—Par $100—Voting
  Entitled to a dividend of $10.00 after dividends are paid on preferred and Class A common, and before any participating dividends.

Tyler's net income for the year 19x2 was $256,000. During the year it it declared a $6.20 per share dividend on its preferred stock, $5.00 per share on Class A, and $10.00 per share on Class B common.

There were no changes in the number of shares outstanding during the year in any class of stock, and Tyler's capital structure at December 31, 19x2 was as follows:

Preferred—Par $100—Issued: 5,000 shares	500,000
Common—Par $100	
Class A—Issued: 5,000 shares	500,000
Class B—Issued: 10,000 shares	1,000,000
	2,000,000

To compute earnings per "ordinary" common share for 19x2, Tyler first deducted from net income the dividends declared on each class of stock. The remaining undistributed income for 19x2 was then allocated in accordance with the claims of each respective security.

The allocation of undistributed net income and the computation of earnings per share are shown in Schedule 10.

CHANGE IN CLASSIFICATION OF CAPITAL STRUCTURE

A change in classification of capital structure from simple to complex can occur if the corporation changes its method of equity funding. Obviously, if a corporation with a simple capital structure initiates the issuance of convertible securities, options, or warrants, the changed nature of its capital accounts would require the structure to be classified as complex.

However, it is important to realize that where rights have accrued to employees, shareholders, or prospective shareholders, which could ultimately increase the number of shares outstanding, such rights are considered common stock equivalents and the capital structure of the company should be classified as complex. Thus, computation of earnings per share must, in such cases, be computed in accordance with the principles of the dilution concept. Examples of such rights are found in stock option plans, deferred compensation stock options, and agreements for issuance of shares contingent upon specified conditions, such as maintenance of current earnings or attainment of specified increased earnings.

ALLOCATION OF UNDISTRIBUTED NET INCOME AND
COMPUTATION OF EARNINGS PER SHARE

UNDISTRIBUTED NET INCOME

Net Income		256,000
Less: Dividends Declared		
Preferred — 5,000 shares × $6.20	31,000	
Common		
Class A — 5,000 shares × $5.00	25,000	
Class B —10,000 shares ×$10.00	100,000	156,000
Undistributed Net Income		100,000

ALLOCATION OF UNDISTRIBUTED NET INCOME

Class of Stock	Number of Shares Outstanding	Percent of Aggregate Shares Outstanding		Undistributed Net Income		Allocation of Undistributed Net Income
Preferred	5,000	25%	×	100,000	=	25,000
Common						
Class A	5,000	25%	×	100,000	=	25,000
Class B	10,000	50%	×	100,000	=	50,000
	20,000	100%				100,000

EARNINGS APPLICABLE TO EACH CLASS OF STOCK

		Common		
	Preferred	Class A	Class B	Total
Dividends Declared	31,000	25,000	100,000	156,000
Allocation of Undistributed Net Income	25,000	25,000	50,000	100,000
	56,000	50,000	150,000	256,000

EARNINGS PER SHARE

	Applicable Earnings	Number of Shares Outstanding	Earnings Per Share
Preferred	56,000	5,000	11.20
Common			
Class A	50,000	5,000	10.00
Class B	150,000	10,000	15.00
	256,000	20,000	

SCHEDULE 10

DISCLOSURE IN FINANCIAL STATEMENTS

In Opinion No. 15 the Board prescribes elaborate and extensive disclosure requirements with respect to earnings per share and related data for corporations having a complex capital structure. However, the rules for reporting such data for a corporation with an incomplex structure are simple, direct, and precise. The text of this chapter is concerned with only the reporting requirements of corporations with simple capital structures.

Presentation on Face of Income Statement

The Opinion requires corporations to present earnings or loss per common share on the face of their income statements, or earnings summaries, for all periods included in the statement or summary. Each presentment must disclose earnings or loss per share for income or loss before extraordinary items, and earnings or loss per share for net income or net loss.

Restatement for Prior Periods

When results of operations of a prior period included in the statement of income or summary of earnings have been restated as a result of a prior period adjustment, earnings per share data given for the prior period should be restated. The effect of the restatement, expressed in per share terms, should be disclosed in the year of restatement.

Rights and Privileges of Outstanding Securities

The financial statements should include a description, in summary form, sufficient to explain the rights and privileges of the outstanding securities. The description should contain information with respect to the following:

(a) dividend preferences,
(b) liquidation preferences,
(c) participation rights, and
(d) unusual voting rights.

Stock Dividends or Splits

Where stock dividends, splits, or reverse splits have been recognized retroactively for the purpose of computing the weighted average number of shares outstanding, details of the method used should be disclosed in the financial statements.

Claims of Senior Securities

The effect of claims of senior securities on the computation of earnings per share should be disclosed.

Cumulative Preferred Dividends in Arrears

The per share and aggregate amounts of cumulative preferred dividends in arrears should be disclosed in the financial statements.

THE DILUTION CONCEPT

The dilution concept infers that securities other than common stock which are substantially equivalent to common stock (convertible securities, warrants, etc.), and contingent issuances of common stock (stock option plans, etc.), should enter into the computation of earnings per share. Thus, the principles of the dilution concept require that the computation of earnings per share for corporations with complex capital structures be based on assumptions made to reflect:

(a) earnings per share computed on outstanding common shares and on those securities that are, in substance, equivalent to common shares, as though common shares had been issued to replace the equivalent securities, and

(b) earnings per share that would have resulted if *all* contingent issuances of common stock had taken place at the beginning of the period.

APB Opinion No. 15 sets forth specific assumptions that must be made for exercise, conversion, and issuance of securities; prices to be applied; and methods to be used in the computation of earnings per share for corporations with complex capital structures so as to reflect the dilution in earnings per common share that would have resulted had such transactions actually occurred.

The computation of earnings per share for corporations with complex capital structures can be a complicated process, and the person who is confronted with such a problem should seek solution direct from APB No. 15 and its accounting interpretation.

4

Nonmonetary Transactions—
Accounting and Tax Treatment and
Determination of Gains and Losses

In May, 1973 the Accounting Principles Board published Opinion No. 29, "Accounting for Nonmonetary Transactions"[1] The fundamental objective of the Opinion was to resolve certain questions concerning amounts to be assigned to nonmonetary assets transferred in nonmonetary transactions, and to provide criteria for determining the conditions under which gain or loss should be recognized in such transactions. Three years prior to the publication of the Opinion, Accounting Principles Board Statement No. 4 had set forth the concept of "fair value" as a basic principle of measurement in financial accounting.[2] In the interim, however, with respect to accounting for nonmonetary transactions, inconsistencies in accounting practice persisted because the views of accountants differed as to the method of valuing assets in nonmonetary transfers and exchanges. To eliminate such inconsistencies, APB Opinion No. 29 affirmed the fair value principle; expanded application of the principle to nonmonetary items; and provided for specific modification of the principle in particular circumstances.

This chapter explains the provisions of the Opinion; develops problems in connection with all types of nonmonetary transactions; and provides illustrations of the prescribed accounting treatment for each respective accounting problem so developed.

MONETARY AND NONMONETARY ITEMS

The directives and procedures set forth in APB Opinion No. 29 apply solely to transfers and exchanges of *nonmonetary* items. Therefore, the key to appropriate application of the provisions of the Opinion lies in a proper classification of balance sheet accounts into monetary and nonmonetary items.

---

[1]*Accounting for Nonmonetary Transactions,* Opinion of the Accounting Principles Board No. 29. (New York, NY: Copyright 1973 by the American Institute of Certified Public Accountants.)
[2]*Basic Concepts and Accounting Principles Underlying Financial Statements of Business Enterprises,* Statement of the Accounting Principles Board No. 4. (New York, NY: Copyright 1970 by the American Institute of Certified Public Accountants.)

Generally, monetary items are those balance sheet accounts that represent cash and claims to cash, and those receivables and payables that are fixed in terms of number of dollars. All other balance sheet accounts are nonmonetary items.[3]

Monetary Items

The following balance sheet accounts are normally classified as monetary items:

> Cash on Hand
> Time and Demand Bank Deposits
> Investment in Bonds
> Accounts and Notes Receivable
> Allowance for Doubtful Accounts and Notes Receivable
> Cash Surrender Value of Life Insurance
> Accounts and Notes Payable
> Accrued Expenses
> Cash Dividends Payable
> Long-term Debt
> Unamortized Premium or Discount on Debt Securities
> Preferred Stock

Nonmonetary Items

The following accounts are generally considered to be nonmonetary items:

> Foreign Currency on Hand, and Claims for Foreign Currency
> Investments in Stocks
> Inventories
> Prepaid Expenses
> Property, Plant, and Equipment
> Accumulated Depreciation of Property, Plant, and Equipment
> Deferred Income Tax Debits
> Intangibles and Deferred Charges
> Goodwill
> Deferred Income
> Obligations under Warranties
> Deferred Income Tax Credits
> Preferred Stock
> Common Stock
> Paid-In Capital
> Retained Earnings

---

[3] The following works contain a more complete explanation of monetary and nonmonetary items:
Reporting the Financial Effects of Price-Level Changes, Accounting Research Study No. 6. (New York, NY: Copyright 1963 by the American Institute of Certified Public Accountants.)
Financial Statements Restated for General Price-Level Changes, Statement of the Accounting Principles Board No. 3. (New York, NY: Copyright 1969 by the American Institute of Certified Public Accountants.)
Financial Reporting in Units of General Purchasing Power, Exposure Draft of Proposed Statement of Financial Accounting Standards. (Stamford, Connecticut, Financial Accounting Standards Board, 1974. Reprinted with permission. Copies of the complete document are available from the FASB.)

Items Having a Dual Nature

The following items have characteristics of both classifications and can be either monetary or nonmonetary:

Bonds. Bonds, including convertible bonds, generally are of a monetary nature when they are intended to be held to maturity and redeemed at a fixed number of dollars. However, if bonds are intended to be sold or converted prior to maturity they are nonmonetary items.

Inventories. Inventories produced under fixed contracts and accounted for at the contract price are monetary. All other inventory items are nonmonetary.

Preferred Stocks. Generally, preferred stock is a monetary item. However, preferred stock carried at less than its redemption value is nonmonetary.

Investments in Equity Securities

If the investment is carried at cost, it is nonmonetary. If it is accounted for by the equity method, it is monetary.

NONMONETARY TRANSACTIONS

The Opinion classifies nonmonetary transactions into two basic categories:

(a) Nonmonetary exchanges, and
(b) Nonreciprocal transfers.

Nonmonetary Exchanges

A nonmonetary exchange is a reciprocal transfer between entities of nonmonetary assets or liabilities or both. The Opinion also applies to exchanges that are essentially nonmonetary, even though they might involve an insignificant monetary consideration, or "boot."

The Opinion lists the following examples of nonmonetary exchanges:

(a) Exchange of a product held for sale in the ordinary course of business (inventory) for dissimilar property as a means of selling the product to a customer;
(b) Exchange of a product held for sale in the ordinary course of business (inventory) for a similar product as an accommodation, and not as a means of selling the product to a customer; and
(c) Exchange of productive assets for similar productive assets.

Nonreciprocal Transfers of Nonmonetary Items

A nonreciprocal transfer of nonmonetary items is a one-directional transfer of nonmonetary assets or services to or from an entity. The Opinion differentiates between owners and others in prescribing procedures to be followed in accounting for nonreciprocal transfers.

Nonreciprocal Transfers to or from Owners. The following are listed by the Opinion as examples of nonreciprocal transfers between the enterprise and its owners:

(a) Distribution of nonmonetary assets, such as marketable securities, to stockholders as dividends;
(b) Distribution of nonmonetary assets, such as marketable securities, to stockholders to redeem or acquire outstanding capital stock of the enterprise;
(c) Distribution of nonmonetary assets, such as capital stock of subsidiaries, to stockholders in corporate liquidations or plans of reorganization that involve disposing of

all or a significant segment of the business (spin-offs, split-ups, split-offs); and

(d) Distribution of nonmonetary assets to groups of stockholders to redeem or acquire shares of capital stock previously issued in a business combination.

Nonreciprocal Transfers to or from Other Than Owners. The Opinion lists the following transactions as nonmonetary transfers between an enterprise and entities other than its owners:

(a) Contribution of nonmonetary assets to charitable organizations; and

(b) Contribution of land by a governmental unit for construction of productive facilities by an enterprise.

APPLICABILITY OF APB OPINION NO. 29

APB Opinion No. 29 specifically exempts the following types of nonmonetary transactions from its provisions:

(a) Business combinations accounted for by the pooling of interests or the purchase method;

(b) Transfer of nonmonetary assets solely between companies or persons under common control;

(c) Acquisitions of nonmonetary assets or services on issuance of the capital stock of an enterprise; and

(d) Stock issued or received in stock dividends and stock splits.

BASIC PRINCIPLE

Generally, accounting for nonmonetary transactions should be based on the "fair value" of the assets or services involved, which is the same basis as that used in monetary transactions. The Opinion states that fair value of a nonmonetary asset transferred to or from an enterprise in a nonmonetary transaction should be determined by:

(a) Referring to estimated realizable values in cash transactions of the same or similar assets;

(b) Independent appraisals;

(c) Estimated fair values of assets or services received in exchange; and

(d) Other available evidence.

Application of the basic principle is not feasible, of course, in situations where fair value is not determinable. Modification of the basic principle in such instances is discussed in a later section of the chapter.

DEFERRED INCOME TAXES

The amount of gain or loss resulting from nonmonetary transactions that is recognized for financial accounting purposes may be different from the amount allowed for tax purposes. If the discrepancy between book income and taxable income constitutes a timing difference that will reverse, the difference should be accounted for as a deferred income tax debit or credit.

The illustrations of nonmonetary transactions set forth in the following sections of this chapter describe the financial accounting procedures; the tax accounting methods; and the timing differences that arise where the respective accounting treatments differ. (Chapter 1 of this volume is devoted to a full explanation of deferred income taxes.)

APPLYING THE BASIC PRINCIPLE

The paragraphs that follow describe conditions and circumstances under which the basic principle of fair value is required to be applied in accounting for nonmonetary transactions and, in each instance, they provide illustrations of appropriate accounting procedures for the exemplified transactions.

Nonmonetary Exchanges

1. *The cost of a nonmonetary asset acquired in exchange for another nonmonetary asset is the fair value of the asset surrendered to obtain it, and a gain or loss should be recognized on the exchange.*

The accounting treatment specified above generally pertains to exchanges of dissimilar assets. It also applies to an exchange of similar assets if the exchange culminates an earnings process.

The following examples illustrate required accounting procedures for both exchanges of dissimilar assets and exchanges of similar assets where the latter exchange culminates an earnings process.

Dissimilar Assets

Development Company acquires land for development by exchanging marketable securities, held as temporary investments, which originally cost $220,000, but have a current market value of $350,000. The entries to be made by Development Company to record the exchange are as follows:

	Debit	Credit
Land	350,000	
Gain on Exchange		130,000
Marketable Securities		220,000

Similar Assets Where Exchange Culminates an Earnings Process

Cement Block Company manufactures expensive-faced cement blocks. The Company plans to build a cement shed on its property, but does not wish to use its own expensive blocks for that purpose. Therefore, it arranges with Concrete Company to exchange 12,000 of its own expensive blocks for 20,000 of Concrete's less expensive blocks. The market value of 12,000 of Cement Company's blocks is $48,000, and the cost to manufacture them is $40,000. Cement Block Company makes the following entries to record the exchange:

	Debit	Credit
Construction in Progress	48,000	
Cost of Sales		40,000
Gain on Exchange		8,000

No deferred income tax is generated in either type of exchange illustrated above because, in each case, the financial accounting treatment is the same as that required for income tax purposes.

2. *The fair value of the asset received should be used to measure the cost if it is more clearly evident than the fair value of the asset surrendered.*

A situation in which the value of the asset received was more clearly evident than the value of the asset relinquished, along with the application of the required accounting procedures, is illustrated in the example that follows:

Land Company owned a parcel of land that was of dubious value. It was carried at its original cost of $40,000, but it had been eroded by weather conditions over the years. Land Company arranged with a development company to exchange the land for marketable securities having a market value of $30,000. The exchange was recorded by Land Company as follows:

	Debit	Credit
Marketable Securities	30,000	
Loss on Exchange	10,000	
Land		40,000

This type of exchange does not develop any deferred income taxes because the prescribed accounting treatment corresponds to that required by income tax regulations.

Nonreciprocal Nonmonetary Transfers

1. *A nonmonetary asset received in a nonreciprocal transfer should be recorded at the fair value of the asset received.*

This type of transfer and the appropriate accounting treatment is illustrated in the following example:

Because of an increase in population, the Town of Atherton needed to add to its dry waste disposal facilities. As an inducement to construct additional facilities, Atherton offered to transfer a tract of land worth $100,000 to Refuse Company. Refuse Company accepted the offer, and recorded the transfer as follows:

	Debit	Credit
Land	100,000	
Donation of Land Received		100,000

The donated land did not constitute taxable income; therefore, taxable income was less than financial pretax accounting income. However, since the land would not be depreciated for accounting purposes, the difference was a permanent difference, and no deferred income tax was developed from the transaction.

2. *A transfer of a nonmonetary asset to a stockholder or to another entity in a nonreciprocal transfer should be recorded at the fair value of the asset transferred, and a gain or loss should be recognized on the disposition of the asset.*

The following illustrations demonstrate the accounting procedures required to record the transfer of nonmonetary assets to stockholders as dividends:

Delta Company declares a property dividend to be paid in shares of stock of Fox Company, which Delta acquired some years ago at a cost of $600,000. The current market value of the block of Fox Company stock held by Delta is $720,000.

Delta records the transfer by making the following entries:

	Debit	Credit
Retained Earnings	720,000	
Gain on Revaluation of Investment		120,000
Investment—Fox Company Stock		600,000
The same effect would derive from the following series of entries:		
Investment—Fox Company Stock	120,000	
Gain on Revaluation of Investment		120,000

Retained Earnings	720,000	
Property Dividend Payable		720,000
Property Dividend Payable	720,000	
Investment—Fox Company Stock		720,000

In the above example the income from revaluation of the investment is recognized, and the value of the dividend is increased by an equivalent amount. A similar situation exists when the transfer of a nonmonetary asset is recorded as an expense, and the fair value of the nonmonetary asset transferred is in excess of its recorded value. In such case the gain from revaluation of the asset should be recognized and stated separately, and the recorded expense should include the amount so recognized. The following example illustrates such a situation:

George Company donates a section of land to the Town of Danbury to be used as a parking lot. The land was recorded at a cost of $40,000, but is currently appraised at $60,000.

George Company makes the following entries to record the donation:

	Debit	Credit
Donated Land	60,000	
Gain on Revaluation of Land		20,000
Land		40,000

The dividend declared by Delta Company in the first example had no tax effect. The type of transaction engaged in by George Company could result in a contribution carryforward for tax purposes, but it would not constitute a timing difference at the time it was made.

3. *Nonmonetary assets distributed in a nonreciprocal transfer to acquire treasury stock or stock for retirement may be valued at the fair value of the entity's own stock.*

Normally, a nonreciprocal transfer of an asset to an owner should be recorded at the fair value of the asset transferred. However, the fair value of an entity's own stock may be a more clearly evident measure of the fair value of the asset transferred than would be an estimate of fair value based on other considerations.

The following example illustrates the accounting treatment of such a nonreciprocal transfer with an owner:

Helwig Company acquired 5,000 shares of treasury stock by transferring to the stockholder a warehouse and the land on which it was situated. On the books of Helwig the land was carried at $50,000 and the building was recorded at a cost of $750,000, with accumulated depreciation of $450,000. At the time of the transfer Helwig's stock had a market value of $120 per share. Management decided that the fair value of Helwig's stock would be a more accurate valuation of the treasury stock than would the estimated fair value of the asset transferred. Therefore Helwig made the following entries to record the transfer to the stockholder:

	Debit	Credit
Treasury Stock	600,000	
Accumulated Depreciation—Building	450,000	
Gain on Revaluation of Building		250,000
Land		50,000
Building		750,000

The gain on the revaluation of the building was not a taxable gain, and had no tax effect. Therefore no deferred taxes were developed by the transaction.

MODIFICATIONS OF THE BASIC PRINCIPLE

The Opinion provides for modifications of the basic principle that accounting for nonmonetary transactions should be based on the fair value of the assets or services involved in the transfer or exchange. As a matter of simple logic, the Opinion states that accounting for a nonmonetary transaction should not be based on the fair values of the assets transferred unless their fair values are determinable within reasonable limits. The Opinion also requires a departure from the basic principle in accounting for:

(a) Nonmonetary exchanges not culminating an earnings process;
(b) Nonmonetary exchanges in which is included a monetary consideration; and
(c) Nonreciprocal transfers of nonmonetary assets to owners.

Prescribed accounting treatment for nonmonetary transactions effected under the conditions or having the characteristics referred to above are described and illustrated in the following paragraphs:

1. *Exchanges Where Fair Value Cannot Be Determined.*
   If neither the fair value of a nonmonetary asset transferred nor the fair value of a nonmonetary asset received in exchange is determinable within reasonable limits, the recorded amount of the asset transferred from the enterprise should be the measure used in the transaction.

   The following case illustrates the accounting procedures to be followed by both parties when the fair value of neither of the assets transferred in an exchange can be determined within reasonable limits:

   James Company transferred a delivery van to Williams, Inc. in exchange for 200 shares of Williams, Inc. $10 par value common stock. Williams, Inc. was a closed corporation and the fair value of the stock could not be determined within reasonable limits. The delivery van exchanged by James was carried at a cost of $12,000 with accumulated depreciation of $9,000. There was no market for this type of van, and therefore a fair value was not determinable. Since the fair value of neither property in the exchange could be determined within reasonable limits the two companies recorded the exchange, respectively, as follows:

   James Company

	Debit	Credit
Investment—Stock in Williams, Inc.	3,000	
Accumulated Depreciation—Delivery Van	9,000	
Delivery Van		12,000

   Williams, Inc.

	Debit	Credit
Delivery Van	2,000	
Capital Stock		2,000

There was no gain or loss recognized by either party to the exchange, and the financial accounting treatment corresponded to the required tax method, and no deferral of income taxes was necessary.

2. *Exchanges That Do Not Culminate an Earnings Process*

   If an exchange of a similar nonmonetary asset between an enterprise and another entity is not essentially the culmination of an earnings process, the transaction should be accounted for based on the recorded amount of the nonmonetary asset relinquished. No gain or loss should be recognized in such transactions.

The Opinion outlines two specific types of nonmonetary exchange transactions that do not culminate an earnings process. The following paragraphs describe and illustrate appropriate accounting procedures for the two types of transactions referred to in the Opinion:

(a) *Exchange of a Product to Facilitate Sales to Customers.*

An exchange does not culminate an earnings process if it is an exchange of a product or property held for sale in the ordinary course of business for a product to be sold in the same line of business to facilitate sales to customers other than the parties to the exchange.

The following example illustrates the exchange of similar inventory items to facilitate the sale of one of the items to a customer:

Smith Lincoln-Mercury, Inc. in Baltimore was negotiating the sale of a Mercury Monarch, but could not close the deal because it did not have the customer's color choice (white) in stock. However, Smith arranged to transfer a green Monarch to Harris Mercury Dealer in Washington in exchange for a white Monarch to be delivered to the customer.

In this case there would be no gain or loss on the exchange, and the only entries necessary to record the exchange would be in the inventory records, to indicate the correct serial numbers, etc.

(b) *Exchange of a Productive Asset for a Similar Productive Asset.*

The following type of exchange does not culminate an earnings process: an exchange of a productive asset not held for sale in the ordinary course of business for a similar productive asset.

The example that follows illustrates the exchange of similar productive assets that do not culminate an earnings process.

Jack's Back Hoe was the successful bidder on an excavation contract that also required digging an extensive ditch. Jack did not have a machine equipped to do that kind of work, so he arranged to transfer a back hoe to Excavators, Inc. in exchange for a ditch-digging machine that would enable him to fulfill his contract. The back hoe transferred was recorded on Jack's books at a cost of $18,000 with accumulated depreciation of $6,000. The entry made by Jack to record the exchange was as follows:

	Debit	Credit
Ditch Digger	12,000	
Accumulated Depreciation—Back Hoe	6,000	
Back Hoe		18,000

No gain or loss was recognized in the transaction, either for tax purposes or for financial accounting purposes. Income tax regulations permitted the new asset to assume the same basis (the "substituted basis") as the old asset and, consequently, depreciation expense in future periods will be the same for both tax and financial reporting. Therefore, no timing difference was created by the exchange.

3. *Nonmonetary Exchanges Which Include a Monetary Consideration*

Special accounting treatment must be accorded to transactions involving an exchange of nonmonetary assets that do not culminate an earnings process, and that include an amount of monetary consideration. Appropriate accounting procedures for both the payer and the recipient of the monetary consideration, and proper recognition of gain or loss with respect to both parties, are described and illustrated in the following paragraphs:

(a) *Recipient of the Monetary Consideration.*

The recipient of the monetary consideration in a transaction such as described above has realized gain on the exchange to the extent that the amount of the monetary receipt exceeds a proportionate share of the recorded amount of the asset surrendered. The portion of the cost applicable to the realized amount should be based on the ratio of the monetary consideration to the total consideration received (monetary consideration plus the estimated fair value of the nonmonetary asset received) or, if more clearly evident, the fair value of the nonmonetary asset transferred.

The portion of the cost referred to in the last sentence of the preceding paragraph can be determined very simply by providing appropriate amounts for the factors contained in the following formula:

Where: C = The portion of cost of the asset that is to be applied to monetary consideration received.

M = The monetary consideration received.

F = Fair value of the asset relinquished or received— whichever is more clearly evident.

R = Recorded cost of assets relinquished.

The formula is:

$$C = \left(\frac{M}{M + F}\right) R$$

The following case illustrates the use of this formula to determine gain or loss on a nonmonetary exchange not culminating an earnings process which includes a monetary consideration:

Trailer Transportation Company exchanged stake-bed trucks costing $500,000 and having a book value of $280,000 with Abbott Trucking Company for trailer trucks having a fair value of $300,000. Abbott paid Trailer $50,000 on the exchange.

It was necessary for Trailer to determine the gain or loss on the exchange, and it did so by applying the aforementioned formula. It was determined that the fair value of the trailers was more clearly evident than that of the trucks relinquished and, therefore, the value of the trailers was used in the computation.

The values of the factors of the equation were:

M — $50,000
F — $300,000
R — $280,000
C — To be determined

The values were placed in the formula and the cost applicable to the monetary consideration was determined as follows:

$$\frac{50,000}{50,000 + 300,000} \times 280,000 = 40,000.$$

The cost of $40,000 applicable to the monetary consideration was deducted from the cash received to compute the gain on the exchange:

Cash Received	50,000
Applicable Cost	40,000
Gain on Exchange	10,000

It was also necessary to determine the carrying value of the new asset by reducing the carrying cost of the old asset by the cost used in determining the gain:

Net Book Value of Asset Relinquished	280,000
Cost Applied in Determining Gain	40,000
Carrying Value of Asset Received	240,000

The following entries were made by Trailer to record the exchange:

	Debit	Credit
Cash	50,000	
Trailers	240,000	
Accumulated Depreciation—Trucks	220,000	
Trucks		500,000
Gain on Exchange		10,000

Income Tax Effects of the Exchange

The above treatment for financial accounting purposes does not correspond to the method required for tax purposes, and results in a timing difference that will be reversed. The full tax effect of this case is illustrated in the following paragraphs.

In the example cited, Trailer Transportation Company recorded a $10,000 gain on the exchange and recorded $240,000 as the depreciable basis of the net asset.

In an exchange of property for like kind by a business entity no taxable gain or loss is generated. However, when such an exchange includes *other* property, or cash, taxable gain is recognized, but not in excess of the cash received plus the fair value of the *other* property (if any) received in exchange. The basis of the net asset for tax purposes becomes the book value of the old asset plus any gain recognized, minus the cash and fair value of the *other* property.

Since only a like asset and cash were received in the exchange of similar assets in the example (no *other* property was involved), the taxable gain on the exchange was computed as follows:

Fair Value of Trucks Received	300,000
Cash Consideration Received	50,000
Fair Value of Assets Received	350,000
Book Value of Assets Relinquished	280,000
Indicated Gain on Exchange	70,000
Amount in Excess of Cash Received	20,000
Taxable Gain on Exchange	50,000

For tax purposes the basis of the net asset became:

Carrying Value of Asset Exchanged	280,000
Plus—Taxable Gain on Exchange	50,000
	330,000
Less—Amount of Cash Received	50,000
Taxable Basis of Net Asset	280,000

Assuming that Trailer Transportation had both pretax accounting income and taxable income of $100,000 before considering the exchange, the effect of the exchange was as follows:

	Pretax Accounting Income	Taxable Income
Income before considering the Exchange	100,000	100,000
Gain on Exchange	10,000	50,000
Income after considering the Exchange	110,000	150,000

Also, after the exchange the depreciable basis of the net asset was:

	Book Basis	Tax Basis
Carrying Value of New Asset	240,000	280,000

The tax paid currently on the $40,000 excess of taxable income over book income was set up by Trailer Transportation Company as a deferred tax debit. The deferred tax is to be amortized over the remaining life of the net asset, which will be depreciated for tax purposes in an amount $40,000 in excess of the amount that will be depreciated for financial accounting purposes.

(b) *Payer of the Monetary Consideration*

> *The entity paying the monetary consideration in a transaction of the nature referred to previously should not recognize any gain on the transaction, but should record the asset received at the amount of the monetary consideration paid, plus the recorded amount of the nonmonetary asset surrendered.*

The case of Abbott Trucking Company can be used to illustrate a situation where indicated gain cannot be recognized by the payer of monetary consideration in an exchange of like property.

For purposes of illustration, assume the following conditions with respect to Abbott's exchange with Trailer Transportation Company:

Estimated Value of Truck Received		280,000
Cost of Trailers Relinquished	450,000	
Allowance for Depreciation— Trailers	230,000	
Net Book Value of Trailers	220,000	
Cash Paid	50,000	270,000
Indicated Gain on Exchange		10,000

The indicated gain of $10,000 could not be recognized by Abbott for financial accounting purposes, and the carrying value of the net asset would be recorded at $270,000, which is the net book value of the asset relinquished plus the amount of cash paid. The method prescribed for financial accounting is the same as that required for tax purposes. So there would be no deferred income tax generated by the exchange.

(c) *Losses*

> *If the terms of a nonmonetary exchange (which includes a monetary consideration) indicate a loss, the entire indicated loss on the exchange should be recognized.*

The following case contains an example of a loss sustained by a party to a nonmonetary exchange involving a monetary consideration, and demonstrates appropriate accounting procedures for recording the exchange and the loss:

Following a program for modernizing its plant, Athol Printing Company transferred a printing press costing $350,000 and having a net book value of $200,000 and a fair value of $150,000 to Bethel Offset Company in exchange for a newer model of the same type machine, which also had a fair value of $150,000. Athol paid $20,000 in cash on the exchange. The press transferred by Bethel was recorded at a cost of $400,000 with accumulated depreciation of $190,000.

Athol Printing Company recorded the transaction as follows:

	Debit	Credit
Printing Press—New	150,000	
Accumulated Depreciation—Old Press	150,000	
Loss on Exchange	70,000	
Printing Press—Old		350,000
Cash		20,000

Bethel made the following entries to record the exchange and recognize the loss:

Cash	20,000	
Printing Press—New	150,000	
Accumulated Depreciation—Old Press	190,000	
Loss on Exchange	40,000	
Printing Press—Old		400,000

Tax Effect

Under no circumstances may a *loss* from an exchange of similar assets be recognized for tax purposes. The tax basis of the property received is the same as that of the property relinquished, plus or minus the cash paid or received by the respective parties to the exchange. The tax accounting for the exchange between Athol and Bethel is summarized as follows:

Tax Basis	Athol	Bethel
Recorded Value of Assets Transferred	200,000	210,000
Plus—Cash Paid on Exchange	20,000	—
Less—Cash Received	—	20,000
Tax Basis of Asset Received	220,000	190,000
Financial Accounting Basis	150,000	150,000
Financial Accounting Loss Recognized	70,000	40,000

The difference between the tax basis and the financial accounting basis of the property of each respective company corresponds to the financial accounting loss to be recorded by each company.

For financial accounting purposes in the current year Athol would record a tax benefit on its $70,000 loss, and Bethel would also record a tax benefit on its accounting loss of $40,000. Both companies would set up an account equivalent to their respective current tax benefits as a deferred income tax debit. These deferred tax debits would be amortized annually over the remaining useful life of the respective assets by applying the tax effect of the excess of depreciation allowed for tax purposes over that recorded for financial accounting purposes.

4. *Nonreciprocal Transfers to Owners*

Accounting for the distribution of nonmonetary assets to owners in a spin-off, a liquidation or another form of reorganization, or in a plan that is the recission of a prior business combination should be based on the recorded amount of the nonmonetary assets distributed. This includes a pro rata distribution to owners of an enterprise of shares of a subsidiary or other investee company that has been or is being consolidated, or that has been or is being accounted for under the equity method.

Accounting for a transfer of nonmonetary assets to owners in a spin-off is illustrated in the following example.

Talbott Motor Company is a dealer in foreign automobiles. In planning to expand its dealership to include additional foreign manufacturers, the company decides to set up its real estate properties in a separate corporation so that it can more accurately distribute the cost of its showrooms, lots, etc. Accordingly, it creates a new corporation, Realty, Inc., and transfers its real property to the new corporation in exchange for all of the new corporation's authorized capital stock. Talbott also plans to distribute to its own shareholders the shares of stock received from Realty, Inc. The real estate transferred to Realty, Inc. was recorded on Talbott's books at a cost of $500,000, with accumulated depreciation amounting to $200,000.

The value of the shares of stock received from Realty, Inc. is based on the net book value of the real estate recorded on Talbott's books, and Talbott makes the following entries to record the exchange and the distribution to its own shareholders:

	Debit	Credit
Stock in Realty, Inc.	300,000	
Accumulated Depreciation—Buildings	200,000	
Land and Building		500,000
To record transfer of real estate to Realty, Inc. in exchange for its capital stock.		
Retained Earnings	300,000	
Stock in Realty, Inc.		300,000
To record pro rata distribution of stock in Realty, Inc. to shareholders of Talbott Motors stock.		
The entry on the books of Realty, Inc. would be:		
Land and Buildings	300,000	
Capital Stock		300,000

The transactions outlined above constitute a tax-free exchange and, accordingly, the specified financial accounting corresponds with the required tax accounting.

INVOLUNTARY CONVERSION

The Opinion specifically states that involuntary conversions of nonmonetary assets are *monetary* transactions where the monetary assets received in the conversion are reinvested in other nonmonetary assets. The reason given in the Opinion for this statement is that the recipient is not obligated to reinvest the monetary consideration in other nonmonetary assets.

DISCLOSURE OF NONMONETARY TRANSACTIONS IN FINANCIAL STATEMENTS

The financial statements should disclose the nature of all significant nonmonetary transactions, the basis of accounting for the assets transferred, and gains and losses recognized in the transfers.

5

Accounting for Capitalized Leases—
Present Value Concepts and
Measurement Techniques

When the Financial Accounting Standards Board was established in 1973 one of the first items it placed on its agenda for consideration was the development of new accounting standards for lease transactions. In November, 1976, after considerable study and deliberation, FASB issued Statement of Financial Accounting Standards No. 13[1] which superseded all prior authoritative literature on the subject of leases. The provisions of the Statement are based on the concept that a lease which transfers substantially all of the benefits and risks incident to ownership of property should be accounted for as the acquisition of an asset and the incurrence of an obligation by the lessee and as a sale or financing transaction by the lessor: all other leases should be accounted for as operating leases. The Statement provides criteria for the classification of leases and establishes standards of accounting and reporting designed to implement the principles of the Board's concept.

While FASB Statement No. 13 establishes certain separate accounting standards for lessors and lessees, nevertheless, many accounting requirements and procedures are common to both, and in the sections of the Statement dealing separately with lessors and lessees descriptions of such common requirements are cross-referenced rather than repeated. In order to maintain a continuity in separate expositions of accounting standards and illustrations of accounting procedures applicable to lessors and lessees, respectively, this book contains two chapters on accounting for leases: lessee transactions are described in this chapter, and lessor transactions are discussed in Chapter 6. Classification criteria, accounting standards, and reporting requirements are repeated in each chapter where they are applicable to both lessors and lessees.

The rules and regulations for the accounting treatment of leases as set forth in the Statement are complex, intricate, and technical; and the text of the Statement itself is difficult to comprehend because of the excessive cross-referencing of interrelated elements. The objectives of this chapter, and of Chapter 6, are to clarify the provisions of the Statement, explain the criteria for classifying leases, illustrate accounting procedures and reporting requirements for lease transactions, and demonstrate computational techniques for the measurement of present values of lease commitments.

---

[1]*Accounting for Leases,* Statement of the Financial Accounting Standards Board No. 13 (Stamford, Connecticut, Financial Accounting Standards Board, 1976. Reprinted with permission. Copies of the complete document are available from the FASB.)

DEFINITIONS OF TERMS

FASB Statement No. 13 contains definitions of certain terms that are peculiar to its text. These definitions, generally, have no conventional acceptance and are valid only for purposes of the Statement. For that reason they are set forth early in the chapter, and are quoted verbatim from the Statement. The reader should use this section for reference when confronted by the terms later in the text.

Related Parties in Leasing Transactions

A parent company and its subsidiaries, an owner company and its joint ventures (corporate or otherwise) and partnerships, and an investor (including a natural person) and its investees, provided that the parent company, owner company, or investor has the ability to exercise significant influence over operating and financial policies of the related party, as significant influence is defined in APB Opinion No. 18, paragraph 17. In addition to the examples of significant influence set forth in that paragraph, significant influence may be exercised through guarantees of indebtedness, extensions of credit, or through ownership of warrants, debt obligations, or other securities. If two or more entities are subject to the significant influence of a parent, owner company, investor (including a natural person), or common officers or directors, those entities shall be considered related parties with respect to each other.

Inception of the Lease

With the exception noted below, the date of the lease agreement or commitment, if earlier. For purposes of this definition, a commitment shall be in writing, signed by the parties in interest to the transaction, and shall specifically set forth the principal terms of the transaction. However, if the property covered by the lease has yet to be constructed or has not been acquired by the lessor at the date of the lease agreement or commitment, the inception of the lease shall be the date that construction of the property is completed or the property is acquired by the lessor.

Fair Value of the Leased Property

The price for which the property could be sold in an arm's-length transaction between unrelated parties. The following are examples of the determination of fair value:

i. When the lessor is a manufacturer or dealer, the fair value of the property at the inception of the lease will ordinarily be its normal selling price, reflecting any volume or trade discounts that may be applicable. However, the determination of fair value shall be made in light of market conditions prevailing at the time, which may indicate that the fair value of the property is less than the normal selling price and, in some instances, less than the cost of the property.

ii. When the lessor is not a manufacturer or dealer, the fair value of the property at the inception of the lease will ordinarily be its cost, reflecting any volume or trade discounts that may be applicable. However, when there has been a significant lapse of time between the acquisition of the property by the lessor and the inception of the lease, the determination of fair value shall be made in light of market conditions prevailing at the inception of the lease, which may indicate that the fair value of the property is greater or less than its cost or carrying amount, if different.

Bargain Purchase Option

A provision allowing the lessee, at his option, to purchase the leased property for a price which is sufficiently lower than the expected fair value of the property at the date the option becomes exercisable that exercise of the option appears, at the inception of the lease, to be reasonably assured.

Bargain Renewal Option

A provision allowing the lessee, at his option, to renew the lease for a rental sufficiently lower than the fair rental of the property at the date the option becomes exercisable that exercise of the option appears, at the inception of the lease, to be reasonably assured.

Lease Term

The fixed noncancelable term of the lease plus:

   i. All periods, if any, covered by bargain renewal options;
   ii. All periods, if any, for which failure to renew the lease imposes a penalty on the lessee in an amount such that the renewal appears, at the inception of the lease, to be reasonably assured;
   iii. All periods, if any, covered by ordinary renewal options during which a guarantee by the lessee of the lessor's debt related to the leased property is expected to be in effect;
   iv. All periods, if any, covered by ordinary renewal options preceding the date as of which a bargain purchase option is exercisable; and
   v. All periods, if any, representing renewal or extensions of the lease at the lessor's option.

However, in no case shall the lease term extend beyond the date a bargain purchase option becomes exercisable.

A lease which is cancelable:

   i. Only upon the occurrence of some remote contingency;
   ii. Only with the permission of the lessor;
   iii. Only if the lessee enters into a new lease with the same lessor; or,
   iv. Only upon payment by the lessee of a penalty in an amount such that continuation of the lease appears, at inception, reasonably assured; shall be considered "noncancelable" for purposes of this definition.

Estimated Economic Life of Leased Property

The estimated remaining period during which the property is expected to be economically usable by one or more users, with normal repairs and maintenance, for the purpose for which it was intended at the inception of the lease, without limitation by the lease term.

Estimated Residual Value of Leased Property

The estimated fair value of the leased property at the end of the lease term.

Unguaranteed Residual Value

The estimated residual value of the leased property exclusive of any portion guaranteed by the lessee or by a third party unrelated to the lessor.

Minimum Lease Payments

   i. From the Standpoint of the Lessee
      The payments that the lessee is obligated to make or can be required to make in connection with the leased property. However, a guarantee by the lessee of the lessor's debt and the lessee's obligation to pay (apart from the rental payments) executory costs such as insurance, maintenance, and taxes in connection with the leased property shall be excluded. If the lease contains a bargain purchase option, only the minimum rental payments over the lease

term and the payment called for by the bargain purchase option shall be included in the minimum lease payments. Otherwise, minimum lease payments include the following:

a. The minimum rental payments called for by the lease over the lease term.
b. Any guarantee by the lessee of the residual value at the expiration of the lease term, whether or not payment of the guarantee constitutes a purchase of the leased property. When the lessor has the right to require the lessee to purchase the property at termination of the lease for a certain or determinable amount, that amount shall be considered a lessee guarantee. When the lessee agrees to make up any deficiency below a stated amount in the lessor's realization of the residual value, the guarantee to be included in the minimum lease payments shall be the stated amount, rather than an estimate of the deficiency to be made up.
c. Any payment that the lessee must make or can be required to make upon failure to renew or extend the lease at the expiration of the lease term, whether or not the payment would constitute a purchase of the leased property. In this connection, it should be noted that the definition of lease term in a preceding paragraph includes "all periods, if any, for which failure to renew the lease imposes a penalty on the lessee in an amount such that renewal appears, at the inception of the lease, to be reasonably assured." If the lease term has been extended because of that provision, the related penalty shall not be included in minimum lease payments.

ii. From the Standpoint of the Lessor

The payments described in (i) above plus any guarantee of the residual value or of rental payments beyond the lease term by a third party unrelated to either the lessee or the lessor, provided the third party is financially capable of discharging the obligations that may arise from the guarantee.

Interest Rate Implicit in the Lease

The discount rate that, when applied to:

(a) The minimum lease payments, excluding that portion of the payments representing executory costs to be paid by the lessor, together with any profits thereon; and
(b) The unguaranteed residual value accruing to the benefit of the lessor,

causes the aggregate present value at the beginning of the lease term to be equal to the fair value of the leased property to the lessor at the inception of the lease, minus any investment tax credit retained by the lessor and expected to be realized by him.

Lessee's Incremental Borrowing Rate

The rate that, at the inception of the lease, the lessee would have incurred to borrow over a similar term the funds necessary to purchase the leased asset.

Initial Direct Costs[2]

Those costs incurred by the lessor that are directly associated with negotiating and consummating completed leasing transactions. Those costs include, but are not necessarily limited to, commissions, legal fees, costs of credit investigations, and

[2]This definition is quoted from FASB Statement No. 17, which was published solely to amend the definition originally published in FASB Statement No. 13. See *Accounting for Leases—Initial Direct Costs,* Statement of the Financial Accounting Standards Board No. 17. (Stamford, Connecticut, Financial Accounting Standards Board, 1977. Reprinted with permission. Copies of the complete document are available from the FASB).

costs of preparing and processing documents for new leases acquired. In addition, that portion of the sales person's compensation, other than commissions, and the compensation of other employees that is applicable to the time spent in the activities described above with respect to completed leasing transactions shall also be included in initial direct costs. That portion of sales person's compensation and the compensation of other employees that is applicable to the time spent in negotiating leases that are not consummated shall not be included in initial direct costs. No portion of supervisory and administrative expenses or other indirect expenses, such as rent and facilities' costs, shall be included in initial direct costs.

PRESENT VALUE CONCEPTS

Prior to 1964 present values generally were conceptually illusive to accountants indoctrinated in the historic basis of accounting, and many did not bother with the concept until they were confronted by it. However, the Accounting Principles Board's (APB) original directives on leasing transactions and its later Opinion on the imputation of interest for receivables and payables established discounted present values as a major accounting principle. The concept is reaffirmed in FASB Statement No. 13, and the accounting principle of the APB persists as an integral part of FASB accounting standards.

There are two concepts of present value involved in accounting for leases under FASB Statement No. 13:

(a) The present value of an annuity; and
(b) The present value of an amount at compound interest.

Present Value of an Annuity

The present value of an annuity coincides with the present value of a series of future payments made at the end of each of a specific number of uniform intervals at a particular interest rate compounded at the end of each interval. For example, the present value of five annual payments of $10,000.00 each at an interest rate of 5% compounded annually is $43,294.77. In other words, $43,294.77 deposited immediately in a bank paying 5% interest compounded annually would amount to $55,256.32 at the end of five years. Thus, $55,256.32 is equivalent to the amount that would be on deposit at the end of five years, if five annual deposits were made at the end of each year and the bank paid interest at 5% compounded annually.

Present Value of a Future Amount at Compound Interest

The present value of an amount at compound interest coincides with the amount required to be deposited immediately and left on deposit over a specific number of intervals at a particular interest rate compounded at the end of each interval, so that the aggregate principal and interest at the end of the period would be equivalent to the stated amount at compound interest. For example, at an interest rate of 5% compounded annually, the present value of a single future payment of $50,000.00 to be made at the end of five years is $39,176.31, and is equivalent to the amount necessary to deposit immediately at 5% interest compounded annually and left on deposit for five years so that at the end of five years the aggregate principal and interest would total $50,000.00.

BASIC FORMULAS

Computations of annuities, amounts at compound interest, and their related present values, all can be performed by the use of four simple algebraic equations, each containing four variables.

The basic formula for each of the four values, respectively, are as follows:[3]

Where:

S = Amount of the annuity
R = Periodic payment of an annuity
A = Present value of an annuity
i = Rate of interest per period
n = Number of intervals—number of interest periods
P = Principal to be invested at a compound interest—present value of an amount at compound interest
C = Compound amount at end of period

Amount at Compound Interest

$$C = P(1+i)^n$$

Present Value of an Amount at Compound Interest

$$P = C \left(\frac{1}{1+i}\right)^n$$

Annuity per Period

$$S = R \left(\frac{(1+i)^n - 1}{i}\right)$$

Present Value of an Annuity per Period

$$A = R\left(\frac{1 - \left(\frac{1}{1+i}\right)^n}{i}\right)$$

COMPUTATIONAL TECHNIQUES

While the basic formulas are simple algebraic equations and easy to solve, nevertheless, the solutions sometimes require extensive computation because the exponent in the term $(1+i)^n$ can represent a large number of interest intervals, and it is the exponent that determines the number of separate calculations that must be made. Because of the time factor involved in such extensive computation, various computational techniques have been developed that reduce the number of separate calculations required to solve the equations. Such techniques include, respectively, applying logarithms as factors in the equations, referring to tables of values, preparing computer programs, and using electronic calculators.[4]

SOLVING THE BASIC EQUATIONS

The basic equations are solved simply by putting the known values in the formula, and solving for the unknown.

Illustrative Problem No. 1

Find the present value of a contract calling for 5 annual payments of $10,000.00 at the end of each year, when the cost of money is 8-¾ %.

$$R = \$10,000.00, i = .0875, n = 5.$$

---

[3] Negative exponents are not used in these equations so as to present them in a configuration that conforms to the shortest possible sequence of algebraic entry into an electronic calculator.

[4] The binomial theorem can be used in approximating, to a given number of decimal points, powers of $(1+i)$. However, expansion of a binomial is a lengthy operation and generally not useful for this purpose.

Placing the known values in the equation, we have:

$$A = 10,000 \left(\frac{1 - \left(\frac{1}{(1.0875)} \right)^{5}}{.0875} \right)$$

Solving for the exponent first we have $(1.0875)^{5} = 1.52106$

Then, $1 \div 1.52106 = .65744$: $1 - .65744 = .34256$: $.34256 \div .0875 = 3.9150$

$3.9150 \times 10,000 = 39,150.$

Therefore, the present value of the contract is $39,150.00.

The above equation can be used to compute the present value of any amount, at any interest rate, for any number of periods.

LOGARITHMS

The use of logarithms to compute powers of $(1+i)$ reduces the number of required manual calculations to a minimum. For example, if there are 120 interest periods involved in a present value problem then $(1+i)$ must be computed to the 120th power, requiring 119 manual operations.

However, the number of operations to compute $(1+i)^{120}$ can be reduced from 119 to 3 by the use of logarithms. Since it has been proven that the logarithm of a power of a positive number is the exponent of the power times the logarithm of the number, a simple computation can be made to carry $(1+i)$ to any power desired by simply finding the logarithm of $(1+i)$, multiplying it by the exponent of the power, and then finding the antilogarithm of the result.

Logarithms can be employed to solve all parts of the equation. However, it is suggested that the use of logarithms be limited to solving $(1+i)^{n}$, and that a desk calculator be used to solve the rest of the equation. That is the method used in the problem described below.

Illustrative Problem No. 2

Find the present value of an annuity of $2,275.00 every six months for 8 years, 6 months, if money is worth 5.4% compounded semiannually.

$$R = 2,275, i = .027 \text{ (semiannual interest rate!), } n = 17.$$

$$A = 2.275 \left(\frac{1 - \left(\frac{1}{(1.027)} \right)^{17}}{.027} \right)$$

Solving first for the exponent by use of logarithms found in 6-place tables:

$$\log 1.027 = .0115704: 17 \times .0115704 = .196697:$$

$$\text{Antilog } .196697 = 1.5729. \text{ Therefore, } (1.027)^{17} = 1.5729$$

Continuing the operation by use of a desk calculator, we have:

$$1 \div 1.5729 = .63577: 1 - .63577 = .36423: .36423 \div .027 = 13.49:$$
$$2,275 \times 13.49 = 30,689.75$$

Therefore, the present value of the annuity is $30,689.75.

PUBLISHED TABLES

One of the simplest methods of finding values of annuities and elements of compound interest is the use of published tables. For example, tables are published for the present value of an annuity of 1 per period. Such tables are generally designated by the following terms:

$$a_{\overline{n}/i} = \frac{1 - (1+i)^{-n}}{i}$$

The symbol $a_{\overline{n}/i}$ is read "a angle n at i" and simply means that for certain i and n, its value is found in the table. Thus, if i = 8.75% and n = 6 interest periods, the present value of its annuity at $1.00 would be found in the 8.75% column, on a line with the sixth period. The term $\frac{1 - (1+i)^{-n}}{i}$ simply indicates what equation the tables are solving.

Illustrative Problem No. 3

Using the tables in Schedule 1 find the present value of 6 annual payments of $4,000.00 each when the current interest rate is 8.75%, compounded annually.

PRESENT VALUE OF ANNUITY OF 1 PER PERIOD

$$a_{\overline{n}/i} = \frac{1 - (1+i)^{-n}}{i}$$

RATE = 8.75%		RATE = 9.00%		RATE = 9.50%	
PERIOD	VALUE	PERIOD	VALUE	PERIOD	VALUE
1	0.91954	1	0.91743	1	0.91324
2	1.76509	2	1.75911	2	1.74725
3	2.54261	3	2.53129	3	2.50890
4	3.25757	4	3.23971	4	3.20448
5	3.91501	5	3.88965	5	3.83970
6	4.51955	6	4.48591	6	4.41982
7	5.07545	7	5.03295	7	4.94961
8	5.58662	8	5.53481	8	5.43343
9	6.05666	9	5.99524	9	5.87528
10	6.48888	10	6.41765	10	6.27879

SCHEDULE 1

Using the symbol $a_{\overline{n}/i}$ we have $a_{\overline{6}/8.75}$, and this indicates that the value of 1 will be found in the 8.75% column on a line with the sixth period. From the table we find the value of 1 to be 4.51955.

To find the present value of the annuity we multiply the value of 1 by the amount of the periodic payment, thus:

$$4,000 \times 4.51955 = 18,078.20$$

Therefore the present value of the six annual payments of $4,000 each at an interest rate of 8.75% compounded annually is $18,078.20.

COMPUTER PROGRAMS

Tables of values of annuities and elements of compound interest are, of course, published for only a limited number of interest rates, but if there is access to a computer, the accountant can, in a matter of minutes, print out tables for any interest rate he may need. However, this is an expensive operation and implementation is not feasible unless an extraordinarily large number of computations would be involved.

ELECTRONIC CALCULATORS

The advent of electronic pocket and desk calculators has revolutionized the method of solving problems involving annuities, amount at compound interest, and their related present values. A basic four-function electronic calculator with processing sequences that produce $y^x, \sqrt[x]{y}, \frac{1}{x}$, $+/-$, log, storage, and recall can solve any such problem almost instantaneously, and absolutely obviate the use of published tables. The more expensive programmable hand calculator can be operated on calculate, run, and learn modes, and thus can be programmed for automatic solution of the type of problems referred to above.

The speed with which problems can be solved on an electronic calculator is absolutely astonishing when compared to a manual process of solution. For example, on an algebraic entry calculator[5] compound interest can be computed by six keystrokes and the present value can be computed by seven strokes. Both routines are illustrated in Schedule 2.

COMPUTATIONAL ROUTINES FOR COMPOUND INTEREST

	Compound Interest		Present Value of Amount at Compound Interest	
	Find compound amount accumulated by 20 annual deposits of $5,000 each at 8% interest compounded annually.		Find present value of a $50,000 payment made at the end of ten years when the current interest rate is 6%, compounded annually.	
	$C = P(1+i)^n$		$P = C\left(\dfrac{1}{1+i}\right)^n$	
	Calculator Operations		Calculator Operations	
Sequence	Key	Display	Key	Display
1	1.08	1.08	1.06	1.06
2	y^x	1.08	1/x	.9433962264
3	20	20	y^x	.9433962264
4	X	4.660957144	10	10
5	5,000	5,000	X	.5583947769
6	=	23,304.78572	50,000	50,000
7			=	27,919.73885

SCHEDULE 2

---

[5] Algebraic entry processing only is illustrated because it is not feasible to demonstrate both algebraic and reverse Polish keystrokes in the space allotted to this chapter.

The solutions to the two problems are $23,304.79 and $27,919.74, respectively. On an algebraic entry electronic calculator the computational routines shown in Schedule 3 can be used to solve for annuities, and present values of annuities, respectively.

The solutions to the two problems are $107,892.82 and $47,656.12, respectively.

COMPUTATIONAL ROUTINES FOR ANNUITIES

Amount of Annuity	Present Value of Annuity
Find amount accumulated by 15 annual payments of $5,000 at interest rate of 5%, compounded annually.	Find present value of 12 annual payments of $6,000 at 7% interest compounded annually.

$$S = R\left(\frac{(1+i)^n - 1}{i}\right) \qquad A = R\left(\frac{1 - \left(\frac{1}{1+i}\right)^n}{i}\right)$$

	Calculator Operations		Calculator Operations	
Sequence	Key	Display	Key	Display
1	1.05	1.05	1.07	1.07
2	y^x	1.05	1/x	.9345794393
3	15	15	y^x	.9345794393
4	−	2.078928179	12	12
5	1	1	=	.4440119592
6	=	1.078928179	+/−	−.4440119592
7	÷	1.078928179	+	−.4440119592
8	.05	.05	1	1
9	=	21.57856359	=	.5559880408
10	X	21.57856359	÷	.5559880408
11	5,000	5,000	.07	.07
12	=	107,892.8179	=	7.942686297
13			X	7.942686297
14			6,000	6,000
15			=	47,656.11778

SCHEDULE 3

CALCULATING IMPLICIT INTEREST RATES

Where the aggregate present value of the minimum lease payments exceeds the fair value of the leased property at the inception of the lease, the Statement requires that an interest rate implicit in the lease be applied to the minimum lease payments so as to cause such payments to be equal to the fair value. This requires a computation of present value where the interest rate is unknown.

The basic formula for the present value of an annuity comprehends four variables, and any one variable can be computed algebraically when the other three are known. However, the interest rate is the one variable that cannot be computed by a simple algebraic equation. The practical method is to solve the equation repeatedly with an *estimated* interest rate until an interest rate that satisfies the equation is found.[6] This method is illustrated in the following problem.

Illustrative Problem No. 4

Brooks Company leased a machine having a fair value of $20,000 from Sanders, Inc. under a lease agreement that fitted the criteria for a capital lease, and required five annual payments of $6,000 at the end of each year.

Brooks' incremental borrowing rate was 8.75% and the present value of the minimum lease payments were computed using that rate as follows:

$$6,000 \times \left(\frac{1 - \left(\frac{1}{1.0875}\right)^5}{.0875} \right) = 6,000 \times 3.915013851 = 23,490.08$$

However, since the fair value of the leased property was less than the present value of the minimum lease payments discounted at 8.75% Brooks was required to use an implicit interest rate that would make the minimum lease payments equivalent to the fair value. Since three of the variables in the formula equation were known, the unknown interest rate was computed on an electronic calculator by testing estimated rates as follows:

The known variables were placed in the equation, and it then became:

$$20,000 = 6,000 \times \left(\frac{1 - \left(\frac{1}{1+i}\right)^5}{i} \right)$$

Since a discount rate of 8.75% gave a present value in excess of the fair value, an estimated interest rate in excess of 8.75% was used for the first test, and the following tests were made on estimates based on the respective preceding tests, as shown below.[7]

$$\text{1st Test—15\%} - \frac{1 - \left(\frac{1}{1.15}\right)^5}{.15} = 3.352155098 \times 6,000 = 20,112.93$$

$$\text{2nd Test—16\%} - \frac{1 - \left(\frac{1}{1.16}\right)^5}{.16} = 3.274293654 \times 6,000 = \underline{19,645.76}$$

$$\underline{467.17}$$

$20,112.93 needed to be reduced by $112.93.
The difference between 15% and 16% was $467.17.
Therefore, $\frac{112.93}{467.17}$ of 1% or .24% was added to 15%.

$$\text{3rd Test} - 15.24\% - \left(\frac{1 - \left(\frac{1}{1.1524}\right)^5}{.1524} \right) = 3.33194701 \times 6,000 = 19,999.17$$

---

[6] A programmable electronic pocket calculator can calculate an unknown interest rate in an annuity present value formula in a matter of seconds by using this iterative method.

[7] Since the results obtained from using different interest rates follow a pattern of geometric progression, this method of interpolation will not always provide the required difference as quickly as is demonstrated in this particular problem. In most cases the interpolation must be repeated in successive tests until the precise required difference is obtained.

Therefore, 15.24% was the rate implicit in the lease. The asset and lease obligation was $20,000 and the payments were distributed as shown in Schedule 4.

DISTRIBUTION OF PERIODIC PAYMENTS BASED ON IMPLICIT INTEREST RATE

	Payment	Applied to Interest Expense	Applied to Lease Obligation	Balance of Lease Obligation
Balance				20,000
1st Year	6,000	3,048	2,952	17,048
2nd Year	6,000	2,598	3,402	13,646
3rd Year	6,000	2,080	3,920	9,726
4th Year	6,000	1,482	4,518	5,208
5th Year	6,000	792	5,208	
	30,000	10,000	20,000	

SCHEDULE 4

COMPUTING THE PRESENT VALUE OF PAYMENTS MADE AT THE BEGINNING OF INTEREST INTERVALS

It is important to remember that the basic formula for the present value of annuities computes the value of the payments when they are made at the end of each interest interval.

When it is necessary to compute the present value of payments made at the *beginning* of the interest intervals, the present value of the first payment is equivalent to the amount of the payment, and the total number of payments minus 1 can then be applied to the equation. This procedure is illustrated in the following problem.

Illustrative Problem No. 5

Find the present value of five annual lease payments of $6,000 made at the beginning of each year at an interest rate of 15.24% compounded annually.

Present value of first payment   6,000
Present value of four subsequent payments:

$$\frac{1 - \left(\dfrac{1}{1.1524}\right)^4}{.1524} = 2.841173573 \times 6,000 =$$ 17,047

Aggregate present value   23,047

The periodic payments would be distributed as outlined in Schedule 5.

DISTRIBUTION OF PERIODIC PAYMENTS PAYMENTS MADE AT BEGINNING OF PERIOD

	Payment	Applied to		Balance of Lease Obligation
		Interest Expense	Lease Obligation	
Balance				23,047
1st Year	6,000		6,000	17,047
2nd Year	6,000	2,598	3,402	13,645
3rd Year	6,000	2,079	3,921	9,724
4th Year	6,000	1,482	4,518	5,206
5th Year	6,000	794	5,206	
	30,000	6,953	23,047	

SCHEDULE 5

COMPUTATION OF PRESENT VALUE WHERE AMOUNT OF PERIODIC PAYMENT CHANGES

In some cases lease agreements provide for a reduced periodic payment after a certain number of payments have been made on the contract. For example, a ten-year lease may call for five annual payments of $4,000 for the first five years and five $3,000 annual payments for the last five years.

Computation of the present value of the minimum lease payments under such a contract requires use of the basic formula for the present value of an annuity for the periods of uniform payment, and use of the basic formula for the present value of an amount at compound interest to compute the amount necessary to provide the annuity present values computed for the later periods of uniform payments.

This method is illustrated in the following problem.

Illustrative Problem No. 6

Tillman Company leased a machine having a fair value of $100,000 under a capital lease agreement requiring five annual payments of $6,000 at the beginning of each of the first five years of the lease; five annual payments of $4,000 at the beginning of each of the last five years of the lease; and a $1,000 payment at the end of the ten year lease term.

Tillman computed the present value of the minimum lease payments, using its incremental borrowing rate of 9.5%, as follows:

	Present Value
Present Value of First Five Payments at $6,000	
First payment	6,000
Four Annual Payments of $6,000	

$$\frac{1 - \left(\dfrac{1}{1.095}\right)^{4}}{.095} = 3.204481121 \times 6,000 \qquad 19,226$$

	25,226

Present Value of Last Five Payments at $4,000

Sixth payment		4,000

Four Annual Payments of $4,000

$$\frac{1 - \left(\frac{1}{1.095}\right)^4}{.095} = 3.204481121 \times 4,000 \qquad 12,818$$

$$16,818$$

Present Value of $16,818 at Compound Interest at the End of Five Years

$$\left(\frac{1}{1.095}\right)^5 = .6352276653 \times 16,818 = \qquad 10,683$$

Present Value of $1,000 Payment at End of 10 Years

$$\left(\frac{1}{1.095}\right)^{10} = .4035141867 \times 1,000 = \qquad 403$$

Aggregate present value $\qquad\qquad$ 36,312

Thus, $36,312 is the aggregate present value of the minimum lease payments, and the periodic payments would be distributed as shown in Schedule 6.

DISTRIBUTION OF PERIODIC PAYMENTS WHERE AMOUNT OF PAYMENT CHANGES

Beginning of	Payment	Applied to Interest Expense	Applied to Lease Obligation	Amount of Lease Obligation
1st Year				36,312
1st Year	6,000		6,000	30,312
2nd Year	6,000	2,879	3,121	27,191
3rd Year	6,000	2,583	3,417	23,774
4th Year	6,000	2,258	3,742	20,032
5th Year	6,000	1,903	4,097	15,935
6th Year	4,000	1,514	2,486	13,449
7th Year	4,000	1,277	2,723	10,726
8th Year	4,000	1,019	2,981	7,745
9th Year	4,000	735	3,265	4,480
10th Year	4,000	425	3,575	905
End of				
10th Year	1,000	95	905	
	51,000	14,688	36,312	

SCHEDULE 6

COMPUTING AMOUNT OF PERIODIC PAYMENT REQUIRED TO AMORTIZE A CAPITAL LEASE OBLIGATION

In some cases the parties to a lease may enter into a contract designed to provide the lessor with a specific amount at a particular interest rate over a given number of interest intervals. In such cases it is necessary to compute the amount of the periodic payment required to amortize the lease obligation in accordance with the agreement. This computation can be made by taking a reciprocal of the annuity present value ratio and multiplying it by the amount of the lease obligation. The formula for the required payment is:

$$R = S\left(\frac{1}{\frac{1 - \left(\frac{1}{1+i}\right)^n}{i}}\right)$$

This equation can be solved easily with an electronic calculator even to the 480th power of the exponential number, as demonstrated in the following problem.

Illustrative Problem No. 7

Green Bros. and Schultz, Inc. entered into an agreement, required to be classified as a capital lease, in which Green contracted to lease a building from Schultz for 40 years at a monthly rental that would pay Schultz a principal amount of $75,000 over the 40 years and interest at an annual rate of 9.75% on the monthly unpaid balance.

Green computed the monthly rate to be $1/12 \times 9.75\%$ or .8125%, and the intervals to be 40×12, or 480. He then put the known variables in the formula

$$R = 75,000\left(\frac{1}{\frac{1 - \left(\frac{1}{1.008125}\right)^{480}}{.008125}}\right)$$

and solved the equation on an electronic calculator as follows:

Sequence	Key Press (left to right)	Display
1	1.008125 $\frac{1}{x}$ y^x 480 =	.0205634191
2	$+/-$ $+$ 1 =	.9794365808
3	$\div$ .008125 =	120.5460407
4	$\frac{1}{x}$ x 75,000 =	622.1689203

Thus, the required monthly payment was determined to be $622.17.

ACCOUNTING AND REPORTING STANDARDS FOR LESSEES

CLASSIFICATION OF LEASES BY LESSEE

Implementation of the principles of the FASB concept of leasing transactions requires lessees to classify all leases into one of two categories, as indicated below:

(a) *Capital Leases*
Leases which transfer substantially all of the benefits and risks incident to ownership of property.
(b) *Operating Leases*
All other leases.

CRITERIA FOR CLASSIFICATION OF LEASES BY LESSEES

The Statement establishes the following criteria for classification of leases by lessees:

Capital Leases

A lease shall be classified as a capital lease if, at its inception, it meets one or more of the following criteria:
(a) The lease transfers ownership of the property to the lessee by the end of the lease term;
(b) The lease contains a bargain purchase option;
(c) The lease terms are equal to 75% or more of the estimated economic life of the leased property; and
(d) The present value of the minimum lease payments equals or exceeds 90% of the fair value of the leased property less any related investment tax credit retained by the lessor.

Neither criterion (c) nor criterion (d) shall be used if the beginning of the lease term falls within the last 25% of the total estimated economic life of the leased property, including earlier years of use.

Operating Leases

A lease that does not meet any one of the criteria for classifying capital leases shall be classified as an operating lease.

EXPLANATION AND ILLUSTRATION OF LESSEE CLASSIFICATION CRITERIA

The criteria set forth in the foregoing subparagraphs (a), (b), and (c) are self-explanatory and need no clarification. It is useful to note, however, that only the criteria in (a) or (b) can be used to classify a lease that begins within the last 25% of the estimated economic life of the property being leased. It is also important to note that the computations required in subparagraph (d) need not be made if the lease is determined to be a capital lease because it meets any one of the criteria set forth in subparagraphs (a), (b), or (c).

With reference to the criterion outlined in subparagraph (d), the Statement provides that the lessee shall compute the present value of the minimum lease payments using his incremental borrowing rate. However, the lessee shall use the lessor's implicit rate where both of the following conditions obtain:

 i. It is practicable for the lessee to learn the implicit rate computed by the lessor; and
 ii. The implicit rate computed by the lessor is less than the lessee's incremental borrowing rate.

Model Case No. 1 illustrates the use of the criterion described in subparagraph (d) for the purpose of classification of leases by a lessee.

MODEL CASE NO. 1

Addison, Inc. entered into two similar lease agreements with Clark Company and Vinson Bros., respectively. Neither of the leases transferred ownership at the end of the lease term, offered the lessee a bargain purchase option, nor began within the last 25% or extended over 75% of the estimated economic life of the leased property. Consequently, it was necessary for Addison to test the criterion in subparagraph (d) above to determine whether or not the agreements should be classified as capital leases. Addison could not learn the rate implicit in the Clark lease, but was able to determine that Vinson's implicit rate was 8.5%, compounded annually. Since Addison's incremental borrowing rate was 10%, the present value of the minimum payments under the Clark lease was computed at 10%, and the present value of the minimum payments under the Vinson lease was computed at the lesser rate of 8.5% implicit in the lease.

Addison made the following computations, based on the terms of the leases, using the discount rate indicated above:

	Clark Lease	Vinson Lease
Fair value of leased property	74,000	75,360
Less: Investment credit retained by lessor	—	7,536
	74,000	67,824

Present Value of Minimum Lease Payments
10 Annual Payments of $10,000 Each

$$\text{Clark} \quad 10,000 \times \frac{1 - \left(\frac{1}{1.10}\right)^{10}}{.10} = \qquad 61,446$$

$$\text{Vinson} \quad 10,000 \times \frac{1 - \left(\frac{1}{1.085}\right)^{10}}{.085} = \qquad\qquad\qquad 65,612$$

$$\text{Residual Guarantee} \quad 5,000 \times \left(\frac{1}{1.085}\right)^{10} = \qquad\qquad\qquad 2,212$$

	Clark Lease	Vinson Lease
Total present value of minimum lease payments	61,446	67,824
Present value as a percentage of fair value	.83%	100%

The present value of the minimum lease payments is less than 90% of the fair value of the property leased from Clark, and exceeds 90% of the fair value of the property leased from Vinson. Consequently, Clark's lease was classified as an operating lease, and Vinson's lease as a capital lease.

APPLICATION OF CLASSIFICATION CRITERIA BY LESSEES TO LEASES INVOLVING REAL ESTATE

Land generally does not depreciate in value over time and therefore leases for land normally are based solely on an interest factor. On the other hand, there is a continuity of deterioration in buildings and equipment, and leases for such property are usually based on compensation for depreciation, plus interest. Because of this distinction in the nature of land and buildings, the Board was constrained to make separate rules for the application of classification criteria to leases for real estate and, in certain instances, to require a separation of the land and building elements in a lease involving both.

Leases for Land Only

If land is the sole item of property leased, and the lease either transfers ownership of the land to the lessee by the end of the lease term or contains a bargain purchase option, the lessee should classify the lease as a capital lease. If these conditional criteria are not met, he should classify it as an operating lease.

Leases Involving Land and Buildings

If the lease for both land and buildings either transfers ownership of the property to the lessee by the end of the lease term or contains a bargain purchase option, the lease is a capital lease, and land and buildings should be separately capitalized by the lessee.

If the lease for both land and buildings neither transfers ownership to the lessee nor contains a bargain purchase option, the lessee should classify the lease according to the ratio of the fair value of the land to the total fair value, as outlined in the two following paragraphs.

Fair Value of Land Less Than 25% of Total Fair Value

If the fair value of the land is less than 25% of the total fair value of the leased property at the inception of the lease, the lessee shall consider the land and building as a single unit. If the lease term is equal to 75% of the estimated economic life of the *building* or if the present value of the minimum lease payments applicable to the single "unit" equals or exceeds 90% of the fair value of the single "unit," the lease shall be classified as a capital lease. If these conditional criteria are not met, the lease shall be classified as an operating lease.

Fair Value of Land 25% or More of the Total Fair Value

If the fair value of the land is 25% or more of the total fair value of the leased property the lessee should treat the land and building as separate components. If the lease term is equal to 75% of the estimated economic life of the building or if the present value of the minimum lease payments applicable to the building equals or exceeds 90% of the fair value of the building, the building element should be classified as a capital lease and the land element as an operating lease. If these conditional criteria are not met, both the building element and the land element should be considered as a single operating lease.

Leases Involving Equipment and Real Estate

If a lease involving real estate also includes equipment, the portion of the minimum lease payments applicable to the equipment element of the lease should be estimated by whatever means are appropriate in the circumstances. The equipment should be considered separately, and the criteria described in the foregoing paragraphs should be applied to the separate components for the purpose of classifying the elements of the lease.

Leases Involving Only a Part of a Building

The classification of leases involving only a part of a building depends upon whether or not the cost and fair value of the leased property is objectively determinable.

If the cost and fair value, or only the fair value, of the leased property is objectively determinable, the same criteria applicable to the lease of a whole building, as outlined in the preceding paragraphs, should be used for the purpose of classifying the lease.

If the fair value of the leased property is not objectively determinable, and the term of the lease is equal to 75% or more of the estimated economic life of the building, the lease should be classified as a capital lease. If these conditional criteria are not met, it should be classified as an operating lease.

ACCOUNTING FOR LEASES BY LESSEES

FASB Statement No. 13 provides two separate sets of accounting standards for lease transactions of lessees: one for operating leases and the other for capital leases.

ACCOUNTING FOR OPERATING LEASES

Leases classified as operating leases in accordance with the criteria described in the preceding paragraphs generally are nothing more than executory contracts covering the right to use property in exchange for future rental payments and, as such, present no special accounting problems. However, the Statement specifically provides that rental on an operating lease normally shall be charged to expense over the lease term as it becomes payable, and if rental payments are not made on a straight-line basis rental expense, nevertheless, shall be recognized on a straight-line basis unless another systematic and rational basis is more representative of the time pattern in which use benefit is derived from the leased property, in which case that basis shall be used.

ACCOUNTING FOR CAPITAL LEASES

The standards of accounting set forth in the Statement for capital leases are technical and complex; they establish abstruse present value methods for measurement and complicated systems for amortization of the asset and obligation involved in the lease transaction. The Statement lays down precise rules and regulations with respect to recording the asset acquired and the obligation assumed under a capital lease, and provides specific instructions as to the method of amortization and liquidation of the asset and obligation so recorded. Special rules applicable to leases for real estate are disclosed separately in the Statement.

RECORDING ASSETS AND OBLIGATIONS UNDER CAPITAL LEASES

Assets acquired and liabilities assumed under capital lease agreements should be recorded in accordance with the following rules:

1. The lessee shall record a capital lease as an asset and an obligation at an amount equal to the present value at the beginning of the lease term of minimum lease payments during the lease term.
2. The portion of the minimum lease payments representing executory costs such as insurance, maintenance, and taxes, to be paid by the lessor, and any profit thereon, shall be excluded in computing the present value to be recorded as an asset and obligation.
3. If the computed present value of the lease payments exceeds the fair value of the leased property at the inception of the lease, the amount recorded as the asset and obligation shall be the fair value.
4. If the portion of the minimum lease payments representing executory costs, including profit thereon, is not determinable from the provisions of the lease, an estimate of the amount shall be made.
5. The discount rate to be used by the lessee in determining present value of the minimum lease payments shall be his incremental borrowing rate. However, the lessee shall use the lessor's implicit rate where both of the following conditions obtain:

(a) It is practicable for the lessee to learn the implicit rate computed by the lessor; and

(b) The implicit rate computed by the lessor is less than the lessee's incremental borrowing rate.

AMORTIZING ASSETS RECORDED UNDER CAPITAL LEASES

In general, assets acquired under a capital lease should be amortized by one of the two methods described below. Special rules for amortization of assets acquired under a capital lease for real estate are outlined in the section immediately following.

1. If the lease transfers ownership of the property to the lessee by the end of the lease term or contains a bargain purchase option, the asset should be amortized in a manner consistent with the lessee's normal depreciation policy for owned assets.
2. If the lease does not transfer ownership or contains a bargain purchase option, the property should be amortized over the life of the lease in accordance with the lessee's normal depreciation policy. The asset shall be amortized to its expected value, if any, to the lessee at the end of the lease term.

As an example, if the lessee guarantees a residual value at the end of the lease term and has no interest in any excess which might be realized, the expected value of the leased property to him is the amount that can be realized from it up to the amount of the guarantee, as illustrated below.

Periodic lease payments	100,000
Guarantee of residual value	5,000
Total minimum lease payments	105,000
Present value to lessee	95,000
Residual value expected by lessee	(5,000)
Maximum amortization allowed to lessee	90,000

AMORTIZATION OF ASSETS ACQUIRED UNDER A CAPITAL LEASE FOR REAL ESTATE

The Statement establishes the following special rules for amortizing assets acquired under a capital lease for real estate:

1. If the land and buildings of a lease are required to be separately capitalized because the lease transfers ownership at the end of the lease term or contains a bargain purchase option, the buildings should be amortized in a manner consistent with the lessee's normal depreciation policy, and the land should not be amortized at all.
2. If no ownership transfer or bargain purchase option is contained in the lease, but the land and buildings are required to be capitalized as a single unit because the fair value of the land element is less than 25% of the total fair value, the unit should be amortized over the lease term.
3. If the lease does not transfer ownership nor offer a bargain purchase option, but the land and buildings are required to be separately capitalized because the fair value of the land is 25% or more of the total fair value, the building element shall be amortized over the life of the lease, and the land element shall be accounted for as an operating lease.
4. If a lease involving only a part of a building is capitalized because the fair value of the leased property is objectively determinable, it shall be amortized in the same manner as that required for the capitalized lease of a whole building. If a lease involving only

a part of a building, where the fair value is not objectively determinable, is capitalized because the lease term extends over 75% or more of the estimated economic life of the leased property, the property shall be amortized over the life of the lease.

DISCLOSURE REQUIREMENTS FOR LESSEES

Paragraph 16 of FASB Statement No. 13 sets forth the information required to be disclosed in a lessee's financial statements, or footnotes thereto, with respect to lease transactions. The subparagraphs of paragraph 16 (quoted verbatim) are:

a. For capital leases:
   i. The gross amount of assets recorded under capital leases as of the date of each balance sheet presented by major classes according to nature of function. This information may be combined with the comparable information for owned assets.
   ii. Future minimum lease payments as of the date of the latest balance sheet presented, in the aggregate and for each of the five succeeding fiscal years, with separate deductions from the total for the amount representing executory costs, including any profit thereon, included in the minimum lease payments and for the amount of the imputed interest necessary to reduce the net minimum lease payments to present value.
   iii. The total of minimum sublease rentals to be received in the future under noncancelable subleases as of the date of the latest balance sheet presented.
   iv. Total contingent rentals (rentals on which the amounts are dependent on some factor other than the passage of time) actually incurred for each period for which an income statement is presented.
b. For operating leases having initial or remaining noncancelable lease terms in excess of one year:
   i. Future minimum rental payments required as of the date of the latest balance sheet presented, in the aggregate and for each of the five succeeding fiscal years.
   ii. The total of minimum rentals to be received in the future under noncancelable subleases as of the date of the latest balance sheet presented.
c. For all operating leases, rental expense for each period for which an income statement is presented, with separate amounts for minimum rentals, contingent rentals, and sublease rentals. Rental payments under leases with terms of a month or less that were not renewed need not be included.
d. A general description of the lessee's leasing arrangements including, but not limited to, the following:
   i. The basis on which contingent rental payments are determined.
   ii. The existence and terms of renewal or purchase options and escalation clauses.
   iii. Restrictions imposed by lease agreements, such as those concerning dividends, additional debt, and further leasing.

CASE STUDY IN ACCOUNTING AND REPORTING FOR LEASE TRANSACTIONS BY LESSEE

Model Case No. 2 illustrates lessee accounting procedures and disclosure requirements for four separate lease agreements that are representative of lease transactions involving land, buildings, and equipment.

MODEL CASE NO. 2

In 19x0 Conroy Corporation adopted a plan to extend its operations over a period of years. On January 2, 19x1, in accordance with the plan, Conroy entered into four separate lease agreements for land, buildings, and machinery with Horizons, Inc., Joy Bros., Rosedale Enterprises, and Webb Company. Analyses of the nature of the leased property and provisions of the lease agreements, computation of classification data, and determination of appropriate classification policy and amortization method are outlined in Schedule 7 for each respective lease.

SCHEDULE OF LEASE PROVISIONS AND DETERMINATION OF APPROPRIATE ACCOUNTING TREATMENT

Lessors	Horizons, Inc.	Joy Bros.	Rosedale Enterprises	Webb Company
Nature of property	Machinery	Machinery	Land and Buildings	Land and Buildings
Fair Value				
Machinery	125,000	130,000	—	—
Land	—	—	90,000	165,000
Buildings	—	—	360,000	385,000
Total fair value	125,000	130,000	450,000	550,000
Percentage of fair value of land to total fair value	—	—	20%	30%
Estimated Economic Life				
Machinery	10 years	16 years	—	—
Buildings	—	—	20 years	20 years
Lease Agreement				
Term	10 years	10 years	20 years	20 years
Annual payment (at end of year)	20,000	22,000	50,000	50,000
Transfer ownership at end of lease term	No	Yes	No	No
Contains bargain purchase option	No	No	No	No
Classification Data				
Minimum lease payments	200,000	220,000	1,000,000	1,200,000
Lessee's incremental borrowing rate	10.5%	10.5%	9.5%	9.5%
Lessor's implicit rate	Unknown	Unknown	Unknown	Unknown
Present value of minimum lease payments (building element only in Webb Company lease)	120,295	132,325	440,619	370,120
Lease term as a percentage of estimated economic life (buildings only in real estate leases)	100%	62.5%	100%	100%
Present value of lease payments as a percentage of total fair value (buildings only for Webb Company lease)	96.23%	101.7885%	97.9153%	96.1351%
Classification of Lease				
Machinery	Capital	Capital	—	—
Land	—	—	Capital	Operating
Buildings	—	—	Capital	Capital
Amortization Period				
Machinery	Lease	Asset	—	—
Land	—	—	Lease	None
Buildings	—	—	Lease	Lease
Lessee's normal depreciation method	S/D	S/D	S/L	S/L

SCHEDULE 7

The classification and measurement bases and the accounting method used by Conroy for each separate lease are described below.

Horizons, Inc.

Conroy computed the present value of the minimum lease payments, using his incremental borrowing rate as follows:

$$20,000 \quad \frac{1 - \left(\frac{1}{1.105}\right)^{10}}{.105} = 120,295$$

The lease was classified as a capital lease because the lease term extended over more than 75% of the estimated economic life of the leased property and because the present value of the minimum lease payments exceeded 90% of the fair value of the leased property. However, since the fair value *did* exceed the present value of the minimum lease payments, and the lessor's implicit rate was unknown, the asset and obligation was recorded by Conroy at $120,295. The lease neither transferred ownership nor contained a bargain purchase option, and, accordingly, Conroy depreciated the property over the life of the lease by his normal policy of using the sum-of-the-digits method.

Conroy's method of liquidating the lease obligation and depreciating the leased property is shown in Schedule 8.

LEASE WITH HORIZONS, INC.
LIQUIDATION AND DEPRECIATION SCHEDULE

Date	Total Payment	Payment Applied To: Interest Expense	Payment Applied To: Lease Obligation	Balance of Lease Obligation	Depreciation Depreciation Expense	Depreciation Remaining Value
1/ 2/x1				120,295		120,295
12/31/x1	20,000	12,631	7,369	112,926	21,872	98,423
12/31/x2	20,000	11,858	8,142	104,784	19,685	78,738
12/31/x3	20,000	11,003	8,997	95,787	17,497	61,241
12/31/x4	20,000	10,058	9,942	85,845	15,310	45,931
12/31/x5	20,000	9,013	10,987	74,858	13,123	32,808
12/31/x6	20,000	7,860	12,140	62,718	10,936	21,872
12/31/x7	20,000	6,585	13,415	49,303	8,749	13,123
12/31/x8	20,000	5,177	14,823	34,480	6,562	6,561
12/31/x9	20,000	3,620	16,380	18,100	4,374	2,187
12/31/y0	20,000	1,900	18,100	—	2,187	—
	200,000	79,705	120,295		120,295	

SCHEDULE 8

Conroy's entries to record the Horizons, Inc. lease at January 2, 19x1, and to record the distribution of the first annual payment at the end of the year were as follows:

		Debit	Credit
January 1, 19x1	— Leased property— Horizons, Inc.	120,295	

		Debit	Credit
December 31, 19x1	Obligation under capitalized leases—Horizons, Inc.		120,295
	— Obligation under capitalized leases—Horizons, Inc.	7,369	
	— Interest expense	12,631	
	— Depreciation of leased property—Horizons, Inc.	21,872	
	Cash		20,000
	Accumulated depreciation—leased property—Horizons, Inc.		21,872

Joy Bros.

Conroy computed the present value of the minimum lease payments using his incremental borrowing rate as follows:

$$22,000 \quad \frac{1 - \left(\frac{1}{1.105}\right)^{10}}{.105} = 132,325$$

The lease was classified as capital because it tranferred ownership of the leased property to Conroy at the end of the lease term. However, since the present value of the minimum lease payments exceeded the fair value of the leased property, Conroy could not record the asset and obligation at $132,325, but had to record it at the fair value of $130,000. Consequently, Conroy had to impute an interest rate that would spread the interest expense of $90,000 over the ten payments of $22,000 by the interest method. The interest rate was computed by testing estimated interest rates until the rate that satisfied the basic formula equation was found, as described in the foregoing Computational Techniques section of this chapter. Conroy computed the rate to be 10.9198%, and that is the rate he used to discount the annual payments. The lease transferred the property to Conroy at the end of the lease period and, therefore, Conroy depreciated the property over its estimated economic life, based on his normal policy of using the sum-of-the-digits method.

Liquidation of the lease obligation and depreciation of the leased property is shown in Schedule 9.

The entries made to record the asset and obligation at the beginning of 19x1 and to distribute the payment and record depreciation expense at the end of the first year for the Joy Bros.' lease were as follows:

		Debit	Credit
January 2, 19x1	— Leased property—Joy Bros.	130,000	
	Obligation under capitalized leases—Joy Bros.		130,000
December 31, 19x1	— Obligation under capitalized leases—Joy Bros.	7,804	
	— Interest expense	14,196	
	— Depreciation of leased property—Joy Bros.	15,294	
	Cash		22,000
	Accumulated depreciation—leased property—Joy Bros.		15,294

LEASE WITH JOY BROS.
LIQUIDATION AND DEPRECIATION SCHEDULE

Date	Total Payment	Payment Applied To: Interest Expense	Payment Applied To: Lease Obligation	Balance of Lease Obligation	Depreciation Depreciation Expense	Depreciation Remaining Value
1/ 2/x1				130,000		130,000
12/31/x1	22,000	14,196	7,804	122,196	15,294	114,706
12/31/x2	22,000	13,344	8,656	113,540	14,338	100,368
12/31/x3	22,000	12,398	9,602	103,938	13,382	86,986
12/31/x4	22,000	11,350	10,650	93,288	12,426	74,560
12/31/x5	22,000	10,187	11,813	81,475	11,471	63,089
12/31/x6	22,000	8,896	13,104	68,371	10,515	52,574
12/31/x7	22,000	7,466	14,534	53,837	9,559	43,015
12/31/x8	22,000	5,879	16,121	37,716	8,603	34,412
12/31/x9	22,000	4,118	17,882	19,834	7,647	26,765
12/31/y0	22,000	2,166	19,834	—	6,691	20,074
	220,000	90,000	130,000			
12/31/y1					5,735	14,339
12/31/y2					4,779	9,560
12/31/y3					3,824	5,736
12/31/y4					2,868	2,868
12/31/y5					1,912	956
12/31/y6					956	—
					130,000	

SCHEDULE 9

Rosedale Enterprises

Conroy computed the present value of the minimum lease payments, using his incremental borrowing rate of 9.5% applicable to long-term loans, as follows:

$$50,000 \cdot \frac{1 - \left(\dfrac{1}{1.095}\right)^{20}}{.095} = 440,619$$

Since the lease did not transfer ownership nor offer a bargain purchase option, and the fair value of the land element was less than 25% of the total fair value of the leased property, Conroy considered the land and building as a single unit and determined that the lease should be classified as capital because the lease extended beyond 75% of the estimated economic life of the building element and also because the present value of the lease payments exceeded 90% of the total fair value of the leased property. Therefore, Conroy recorded the asset and obligation at $440,619 and depreciated the leased property as a single unit over the term of the lease in accordance with their usual policy of depreciating real estate on a straight-line basis.

The liquidation of the lease obligation and depreciation of the leased property is shown in Schedule 10.

LEASE WITH ROSEDALE ENTERPRISES
LIQUIDATION AND DEPRECIATION SCHEDULE

Date	Total Payment	Payment Applied To:		Balance of Lease Obligation	Depreciation	
		Interest Expense	Lease Obligation		Depreciation Expense	Remaining Value
1/ 1/x1				440,619		440,619
12/31/x1	50,000	41,859	8,141	432,478	22,031	418,588
12/31/x2	50,000	41,086	8,914	423,564	22,031	396,557
12/31/x3	50,000	40,239	9,761	413,803	22,031	374,526
12/31/x4	50,000	39,311	10,689	403,114	22,031	352,495
12/31/x5	50,000	38,296	11,704	391,410	22,031	330,464
12/31/x6	50,000	37,185	12,815	378,595	22,031	308,433
12/31/x7	50,000	35,967	14,033	364,562	22,031	286,402
12/31/x8	50,000	34,633	15,367	349,195	22,031	264,371
12/31/x9	50,000	33,171	16,829	332,366	22,031	242,340
12/31/y0	50,000	31,575	18,425	313,941	22,031	220,309
12/31/y1	50,000	29,825	20,175	293,766	22,031	198,278
12/31/y2	50,000	27,907	22,093	271,673	22,031	176,247
12/31/y3	50,000	25,810	24,190	247,483	22,031	154,216
12/31/y4	50,000	23,511	26,489	220,994	22,031	132,185
12/31/y5	50,000	20,994	29,006	191,988	22,031	110,154
12/31/y6	50,000	18,239	31,761	160,227	22,031	88,123
12/31/y7	50,000	15,221	34,779	125,448	22,031	66,092
12/31/y8	50,000	11,916	38,084	87,364	22,031	44,061
12/31/y9	50,000	8,299	41,701	45,663	22,031	22,030
12/31/z0	50,000	4,337	45,663	—	22,030	—
	1,000,000	559,381	440,619		440,619	

SCHEDULE 10

The entries made by Conroy to record the asset and obligation at the beginning of 19x1 and to liquidate the lease obligation and record depreciation at the end of the first year were as follows:

		Debit	Credit
January 2, 19x1	— Leased property—Rosedale Enterprises	440,619	
	Obligation under capital leases—Rosedale Enterprises		440,619
December 31, 19x1	— Obligation under capital leases—Rosedale Enterprises	8,141	
	— Interest expense	41,859	
	— Depreciation of leased property—Rosedale Enterprises	22,031	
	Cash		50,000
	Accumulated depreciation— leased property— Rosedale Enterprises		22,031

Webb Company

The fair value of the land element in the lease was 30% of the total fair value of the leased property. Therefore the minimum lease payments and the periodic payments were allocated as follows:

	Land (30%)	Building (70%)	Total
Fair value	165,000	385,000	550,000
Minimum lease payments	360,000	840,000	1,200,000
Periodic rent	18,000	42,000	60,000

Conroy computed the present value of the minimum lease payments applicable to the building element using his long-term incremental borrowing rate of 9.5% as follows:

$$42,000 \left(\frac{1 - \left(\frac{1}{1.095} \right)^{20}}{.095} \right) = 370,120$$

Since the lease did not transfer ownership nor contain a bargain purchase option, and the fair value of the land element exceeded 25% of the total fair value of the leased property, Conroy considered the land and building as separate units, and determined that the building element should be classified as a capital lease because the present value of the minimum lease payments applicable to the building exceeded 90% of the total fair value of the building. Therefore, Conroy recorded an asset for $370,120, representing the present value of the minimum lease payments applicable to the building, and a lease obligation for the same amount. The asset was depreciated over the life of the lease by Conroy's usual policy of using the straight-line method for buildings. The portion of the periodic payment applicable to the land element in the lease was considered to be annual payments on an operating lease.

The liquidation of the lease obligation, rental expense on the operating lease, and depreciation of the building are shown in Schedule 11.

The entries Conroy made at January 2, 19x1 to record the asset and lease obligation and at December 31, 19x1 to record liquidation of the lease obligation, depreciation, and rent expense were as follows:

		Debit	Credit
January 2, 19x1	— Leased property—building— Webb Company	370,120	
	Obligation under capital leases—Webb Company		370,120
December 31, 19x1	— Obligation under capital leases—Webb Company	6,839	
	— Interest expense	35,161	
	— Depreciation of leased property—Webb Company	18,506	

LEASE WITH WEBB COMPANY

SCHEDULE OF LIQUIDATION, DEPRECIATION, AND RENT EXPENSE

Date	Total Payment	Payment Applied to: Interest Expense	Lease Obligation	Balance of Lease Obligation	Rent Expense	Depreciation: Depreciation Expense	Remaining Value
1/1/x1				370,120			370,120
12/31/x1	42,000	35,161	6,839	363,281	18,000	18,506	351,614
12/31/x2	42,000	34,512	7,488	355,793	18,000	18,506	333,108
12/31/x3	42,000	33,800	8,200	347,593	18,000	18,506	314,602
12/31/x4	42,000	33,021	8,979	338,614	18,000	18,506	296,096
12/31/x5	42,000	32,168	9,832	328,782	18,000	18,506	277,590
12/31/x6	42,000	31,234	10,766	318,016	18,000	18,506	259,084
12/31/x7	42,000	30,212	11,788	306,228	18,000	18,506	240,578
12/31/x8	42,000	29,092	12,908	293,320	18,000	18,506	222,072
12/31/x9	42,000	27,865	14,135	279,185	18,000	18,506	203,566
12/31/y0	42,000	26,523	15,477	263,708	18,000	18,506	185,060
12/31/y1	42,000	25,052	16,948	246,760	18,000	18,506	166,554
12/31/y2	42,000	23,442	18,558	228,202	18,000	18,506	148,048
12/31/y3	42,000	21,680	20,320	207,882	18,000	18,506	129,542
12/31/y4	42,000	19,749	22,251	185,631	18,000	18,506	111,036
12/31/y5	42,000	17,635	24,365	161,266	18,000	18,506	92,530
12/31/y6	42,000	15,321	26,679	134,587	18,000	18,506	74,024
12/31/y7	42,000	12,786	29,214	105,373	18,000	18,506	55,518
12/31/y8	42,000	10,011	31,989	73,384	18,000	18,506	37,012
12/31/y9	42,000	6,972	35,028	38,356	18,000	18,506	18,506
12/31/z0	42,000	3,644	38,356	—	18,000	18,506	—
	840,000	469,880	370,120		360,000	370,120	

SCHEDULE 11

— Rent expense	18,000	
Cash		60,000
Accumulated depreciation— leased property—Webb Company		18,506

Disclosure in Conroy's Financial Statements

At December 31, 19x1 Conroy prepared Schedule 12 from information contained in Schedules 8, 9, 10, and 11 for the purpose of making the the disclosures prescribed by FASB Statement No. 13, which are outlined in a preceding section of this chapter.

SCHEDULE OF INFORMATION NECESSARY FOR DISCLOSURE OF LEASE TRANSACTIONS

Lessor:	Horizons Schedule 8	Joy Schedule 9	Rosedale Schedule 10	Webb Schedule 11	Total
Capital Leases					
Leased Property					
Buildings	—	—	440,619	370,120	810,739
Machinery	120,295	130,000	—	—	250,295
Total	120,295	130,000	440,619	370,120	1,061,034
Accumulated Depreciation					
Buildings	—	—	22,031	18,506	40,537
Machinery	21,872	15,294	—	—	37,166
Total	21,872	15,294	22,031	18,506	77,703
Leased property—net of depreciation	98,423	114,706	418,588	351,614	983,331
Minimum Lease Payments					
19x2	20,000	22,000	50,000	42,000	134,000
19x3	20,000	22,000	50,000	42,000	134,000
19x4	20,000	22,000	50,000	42,000	134,000
19x5	20,000	22,000	50.000	42,000	134,000
19x6	20,000	22,000	50,000	42,000	134,000
Subsequent	80,000	88,000	700,000	588,000	1,456,000
Total	180,000	198,000	950,000	798,000	2,126,000
Less: Amount representing interest	67,074	75,804	517,522	434,719	1,095,119
Present value of minimum lease payments	112,926	122,196	432,478	363,281	1,030,881
Current portion of lease obligation	8,142	8,65ʋ	8,914	7,488	33,200
Long-term portion of lease obligation	104,784	113,540	423,564	355,793	997,681
Operating Lease					
Minimum Lease Payments					
19x2				18,000	18,000
19x3				18,000	18,000
19x4				18,000	18,000
19x5				18,000	18,000
19x6				18,000	18,000
Subsequent				252,000	252,000
Total				342,000	342,000
Rental expense—19x1				18,000	18,000

SCHEDULE 12

The following extracts were taken from the balance sheet and notes contained in Conroy's financial statements at December 31, 19x1:

CONROY CORPORATION

Balance Sheet
December 31, 19x1

Assets		Liabilities	
Plant and Equipment		**Current**	
* * * * * * * * * * * * * * *		* * * * * * * * * * * * * * * *	
Leased property under capital leases—net of depreciation of $77,703—Note 4	983,331	Obligations under capital leases—Note 4	33,200
		* * * * * * * * * * * * * * * *	
* * * * * * * * * * * * * * *		**Long-Term**	
		Obligations under capital leases—Note 4	997,681
		* * * * * * * * * * * * * * * * *	

CONROY CORPORATION

Notes to Financial Statements
December 31, 19x1

Note 1—Summary of Significant Accounting Policies

In the current year, in accordance with a plan of expansion adopted in the preceding year, the company entered into four long-term lease agreements for the purpose of acquiring additional plant and equipment. Two leases for machinery are capitalized; one lease involving land and buildings is capitalized as a single unit; and one lease involving land and buildings is capitalized with respect to the building element and accounted for as an operating lease with respect to the land element. Capitalized buildings are depreciated over 20 years by the straight-line method, and capitalized machinery is depreciated over 10 to 16 years by the sum-of-the-digits method. The period of the lease extends to the total economic life of the leased properties in every case except one, in which case the property is transferred to the company at the end of the lease term.

* * * * * * * * * * *

Note 4—Capital Leases

The major classifications of leased property under capital leases are as follows:

Buildings	810,739
Machinery	250,295
	1,061,034
Less: Accumulated depreciation	77,703
	983,331

Future minimum lease payments under capital leases, and the present value of the aggregate of such payments, are as follows:

Year ended December 31,—	
19x2	134,000
19x3	134,000
19x4	134,000
19x5	134,000
19x6	134,000
Subsequent to 19x6	1,456,000
	2,126,000
Less: Amount representing interest	1,095,119
Present value of future minimum lease payments	1,030,881

Note 5—Operating Lease

The future minimum rental payments required under the operating lease for land, referred to in Note 1, are as follows:

Year ended December 31,—	
19x2	18,000
19x3	18,000
19x4	18,000
19x5	18,000
19x6	18,000
Subsequent to 19x6	252,000
Total future minimum rental payments	342,000

Rental expense under the operating lease for the current year was 18,000.

* * * * * * * * * * *

CHANGES IN PROVISIONS OF A CAPITAL LEASE

If at any time the lessee and lessor agree to change the provisions of a capital lease in a manner that would have resulted in a different classification had the original lease contained the changed provisions, or agree to extend a capital lease beyond the expiration of the existing lease terms, the revised agreement shall be considered a new lease, and shall be reclassified in accordance with appropriate classification criteria applied to the new terms.

If the new agreement resulting from renewal, extension, or termination of the existing capital lease is classified as a capital lease, the present balances of the asset and obligation shall be adjusted to conform to the present value of the minimum lease payments under the new agreement, discounted at the interest rate used initially to record the lease.

If the new agreement resulting from termination of an existing lease is classified as an operating lease, the asset and obligation under the lease shall be removed, gain or loss recognized for the difference, and the new agreement shall thereafter be accounted for as any other operating lease. However, if a new agreement resulting from renewal or extension of an existing lease is classified as an operating lease, the existing lease shall be accounted for as a capital lease to the end of its original term, and as an operating lease for the remainder of the renewal or extension period.

LEVERAGED LEASES

Lessees shall classify and account for leverage leases in the same manner as nonleveraged leases are treated.

LEASES BETWEEN RELATED PARTIES

Generally, leases between related parties shall be classified and accounted for in the same manner as similar leases between unrelated parties.

SALE-LEASEBACK TRANSACTIONS

The seller-lessee shall classify and account for the lease in accordance with the classification criteria and accounting standards applicable to lease transactions by lessees. Any profit or loss on the sale shall be deferred and amortized in proportion to the leased asset if a capital lease, or in proportion to the rental payments over the period of time the asset is expected to be used, if an operating lease. However, when the fair value of the property at the time of the transaction is less than the undepreciated cost, a loss shall be recognized immediately up to the amount of the undepreciated cost and fair value.

SUBLEASES

A lessee may enter into sublease agreements that may or may not relieve him of the primary obligation under the original lease. The general rules for lessee accounting for sublease transactions under each of the two conditions referred to are as follows:

(a) Where the original lessee of a capital lease is relieved of primary obligation under the lease, the asset and obligation shall be removed from the accounts, and gain or loss shall be recognized for the difference. If the original lessee is secondarily liable the loss contingency shall be treated as provided in FASB Statement No.5, "Accounting for Contingencies."

(b) Where the original lessee is not relieved of the primary obligation under the lease, he becomes the sublessor and shall classify and account for the sublease in accordance with classification criteria and accounting standards applicable to lessors, as outlined in Chapter 6 of this volume. However, the lessee shall continue to account for the obligation related to the original lease as before.

RESTATEMENT OF FINANCIAL STATEMENTS

The Statement requires retroactive application of its accounting and reporting standards for purposes of financial statements for calendar or fiscal years beginning after December 31, 1980. The cumulative effect of applying the accounting principles of the Statement on retained earnings at the beginning of the earliest period restated shall be included in determining the net income of that period. The effect on net income of applying the changed standards in the period in which the cumulative effect is included in determing net income shall be disclosed for that period, and the reason for not restating the prior periods shall be explained.

6

Accounting for Lessor Transactions—
Sales-Type, Direct-Financing and
Leveraged Leases

A logical analysis of the accounting standards prescribed by FASB Statement No. 13[1] for leasing transactions requires separate expositions of accounting and reporting standards applicable to lessees and lessors, respectively. To that end, two chapters on lease accounting have been prepared for this book: lessee transactions are described in the preceding chapter and lessor transactions are treated in this chapter.

The present chapter deals with lessor transactions exclusively and its purpose is to clarify the provisions of the Statement, explain the criteria for classifying leases, illustrate accounting procedures and reporting requirements, and demonstrate computational techniques for the measurement of present values of lease commitments.

DEFINITION OF TERMS

FASB Statement No. 13 contains definitions of certain terms that are peculiar to its text. These definitions, generally, have no conventional acceptance and are valid only for purposes of the Statement. The definitions are set forth at the beginning of Chapter 5 and therein are quoted verbatim from the Statement. The definitions are not repeated in this chapter, and the reader should use Chapter 5 for reference when confronted by the terms later in the text.

PRESENT VALUE CONCEPTS

The concept of present value received initial official recognition as an accounting principle in 1964 by the Accounting Principles Board.[2] The concept is reaffirmed by the Financial Accounting Standards Board in its Statement No. 13, and is outlined

---

[1]*Accounting for Leases*, Statement of the Financial Accounting Standards Board No. 13. (Stamford, Connecticut, Financial Accounting Standards Board, 1976. Reprinted with permission. Copies of the complete document are available from the FASB.)

[2]*Reporting of Leases in Financial Statements of Lessee*, Opinion of Accounting Principles Board No. 5. (New York, NY: Copyright 1964 by the American Institute of Certified Public Accountants.)

briefly in a section of the preceding chapter. A description of the concept is not repeated here, but the reader can refer to the relevant section in Chapter 5 for introduction to, or reflection upon, the elements of the concept that are involved in lease transactions.

BASIC FORMULAS

Computations of annuities, amounts at compound interest, and their related present values can be performed by the use of four simple algebraic equations, each containing four variables.

The basic formulas for each of the four values, respectively, are as follows:[3]

Where:
   S = Amount of the annuity
   R = Periodic payment of an annuity
   A = Present value of an annuity
   i = Rate of interest per period
   n = Number of intervals—number of interest periods
   P = Principal to be invested at compound interest—present value of an amount at compound interest
   C = Compound amount at end of period

Amount at Compound Interest

$$C = P(1+i)^n$$

Present Value of an
Amount at Compound Interest

$$P = C \left(\frac{1}{1+i}\right)^n$$

Annuity per Period

$$S = R \left(\frac{(1+i)^n - 1}{i}\right)$$

Present Value of an
Annuity per Period

$$A = R \left(\frac{1 - \left(\frac{1}{1+i}\right)^n}{i}\right)$$

COMPUTATIONAL TECHNIQUES

Chapter 5 comprehends fairly exhaustive descriptions and demonstrations of computational techniques for solving the basic formulas, using actual, implicit, imputed, and unknown interest rates for both uniform and varying periodic payments by algebraic, logarithmic, tabular, computer, and electronic calculator methods of solution. The reader should use the relevant sections in Chapter 5 as a reference in connection with the solution of present value and implicit interest rate problems involved in accounting for lessor transactions described in this chapter.

---

[3]Negative exponents are not used in these equations so as to present them in a configuration that conforms to the shortest possible sequence of algebraic entry into an electronic calculator.

ACCOUNTING AND REPORTING STANDARDS FOR LESSORS

CLASSIFICATION OF LEASES BY LESSORS

To accommodate implementation of the principles of its concept that a lease which transfers substantially all of the benefits and risks incident to ownership of property should be accounted for as a sale or financing transaction by the lessor, the Board directed that a lessor should classify all leases into one of the following four categories:

(a) Sales-type leases,
(b) Direct-financing leases,
(c) Leveraged leases, or
(d) Operating leases.

CRITERIA FOR CLASSIFYING LEASES BY LESSORS

The Board's concept of leasing transactions also comprehends the principle that the same characteristics of a leasing transaction that identify the lease as a capital lease for lessees should be the same attributes that determine the classification of a direct-financing, sales-type, or leveraged lease, as distinct from an operating lease, for lessors. However, the Board felt that, to be classified as other than an operating lease by lessors, a lease should be surrounded by two specific conditions: the collectibility of the minimum lease payments should be reasonably predictable; and no important uncertainties should surround the unreimbursable costs yet to be incurred by the lessor. To achieve standardization of classification for the purpose of applying appropriate accounting procedures in accordance with its concept of leasing transactions, the Board established the following general criteria for classifying sales-type, direct-financing, and leveraged leases, as distinct from operating leases.

Capital Lease Criteria

To be classified as other than an operating lease by a lessor the lease must meet one or more of the following criteria:
(a) The lease transfers ownership of the property to the lessee by the end of the lease term;
(b) The lease contains a bargain purchase option;
(c) The lease term is equal to 75% or more of the estimated economic life of the leased property; and
(d) The present value of the minimum lease payments equals or exceeds 90% of the fair value of the leased property, less any related investment tax credit retained by the lessor.
Neither criterion (c) nor criterion (d) shall be used if the beginning of the lease term falls within the last 25% of the total estimated economic life of the leased property, including earlier years of use.

Conditional Criteria

To be classified as other than an operating lease by a lessor, in addition to meeting one or more of the capital lease criteria listed above, the lease must meet both of the following:
(a) Collectibility of the minimum lease payments is reasonably predictable; and
(b) No important uncertainties surround the amount of unreimbursable costs yet to be incurred by the lessor under the lease.

APPLICATION OF GENERAL CLASSIFICATION CRITERIA TO SPECIFIC LEASE TRANSACTIONS

The general classification criteria is a guide to distinguishing sales-type, direct-financing, and leveraged leases, as a group, from ordinary operating leases. However, certain characteristics of the *nature* of the leasing transaction serve as criteria for the reclassification of leases into the separate categories of sales-type, direct-financing, and leveraged leases.

Sales-Type Leases

Leases which give rise to a manufacturer's or dealer's profit to the lessor, and meet one or more of the capital lease criteria and both of the conditional criteria, shall be classified as sales-type lease.

Direct Financing Lease

Leases which meet one or more of the capital lease criteria and both conditional criteria, but do not give rise to a manufacturer's or dealer's profit, *and* are not classified as leveraged leases, shall be classified as direct-financing leases.

Leveraged Leases

Leases which meet one or more of the capital lease criteria and both of the conditional criteria, but do not give rise to a manufacturer's or dealer's profit, *and* are not classified as direct-financing leases, shall be classified as leveraged leases provided the lease has the following additional characteristics:
(a) It involves at least three parties: a lessee, a long-term creditor, and a lessor.
(b) The financing provided by the long-term creditor is nonrecourse as to the general credit of the lessor, although the creditor may have recourse to the specific property leased and the unremitted rentals relating to it. The amount of the financing is sufficient to provide the lessor with substantial "leverage" in the transaction.
(c) The lessor's net investment declines during the early years once the investment has been completed and rises during the later years of the lease before its final elimination.

Operating Leases

Leases that do not meet any one of the capital lease criteria shall be classified as operating lease.

EXPLANATION OF LESSOR CLASSIFICATION CRITERIA

With reference to the capital lease criteria set forth in the foregoing subparagraphs (a), (b), and (c)—they are self-explanatory and need no clarification. It is useful to note, however, that only the criteria in (a) or (b) can be used to classify a lease that begins within the last 25% of the estimated economic life of the property being leased. It is also important to note that the computations required in subparagraph (d) need not be made if the lease is determined to be other than an operating lease because it meets any one of the criteria set forth in subparagraphs (a), (b), or (c).

In connection with the criterion outlined in subparagraph (d) it is important to note that the lessor must use the *interest rate implicit in the lease* to compute the present value of the minimum lease payments. While the lessee can compute the present value of the minimum lease payments at his incremental borrowing rate, the lessor must, in almost every case, compute the present value of the minimum lease payments by an imputed interest rate, which rate is *not known* to him at the commencement of the computation. The alternative to the lessor's using an *imputed* interest rate is for him to set the periodic payments in an amount that will provide a *predetermined* rate of return. The computational techniques for computing present value when the interest rate is unknown is demonstrated in Chapter 5, and the method is also reviewed in the model cases that follow in this chapter.

Sales-Type Leasing Criteria

A lessor need not be a dealer to realize a dealer's profit or loss in a transaction. For example, if a lessor who is not a dealer leases an asset that has a fair value that is greater or less than the cost or carrying amount, such a transaction is a sales-type lease, and not a direct-financing lease, assuming the other criteria are met.

A renewal or extension of an existing sales-type lease or direct-financing lease shall not be classified as a sales-type lease. However, if it meets the capital lease criteria and the conditional criteria, it shall be classified as a direct-financing lease.

Direct Financing Lease Criteria

In a direct-financing lease the cost or carrying amount of the leased property will coincide with the fair value at the inception of the lease. However, if a direct-financing lease is renewed or extended, the fact that the carrying value is different from its fair value at the date of the extension or renewal will not preclude the classification of the renewal or extension as a direct-financing lease, as outlined in the preceding paragraph.

APPLICATION OF CLASSIFICATION CRITERIA TO LEASES INVOLVING REAL ESTATE

Leases for land are generally based solely on an interest factor, while leases for buildings are normally based on compensation for depreciation, as well as for interest. Consequently, FASB Statement No. 13 provides separate rules for the application of classification criteria to leases involving real estate and, in some instances, requires a separation of the land and building elements in a lease involving both.

Leases for Land Only

If land is the sole item of property leased, and the lease either transfers ownership of the land to the lessee by the end of the lease term or contains a bargain purchase option, *and* meets the conditional criteria, the lessor shall classify the lease as a sales-type or direct-financing lease, whichever is appropriate.

Leases Involving Land and Buildings

If the lease for both land and buildings either transfers ownership of the property to the lessee by the end of the lease term or contains a bargain purchase option, *and* meets the conditional criteria, the lessor shall consider the lease as a single unit and classify it as a sales-type or direct-financing lease, whichever is appropriate. If the conditional criteria are *not* met, the lessor shall classify the lease as an operating lease.

If the lease for both land and buildings neither transfers ownership to the lessee nor contains a bargain purchase option, the lessor should classify the lease according to the percentage of the fair value of the land to the total fair value, as outlined in the two paragraphs following.

Fair Value of Land Less Than 25% of Total Fair Value

If the fair value of the land is less than 25% of the total fair value of the leased property at the inception of the lease, the lessor shall consider the lease as a single unit. If the lease term is equal to 75% of the estimated economic life of the *buildings,* or if the present value of the minimum lease payments applicable to the single "unit" equals or exceeds 90% of the fair value of the single unit, *and* the lease meets the conditional criteria, the lease shall be classified as a sales-type or direct-financing lease, whichever is appropriate; otherwise, the lease shall be classified as an operating lease.

Fair Value of Land 25% or More of Total Fair Value

If the fair value of the land is 25% or more of the total fair value of the leased property, the lessor should treat the land and buildings as separate components. If the lease term is equal to 75% of the estimated economic life of the buildings, or if the present value of the minimum lease payments applicable to the building equals or exceeds 90% of the fair value, *and* the conditional criteria are met, the building element should be classified as a sales-type or direct-financing lease, whichever is appropriate. The land element shall be classified as an operating lease. If the building element does *not* meet the criteria referred to above, both the building element and the land element shall be classified as a single operating lease.

Leases Involving Equipment and Real Estate

If a lease involving real estate also includes equipment, the portion of the minimum lease payments applicable to the equipment element of the lease should be estimated by whatever means are appropriate in the circumstances. The equipment should be considered separately, and the criteria described in the foregoing paragraphs should be applied to the separate components for the purpose of classifying the elements of the lease.

Leases Involving Only a Part of a Building

Where a lease covers only a part of a building, if either the cost or the fair value of the leased property is not objectively determinable, the lease shall be classified as an operating lease.

ACCOUNTING FOR LEASES BY LESSOR

FASB Statement No. 13 prescribes separate sets of accounting standards for each of the four categories into which leases may be classified by lessors.

ACCOUNTING FOR OPERATING LEASES

The leased property under an operating lease shall have the same accounting treatment as other property of the lessor.

Rent shall be reported as income over the lease term as it becomes receivable according to the provisions of the lease. However, if the rentals vary from the straight-line basis, the income should be recognized on a straight-line basis unless another systematic and rational basis is more representative of the time pattern in which use benefits from the leased property are diminished, in which case that basis should be used.

Initial direct costs may be charged to expense as incurred if the effect is not material with respect to rental income. If such costs are material with respect to rental income they shall be deferred and allocated over the lease term in proportion to the recognition of rental income.

ACCOUNTING FOR SALES-TYPE LEASES

The Statement defines the elements of a sales-type lease transaction, and establishes standards for measuring, recording, and reporting the elements defined.

ACCOUNTING ELEMENTS OF A SALES-TYPE LEASE

The accounting elements of a sales-type lease transaction, as set forth in the Statement, are the following:

1. *Gross Investment in the Lease*
   The minimum lease payments plus any unguaranteed residual value accruing to the benefit of the lessor.
2. *Unearned Income*
   The gross investment in the lease, less the present value of the two components of gross investment in the lease.
3. *Net Investment in the Lease*
   The difference between the gross investment in the lease, and unearned income.
4. *Sales Price*
   Present value of the minimum lease payments.
5. *Charges to Current Income*
   Cost, or carrying value, of the leased property, plus any initial direct costs, less the present value of the unguaranteed residual value accruing to the benefit of the lessor.

ACCOUNTING STANDARDS FOR SALES-TYPE LEASES

The following accounting standards are prescribed in the Statement for sales-type lease transactions.

1. Entries shall be made to record gross investment in the lease and current charges to income; these entries shall be offset by entries to record sales, unearned income, and disposition of the asset under the lease.
2. The investment in the lease shall be presented net of unearned income on the balance sheet, and it shall be classified as current and noncurrent in a classified balance sheet.
3. The discount rate to be used in determining the present value shall be the interest rate implicit in the lease.
4. Unearned income shall be amortized to income over the lease term so as to produce a constant periodic rate of return on the net investment in the lease.
5. Contingent rentals, such as rentals based on variations in the prime interest rate, etc., shall be credited to income when they become receivable.

CASE STUDY IN ACCOUNTING FOR SALES-TYPE LEASES

Model Case No. 1 illustrates lessor accounting procedures for two sales-type lease agreements: one a simple, commonplace sales-type lease, and the other a contract complicated by an unguaranteed residual value accruing to the benefit of the lessor.

MODEL CASE NO. 1

Barber & Company is a dealer in heavy construction equipment. In 19x0 the company purchased outright a bulldozer and a backhoe for the purpose of leasing the equipment to Dunton, Inc. Analyses of the nature of the leased property and provisions of the lease agreements; computation of classification date; and determination of appropriate classification are outlined in Schedule 1 for each respective lease.

ANALYSIS OF LEASE PROVISIONS AND CLASSIFICATION DATA

Leased property	Bulldozer	Backhoe
Fair value	120,000	65,000
Cost	85,000	50,000
Estimated economic life	5 years	12 years
Lease agreement		
Term	5 years	10 years
Annual rental (at end of year)	30,000	10,000
Transfers ownership at end of lease	Yes	No
Contains bargain purchase option	No	No
Classification Data		
Minimum lease payments	150,000	100,000
Interest rate implicit in lease	7.9731%	8.7114%
Present value of minimum lease payments	120,000	65,000
Lease term as a percentage of estimated economic life	100%	83.33%
Present value of minimum lease payments as a percentage of total fair value	100%	100%
Collectibility of minimum lease payments reasonably predictable	Yes	Yes
Important uncertainties concerning future unreimbursable costs	None	None
Classification of lease	Sales-type	Sales-type

SCHEDULE 1

From the information outlined in Schedule 1, Barber prepared Schedule 2 to analyze the accounting elements inherent in the nature of each lease transaction.

SCHEDULE OF ACCOUNTING ELEMENTS IN LEASES

	Lease for Bulldozer	Lease for Backhoe
Gross Investment in Lease		
1. Minimum lease payments	150,000	100,000
2. Unguaranteed residual value of leased property	—	5,000
3. Total gross investment in lease	150,000	105,000
Present Value of Gross Investment in Lease		
4. Minimum lease payments	120,000	65,000
5. Unguaranteed residual value of leased property	—	2,169
6. Total present value of gross investment in lease	120,000	67,169
Unearned Income		
7. Total gross investment in lease—line 3	150,000	105,000
8. Total present value of gross investment in lease—line 6	120,000	67,169
9. Unearned income	30,000	37,831
Net Investment in Lease		
10. Total gross investment in lease—line 3	150,000	105,000
11. Unearned income—line 9	30,000	37,831
12. Net investment in lease	120,000	67,169
Sales Price		
13. Present value of minimum lease payments —line 4	120,000	65,000
Charges to Current Income		
14. Cost of leased property	85,000	50,000
15. Present value of residual value of leased property	—	2,169
16. Net charge to current income	85,000	47,831

SCHEDULE 2

The classification and measurements bases used by Barber for each separate lease were as follows:

LEASE FOR BULLDOZER

The fair value of the leased property was $120,000 and, consequently, the present value of the minimum lease payments of $150,000 coincided with the fair value. The interest rate implicit in the lease was calculated by repeatedly solving the basic formula for the present value of an annuity, using estimated interest rates, until the precise rate that satisfied the equation was found. The final computation was as follows:

$$30,000 \left(\frac{1 - \left(\frac{1}{1.07931} \right)^{5}}{.07931} \right) = 120,000$$

The lease was classified as other than an operating lease because it transferred ownership of the property to the lessee at the end of the lease term, and also met the conditional criteria for collectibility of the minimum lease payments and no important uncertainties concerning future unreimbursable costs. It was classified specifically as a sales-type lease because the fair value of the leased property exceeded its cost at the inception of the lease.

From the information displayed in Schedules 1 and 2, Barber made the following entry at January 1, 19x0 to record the lease investment, and then prepared Schedule 3

SCHEDULE OF ACCOUNTING ENTRIES FOR BULLDOZER LEASE

Date	Cash Payment Received Cr. Minimum Lease Payments Receivable	Journal Entry Dr. Unearned Interest Income Cr. Interest Income	Minimum Lease Payments Receivable (Gross Investment in Lease)	Unearned Interest Income	Net Investment in Lease
January 1, 19x0	—	—	150,000	30,000	120,000
December 31, 19x0	30,000	9,517	120,000	20,483	99,517
December 31, 19x1	30,000	7,893	90,000	12,590	77,410
December 31, 19x2	30,000	6,139	60,000	6,451	53,549
December 31, 19x3	30,000	4,247	30,000	2,204	27,796
December 31, 19x4	30,000	2,204	—	—	—
	150,000	30,000			

SCHEDULE 3

to provide guidelines for accounting for the lease transaction at the end of each year during the lease term.

	Debit	Credit
Minimum lease payments receivable	150,000	
Cost of goods sold	85,000	
Sales		120,000
Inventory—bulldozer		85,000
Unearned interest income		30,000
To record investment in lease for bulldozer.		

The entry made by Barber at December 31, 19x0 was as follows:

	Debit	Credit
Cash	30,000	
Unearned interest income	9,517	
Minimum lease payments receivable		30,000
Interest income		9,517

Similar entries, reflecting the appropriate reduction in unearned income indicated in Schedule 3, were made at the end of each year during the term of the lease.

LEASE FOR BACKHOE

The lease for the backhoe was classified as a sales-type lease because the fair value of the leased property exceeded its cost, and the lease agreement extended over more than 75% of the estimated economic life of the leased property and met the conditional criteria for collectibility of the minimum lease payments and no important uncertainties concerning future unreimbursable costs.

The interest rate implicit in the lease was calculated by the trial-and-error method in the same manner as that used to compute the present value of the minimum lease payments on the lease for the bulldozer. The final computation for the present value of the minimum lease payments was as follows:

$$10,000 \left(\frac{1 - \left(\frac{1}{1.087114}\right)^{10}}{.087114} \right) = 65,000$$

Using the implicit interest rate above, the present value of the unguaranteed residual value was computed by the basic formula for the present value of an amount at compound interest, as follows:

$$5,000 \left(\frac{1}{1.087114} \right)^{10} = 2,169$$

From the information shown in Schedules 1 and 2 Barber made the following entry at January 1, 19x0 to record the lease investment, and then prepared Schedule 4 to

SCHEDULE OF ACCOUNTING ENTRIES FOR BACKHOE LEASE

Date	Cash Payment Received Cr. Minimum Lease Payments Receivable	Journal Entry Dr. Unearned Interest Income Cr. Interest Income	Minimum Lease Payments Receivable	Unguaranteed Residual Value	Gross Investment in Lease	Unearned Interest Income	Net Investment in Lease
January 1, 19x0	—	—	100,000	5,000	105,000	37,831	67,169
December 31, 19x0	10,000	5,851	90,000	5,000	95,000	31,980	63,020
December 31, 19x1	10,000	5,490	80,000	5,000	85,000	26,490	58,510
December 31, 19x2	10,000	5,097	70,000	5,000	75,000	21,393	53,607
December 31, 19x3	10,000	4,670	60,000	5,000	65,000	16,723	48,277
December 31, 19x4	10,000	4,206	50,000	5,000	55,000	12,517	42,483
December 31, 19x5	10,000	3,701	40,000	5,000	45,000	8,816	36,184
December 31, 19x6	10,000	3,152	30,000	5,000	35,000	5,664	29,336
December 31, 19x7	10,000	2,556	20,000	5,000	25,000	3,108	21,892
December 31, 19x8	10,000	1,906	10,000	5,000	15,000	1,202	13,798
December 31, 19x9	10,000	1,202	—	5,000	5,000	—	5,000
	100,000	37,831					

SCHEDULE 4

provide guidelines for accounting for the lease transaction at the end of each year during the term of the lease.

	Debit	Credit
Minimum lease payments receivable	100,000	
Unguaranteed residual value	5,000	
Cost of goods sold	47,831	
Sales		65,000
Inventory—backhoe		50,000
Unearned interest income		37,831
To record investment in lease for backhoe.		

Barber made the following entry at December 31, 19x0:

	Debit	Credit
Cash	10,000	
Unearned interest income	5,851	
Minimum lease payments receivable		10,000
Interest income		5,851

Similar entries, reflecting the appropriate reduction in unearned interest income indicated in Schedule 4, were made at the end of each year during the term of the lease. At the end of the lease term, on December 31, 19x9, Barber made the following entry to close out the lease transaction:

	Debit	Credit
Cash	5,000	
Unguaranteed residual value		5,000

ACCOUNTING FOR DIRECT FINANCING LEASES

The accounting elements of a direct financing lease, as set forth in the Statement, are the following:

1. *Gross Investment in the Lease*
   The minimum lease payments plus any unguaranteed residual value accruing to the benefit of the lessor.

2. *Gross Unearned Income*
   The gross investment in the lease, less the cost or carrying amount of the leased property.

3. *Net Unearned Income*
   Gross unearned income less initial direct costs taken into income.

4. *Net Investment in the Lease*

The difference between the gross investment in the lease and unearned income.

ACCOUNTING STANDARDS FOR DIRECT FINANCING LEASES

The Statement prescribes the following accounting standards for direct financing leases.

1. Entries shall be made to record gross investment in the lease and to charge initial direct costs to income. These entries shall be offset by entries to record unearned income, a credit to current income equal to initial direct costs paid, and disposition of the asset under the lease.
2. The investment in the lease shall be presented net of unearned income on the balance sheet, and it shall be classified as current and noncurrent in a classified balance sheet.
3. Initial direct costs shall be charged against income as incurred, and a portion of unearned income equal to the initial direct costs shall be recognized as income in the same period.
4. The remaining unearned income shall be amortized to income over the lease term so as to produce a constant periodic rate of return on the net investment in the lease.
5. Contingent rentals, such as rentals based on variations in the prime interest rate, etc. shall be credited to income when they become receivable.

CASE STUDY IN ACCOUNTING FOR DIRECT FINANCING LEASES

Model Case No. 2 illustrates lessor accounting procedures for two direct financing leases. One of the leases is a typical, simple direct-financing lease, and the other is a financing lease contract complicated by initial direct costs and guaranteed and unguaranteed residual values accruing to the benefit of the lessor. Both leases are representative of the type of lease agreements that require an imputed discount rate based on the relation of minimum lease payments to unearned income.

MODEL CASE NO. 2

On January 1, 19x0 Willard Finance Corporation purchased twenty-five dumpsters and a mobile concrete mixer for the purpose of leasing the properties to the County Sanitary District. The dumpsters were to be used by the District as trash depositories throughout the county, and the mobile concrete mixer was intended for use in sewer construction work. Analyses of the nature of the leased property and provisions of the lease agreements; computation of classification data; and determination of appropriate classification are outlined in Schedule 5 for each respective lease.

ANALYSIS OF LEASE PROVISIONS AND CLASSIFICATION DATA

Leased property	Dumpsters	Concrete Mixer
Fair value	25,000	45,600
Unguaranteed residual value at end of lease term	—	2,000
Cost and carrying amount	25,000	45,000
Estimated economic life	10 years	6 years
Guaranteed residual value	—	1,000
Initial direct costs	—	600
Lease agreement		
Term	10 years	6 years
Annual rental (at end of year)	4,000	10,000
Transfers ownership at end of lease term	No	No
Contains bargain purchase option	No	No
Classification Data		
Minimum lease payments	40,000	61,000
Interest rate implicit in lease	9.605%	—
Imputed interest rate	—	9.742%
Present value of minimum lease payments	25,000	—
Lease term as a percentage of estimated economic life	100%	75%
Present value of minimum lease payments as a percentage of total fair value	100%	—
Collectibility of minimum lease payments predictable	Yes	Yes
Important uncertainties concerning future unreimbursable costs	None	None

SCHEDULE 5

From the information outlined in Schedule 5 Willard prepared Schedule 6 to analyze the accounting elements involved in each lease.

The classification and measurement bases used by Willard were as follows.

LEASE FOR DUMPSTERS

The lease was classified as other than an operating lease because the lease agreement extended over 100% of the estimated economic life of the leased property, and also met the conditional criteria for collectibility of the minimum lease payments and no important uncertainties concerning future unreimbursable costs. It was classified specifically as a direct financing lease because the fair value of the leased property was exactly equal to the cost.

The unearned income of $15,000 was required to be amortized to income over ten years in a manner that would provide a constant rate of return on the net investment in the lease. Therefore, Willard computed the interest rate implicit in the lease by repeatedly solving the basic formula for the present value of an annuity using estimated

SCHEDULE OF ACCOUNTING ELEMENTS IN LEASES

	Lease for Dumpsters	Lease for Mixer
Minimum Lease Payments		
1. Total of periodic payments	40,000	60,000
2. Guaranteed residual value	—	1,000
3. Total minimum lease payments	40,000	61,000
Gross Investment in Lease		
4. Minimum lease payments—line 3	40,000	61,000
5. Unguaranteed residual value	—	2,000
6. Gross investment in lease	40,000	63,000
Gross Unearned Income		
7. Gross investment in lease—line 6	40,000	63,000
8. Less—cost of leased property (fair value)	25,000	45,000
9. Gross unearned income	15,000	18,000
Net Unearned Income		
10. Gross unearned income—line 9	15,000	18,000
11. Less—initial direct costs	—	600
12. Net unearned income	15,000	17,400
Net Investment in Lease		
13. Gross investment in lease—line 6	40,000	63,000
14. Less—net unearned income—line 12	15,000	17,400
15. Net investment in lease	25,000	45,600

SCHEDULE 6

interest rates until the precise rate that satisfied the equation was found. The final computation was as follows:

$$4,000 \left(\frac{1 - \left(\frac{1}{1.09605} \right)^{10}}{.09605} \right) = 25,000$$

From the information shown in Schedules 5 and 6, Willard made the following entry to record the lease investment, and then prepared Schedule 7 to provide guidelines for accounting for the lease transaction at the end of each year during the lease term.

	Debit	Credit
Minimum lease payments receivable	40,000	
Unearned interest income		15,000
Inventory—dumpsters		25,000
To record investment in dumpsters lease.		

SCHEDULE OF ACCOUNTING ENTRIES FOR DUMPSTER LEASE

Date	Cash Payment Received Cr. Minimum Lease Payments Receivable	Journal Entry Dr. Unearned Interest Income Cr. Interest Income	Minimum Lease Payments Receivable (Gross Investment in Lease)	Unearned Interest Income	Net Investment in Lease
January 1, 19x0	—	—	40,000	15,000	25,000
December 31, 19x0	4,000	2,401	36,000	12,599	23,401
December 31, 19x1	4,000	2,248	32,000	10,351	21,649
December 31, 19x2	4,000	2,079	28,000	8,272	19,728
December 31, 19x3	4,000	1,895	24,000	6,377	17,623
December 31, 19x4	4,000	1,693	20,000	4,684	15,316
December 31, 19x5	4,000	1,472	16,000	3,212	12,788
December 31, 19x6	4,000	1,229	12,000	1,983	10,017
December 31, 19x7	4,000	962	8,000	1,021	6,979
December 31, 19x8	4,000	671	4,000	350	3,650
December 31, 19x9	4,000	350	—	—	—
	40,000	15,000			

SCHEDULE 7

Willard made the following entry at December 31, 19x0:

	Debit	Credit
Cash	4,000	
Unearned interest income	2,401	
Minimum lease payments receivable		4,000
Interest income		2,401

Similar entries reflecting the reduction in unearned income indicated in Schedule 7 were made at the end of each year during the term of the lease.

LEASE FOR MOBILE CONCRETE MIXER

The lease was classified as other than an operating lease because the lease term extended over 75% of the economic life of the leased property, and also met the conditional criteria for collectibility of the minimum lease payments and no uncertainties concerning future unreimbursable costs. It was classified specifically as a direct-financing lease because the fair value of the leased property was the same as its cost and carrying value.

The complications in accounting for this lease transaction, compared to accounting for the dumpster lease, arose from the fact that guaranteed residual value, unguaranteed residual value, and initial direct costs were involved in the lease for the concrete mixer.

The interest rate implicit in the lease could not be used to discount the periodic and final payments because the interest income was required to provide a constant periodic rate of return based on the *net investment in the lease,* and the net investment in the lease was increased by the initial direct costs paid at the inception of the lease. Therefore, Willard had to calculate an *imputed* interest rate by the trial-and-error method in the same manner as that used to calculate the interest rate implicit in the dumpster lease. The final computation was as follows:

Uniform periodic payments:

$$10,000 \left(\frac{1 - \left(\frac{1}{1.09742} \right)^6}{.09742} \right) = 43,884$$

Payment at end of lease term:

$$3,000 \left(\frac{1}{1.09742} \right)^6 = \underline{1,716}$$

Net investment in lease $\qquad\qquad\qquad$ $\underline{\underline{45,600}}$

From the information contained in Schedules 5 and 6, Willard prepared the following entries to record the investment in the lease. Schedule 8 was then prepared to provide guidelines for accounting for the lease transaction at the end of each year during the term of the lease.

	Debit	Credit
(1)		
Minimum lease payments receivable	61,000	
Unguaranteed residual value	2,000	
$\quad$ Inventory—concrete mixer		45,000
$\quad$ Unearned income		18,000
(2)		
Initial direct costs (expense)	600	
$\quad$ Cash		600
(3)		
Unearned interest income	600	
$\quad$ Interest income		600

SCHEDULE OF ACCOUNTING ENTRIES FOR CONCRETE MIXER LEASE

Date	Cash Payment Received Cr. Minimum Lease Payments Receivable	Journal Entry Dr. Unearned Interest Income Cr. Interest Income	Minimum Lease Payments Receivable	Unguaranteed Residual Value	Gross Investment in Lease	Unearned Interest Income	Net Investment in Lease
January 1, 19x0	—	—	61,000	2,000	63,000	17,400	45,600
December 31, 19x0	10,000	4,442	51,000	2,000	53,000	12,958	40,042
December 31, 19x1	10,000	3,901	41,000	2,000	43,000	9,057	33,943
December 31, 19x2	10,000	3,307	31,000	2,000	33,000	5,750	27,250
December 31, 19x3	10,000	2,655	21,000	2,000	23,000	3,095	19,905
December 31, 19x4	10,000	1,940	11,000	2,000	13,000	1,155	11,845
December 31, 19x5	10,000	1,155	1,000	2,000	3,000	—	3,000
	60,000	17,400					

SCHEDULE 8

Willard made the following entries at December 31, 19x0:

	Debit	Credit
Cash	10,000	
Unearned interest income	4,442	
Minimum lease payments receivable		10,000
Interest income		4,442

Similar entries were made at the end of each year during the lease term, reflecting the periodic payment received and the amortization of unearned interest income as indicated by Schedule 8 for each respective year.

In addition, at the end of the lease term on December 31, 19x5, Willard made the following entry to record payment of the residual value and to close out the lease transaction:

	Debit	Credit
Cash	3,000	
Minimum lease payments receivable		1,000
Unguaranteed residual value		2,000

LEASES BETWEEN RELATED PARTIES

Generally, leases between related parties should be classified and accounted for in the same manner as similar leases between unrelated parties.

SALES-LEASEBACK TRANSACTIONS

If the lease in a sales-leaseback transaction meets the capital and conditional criteria, the purchaser-lessor shall record the transaction as a purchase and direct-financing lease. If these criteria are not met, he shall record the transaction as a purchase and operating lease.

SUBLEASES

Leasing activities sometimes involve such transactions as subleasing by the lessee, substituting a new lessee under the original lease agreement, selling or transferring the original lease to a third party, and contracting with a new lessee through a new agreement. The general rules for lessor accounting for such transactions are as follows:

(a) If the original lessee enters into a sublease or the original lease agreement is sold or transferred by the original lessee to a third party, the original lessor shall continue to account for the lease as before.

(b) If the original lease agreement is replaced by a new agreement with a new lessee, the lessor shall account for the termination of the original lease in accordance with the rules for renewals and extensions outlined in a following paragraph, and shall classify and account for the new lease as a separate transaction.

ANNUAL REVIEW OF ESTIMATED RESIDUAL VALUE

The estimated residual value accruing to the benefit of the lessor shall be reviewed annually. If the residual value reflects a permanent decline in value, the resulting reduction in net investment should be recognized as a loss in the period in which the estimate changed. An upward adjustment of the estimated residual value shall not be made.

CHANGE, RENEWAL, EXTENSION, AND TERMINATION OF LEASE AGREEMENTS

Prior to the termination of a lease term, a change in the provisions of a lease, a renewal or extension of an existing lease, and termination of a lease shall be accounted for as follows.

Change in Lease Provisions

If a change in the provisions of a sales-type or direct-financing lease changes the amount of the remaining minimum lease payments, the balance of the minimum lease payments receivable shall be adjusted to reflect the change and the net adjustment shall be charged or credited to income.

If a change in the provisions of a sales-type or direct-financing lease gives rise to a new agreement classified as an operating lease, the remaining investment shall be removed from the accounts, the leased asset shall be recorded as an asset at the lower of its original cost, present fair value, or present carrying amount, and the net adjustment shall be charged to income of the period. The new lease shall thereafter be accounted for as any other operating lease.

Renewal or Extension of Lease Agreement

A renewal or extension of a sales-type or direct-financing lease shall be accounted for as follows:
(a) If the renewal or extension is classified as a sales-type or direct-financing lease, it shall be accounted for in the same manner as that prescribed for a change in lease provisions, as described in the preceding paragraph.
(b) If the renewal or extension of a sales-type or direct financing lease is classified as an operating lease, the existing lease shall continue to be accounted for in the same manner as previously treated until the end of the original term, and the renewal or extension shall be accounted for as any other operating lease.

Termination of Lease Agreement

A termination of a lease shall be accounted for by removing the net investment from the accounts, recording the leased asset at the lower of its original cost, present fair value, or present carrying amount, and the net adjustment shall be charged to income of the period.

LESSOR'S DISCLOSURE REQUIREMENTS FOR SALES-TYPE, DIRECT-FINANCING, AND OPERATING LEASES

Paragraph 23 of FASB Statement No. 13 establishes specific disclosure requirements for lessors:

When leasing, exclusive of leveraged leasing, is a significant part of the lessor's business activities in terms of revenue, net income, or assets, the following information with respect to leases shall be disclosed in the financial statements, or footnotes thereto.

a. For sales-type and direct-financing leases:
  i. The components of the net investment in sales-type and direct-financing leases as of the date of each balance sheet presented.
     a. Future minimum lease payments to be received with separate deductions for:
        (1) amounts representing executory costs, including any profit thereon, included in the minimum lease payments; and
        (2) the accumulated allowance for uncollectible minimum lease payments receivable.
     b. The unguaranteed residual values accruing to the benefit of the lessor.
     c. Unearned income.
  ii. Future minimum lease payments to be received for each of the five succeeding years as of the date of the latest balance sheet presented.
  iii. The amount of unearned income included in income to offset initial direct costs charged against income for each period for which an income statement is presented. (For direct-financing leases only.)
  iv. Total contingent rentals included in income for each period for which an income statement is presented.

b. For operating leases:
  i. The cost and carrying amount, if different, of property on lease or held for leasing by major classes of property according to nature or function, and the amount of accumulated depreciation in total as of the date of the latest balance sheet presented.
  ii. Minimum future rentals on noncancelable leases as of the date of the latest balance sheet presented, in the aggregate and for each of the five succeeding fiscal years.
  iii. Total contingent rentals included in income for each period for which an income statement is presented.

c. A general description of the lessor's leasing arrangements.

ILLUSTRATION OF DISCLOSURE OF SALES-TYPE AND DIRECT-FINANCING LEASE TRANSACTIONS

The financial statements of Willard Financial Corporation at December 31, 19x0, (Model Case No. 2) illustrate required disclosure of direct-financing lease transactions. This illustration also applies to sales-type lease transactions since the disclosure requirements are the same for both types of leases.

At December 31, 19x0 Willard prepared Schedule 9 from the information contained in Schedules 7 and 8 for the purpose of making the disclosures required by FASB Statement No. 13.

SCHEDULE OF COMPONENTS OF NET INVESTMENT IN DIRECT-FINANCING LEASES

	Lease for Dumpster	Lease for Mixer	Total
Minimum lease payments to be received			
19x1	4,000	10,000	14,000
19x2	4,000	10,000	14,000
19x3	4,000	10,000	14,000
19x4	4,000	10,000	14,000
19x5	4,000	10,000	14,000
19x6	4,000	1,000	5,000
19x7	4,000	—	4,000
19x8	4,000	—	4,000
19x9	4,000	—	4,000
	36,000	51,000	87,000
Unguaranteed residual value	—	2,000	2,000
	36,000	53,000	89,000
Less—unearned interest income	12,599	12,958	25,557
Net investment in direct-financing leases	23,401	40,042	63,443
Balance sheet classification			
Minimum lease payments to be received in 19x1	4,000	10,000	14,000
Less—unearned income to be amortized in 19x1	2,248	3,901	6,149
Current net investment in leases	1,752	6,099	7,851
Noncurrent net investment in leases	21,649	33,943	55,592

SCHEDULE 9

The following extracts were taken from the balance sheet and notes contained in Willard's financial statements at December 31, 19x0.

WILLARD FINANCIAL CORPORATION

Balance Sheet
December 31, 19x0

ASSETS   LIABILITIES

Current

* * * * *

Net investment in direct-financing leases (Note 2)   7,851   * * * * * *

* * * * *

Long-term
  Net investment in direct-
    financing leases (Note 2)   55,592

* * * * *

WILLARD FINANCIAL CORPORATION

Notes to Financial Statements
December 31, 19x0

Note 1—Summary of Significant Accounting Policies

The Company's principal operations consist of making loans secured by personal property. In 19x0, however, the Company adopted a plan of expansion involving eventual significant leasing activity. In accordance with the plan, during the current year the Company entered into two long-term direct financing leases for heavy equipment: one for 25 trash dumpsters expires in 9 years, and the other for a mobile concrete mixer expires in 5 years.

Note 2—Net Investment in Direct-Financing Leases

Following are the components of the Company's net investment in direct-financing leases at December 31, 19x0.

Total minimum lease payments to be received	87,000
Estimated unguaranteed residual value of leased property	2,000
	89,000
Less—unearned interest income	25,557
Net investment in direct-financing lease	63,443

ACCOUNTING FOR LEVERAGED LEASES

The Board's concept of leveraged leasing transactions comprehends the *overall* economic effect of such leases, and the principles of the concept equate income with the excess of total cash flow over the original cash investment. Accordingly, FASB Statement No. 13 establishes the standards of accounting for leveraged leases and the rules for recognition of income therefrom, listed below.

1. The lessor shall record his investment in a leveraged lease net of the nonrecourse debt. The net of the balances of the following accounts shall represent the initial and continuing investment in leveraged leases:
   (a) rentals receivable, net of that portion of rental applicable to principal and interest on the nonrecourse debt;
   (b) a receivable for the amount of the investment tax credit to be realized on the transaction;
   (c) the estimated residual value of the leased asset;
   (d) unearned and deferred income consisting of
      (i) the estimated pretax lease income or loss, after deducting initial direct costs, remaining to be allocated to income over the lease term; and
      (ii) the investment tax credit remaining to be allocated to income over the lease term.

2. The investment in leveraged leases less deferred taxes arising from differences between pretax accounting income and taxable income should represent the lessor's net investment in leveraged leases for purposes of computing periodic net income from the lease.

3. Rate of return shall be computed, using projected cash receipts and disbursements, applied to net investment in years when it is positive.

4. The computed rate, when applied to the net investment in years when the net investment is positive, will distribute the net income to those years. The rate is distinct from the interest rate implicit in the lease.

5. In each year, whether positive or not, the difference between the net cash flow and the amount of income recognized, if any, shall serve to increase or reduce the net investment balance.

6. The net income realized shall be composed of these elements:
   (a) pretax lease income or loss;
   (b) investment tax credit; and
   (c) the tax effect of the pretax lease income or loss recognized.

      Pretax lease income or loss and investment tax credit shall be allocated in proportional amounts from unearned and deferred income included in net investment.

      The tax effect of the pretax lease income or loss recognized shall be reflected in tax expense for the year.

7. The tax effect of the difference between pretax accounting income or loss and taxable income or loss shall be charged to deferred income taxes.

8. If the projected net cash receipts over the term of the lease are less than the lessor's initial investment, the deficiency shall be recognized as a loss at the inception of the lease.

9. If at any time during the lease term, the application of the accounting methods described in the foregoing paragraphs could result in a loss being allocated to future years, the loss should be recognized immediately.

10. Any estimated residual value and all other important assumptions affecting estimated total net income from the lease shall be reviewed at least annually. If during the lease term, the estimate of the residual value is determined to be excessive and the decline in the residual value is judged to be other than temporary, or if the revision of another important assumption changes the estimated total net income from the lease, the rate of return and the allocation of income to positive investment years shall be recalculated from the inception of the lease following the method described previously, and using the revised assumption. The accounts constituting the net investment balance shall be adjusted to conform to the recalculated balances, and the change in the net investment shall be recognized as a gain or loss in the year in which the assumption is changed. An upward adjustment of the estimated residual value shall not be made.

11. If the investment tax credit is accounted for other than as prescribed in this section, a lease otherwise fitting the criteria for a leveraged lease shall be classified as a direct-financing lease and accounted for as provided for such leases.

DISCLOSURE REQUIREMENTS

The following disclosure requirements are set forth in the Statement.

1. For purposes of presenting the investment in a leveraged lease in the lessor's balance sheet, the amount of related deferred taxes shall be presented separately from the remainder of the net investment.

2. The income statement, or notes thereto, shall present separately the following information:

    (a) pretax income from the leveraged lease;

    (b) the tax effect of pretax income; and

    (c) the amount of investment credit recognized as income during the period.

3. When leveraged leasing is a significant part of the lessor's business activities in terms of revenue, net income, or assets, the components of the net investment balance in leveraged leases, as outlined in a preceding paragraph, shall be disclosed in a footnote to the financial statements.

COMPUTATIONAL TECHNIQUES FOR RATE OF RETURN

A strenuous computation is required to obtain a rate of return that, when applied to periodic net cash flow, will distribute net income from the lease over its term. In the early stage of the lease cash flow will normally be excessive due to tax benefits of accelerated depreciation and the investment tax credit; during the midterm of the lease the net cash flow may be negative because no tax benefits are derived from depreciation, and the payments to the nonrecourse creditor may exceed the cash rental payments. At the end of the term the cash flow may again become excessive due to the benefits from disposition of the leased property at its estimated residual value. Under such conditions it is obvious that if income were based solely on net cash flow, it would not be distributed properly over the term of the lease. Therefore, the rules for recognition of income require that a rate of return be established that will distribute the income over the period of the lease based on the *net* investment at the end of each period. Thus, a portion of the cash flow at the end of each period will be applied to investment, and a portion to income, so that at the end of the lease term the rate of return has provided income that is exactly equivalent to the difference between the net cash flow and the original cash investment in the leased property.

There is no simple method for computing the appropriate rate of return, and there is no simple algebraic equation to which variable factors can be applied to obtain a solution. FASB Statement No. 13 indicates that the rate of return used for an example illustrated therein was calculated by a trial-and-error method. The method comprehends the selection of an initial estimate of the rate as a starting point. If the total allocated to income by the initial rate differs from the net cash flow, the estimated rate is increased or decreased as appropriate to derive a revised allocation. The process is repeated until a rate is selected which develops a total amount allocated to income that is precisely equal to the net cash flow.

The Statement suggests that, as a practical matter, a computer program be used to make the calculation under successive iterations until the correct rate is determined. Also, such iterated calculations can be programmed for an electronic pocket calculator: a calculator having 19 memory units can be programmed to compute the rate of return on a ten-year lease; leases for longer periods would require a calculator with additional memory functions.

In any event, manual calculation of the appropriate rate of return on a leveraged lease is cumbersome and time consuming, and a company anticipating extensive leveraged lease transactions should provide for preparation of a computer program, or should obtain an electronic pocket calculator.

CASE STUDY IN ACCOUNTING FOR LEVERAGED LEASES

A typical leveraged lease transaction is outlined in Model Case No. 3. The example illustrates applicable accounting and reporting standards, computational techniques for measurement of present values and rate of return, appropriate recognition of income and the accounting procedures necessary to record the transaction throughout the term of the lease.

MODEL CASE NO. 3

Bennett & Company purchased a machine on January 1, 19x1 at a cost of $740,000 for the purpose of leasing it to Tudor, Inc. for a period of ten years at an annual rental of $100,000 per year. Bennett paid $300,000 of the purchase price from its own funds and borrowed $440,000 from Wilder Finance Corporation to complete the deal. An analysis of the leasing provisions and financing arrangements is outlined in Schedule 10.

SCHEDULE OF LEASE AGREEMENT AND FINANCING ARRANGEMENTS

Nature of leased property		Machinery
Cost of leased property		740,000
Lease term		10 years
Lease rental payments		
10 annual payments of $100,000, due on last day of each year		1,000,000
Estimated residual value—realized one year after end of lease term		150,000
Depreciation allowed for tax purposes		
3 year life—double declining balance method—depreciated to a		
salvage value of 74,000		666,000
Investment tax credit—realized on last day of first year		74,000
Estimated effective annual income tax rate		50%
Financing method		
Equity investment by lessor	300,000	
Long-term nonrecourse loan		
Principal amount of loan—678,080.		
Repayable in 10 annual installments of 67,808 on the last day of each		
year with interest at 8.75% per annum.		
Net proceeds	440,000	740,000

SCHEDULE 10

Bennett computed the required ten annual payments on the $440,000 loan with interest at 8.75% to be $67,808 as shown below, and then completed Schedule 11 to reflect the distribution of the respective payments to interest expense and principal payment on the loan.

$$440,000 \left(\frac{1 - \left(\frac{1}{1.0875} \right)^{10}}{.0875} \right) = 67,808$$

LOAN AMORTIZATION SCHEDULE

Year	Amount of Payment	Payment applied to: Interest (8.75%)	Payment applied to: Principal	Principal Balance— End of Year
Beginning Balance	—	—	—	440,000
19x1	67,808	38,500	29,308	410,692
19x2	67,808	35,935	31,873	378,819
19x3	67,808	33,146	34,662	344,157
19x4	67,808	30,113	37,695	306,462
19x5	67,808	26,815	40,993	265,469
19x6	67,808	23,228	44,580	220,889
19x7	67,808	19,328	48,480	172,409
19x8	67,808	15,086	52,722	119,687
19x9	67,808	10,473	57,335	62,352
19y0	67,808	5,456	62,352	—
	678,080	238,080	440,000	

SCHEDULE 11

The depreciation allowable for tax purposes was computed, and the details are shown on Schedule 12.

SCHEDULE OF DEPRECIATION — LEASED PROPERTY

Year	Depreciable Basis— Beginning of Year	Depreciation Rate	Annual Depreciation	Accumulated Depreciation	Net Book Value— End of Year
19x1	740,000	66.6667%	493,333	493,333	246,667
19x2	246,667	66.6667%	164,445	657,778	82,222
19x3	82,222	—	8,222	666,000	74,000
			666,000		

SCHEDULE 12

As a preliminary to computing the projected cash flow over the life of the lease, Bennett had to compute the tax benefits and charges that would originate during the period. These computations are shown in Schedule 13.

SCHEDULE OF TAXABLE INCOME DERIVED FROM LEASE

Year	Cash Rental Payments	Residual Value	Depreciation	Depreciable Cost of Residual Value	Loan Interest	Taxable Income (Loss)	Income Tax Credits (Charges) Rate—50%
	(Schedule 10)	(Schedule 10)	(Schedule 12)	(Schedule 12)	(Schedule 11)		
19x1	100,000	—	(493,333)	—	(38,500)	(431,833)	215,917
19x2	100,000	—	(164,445)	—	(35,935)	(100,380)	50,190
19x3	100,000	—	(8,222)	—	(33,146)	58,632	(29,316)
19x4	100,000	—	—	—	(30,113)	69,887	(34,944)
19x5	100,000	—	—	—	(26,815)	73,185	(36,593)
19x6	100,000	—	—	—	(23,228)	76,772	(38,386)
19x7	100,000	—	—	—	(19,328)	80,672	(40,336)
19x8	100,000	—	—	—	(15,086)	84,914	(42,457)
19x9	100,000	—	—	—	(10,473)	89,527	(44,763)
19y0	100,000	—	—	—	(5,456)	94,544	(47,272)
19y1	—	150,000	—	(74,000)	—	76,000	
							(38,000)
	1,000,000	150,000	(666,000)	(74,000)	(238,080)	171,920	(85,960)

SCHEDULE 13

SCHEDULE OF ANNUAL CASH FLOW

Year	Lease Rentals and Residual Value	Income Tax Credits (Charges)	Investment Tax Credit Realized	Loan Payments	Annual Cash Flow	Cumulative Cash Flow
	(Schedule 13)	(Schedule 13)	(Schedule 10)	(Schedule 11)		
Initial Investment						(300,000)
19x1	100,000	215,917	74,000	(67,808)	322,109	22,109
19x2	100,000	50,190	—	(67,808)	82,382	104,491
19x3	100,000	(29,316)	—	(67,808)	2,876	107,367
19x4	100,000	(34,944)	—			
				(67,808)	(2,752)	104,615
19x5	100,000	(36,593)	—	(67,808)	(4,401)	100,214
19x6	100,000	(38,386)	—	(67,808)	(6,194)	94,020
19x7	100,000	(40,336)	—	(67,808)	(8,144)	85,876
19x8	100,000	(42,457)	—	(67,808)	(10,265)	75,611
19x9	100,000	(44,763)	—	(67,808)	(12,571)	63,040
19y0	100,000	(47,272)	—	(67,808)	(15,080)	47,960
19y1	150,000	(38,000)	—	—	112,000	159,960
	1,150,000	(85,960)	74,000	(678,080)	459,960	

SCHEDULE 14

Assuming that tax benefits would result in a conservation of cash, and that tax charges would increase cash expenditures, Bennett set up annual rentals receivable, realization of the investment tax credit and the indicated tax refunds as projected cash inflow, and combined the payments on the loan and income tax charges, respectively, to reflect projected outflow. These computations are shown on Schedule 14.

The cumulative cash flow of $159,960 shown in Schedule 14 represents income that would be realized over the term of the lease. In order to allocate the income over the lease period based on its net investment in the leasing transaction, Bennett had to compute a rate of return that, when uniformly applied to the fluctuating balance of its investment in the lease, would distribute the annual cash flow in such a manner that an aggregate of precisely $159,960 would be reflected in income for the entire lease period.

Bennett computed the rate of return by the trial-and-error method previously described in the text under "Computational Techniques," and found it to be 28.1123%. The application of this rate of return to the fluctuating balance of the net investment, when such balance was positive, is set forth in Schedule 15.

ALLOCATION OF ANNUAL CASH FLOW TO INVESTMENT AND INCOME

Year	Investment at Beginning of Year	Annual Cash Flow Total (Schedule 14)	Applied to: Investment	Income (28.1123%)	Percent of Annual Income to Total Income	Investment at End of Year
19x1	300,000					
		322,109	237,772	84,337	52.7238%	62,228
19x2	62,228	82,382	64,888	17,494	10.9365%	2,660
19x3	(2,660)	2,876	2,876	—	—	5,536
19x4	(5,536)	(2,752)	(2,752)	—	—	2,784
19x5	(2,784)	(4,401)	(4,401)	—	—	1,617
19x6	1,617	(6,194)	(6,649)	455	.2844%	8,266
19x7	8,266	(8,144)	(10,468)	2,324	1.4529%	18,734
19x8	18,734	(10,265)	(15,532)	5,267	3.2927%	34,266
19x9	34,266	(12,571)	(22,204)	9,633	6.0221%	56,470
19y0	56,470	(15,080)	(30,954)	15,874	9.9237%	87,424
19y1	87,424	112,000	87,424	24,576	15.3639%	—
		459,960	300,000	159,960	100.%	

SCHEDULE 15

The income of $159,960 shown in Schedule 15 represents *net* income from the lease. For reporting purposes it was necessary for Bennett to compute the related pretax income, tax effects of pretax income, distribution of the benefits derived from the investment credit, income tax expense, and the resulting net income for each respective year. This was accomplished by determining the percentage of net income for each year to total net income of $159,960, and applying these yearly percentages to the totals of taxable income and the investment tax credit. The tax effects of pretax income were calculated by applying the effective annual tax rate of 50% to the pretax income calculated for each year, income tax expense was computed to be the difference between the tax effects of pretax income and the allocated investment tax credit, and net income, of course, was computed as the difference between pretax income and income tax expense. These calculations are shown on Schedule 16.

SCHEDULE OF COMPONENTS OF INCOME

Year	Applicable Annual Percentage (Schedule 15)	Pretax Accounting Income (Taxable Income) (Schedule 13)	Tax Effects of Pretax Income (Charge) Credit (Schedule 13)	Investment Tax Credit (Schedule 10)	Income Tax Expense	Net Income from Lease (Schedule 14)
Allocation Base-Totals for Period of Lease	100. %	171,920	(85,960)	74,000		159,960
Allocated to:						
19x1	52.7238%	90,643	(45,322)	39,016	(6,306)	84,337
19x2	10.9365%	18,802	(9,401)	8,093	(1,308)	17,494
19x3	—	—	—	—	—	—
19x4	—	—	—	—	—	—
19x5	—	—	—	—	—	—
19x6	.2844%	489	(244)	210	(34)	455
19x7	1.4529%	2,498	(1,249)	1,075	(174)	2,324
19x8	3.2927%	5,660	(2,830)	2,437	(393)	5,267
19x9	6.0221%	10,353	(5,176)	4,456	(720)	9,633
19y0	9.9237%	17,061	(8,531)	7,344	(1,187)	15,874
19y1	15.3639%	26,414	(13,207)	11,369	(1,838)	24,576
	100. %	171,920	(85,960)	74,000	(11,960)	159,960

SCHEDULE 16

On January 1, 19x1, Bennett made the following entry to record its investment in the leasing transaction:

	Debit	Credit
Rents receivable	1,000,000	
Investment tax credit receivable	74,000	
Estimated residual value	150,000	
Loan obligation		678,080
Unearned income		171,920
Deferred income from investment tax credit		74,000
Cash		300,000

To record investment in leveraged lease transaction.

Bennett made the following entries at the end of 19x1 and 19x2, respectively, to record the changes in the lease investment during the years indicated:

	Debit	Credit
December 31, 19x1		
(1)		
Cash	100,000	
Rents receivable		100,000
To record cash received for rent.		
(2)		
Loan obligation	67,808	
Cash		67,808
To record payment on nonrecourse debt.		
(3)		
Cash	74,000	
Investment tax credit receivable		74,000
To record receipt of cash for investment credit.		
(4)		
Cash	215,917	
Unearned income	90,643	
Deferred income from investment tax credit	39,016	
Income tax expense	6,306	
Deferred income tax credits		261,239
Income under lease		90,643
To record income under lease; set up deferred tax credits; amortize unearned income and deferred income from investment tax credit; record income tax expense and cash received from tax benefits of taxable loss.		
December 31, 19x2		
(1)		
Cash	100,000	
Rents receivable		100,000
(2)		
Loan obligation	67,808	
Cash		67,808
(3)		
Cash	50,190	
Unearned income	18,802	
Deferred income from investment tax credit	8,093	
Income tax expense	1,308	
Income under lease		18,802
Deferred income tax credits		59,591

Similar appropriate entries were made at the end of each year during the lease term. At December 31, 19y1, Bennett made the following entry to close out the lease transactions:

	Debit	Credit
Cash	150,000	
Unearned income	26,414	
Deferred income from investment tax credit	11,369	
Deferred income tax credits	24,793	
Income tax expense	1,838	
Estimated residual value		150,000
Income under lease		26,414
Cash		38,000

To record disposition of leased property; closing of deferred income and income tax credit accounts; income under the lease; cash received from disposition of leased property; and cash paid for income tax liability.

An analysis of the journal entries made from the inception of the lease on January 1, 19x1 to the disposition of the leased property on December 31, 19y1 is set forth in Schedule 17.[4]

At December 19x2 and 19x1, Bennett's post-closing trial balances reflected the following respective balances in the lease transaction accounts:

| | December 31, | |
	19x2	19x1
	Debit (Credit)	
Rents receivable	800,000	900,000
Estimated residual value	150,000	150,000
Loan obligation	(542,464)	(610,272)
Unearned income	(62,475)	(81,277)
Deferred income from investment tax credit	(26,891)	(34,984)
Gross investment in lease	318,170	323,467
Deferred income tax credits	(320,830)	(261,239)
Net investment in lease (Schedule 15)	(2,660)	62,228

[4] This example follows the example in the Statement in that receipts of the investment tax credit and other tax benefits are shown as cash receipts for simplicity only. In actual practice, these receipts would not normally be in the form of immediate cash flow, but would be in the form of reduced tax payments on other income of the lessor.

SCHEDULE OF ENTRIES REQUIRED TO RECORD LEASE TRANSACTION

Debit (Credit)

Date	Cash	Rents Receivable	Investment Tax Credit	Estimated Residual Value	Loan Obliga-tion	Unearned Income	Deferred Income From Investment Credit	Deferred Income Tax Credits	Income Under Lease	Income Tax Expense
Original Investment	(300,000)	1,000,000	74,000	150,000	(678,080)	(171,920)	(74,000)	—	—	—
December 31,										
19x1	322,109	(100,000)	(74,000)	—	67,808	90,643	39,016	(261,239)	(90,643)	6,306
19x2	82,382	(100,000)	—	—	67,808	18,802	8,093	(53,591)	(18,802)	1,308
19x3	2,876	(100,000)	—	—	67,808	—	—	29,316	—	—
19x4	(2,752)	(100,000)	—	—	67,808	—	—	34,944	—	—
19x5	(4,401)	(100,000)	—	—	67,808	—	—	35,593	—	—
19x6	(6,194)	(100,000)	—	—	67,808	489	210	33,142	(489)	34
19x7	(8,144)	(100,000)	—	—	67,808	2,498	1,075	33,087	(2,498)	174
19x8	(10,265)	(100,000)	—	—	67,808	5,660	2,437	33,627	(5,660)	393
19x9	(12,571)	(100,000)	—	—	67,808	10,353	4,456	33,587	(10,353)	720
19y0	(15,080)	(100,000)	—	—	67,808	17,061	7,344	33,741	(17,061)	1,187
19y1	112,000	—	—	(150,000)	—	26,414	11,369	24,793	(26,414)	1,838
	159,960	—	—	—	—	—	—	—	(171,920)	11,960

SCHEDULE 17

The following is extracted from Bennett's financial statements at December 31, 19x2:

BENNETT & COMPANY

Balance Sheet

	December 31,				December 31,	
	19x2	19x1			19x2	19x1
Assets				Liabilities		
* * * * * *				* * * * * *		
Investment in leveraged leases	318,170	323,467		Deferred income taxes arising from leveraged leases	320,830	261,239
* * * * * *				* * * * * *		

BENNETT & COMPANY

Notes to Financial Statements
December 31, 19x2

Note 1—Summary of Significant Accounting Policies

* * * * * * * *

Investment in Leveraged Leases

The Company is the lessor in a leveraged lease agreement entered into in 19x1 under which heavy equipment having an estimated economic life of 10 years was leased for a term of 10 years. The Company's equity investment represented 40% of the purchase price; the remaining 60% was furnished by third-party financing in the form of long-term debt that provides for no recourse against the Company, and is secured by a first lien on the property. At the end of the lease term, the equipment is turned back to the Company. The residual value at that time is estimated to be 20% of cost. For federal income tax purposes, the Company receives the investment tax credit and has the benefit of tax deductions for depreciation on the entire leased asset and for interest on the long-term debt. Since during the early years of the lease those deductions exceed the lease rental income, substantial excess deductions are available to be applied against the Company's other income. In the later years of the lease, rental income will exceed the deductions and taxes will be payable. Deferred taxes are provided to reflect this reversal.

* * * * * * * *

Note 5—Net Investment in Leveraged Leases

The Company's new investment in leveraged leases is composed of the following elements:

	19x2	19x1
Rents receivable (net of principal and interest on nonrecourse debt)	257,536	289,728
Estimated residual value of leased assets	150,000	150,000
	407,536	439,728
Less: Unearned and deferred income	89,366	116,261
Gross investment in leveraged leases	318,170	323,467
Less: Deferred taxes arising from leveraged leases	320,830	261,239
Net investment in leveraged leases	(2,660)	62,228

Note 6—Summary of Income from Leveraged Leases

A summary of income from leveraged leases is as follows:

	19x2	19x1
Income from leveraged leases	18,802	90,643
Less: Income tax expense		
Current	9,401	45,322
Investment credit recognized	(8,093)	(39,016)
	1,308	6,306
Net income from leveraged leases	17,494	84,337

DECLINE IN RESIDUAL VALUE

If at any time during the period of the lease it is determined that the original estimate of the residual value was excessive, or if there is a decline, other than temporary, in the residual value of the leased property, the lessor must recalculate the rate of the return to be used for the remainder of the lease term. This revised rate of return must also be applied retroactively, and the resulting change in net investment must be recognized as a gain or loss in the year in which the residual value is changed. Model Case No. 4 illustrates the procedure to be followed in a situation where the original estimate of residual value is reduced, and the rate of return recalculated on the basis of the new assumption.

MODEL CASE NO. 4

This example is based on the leveraged lease transaction of Bennett & Company which was analyzed in Model Case No. 3. For the purpose of this illustration, it is assumed that at the end of the sixth year Bennett determined that the estimate of the residual value of the leased property should be reduced by $50,000; from $150,000 to $100,000.

The first step taken by Bennett in accounting for the change was to revise his schedule of allocation of annual cash flow to investment and income, Schedule 15, by reducing the cash flow in 19y1 by $25,000, and recalculating a rate of return for the entire period of the lease based on the revised cash flow. The cash flow was reduced by only $25,000 in 19yl because Bennett would get a tax benefit of $25,000 due to the reduction of $50,000 in residual value. The rate of return was computed by the trial-and-error method, and found to be 26.7461%. The revised calculations are set forth in Schedule 18.

REVISED SCHEDULE ALLOCATION OF CASH FLOW TO INVESTMENT AND INCOME

Year	Investment at Beginning of Year	Annual Cash Flow Total	Applied to: Investment	Applied to: Income (26,7461%)	Percent of Annual Income to Total Income	Investment at End of Year
19x1	300,000	322,109	241,871	80,238	59.4532%	58,129
19x2	58,129	82,382	66,835	15,547	11.5197%	(8,706)
19x3	(8,706)	2,876	2,876	—	—	(11,582)
19x4	(11,582)	(2,752)	(2,752)	—	—	(8,830)
19x5	(8,830)	(4,401)	(4,401)	—	—	(4,429)
19x6	(4,429)	(6,194)	(6,194)	—	—	1,765
19x7	1,765	(8,144)	(8,616)	472	.3497%	10,381
19x8	10,381	(10,265)	(13,042)	2,777	2.0576%	23,423
19x9	23,423	(12,571)	(18,836)	6,265	4.6421%	42,259
19y0	42,259	(15,080)	(26,382)	11,302	8.3743%	68,641
19y1	68,641	87,000	68,641	18,359	13.6034%	—
		434,960	300,000	134,960	100. %	

SCHEDULE 18

The reduction of $50,000 in residual value operated to reduce Bennett's projected pretax income by $50,000, the tax effect of pretax income by $25,000, and net income from the lease by $25,000. Bennett, therefore, revised his original schedule of the components of income (shown on Schedule 16) by reducing pretax and net income by the amounts referred to above, and applying the new percentages of annual income. Schedule 19 was prepared to reflect the revised computations of components of income.

REVISED SCHEDULE
COMPONENTS OF INCOME

Year	Applicable Annual Percentage	Pretax Accounting Income (Tax-able income)	Tax Effects of Pretax Income (Charge) Credit	Investment Tax Credit	Income Tax Expense	Net Income from Lease
Allocation Base-Totals for Period of Lease	100. %	121,920	(60,960)	74,000		134,960
Allocated to:						
19x1	59.4532%	72,485	(36,243)	43,995	7,752	80,237
19x2	11.5197%	14,045	(7,022)	8,525	1,503	15,548
19x3	—	—	—	—	—	—
19x4	—	—	—	—	—	—
19x5	—	—	—	—	—	—
19x6	—	—	—	—	—	—
Subtotals		86,530	(43,265)	52,520	9,255	95,785
19x7	.3497%	426	(213)	259	46	472
19x8	2.0576%	2,509	(1,255)	1,523	268	2,777
19x9	4.6421%	5,660	(2,830)	3,435	605	6,265
19y0	8.3743%	10,210	(5,105)	6,197	1,092	11,302
19y1	13.6034%	16,585	(8,292)	10,066	1,774	18,359
Subtotals		35,390	(17,695)	21,480	3,785	39,175
	100. %	121,920	(60,960)	74,000	13,040	134,960

SCHEDULE 19

Bennett then calculated the changes to be made in the lease investment accounts, and the net loss to be recognized in the current period, as follows:

Cumulative effect charged to current income

Reduction in residual value		50,000
Less: Reduction of unearned income attributable to future years		
Balance of pretax income at end of 19x6—Schedule 16	61,986	
Less: Revised balance—Schedule 19	35,390	26,596
Net loss in current period		23,404

Cumulative effect credited to current income tax expense

Net loss in current period, above, at 50%		11,702
Reduction in deferred income from investment tax credit		
Balance at end of 19x6—Schedule 16	26,681	
Less: Revised balance—Schedule 19	21,480	5,201
Credit to income tax expense in current period		16,903

Bennett then made the following journal entry to record the change in the lease investment accounts, to recognize the loss in lease income; and to make an appropriate adjustment of income tax expense for the current period.

	Debit	Credit
Loss from revaluing residual value of leased property	23,404	
Unearned income	26,596	
Deferred income from investment tax credit	5,201	
Deferred income tax credits	11,702	
Estimated residual value		50,000
Income tax expense		16,903

Schedule 20 sets forth the balances in the lease investment accounts at December 31, 19x6; reflects the effect of the above journal entry made on that date; and shows the entries made at the end of each subsequent year during the remaining term of the lease.

RESTATEMENT OF FINANCIAL STATEMENTS

The Statement requires retroactive application of its accounting and reporting standards for purposes of financial statements for calendar or fiscal years beginning after December 31, 1980. The cumulative effect of applying the accounting principles of the Statement on retained earnings at the beginning of the earliest period restated shall be included in determining the net income of that period. The effect on net income of applying the changed standards in the period in which the cumulative effect is included in determining net income shall be disclosed for that period, and the reason for not restating the prior periods shall be explained.

REVISED SCHEDULE OF ENTRIES REQUIRED TO RECORD LEASE TRANSACTIONS

Debit (Credit)

Date	Cash	Rents Receivable	Investment Tax Credit	Estimated Residual Value	Loan Obliga-tion	Unearned Income	Deferred Income from Investment Credit	Deferred Income Tax Credits	Income Under Lease	Income Tax Expense
December 31, 19x6—Balance In Asset and Liability Accounts and Total Income and Expenses to Date	94,020	400,000	—	150,000	(271,232)	(61,986)	(26,681)	(181,835)	(109,934)	7,648
Adjustment	—	—	—	(50,000)	—	26,596	5,201	11,702	23,404	(16,903)
Revised Balances December 31,	94,020	400,000	—	100,000	(271,232)	(35,390)	(21,480)	(170,133)	(86,530)	(9,255)
19x7	(8,144)	(100,000)	—	—	67,808	426	259	40,123	(426)	(46)
19x8	(10,265)	(100,000)	—	—	67,808	2,509	1,523	41,202	(2,509)	(268)
19x9	(12,571)	(100,000)	—	—	67,808	5,660	3,435	41,933	(5,660)	(605)
19y0	(15,080)	(100,000)	—	—	67,808	10,210	6,197	42,167	(10,210)	(1,092)
19y1	87,000	(100,000)	—	(100,000)	—	16,585	10,066	4,708	(16,585)	(1,774)
	134,960	—	—	—	—	—	—	—	(121,920)	(13,040)

SCHEDULE 20

7

Marketable Securities—
Valuation Standards, Accounting Procedures
and Reporting Requirements

For many years the advance, decline, and recovery cycle of stock market prices created considerable problems in accounting for marketable equity securities. The major authoritative literature on the general subject of marketable securities consisted of an Accounting Research Bulletin adopted in 1947, an APB Opinion published in 1975, and a series of AICPA industry audit guides circulated at various times. The enormous disparity in these official directives created confused concepts and served to promote divergent principles with respect to accounting for marketable securities. The decline in stock market prices that occurred during 1973 and 1974, and the substantial recovery that developed in 1975, finally prompted the FASB to urgently consider the problems of accounting for marketable equity securities. As a result of its inquiry, in December, 1975 the Board published Statement No. 12, "Accounting for Certain Marketable Securities," ostensibly designed to provide accounting standards that would accommodate fluctuations in market prices and be applicable to both single business entities and conglomerate business enterprises.[1] However, the Statement is the result of a project of limited scope, and its provisions are confined to consideration of marketable securities in circumstances where there is a decline (or recovery from a previous decline) in their market value, and to consideration of subsidiary and investee-owned marketable securities reported in consolidated or parent company financial statements.

The text of FASB Statement No. 12 is, at once, sparse, redundant, and incoherent, and its provisions create a confusion of artificial dichotomies by prescribing the following division of accounting elements and functions for the purpose of applying its standards: current and noncurrent portfolios, classified and unclassified balance sheet items, temporary and permanent decline in market value, and enterprises in industries that do, or do not, have specialized accounting practices. The objective of this chapter is to analyze, simplify, and illustrate the valuation standards, accounting procedures, and reporting requirements prescribed by the Statement, and to present them in logical and coherent continuity.

---

[1] Accounting for Certain Marketable Securities, Statement of the Financial Accounting Standards Board No. 12. (Stamford, Connecticut, Financial Accounting Standards Board, 1975. Reprinted with permission. Copies of the complete document are available from the FASB.)

APPLICABILITY

FASB Statement No. 12 does not apply to the following:

(a) nonprofit organizations,
(b) mutual life insurance companies, and
(c) employee benefit plans.

APPLICATION TO CERTAIN INDUSTRIES

In its deliberations on the issue of accounting for marketable equity securities, the Board concluded that changes in specialized accounting practices accepted in certain industries would require it to expand the scope of its project because consideration of the fundamental issues that led to the adoption of those specialized practices would be required. Because of the urgency of the matter at hand, the Board decided not to require changes in the specialized accounting methods of such industries except for those entities which carried marketable equity securities on the basis of cost, and it therefore directed that the Statement be divided into three sections: the first section applicable to entities in those industries not having specialized accounting practices with respect to marketable equity securities; the second section directed to entities within industries that *do* have such specialized accounting practices; and the last section devoted to consideration of entities having differing accounting practices.

DEFINITION OF EQUITY SECURITIES

The definitions set forth in the Statement are all self-explanatory and conventionally recognized. However, it is important to recognize all the component elements comprising equity securities as defined in the Statement, and for that purpose the definition (quoted verbatim) contained therein is:

> "Equity security" encompasses any instrument representing ownership shares (e.g., common, preferred, and other capital stock), or the right to acquire (e.g., warrants, rights, and call options) or dispose of (e.g., put options) ownership shares in an enterprise at fixed or determinable prices. The term does not encompass preferred stock that by its terms either must be redeemed by the issuing enterprise or is redeemable at the option of the investor, nor does it include treasury stock or convertible bonds.

ENTERPRISES IN INDUSTRIES NOT HAVING SPECIALIZED ACCOUNTING PRACTICES WITH RESPECT TO MARKETABLE SECURITIES

This chapter adopts the general format of FASB Statement No. 12 which sets forth the accounting standards of the Statement in three separate sections. This section deals exclusively with the standards applicable to those entities in industries not having specialized accounting practices with respect to marketable equity securities. For convenience in exposition, the standards applicable to such entities are further classified in the chapter as general standards applicable under all circumstances, and as consolidation and equity method standards that are applicable in circumstances indicated by the classification.[2]

---

[2] This classification is made solely for exposition purposes for this chapter; it does not appear in the Statement.

GENERAL STANDARDS

The following general accounting standards are applicable to all enterprises in industries not having specialized accounting practices with respect to marketable equity securities.

1. The carrying amount of a marketable equity securities portfolio shall be the lower of its aggregate cost or market value, determined at the balance sheet date. The amount by which aggregate cost of the portfolio exceeds market value shall be accounted for as the valuation allowance.
2. In the case of a classified balance sheet, marketable equity securities owned by an entity shall be grouped into separate portfolios according to the current or noncurrent classification of the securities for the purpose of comparing aggregate cost and market value to determine carrying amount.
3. In the case of an unclassified balance sheet, marketable equity securities shall, for the purpose of the Statement, be considered as noncurrent assets.
4. Realized gains and losses shall be included in the determination of net income of the period in which they occur.
5. Changes in the valuation allowance for a marketable equity securities portfolio included in current assets shall be included in the determination of net income of the period in which they occur.
6. Accumulated changes in the valuation allowance for a marketable equity securities portfolio included in noncurrent assets or in an unclassified balance sheet shall be included in the equity section of the balance sheet and shown separately.
7. If there is a change in the classification of a marketable equity security between current and noncurrent, the security shall be transferred between the corresponding portfolios at the lower of its cost or market value at date of transfer. If market value is less than cost, the market value shall become the new cost basis, and the difference shall be accounted for as if it were a realized loss and included in the determination of net income.
8. For those marketable equity securities for which the effect of a change in carrying amount is included in stockholders' equity rather than in net income (including marketable securities in unclassified balance sheets), a determination must be made as to whether or not a decline in market value below cost as of the balance sheet date of an individual security is other than temporary. If the decline is judged to be other than temporary, the cost basis of the individual security shall be written down to a new cost basis and the amount of the write-down shall be accounted for as a realized loss. The new cost basis shall not be changed for subsequent recoveries in market value.
9. Unrealized gains and losses on marketable equity securities, whether or not recognized in net income or included in the equity section of the balance sheet, shall be considered as timing differences, and the provisions of APB Opinion No. 11, "Accounting for Income Taxes," shall be applied in determining whether or not such net unrealized gain or loss shall be reduced by the applicable income tax effect. A tax effect shall be recognized on an unrealized capital loss only when there exists assurance beyond a reasonable doubt that the benefit will be realized by an offset of the loss against capital gains.

ILLUSTRATION AND EXPLANATION OF GENERAL ACCOUNTING STANDARDS FOR MARKETABLE EQUITY SECURITIES

The following annotations explain and illustrate the indicated elements comprehended in the general accounting standards for marketable equity securities.

Valuation Allowance

Separate valuation allowance accounts should be maintained for current and noncurrent portfolios. The balance in the accounts will represent the excess of the aggregate cost of the respective portfolios over their aggregate market values, and will always carry credit balances. When the aggregate market value of a portfolio increases to a point where it equals or exceeds the portfolio's aggregate cost, the portfolio will then be carried at aggregate cost, and the valuation allowance account will be eliminated.

Current and Noncurrent Classification of Securities

Classification of marketable equity securities into current and noncurrent assets generally depends upon management's intentions, and its ability to fulfill its intentions. Generally, if management intends the security to be available for conversion into cash for use in ordinary operations, and the security is readily marketable, it should be classified as current; all others should be classified as noncurrent.

Transfers Between Portfolios

The Statement requires that a new cost basis be established for a security transferred between current and noncurrent portfolios where the market value of the security is lower than its cost at the date of transfer. In such cases the adjustment should be made directly to the security account, and not to a separate valuation account.

Decline in Market Value Other Than Temporary

Where the market value of a noncurrent marketable equity security declines below cost, and the decline is determined to be other than temporary, the Statement requires that the cost basis of the security be written down to market, and the adjustment treated as a realized loss. In such cases the adjustment should be made directly to the security account, and not to a separate valuation account.

The Statement also prescribes that a new cost basis for such securities shall not be changed for subsequent recoveries in market value. However, a subsequent recovery will affect the *aggregate* market value of the portfolio in the same manner as any other security, and will be a factor in the comparison of the aggregate market value of the portfolio to its aggregate cost.

The term "other than temporary" is not synonymous with "permanent." Therefore, a decline in market value considered to be lengthy or protracted would fit the criterion of "other than temporary" for purposes of writing the cost down to market value.

Allocation of Income Taxes

Tax effects of timing differences arising from unrealized gains and losses on marketable securities which are included in the determination of net income for a period should be charged or credited to income tax expense for that period, and the related deferred income tax account should be classified as a current item in the balance sheet. Unrealized gains and losses on marketable securities which are charged or credited to stockholders' equity should be adjusted for any recognized tax effects of timing differences, and the related deferred income tax account should be classified as a noncurrent item in the balance sheet.

The Statement requires that a tax effect shall be recognized on an unrealized capital loss only where there exists assurance beyond a reasonable doubt that the benefit will be realized by an offset of the loss against capital gains. However, the determination as to whether or not the tax benefits of capital losses will ultimately be realized is extremely difficult to make because capital losses are not deductible as such for income tax purposes, but must be applied to offset capital gains. The problem is further complicated by the fact that income tax regulations permit a carryforward and carryback of unused capital losses. An appropriate determination, therefore, must be carefully formulated, and must take into consideration all of the positive actions and alternatives open to management in its forecast of future securities transactions.

GENERAL DISCLOSURE REQUIREMENTS

The Statement sets forth specific information with respect to marketable equity securities that must be disclosed either in the body of the financial statements or in accompanying notes. The disclosure requirements that follow are quoted verbatim from the Statement.

1. As of the date of each balance sheet presented, aggregate cost and market value (each segregated between current and noncurrent portfolios when a classified balance sheet is presented) with identification as to which is the carrying amount.
2. As of the date of the latest balance sheet presented, the following, segregated between current and noncurrent portfolios when a classified balance sheet is presented:
   (a) Gross unrealized gains representing the excess of market value over cost for all marketable equity securities in the portfolio having such an excess.
   (b) Gross unrealized losses representing the excess of cost over market value for all marketable equity securities in the portfolio having such an excess.
3. For each period for which an income statement is presented:
   (a) Net realized gain or loss included in the determination of net income.
   (b) The basis on which cost was determined in computing realized gain or loss (i.e., average cost or other method used).
   (c) The change in valuation allowances that has been included in the equity section of the balance sheet during the period and, when a classified balance sheet is presented, the amount of such change included in the determination of net income.

SUBSEQUENT EVENTS

Financial statements shall not be adjusted for realized gains or losses, or for changes in market prices with respect to marketable equity securities when such gains, losses, or changes occur after the date of the financial statements, but prior to their issuance (except for disclosure of adjustments made for a decline in market value determined to be other than temporary). However, significant net realized and net unrealized gains and losses arising after the date of the financial statements, but prior to their issuance, applicable to marketable equity securities owned at the date of the most recent balance sheet shall be disclosed.

ILLUSTRATION OF ACCOUNTING FOR MARKETABLE EQUITY SECURITIES

Model Case No. 1 is an example of an enterprise within an industry not having specialized accounting practices with respect to marketable equity securities, and it illustrates valuation methods, accounting procedures, and reporting requirements prescribed by FASB Statement No. 12.

MODEL CASE NO. 1

Bauer Development Company maintained two separate investment portfolios: one contained marketable equity securities purchased for the purpose of temporarily employing excess funds, and the other was made up of similar securities acquired in connection with an ongoing investment program. Bauer accounted for marketable equity securities in accordance with the provisions of FASB Statement No. 12 and, consequently, the two portfolios were classified as current and noncurrent, respectively, on Bauer's balance sheet.

Schedule 1 sets forth cost, the market value, and the required valuation allowance for each individual security contained in the portfolios at December 31, 19x1.

SCHEDULE OF MARKETABLE SECURITIES

December 31, 19x1

	Cost	Market Value at Quoted Market Price	Valuation Allowance Excess (Deficiency) of Cost Over Market
CURRENT PORTFOLIO			
Allied Chemical	47,000	34,120	12,880
American Telephone & Telegraph	61,000	56,870	4,130
Eastman Kodak	75,000	43,120	31,880
General Electric	43,000	57,250	(14,250)
Memorex	27,000	34,500	(7,500)
	253,000	225,860	27,140
NONCURRENT PORTFOLIO			
Baltimore Gas & Electric	24,000	28,500	(4,500)
Bethlehem Steel	25,000	29,370	(4,370)
Consolidated Edison	30,000	22,870	7,130
Maryland Railroad	68,000	66,000	2,000
Mesabi Trust	16,000	9,370	6,630
National Starch and Chemical	72,000	68,370	3,630
	235,000	224,480	10,520

SCHEDULE 1

At December 31, 19x1 Bauer carried two separate security valuation allowances on its books. The valuation allowance of $27,140 for securities in the current portfolio had developed from net charges to current operations; and the allowance of $10,520 for securities in the noncurrent portfolio evolved from net charges to an account captioned "Stockholders' Equity-Net Unrealized Loss on Marketable Equity Securities." This account was reported separately in the shareholders' equity section of Bauer's balance sheet and was precisely equivalent in amount to the valuation allowance account for noncurrent marketable equity securities. The market value of some of the securities in both portfolios exceeded their respective cost. However, since FASB Statement No. 12 requires that a marketable equity security portfolio be carried and reported at the lower of its *aggregate* cost or market value, the excess of market over cost of individual securities was offset by the excess of cost over market of other securities, and the net excess or deficiency of cost over market was equivalent to the difference between aggregate cost and aggregate market value.

Transactions in Marketable Equity Securities in 19x2 and 19x3

During the years 19x2 and 19x3 the following transactions occurred in connection with the marketable equity securities portfolios.

Year Ended December 31, 19x2

CURRENT PORTFOLIO
Purchases
1,000 shares of E. I. duPont de Nemours & Company at 95

Sales
1,000 shares of American Telephone and Telegraph Company at 65-7/8, resulting in a gain of $4,870
1,000 shares of General Electric Company at 41, resulting in a loss of $2,000

Valuation Allowance
At year end the excess of aggregate cost over aggregate market value was $48,510, which reflected an increase of $21,370 in such excess during the year.

NONCURRENT PORTFOLIO
Purchases
1,000 shares of Hewlett-Packard Company at 87

Sales
1,000 shares of Baltimore Gas & Electric Company at 25-7/8, resulting in a gain of $1,800
1,000 shares of Mesabi Trust at 13-7/8, resulting in a loss of $2,130.

Write-Down
During 19x2 the market price of Maryland Railroad Company shares dropped from 66 at the beginning of the year to 26 at year end. At that time it was determined by management that the decline in market value was other than temporary and consequently the security was written down from its original cost of $68,000 to a new cost basis of $26,000, resulting in a $42,000 loss.

Valuation Allowance

At December 31, the excess of aggregate cost over aggregate market value was $7,125, which reflected a decrease in such excess during the year in the amount of $3,395.

Year Ended December 31, 19x3

CURRENT PORTFOLIO

Purchases

1,000 shares of Babcock & Wilcox Company at 62
1,000 shares of Honeywell, Inc. at 49

Sales

1,000 shares of Allied Chemical Corporation at 50, resulting in a gain of $3,000
1,000 shares of Eastman-Kodak Company at 60, resulting in a loss of $15,000

Transfer to Noncurrent Portfolio

On January 2, 19x3 management decided to increase its long-term investment in marketable equity securities by transferring 1,000 shares of duPont de Nemours & Company from its current portfolio to its noncurrent holdings. The stock was transferred between the portfolios at the lower of its $95,000 cost and its $90,000 market value, resulting in a loss of $5,000 that was treated as a realized loss.

Valuation Allowance

During the year the excess of cost over market value of the portfolio decreased from $48,510 to $1,500, reflecting an unrealized gain of $47,010.

NONCURRENT PORTFOLIO

Purchases

1,000 shares of Monsanto Company at 59
1,000 shares of Wells-Fargo at 28

Sales

1,000 shares of Maryland Railroad Company at 20, resulting in a loss of $6,000
1,000 shares of National Starch & Chemical Company at 70, resulting in a loss of $2,000

Transfer from Current Portfolio

1,000 shares of duPont de Nemours & Company transferred from the current portfolio at a stipulated cost of 90.

Valuation Allowance

At December 31, 19x3 the excess of cost over market value of the portfolio was $8,375, which reflected an unrealized loss of $1,250 during the year.

Summary of Marketable Equity Security Transactions

Schedules 2 and 3 are summaries of marketable equity security transactions engaged in by Bauer during 19x2 and 19x3, and they reflect both the realized and the unrealized gain or loss developed from sales, write-downs, transfers between portfolios, and changes in the valuation allowance occurring during the two years.

SCHEDULE OF TRANSACTIONS IN CURRENT PORTFOLIO

Security	December 31, 19x1			Transactions in 19x2				December 31, 19x2			
	Cost	Market	Excess of Cost Over Market	Purchased (Cost)	Sold (Sales Price)	Transferred to Non-Current Portfolio (at Cost)	Realized Gain (Loss)	Cost	Market	Unrealized (Gain) Loss	Excess of Cost Over Market
Allied Chemical	47,000	34,120	12,880	–	–	–	–	47,000	35,370	(1,250)	11,630
American T & T	61,000	56,870	4,130	–	(65,870)	–	4,870	–	–	(4,130)	–
Dupont	–	–	–	95,000	–	–	–	95,000	90,000	5,000	5,000
Eastman-Kodak	75,000	43,120	31,880	–	–	–	–	75,000	43,370	(250)	31,630
General Electric	43,000	57,250	(14,250)	–	(41,000)	–	(2,000)	–	–	14,250	–
Memorex	27,000	34,500	(7,500)	–	–	–	–	27,000	26,750	7,750	250
	253,000	225,860	27,140	95,000	(106,870)	—	2,870	244,000	195,490	21,370	48,510

Security	December 31, 19x2			Transactions in 19x3				December 31, 19x3			
	Cost	Market	Excess of Cost Over Market	Purchased (Cost)	Sold (Sales Price)	Transferred to Non-Current Portfolio (at Cost)	Realized Gain (Loss)	Cost	Market	Unrealized (Gain) Loss	Excess of Cost Over Market
Allied Chemical	47,000	35,370	11,630	–	(50,000)	–	3,000	–	–	(11,630)	–
Babcock & Wilcox	–	–	–	62,000	–	–	–	62,000	60,625	1,375	1,375
Dupont	95,000	90,000	5,000	–	–	(90,000)	(5,000)	–	–	(5,000)	–
Eastman-Kodak	75,000	43,370	31,630	–	(60,000)	–	(15,000)	–	–	(31,630)	–
Honeywell	–	–	–	49,000	–	–	–	49,000	47,875	1,125	1,125
Memorex	27,000	26,750	250	–	–	–	–	27,000	28,000	(1,250)	(1,000)
	244,000	195,490	48,510	111,000	(110,000)	(90,000)	(17,000)	138,000	136,500	(47,010)	1,500

SCHEDULE 2

SCHEDULE OF TRANSACTIONS IN NONCURRENT PORTFOLIO

Security	December 31, 19x1			Transactions in 19x2				December 31, 19x2			
	Cost	Market	Excess of Cost Over Market	Purchased (Cost)	Sold (Sales Price)	Transferred from Current Portfolio (at Cost)	Realized Gain (Loss)	Cost	Market	Unrealized (Gain) Loss	Excess of Cost Over Market
Baltimore G & E	24,000	28,500	(4,500)	–	(25,800)	–	1,800	–	–	4,500	–
Bethlehem Steel	25,000	29,370	(4,370)	–	–	–	–	25,000	29,500	(130)	(4,500)
Con. Edison	30,000	22,870	7,130	–	–	–	–	30,000	21,625	1,245	8,375
Hewlett-Packard	–	–	–	87,000	–	–	–	87,000	85,500	1,500	1,500
Maryland RR	68,000	66,000	2,000	–	–	–	(42,000)	26,000	26,000	(2,000)	–
Mesabi Trust	16,000	9,370	6,630	–	(13,870)	–	(2,130)	–	–	(6,630)	–
National Starch	72,000	68,370	3,630	–	–	–	–	72,000	70,250	(1,880)	1,750
	235,000	224,480	10,520	87,000	(39,670)	–	(42,330)	240,000	232,875	(3,395)	7,125

Security	December 31, 19x2			Transactions in 19x3				December 31, 19x3			
	Cost	Market	Excess of Cost Over Market	Purchased (Cost)	Sold (Sales Price)	Transferred from Current Portfolio (at Cost)	Realized Gain (Loss)	Cost	Market	Unrealized (Gain) Loss	Excess of Cost Over Market
Bethlehem Steel	25,000	29,500	(4,500)	–	–	–	–	25,000	29,000	500	(4,000)
Con. Edison	30,000	21,625	8,375	–	–	–	–	30,000	23,875	(2,250)	6,125
Dupont	–	–	–	–	–	90,000	–	90,000	91,000	(1,000)	(1,000)
Hewlett-Packard	87,000	85,500	1,500	–	–	–	–	87,000	86,000	(500)	1,000
Maryland RR	26,000	26,000	–	–	(20,000)	–	(6,000)	–	–	–	–
Monsanto	–	–	–	59,000	–	–	–	59,000	50,500	8,500	8,500
National Starch	72,000	70,250	1,750	–	(70,000)	–	(2,000)	–	–	(1,750)	–
Wells-Fargo	–	–	–	28,000	–	–	–	28,000	30,250	(2,250)	(2,250)
	240,000	232,875	7,125	87,000	(90,000)	90,000	(8,000)	319,000	310,625	1,250	8,375

SCHEDULE 3

Accounting for Marketable Equity Security Transactions

The entries made by Bauer during the two-year period to account for the transactions in marketable equity securities were as follows:

<u>CURRENT PORTFOLIO</u>
(Schedule 2)
<u>Year Ended December 31, 19x2</u>

	Debit	Credit
(1) Marketable equity securities—current	95,000	
Cash		95,000
To record purchase of 1,000 shares of duPont de Nemours & Company.		
(2) Cash	106,870	
Marketable equity securities—current		104,000
Income from sale of marketable equity securities		2,870
To record sale of 1,000 shares each of American Telephone and Telegraph Company and General Electric Company.		
(3) Unrealized loss on marketable equity securities	21,370	
Valuation allowance—marketable equity securities—current		21,370
To record increase in valuation account at December 31, 19x2		

<u>Year Ended December 31, 19x3</u>

	Debit	Credit
(1) Marketable equity securities—current	111,000	
Cash		111,000
To record purchase of 1,000 shares each of Babcock & Wilcox Company and Honeywell, Inc.		
(2) Cash	110,000	
Loss on sale of marketable equity securities	12,000	
Marketable equity securities—current		122,000
To record sale of 1,000 shares each of Allied Chemical Corporation and Eastman-Kodak Company.		
(3) Marketable equity securities—noncurrent	90,000	
Unrealized loss on marketable equity securities	5,000	
Marketable equity securities—current		95,000
To record transfer of 1,000 shares of duPont de Nemours & Company from current to noncurrent portfolio at cost, and to record unrealized loss for difference between original cost and market value at date of transfer.		

	Debit	Credit
(4) Valuation allowance—marketable equity securities—current	47,010	
Unrealized gain on marketable equity securities		47,010
To record decrease in valuation account at December 31, 19x3.		

NONCURRENT PORTFOLIO
(Schedule 3)
Year Ended December 31, 19x2

	Debit	Credit
(1) Marketable equity securities—noncurrent	87,000	
Cash		87,000
To record purchase of 1,000 shares of Hewlett-Packard Company.		
(2) Cash	39,670	
Loss on sale of marketable equity securities	330	
Marketable equity securities—noncurrent		40,000
To record sale of 1,000 shares each of Baltimore Gas & Electric Company and Mesabi Trust.		
(3) Unrealized loss on marketable equity securities	42,000	
Marketable equity securities—noncurrent		42,000
To adjust cost basis of 1,000 shares of Maryland Railroad Company to make it equivalent to market value at January 1, 19x2.		
(4) Valuation allowance—marketable equity securities—noncurrent	3,395	
Stockholders' equity—net unrealized loss on marketable equity securities		3,395
To record decrease in valuation account at December 31, 19x2.		

Year Ended December 31, 19x3

	Debit	Credit
(1) Marketable equity securities—noncurrent	87,000	
Cash		87,000
To record purchase of 1,000 shares each of Monsanto Company and Wells-Fargo.		
(2) Cash	90,000	
Loss on sale of marketable equity securities	8,000	
Marketable equity securities—noncurrent		98,000
To record sale of 1,000 shares each of Maryland Railroad Company and National Starch & Chemical Company.		

(3) Stockholders' equity—net unrealized loss on
    marketable equity securities   1,250
        Valuation allowance—marketable equity
        securities—noncurrent   1,250
    To record increase in valuation account at
    December 31, 19x3.

Accounting for Deferred Income Taxes

Management of Bauer Development Company determined that annual changes in the valuation allowance account for its current portfolio were timing differences and that income taxes, at current rates, should be allocated to such differences. Management based its conclusions on the assumption that the high rate of turnover in the current portfolio would preclude long-term capital gains treatment of taxable gains and losses, and subject them to current tax rates applicable to ordinary income.[3]

Further, management determined that it could control the sale of profitable securities in a manner that would absorb all capital losses sustained from sales of securities in the current portfolio, and thus assure the tax benefits from such losses beyond any reasonable doubt. At the same time, management determined that the long-term nature of the investment program for its noncurrent portfolio precluded reasonable assurance that tax benefits would be realized from the capital losses indicated by the noncurrent valuation allowance account and, therefore, no allocation of income taxes should be made in connection with the noncurrent portfolio.

At December 31, 19x1 deferred income tax debits in the amount of $13,570 had been accumulated on the current portfolio valuation allowance account, and at the end of 19x2 and 19x3, respectively, Bauer made the following entries to adjust its deferred income tax debits account for changes occurring in the current valuation allowance account, as indicated in Schedule 2.[4]

December 31, 19x2

	Debit	Credit
Deferred income tax debits	10,685	
Income tax expense		10,685
To record tax effects of change in valuation allowance of current marketable equity securities portfolio for year ended December 31, 19x2.		

December 31, 19x3

	Debit	Credit
Income tax expense	23,505	
Deferred income tax debits		23,505
To record tax effects of change in valuation allowance of current marketable equity securities portfolio for year ended December 31, 19x3.		

---

[3] The example of the *noncurrent* portfolio in this case study also indicates a high rate of turnover, but the activity in the portfolio was deliberately accelerated for illustrative purposes. Generally, a long-term investment portfolio is relatively inactive.

[4] The method of accounting for deferred income taxes on timing differences illustrated in the case study is based on *net change* in the valuation allowance for the current portfolio of marketable equity securities. Bauer could have accounted for the tax effect of the timing differences created by each individual security.

Disclosure of Transactions in Marketable Equity Securities

The following balance sheet, statement of income and retained earnings, and notes to the financial statements are extracted from Bauer's annual report for 19x3 for the purpose of illustrating disclosure of transactions in marketable equity securities for the years ended December 31, 19x3 and 19x2:

BAUER DEVELOPMENT COMPANY
BALANCE SHEET

	December 31,	
	19x3	19x2
ASSETS		
Current		
Cash	23,885	21,566
Marketable equity securities—at lower of cost or market—(Cost: 19x3, $138,000; 19x2, $244,000)	136,500	195,490
Accounts and notes receivable	165,152	149,034
Inventories	106,498	91,659
Deferred income taxes	750	24,255
Other current assets	22,039	21,848
Total current assets	454,824	503,852
Property, plant and equipment—(net of accumulated depreciation—19x3, $98,596; 19x2, $55,677)	230,059	222,711
Other		
Investment in marketable equity securities— at lower of cost or market—(Cost: 19x3, $319,000; 19x2, $240,000)	310,625	232,875
	995,508	959,438

LIABILITIES AND STOCKHOLDERS' EQUITY

Current Liabilities		
Notes and accounts payable	75,449	82,840
Current maturities of long-term debt	12,880	10,519
Accrued expenses	109,351	94,006
Total current liabilities	197,680	187,365
Long-term debt	263,422	250,775
Stockholders' Equity		
Common stock—par value $100—authorized and issued: 4,000 shares	400,000	400,000
Net unrealized loss on marketable equity securities	(8,375)	(7,125)
Retained earnings	142,781	128,423
Total stockholders' equity	534,406	521,298
	995,508	959,438

BAUER DEVELOPMENT COMPANY
STATEMENT OF INCOME AND RETAINED EARNINGS

	For Year Ended December 31,	
	19x3	19x2
Net Sales	1,263,975	1,140,682
Cost of sales	1,014,027	875,114
	249,948	265,568
Selling and administrative expenses	129,208	83,561
Interest expense	21,213	17,458
Net realized loss (gain) on marketable equity securities	(22,010)	60,830
	128,411	161,849
Income before income taxes	121,537	103,719
Provision for income taxes	59,179	49,391
Net income	62,358	54,328
Retained earnings—beginning of year	128,423	114,095
	190,781	168,423
Dividends paid	48,000	40,000
Retained earnings—end of year	142,781	128,423
Earnings per common share	15.59	13.58

BAUER DEVELOPMENT COMPANY

NOTES TO FINANCIAL STATEMENTS

December 31, 19x3

Note 1—Summary of Significant Accounting Policies

* * * * * * * * *

Investments in Securities

Investments in securities are carried at the lower of aggregate cost or market determined at the end of the year. Security transactions are accounted for on the date they are purchased or sold and realized gains or losses are determined on the basis of specific identification of the securities sold. Dividend income is recorded on the ex-dividend date. The company maintains two separate investment portfolios each made up exclusively of marketable equity securities. The portfolio of securities purchased for temporary investment of excess funds is classified as a current asset and the portfolio containing securities purchased in connection with the continuing investment program of the company is classified as noncurrent. A valuation allowance has been established for each portfolio, respectively, to reduce cost to market value. Changes in the valuation allowance for the current portfolio are included in the determination of current net income and changes in the valuation allowance for the noncurrent portfolio are recorded in stockholders' equity.

* * * * * * * *

Note 5—Marketable Equity Securities

The results of transactions in the current and noncurrent portfolios of marketable equity securities, and the changes in their respective valuation allowances, are shown in the following tabulation for the years ended December 31, 19x3 and 19x2:

	19x3	19x2
Net Realized Gain (Loss) on Marketable Equity Securities Included in Determination of Net Income		
Current Portfolio		
Net gain (loss) on sales of securities	(12,000)	2,870
Net (loss) on transfer of securities to noncurrent portfolio	(5,000	—
Net gain (loss) from (increases) decreases in valuation allowance	47,010	(21,370)
	30,010	(18,500)
Noncurrent Portfolio		
Net gain (loss) on sale of securities	(8,000)	(330)
(Loss) from write-down of security from cost to market	—	(42,000)
	(8,000)	(42,330)
Net realized gain (loss) included in determination of net income	22,010	(60,830)
Changes in Valuation Allowance Included in Stockholders' Equity Section of Balance Sheet		
Balance at beginning of year	7,125	10,520
Increase (decrease) in valuation allowance for noncurrent portfolio	1,250	(3,395)
Balance at end of year	8,375	7,125

Gross unrealized gains and losses representing the excess of market over cost and the excess of cost over market, respectively, are shown in the following tabulation for the years ended December 31, 19x3 and 19x2:

	19x3	19x2
Gross Unrealized Losses		
Current portfolio	2,500	48,510
Noncurrent portfolio	15,625	11,625
	18,125	60,135

Gross Unrealized Gains

Current portfolio	1,000	—
Noncurrent portfolio	7,250	4,500
	8,250	4,500

* * * * * * * *

Note 7—Income Taxes

Provision for deferred income taxes reflects the effects of timing differences in computing income for financial reporting and income tax purposes. Such differences have occurred in the current reporting period from nontaxable gains and losses developed from changes in the valuation allowance for the current portfolio of marketable equity securities which were included in the determination of net income for financial reporting purposes. The nature of income tax expense reported for the years ended December 31, 19x3 and 19x2 follows:

	19x3	19x2
Income taxes currently payable	35,674	60,076
Deferred income taxes	23,505	(10,685)
	59,179	49,391

* * * * * * * *

CONSOLIDATION STANDARDS

The following standards are applicable to the consolidation policy of entities in industries that do not follow specialized accounting practices with respect to marketable equity securities.

1. The current portfolios of entities that are consolidated in financial statements shall be treated as a single consolidated portfolio for the comparison of aggregate cost and market value.
2. The noncurrent portfolios of entities that are consolidated in financial statements shall be treated as a single consolidated portfolio for the comparison of aggregate cost and market value.
3. The portfolios of marketable equity securities owned by an entity (subsidiary or investee) that is accounted for by the equity method shall not be combined with the portfolios of marketable equity securities owned by any other entity included in the financial statements. However, such an entity is, itself, subject to the requirements of the Statement.

ILLUSTRATION AND EXPLANATION OF CONSOLIDATION STANDARDS FOR PORTFOLIOS OF MARKETABLE EQUITY SECURITIES

Marketable equity securities accounted for by the equity method and owned by an entity in an industry not having specialized accounting practices do not come under the provisions of FASB Statement No. 12. However, the Statement does specifically prohibit combining such securities with the portfolios of marketable equity securities owned by any other entity included in consolidated financial statements. The Statement footnotes the fact that this prohibition constitutes an exception to paragraph 19 of APB Opinion No. 18, which states that an investor's net income for the period and its stockholder's equity at the end of the period are the same whether an investment in a subsidiary is accounted for under the equity method or the subsidiary is consolidated. The exception operates in those cases in which a subsidiary accounted for under the equity method has a net unrealized gain or loss on a portfolio of marketable equity securities that would serve to offset the net unrealized gain or loss on a comparable portfolio of marketable equity securities of the parent. In such cases the consolidated net income of the parent would not be the same as net income reported in unconsolidated financial statements.

Model Case No. 2 illustrates accounting for marketable equity securities in both consolidated and unconsolidated financial statements of entities in industries not having specialized accounting practices. The case study also demonstrates the differences in net income of the parent company resulting from preparing consolidated as opposed to parent company financial statements.

MODEL CASE NO. 2

In 19x1 Reynolds, Inc. adopted a policy of temporarily investing excess operating funds in marketable equity securities, and it directed its wholly-owned subsidiary, Hopkins & Company, to pursue a similar policy. Accordingly, both the parent company and its subsidiary engaged in the purchase of marketable equity securities in 19x1, and at the end of the year both held portfolios of such securities. Schedule 4 sets forth the cost, market value, and excess or deficiency of cost over market at December 31, 19x1 for the individual securities in each portfolio, respectively, and also shows the effect of combining the two portfolios for the purpose of presentation in consolidated financial statements.

Schedule 4 indicates that the differences between cost and market value of the two respective portfolios resulted in an unrealized gain of $10,500 for Reynolds, Inc. and an unrealized loss of $14,000 for Hopkins & Company. In separate financial statements Reynolds could not reflect its unrealized gain in income, but Hopkins, on the other hand, would be required to report its unrealized loss. Therefore, if the subsidiary were accounted for under the equity method by the parent, the parent's net income would be $5,250 less than it would be if the subsidiary were consolidated. This difference of $5,250 arises from the fact that in consolidated statements the parent's unrealized gain of $10,500 would partially offset the subsidiary's unrealized loss of $14,000.

SCHEDULE OF SEPARATE AND COMBINED PORTFOLIOS OF MARKETABLE EQUITY SECURITIES — DECEMBER 31, 19x1

Security	Reynolds, Inc.			Hopkins & Company			Consolidated Portfolio		
	Cost	Market	Excess (Deficiency) of Cost Over Market	Cost	Market	Excess (Deficiency) of Cost Over Market	Cost	Market	Excess (Deficiency) of Cost Over Market
Aetna Life Insurance Company	33,875	35,500	(1,625)	—	—	—	33,875	35,500	(1,625)
Allied Chemical Corporation	—	—	—	48,875	46,375	2,500	48,875	46,375	2,500
American Cyanamid Company	23,375	21,625	1,750	23,375	21,625	1,750	46,750	43,250	3,500
Borg-Warner Corporation	26,500	27,500	(1,000)	—	—	—	26,500	27,500	(1,000)
Dow Chemical Company	46,000	48,000	(2,000)	23,000	24,000	(1,000)	69,000	72,000	(3,000)
Exxon Corporation	43,625	48,375	(4,750)	—	—	—	43,625	48,375	(4,750)
Hormel & Company	23,875	24,125	(250)	—	—	—	23,875	24,125	(250)
Lukens Steel Company	28,500	25,500	3,000	14,250	12,750	1,500	42,750	38,250	4,500
Moore-McCormack Resources	27,875	28,000	(125)	—	—	—	27,875	28,000	(125)
Pacific Petroleums, Ltd.	—	—	—	36,000	29,250	6,750	36,000	29,250	6,750
Raytheon Company	34,000	33,000	1,000	17,000	16,500	500	51,000	49,500	1,500
RCA Corporation	—	—	—	24,365	20,865	3,500	24,365	20,865	3,500
Scott-Foresman & Company	27,875.	30,625	(2,750)	—	—	—	27,875	30,625	(2,750)
Sears, Roebuck & Company	23,500	26,500	(3,000)	11,750	13,250	(1,500)	35,250	39,750	(4,500)
Texaco, Inc.	49,125	48,875	250	98,250	97,750	500	147,375	146,625	750
Xerox Corporation	42,000	43,000	(1,000)	21,000	21,500	(500)	63,000	64,500	(1,500)
	430,125	440,625	(10,500)	317,865	303,865	14,000	747,990	744,490	3,500

SCHEDULE 4

For the year ended December 31, 19x1 the operating income, before considering unrealized gains and losses from marketable equity securities, was $150,000 and $80,000 for Reynolds, Inc. and Hopkins & Company, respectively. Schedule 5 sets forth the lower section of the income statement required for parent company, subsidiary, and consolidated financial statements, respectively, and indicates the difference between the net income reported in consolidated statements and that reported in only the parent company statements.

REPORTING GAINS AND LOSSES ON MARKETABLE EQUITY SECURITIES
IN PARENT, SUBSIDIARY, AND CONSOLIDATED FINANCIAL STATEMENTS

	Reynolds, Inc.	Hopkins & Company	Consolidated
Operating income	150,000	80,000	230,000
Unrealized (loss) on marketable equity securities	—	(14,000)	(3,500)
Increase in equity in subsidiary	33,000	—	—
Income before income taxes	183,000	66,000	226,500
Provision for Income Taxes			
Current	75,000	40,000	115,000
Deferred	—	(7,000)	(1,750)
	75,000	33,000	113,250
Net income	108,000	33,000	113,250

SCHEDULE 5

ENTERPRISES IN INDUSTRIES HAVING SPECIALIZED ACCOUNTING PRACTICES WITH RESPECT TO MARKETABLE SECURITIES

This section of the chapter deals with standards applicable to enterprises in industries having specialized accounting practices with respect to marketable equity securities. Generally, FASB Statement No. 12 does not alter any industry's specialized accounting practice. However, it does set forth specific accounting standards for entities within such industries in connection with:

(a) accounting procedures for entities that carry marketable equity securities at *cost;*
(b) accounting and reporting procedures for securities where a decline in their market value is determined to be other than temporary; and
(c) interperiod allocation of income taxes.

CONTINUITY IN THE EXPOSITION OF ACCOUNTING STANDARDS

There is little or no continuity in the text of FASB Statement No. 12 because of excessive back-, forward-, and cross-referencing of elements in the respective accounting standards. This is especially evident in the section of the Statement concerning industries having specialized accounting practices with respect to marketable securities where, in some instances, basic principles are established by footnote, and in others the essentials of the accounting standards are established with such language as: ". . . the provisions of paragraphs 7-9 shall be applied with the exception of the third sentence of paragraph 9."

This section of the chapter sets forth the standards in logical continuity; where feasible, they are quoted verbatim but, where necessary, they are paraphrased from the Statement.

STANDARDS APPLICABLE TO ENTITIES THAT CARRY MARKETABLE EQUITY SECURITIES AT COST

The following standards apply only to those entities that carry marketable equity securities at *cost*. They do *not* apply to entities in any industry that carry marketable equity securities on any other basis, where such practice is accepted in the industry.

GENERAL STANDARDS

1. The carrying amount of a marketable equity securities portfolio shall be the lower of its aggregate cost or market value, determined at the balance sheet date. The amount by which aggregate cost of the portfolio exceeds market value shall be accounted for as the valuation allowance.
2. Marketable equity securities owned by an entity, in the case of a classified balance sheet, shall be grouped into separate portfolios according to the current or noncurrent classification of the securities for the purpose of comparing aggregate cost and market value to determine carrying amount.
3. In the case of an unclassified balance sheet, marketable equity securities, for the purposes of the Statement, shall be considered as noncurrent assets.
4. Gains and losses, whether realized or unrealized, for marketable equity securities will be reported in accordance with the entity's specialized industry accounting practice.
5. For securities considered to be marketable securities by the entity's specialized industry and for which the effect of a change in carrying amount is included in stockholders' equity rather than in net income (including marketable securities in unclassified balance sheets), a determination must be made as to whether a decline in market value below cost as of the balance sheet date of an individual security is other than temporary. If the decline is judged to be other than temporary, the cost basis of the individual security shall be written down to a new cost basis and the amount of the write-down shall be accounted for as a realized loss. The new cost basis shall not be changed for subsequent recoveries in market value.
6. Unrealized gains and losses on securities considered to be marketable securities by the entity's specialized industry, whether recognized in net income or included in the equity section of the balance sheet, shall be considered as timing differences, and the provisions of APB Opinion No. 11, "Accounting for Income Taxes," shall be applied in determining whether or not such net unrealized gain or loss shall be reduced by the applicable income tax effect. A tax effect shall be recognized on an unrealized capital loss only when there exists assurance beyond a reasonable doubt that the benefit will be realized by an offset of the loss against capital gains.

CONSOLIDATION STANDARDS

1. The portfolios of entities that are consolidated in financial statements and that follow the same specialized industry accounting practices with respect to market-

able equity securities shall be treated as a single portfolio for the comparison of aggregate cost and market value.

2. The portfolios of marketable equity securities owned by an entity (subsidiary or investee) that is accounted for by the equity method shall not be combined with the portfolios of marketable equity securities owned by any other entity included in the financial statements. However, such an entity is, itself, subject to the requirements of the Statement.

DISCLOSURE

Entities having securities considered to be marketable securities by the entity's specialized industry that do not include unrealized gains and losses, as defined by that industry, in the determination of net income, but do include them in the equity section of the balance sheet, shall disclose the following information, either in the body of the financial statements or in the accompanying notes:

(a) Gross unrealized gains and gross unrealized losses as of the date of the latest balance sheet presented.

(b) Change in net unrealized gain or loss (the amount by which equity has been increased or decreased as a result of unrealized gains and losses) for each period for which an income statement is presented.

SUBSEQUENT EVENTS

Financial statements shall not be adjusted for realized gains or losses or for changes in market prices with respect to marketable equity securities when such gains or losses or changes occur after the date of the financial statements, but prior to their issuance, except for disclosure of adjustments made for a decline in market value determined to be other than temporary. However, significant net realized and net unrealized gains and losses arising after the date of the financial statements, but prior to their issuance, applicable to marketable equity securities owned at the date of the most recent balance sheet, shall be disclosed.

EXPLANATION OF ACCOUNTING STANDARDS FOR MARKETABLE EQUITY SECURITIES

The accounting standards for marketable equity securities, applicable to those entities that carry such securities at *cost* and are within industries that have specialized accounting practices, are almost precisely the same as those applicable to entities that are within industries that do *not* have specialized accounting practices. The major difference is that entities within industries having specialized accounting practices are permitted to report realized and unrealized gains and losses in accordance with the industry's practice. Such entities also are not required by the Statement to report gains and losses from transfers from one portfolio to another.

The explanations for valuation allowances, current and noncurrent classification of securities, declines in market value other than temporary, and allocation of income taxes set forth in the first section of the chapter apply to entities discussed in that section, and to those exposed in this section in precisely the same manner.

It is important to note, however, that all the foregoing standards apply only to *equity* securities except the standards for reporting declines in market values determined to be other than temporary, and the interperiod allocation of income taxes. The last two standards apply to all securities considered to be marketable securities by the respective specialized industry, whether or not they are *equity* securities.

ILLUSTRATION OF ACCOUNTING FOR MARKETABLE EQUITY SECURITIES

Model Case No. 1 in the preceding section of the chapter can be used as an illustration of accounting for marketable equity secuirities by entities that carry them at cost and are within industries that have specialized accounting practices with respect to such securities, as well as for entities that are *not* within such industries. The only differences that could develop in the applicability of the illustrated accounting procedures to both types of entities could be that the entity in the specialized industry would be permitted to record gains and losses in some other manner, and *not* be required to record gains and losses on reclassification of securities between current and noncurrent portfolios, in accordance with the practices acceptable in that industry. Otherwise the accounting standards are identical.

ENTERPRISES THAT INCLUDE ENTITIES WHOSE ACCEPTED ACCOUNTING PRACTICES DIFFER WITH RESPECT TO MARKETABLE SECURITIES

FASB Statement No. 12 was not formulated for the purpose of prescribing accounting standards for entities in industries having specialized accounting practices for marketable securities, except where such entities carry marketable equity securities at cost. However, to insure uniformity in consolidation policies for combining entities within and without such specialized industries, the Board set forth the following accounting standards and disclosure requirements in connection with consolidated financial statements.

ACCOUNTING STANDARDS FOR CONSOLIDATION OF ENTITIES HAVING DIFFERING ACCOUNTING PRACTICES

1. If an investee accounted for by the equity method or a subsidiary follows accepted accounting practices that are different from those of the parent or investor with respect to securities considered to be marketable securities by the specialized industry comprehending the investee or subsidiary, those practices shall be retained in the consolidated or parent company financial statements in which those entities are included. As an exception to this requirement, if it is the practice of the parent or investor to include realized gains and losses in the determination of net income, or would so include them if present, the accounting treatment of a subsidiary or an investee that does not follow such practice shall be conformed to that of the parent or investor in that particular respect in consolidated or parent company financial statements.
2. If the parent company in a consolidation follows specialized industry accounting practices with respect to marketable securities, but two or more consolidated subsidiaries do not (and hence are subject to the standards applicable to enterprises not having specialized accounting practices), the current and noncurrent portfolios of marketable *equity* securities of such subsidiaries shall be consolidated as separate current and noncurrent portfolios, exclusive of the portfolio of the parent company, for the purpose of establishing their individual carrying value at the lower of aggregate cost or market value of their respective portfolios.

DISCLOSURE

If the consolidated financial statements reflect more than one accepted practice of accounting for marketable securities, the disclosures required by the Statement and those encompassed by specialized industry practice, as applicable, shall be disclosed either in the body of the financial statements or in the accompanying notes for the marketable securities accounted for under each such practice.

EXPLANATION OF ACCOUNTING STANDARDS FOR CONSOLIDATION ENTITIES HAVING DIFFERING ACCOUNTING PRACTICES

The accounting standards and disclosure requirements set forth in this section of the chapter are self-explanatory and readily understandable. However, it is important to note that the first of the standards for entities having differing accounting practices applies to marketable securities as that term is used in the particular industry concerned, whether or not they are equity securities, while the second standard deals only with marketable *equity* securities.

ILLUSTRATION OF THE CONSOLIDATION OF ENTITIES HAVING DIFFERING ACCOUNTING PRACTICES

While the accounting standards for consolidating entities having differing accounting practices are clear and precise, it is difficult to illustrate their general applicability because of the multiplicity of industries that follow specialized accounting practices with respect to marketable securities.

Model Case No. 3 illustrates a consolidation where the parent is a finance company subject to the provisions of FASB Statement No. 12, and the subsidiaries and an equity method investee are stock life insurance companies having specialized accounting practices acceptable in the life insurance industry.

MODEL CASE NO. 3

Federated Credit Corporation is a commercial loan company whose wholly-owned subsidiaries include several stock life insurance companies. Federated comes under the provisions of FASB Statement No. 12 and, since it has an unclassified balance sheet, its marketable equity securities portfolio is classified as noncurrent and carried at the lower of aggregate cost of market value, and changes in the valuation allowance for the portfolio are reflected in shareholders' equity. In accordance with accepted practice, the life insurance subsidiaries carry marketable securities at market value.

The following financial statements and notes thereto are extracted from Federated's 19x2 annual report.[5]

---

[5] The format of the statements and notes illustrated in this case study follows that of the actual annual report published by a similar company.

FEDERATED CREDIT CORPORATION

Consolidated Balance Sheets

	December 31,	
	19x2	19x1

Assets

	19x2	19x1
Cash	118,352	87,293
Investment in marketable securities	417,013	336,914
Finance and related receivables	3,617,912	3,637,501
Less—Reserves for		
Unearned income	400,299	416,555
Losses on receivables	51,569	53,359
Total	451,868	469,914
Net finance and related receivables	3,166,044	3,167,587
Investment in Western Insurance Company—at cost	31,662	—
Land, buildings, and equipment—less accumulated depreciation	28,535	31,051
Other assets	173,827	191,344
	3,935,433	3,814,189

Liabilities and Stockholders' Equity

	19x2	19x1
Notes due within one year	1,189,075	1,226,780
Dealers' reserves and reserves for losses	119,324	114,155
Deferred income taxes	35,005	28,335
Other payables	523,474	498,080
Long-term notes	1,526,475	1,468,451
Stockholders' Equity		
Common stock—no par—authorized: 20,000 shares; issued: 1,000 shares at stated value	40,000	40,000
Additional paid-in capital	73,068	73,068
Net unrealized loss on marketable equity securities	(45,472)	(75,177)
Retained earnings	474,484	440,497
Total stockholders' equity	542,080	478,388
	3,935,433	3,814,189

FEDERATED CREDIT CORPORATION

Consolidated Income and Retained Earnings

	For Years Ended December 31,	
	19x2	19x1
Gross Income		
Finance discounts	394,405	419,282
Insurance premiums	194,528	188,927
Income on gains realized on sale of investments	18,718	15,118
Other income	6,633	13,779
Total	614,284	637,106
Expenses		
Operating expenses	203,522	196,650
Interest	177,532	203,430
Provision for losses	27,387	31,895
Insurance losses and loss expense	144,892	157,620
Total	553,333	589,595
Earnings before income taxes	60,951	47,511
Provision for income taxes	26,964	20,694
Net earnings	33,987	26,817
Retained earnings, January 1	440,497	430,680
Less: Cash dividends	—	(17,000)
Retained earnings, December 31	474,484	440,497

Consolidated Net Unrealized Loss on Marketable Equity Securities

Balance, January 1	(75,177)	(98,482)
Net realized gain	29,705	23,305
Balance, December 31	(45,472)	(75,177)

FEDERATED CREDIT CORPORATION

Notes to Consolidated Financial Statements

Summary of Significant Accounting Policies

* * * * * * * * *

Marketable Securities

Investments in bonds and notes are carried at amortized cost. As to equity securities, the investments of the insurance company subsidiaries are carried at quoted market values and the investments of other consolidated companies are carried at the lower of aggregate cost or quoted market values. Net realized gains or losses resulting from disposals or permanent impairment in value of investments are reflected in income.

* * * * * * * * *

Note C. Investments in Marketable Securities

The investment in marketable securities at December 31, 19x2 and 19x1 is summarized as follows:

	19x2	19x1
Bonds and notes at cost or amortized value (market: 19x2—$266,584, 19x1—$198,215)	270,772	223,886
Equity Securities		
Investments of insurance company subsidiaries at quoted market:		
Preferred stocks (cost: 19x2—$17,166, 19x1—11,943)	17,842	10,876
Common stocks (cost: 19x2—$165,232, 19x1—166,977)	123,083	98,323
Investments of other consolidated companies, at quoted market: (cost: 19x2—$9,315, 19x1—9,286)	5,316	3,829
Total equity securities	146,241	113,028
Total investment in marketable securities	417,013	336,914

The company had adopted the market basis of accounting for marketable equity securities permissible for insurance companies and, pursuant to the requirements of Statement No. 12 of the Financial Accounting Standards Board, has adopted the policy of carrying marketable equity securities investments of consolidated companies other than insurance companies at lower of cost or quoted market (which policy resulted in such securities being carried at quoted market at December 31, 19x2 and 19x1).

In connection with the utilization of the foregoing basis of accounting for equity securities, a valuation allowance representing the net unrealized loss on such securities has been established by charge to shareholders' equity. The valuation allowance of $45,472 at December 31, 19x2 and $75,177 at December 31, 19x1, respectively, reflected the net unrealized loss at those dates on the equity securities held by the insurance company subsidiaries ($41,472 and $69,720) and by consolidated companies other than insurance subsidiaries ($4,000 and $5,457).

At December 31, 19x2 gross unrealized gains and gross unrealized losses pretaining to the marketable equity securities investment at that date were $12,833 and $58,305, respectively. Net realized gains (losses) (based on the specific identification method of determining the cost of securities sold) of $187 and $105, after giving effect to related income taxes, on the sale of marketable equity securities are included in the determination of net earnings for the years ended December 31, 19x2 and 19x1, respectively.

8

Capital Changes—Accounting for Nonrevenue Adjustments in Stockholders' Equity Accounts

Official accounting directives and generally accepted accounting principles that specifically affect capital changes are not presented in any kind of coherently comprehensive manner in authoritative accounting literature. On the contrary, the available official guidelines for accounting for capital changes are obscurely embodied in an irregular series of official publications that date from 1934 to the present. The purpose of this chapter is to focus on official directives that affect capital changes, and present them in logical and continuous order: to identify each specific directive, set forth its provisions, and illustrate accounting procedures that comply with its requirements.

THE NATURE OF CAPITAL CHANGES

The term "stockholders' equity" is defined in Accounting Principles Board Statement No. 4[1] as the interest of owners in an enterprise which is equivalent to the excess of the enterprise's assets over its liabilities. The Statement indicates that, while the definition isolates stockholders' equity as a separate element of financial position, nevertheless, the definition as stated is comprehended within the limits of the definition suggested in Accounting Terminology Bulletin No. 1,[2] wherein stockholders' equity is defined as a liability that represents balances to be accounted for.[3] The Statement also reveals that, generally, stockholders' equity of corporations is conveniently classified including par or stated amount of capital stock, additional paid-in capital, and retained earnings.[4]

---

[1] *Basic Concepts and Accounting Principles Underlying Financial Statements of Business Enterprises,* Statement of the Accounting Principles Board No. 4. (New York, NY: Copyright 1970 by the American Institute of Certified Public Accountants. Paragraph 132.)

[2] *Review and Resume,* Accounting Terminology Bulletin No. 1. (New York, NY: American Institute of Accountants, 1953.)

[3] For the purpose of consistency certain passages in APB Statement No. 4; Accounting Terminology Bulletin No. 1; and other publications; are paraphrased in this chapter to the extent of substituting herein the term "stockholders' equity" for all synonymous terms, such as "owners' equity," "proprietary accounts," etc. which appear in the quoted reference source.

[4] *Basic Concepts and Accounting Principles Underlying Financial Statements of Business Enterprises,* Statement of the Accounting Principles Board No. 4. (New York, NY: Copyright 1970 by the American Institute of Certified Public Accountants. Paragraph 198.)

Changes in stockholders' equity accounts arise largely from transfers among the categories of such accounts, net income or loss, prior period adjustments, and transactions in the enterprise's own capital stock and convertible debt. Specifically, net income or loss for a period, reported in accordance with generally accepted accounting principles, represents the results of operations of the enterprise and, accordingly, encompasses all its revenue[5] transactions made during the reporting period. Changes that occur in the stockholders' equity accounts, other than the direct charge or credit to retained earnings representing net income or loss, are therefore nonrevenue adjustments to such accounts. The term "capital changes" is conventionally accepted in accounting literature, and it is used in this chapter in connection with all changes that occur in stockholders' equity accounts other than those resulting from the net income or loss reported in the income statement.

REQUIREMENT TO DISCLOSE CAPITAL CHANGES

Accounting Principles Board Opinion No. 12[6] states that when both financial position and results of operations are presented, disclosure of changes in the separate accounts comprising stockholders' equity, and of the change in the number of shares of equity securities during at least the most recent annual fiscal period, and any subsequent interim period presented, is required to make the financial statements sufficiently informative. Disclosure of such changes may take the form of separate statements or may be made in the basic financial statements or notes thereto.[7]

The requirement to disclose capital changes is extended to reporting the capital changes of an investee accounted for by the equity method by the provisions of APB Opinion No. 18, which state that a transaction of an investee of a capital nature that affects the investor's share of stockholders' equity of the investee should be accounted for as if the investee were a consolidated subsidiary.[8]

COMMON STOCK

GENERAL ACCOUNTING PROCEDURES FOR RECORDING CHANGES IN COMMON STOCK

Common stock is that part of stockholders' equity represented by shares that carry no preferences over other shares as to dividends or participation in profits, redemption or liquidation values, or call and conversion prices. Common stock is defined in official literature as stock which is subordinate to all other shares of the issuer.[9] While common stock has no preferences as to participation in profits, etc., generally its significantly distinguishing feature is that it carries exclusive voting rights, and thus is held by individuals and entities that have ultimate management control over the corporation.

---

[5]Paragraph 134 of APB Statement No. 4 defines "revenue" as gross increases in assets or gross decreases in liabilities recognized and measured in conformity with generally accepted accounting principles that result from those types of *profit directed activities* that can change stockholders' equity. (Emphasis added.)

[6]Opinions of the Accounting Principles Board were published by the American Institute of Certified Public Accountants, New York, N.Y. over a period extending from November, 1962 to June, 1973 and, as amended, are the official directives of the disciplinary body. In this chapter footnote reference to the Opinions will simply use the designation "APB Opinion," and indicate the opinion and paragraph numbers referred to.

[7]APB Opinion No. 12, paragraph 10.

[8]APB Opinion No. 18, paragraph 19(e).

[9]APB Opinion No. 15—Appendix D.

Common stock can be issued for cash, property, or services, and the basic accounting entries for recording the issuance of capital stock are very elementary, and are outlined as follows.

Par Value Stock

When par value stock is issued, an account representing the consideration received for the stock is debited for an amount equivalent to the fair value of the consideration; the account for capital stock is credited for the par value of the stock issued; and the value of any consideration received which is in excess of par value is credited to a paid-in capital account. [10]

No Par Value Stock

The laws of most states permit corporations to assign a "stated" value to its no par value stock, and where corporate Boards of Directors have assigned such values, the entries for recording issuance of no par common stock are exactly the same as those for par value, except that the common stock account is credited for the stated value of the shares, and the amount of any consideration received which is in excess of *stated* value is credited to a paid-in capital account.

In states where laws prohibit reference to stated value, no premium can be recognized. Issuance of common stock in those circumstances simply requires a debit to an account representing the consideration received in an amount equivalent to the fair value of the consideration, and a credit in the same amount to the common stock account.

There are some variations in the basic entries for recording issuance of capital stock outlined above. Some companies, for example, make an entry for the entire amount of the par value of its *authorized* capital stock and credit the amount to an account bearing that name: an offsetting debit in an equivalent amount is made to an account for unissued capital stock. When stock is actually issued, the account for unissued capital stock, and paid-in capital, if appropriate, is credited, and a debit in the amount of the fair credit of the consideration received is made to an account representing that consideration. The difference between the account for authorized capital stock and that for unissued capital stock, at any particular time, represents the par value of the issued stock, and is the amount reported on the balance sheet. In some instances corporations permit capital stock to be subscribed for in advance, and paid for at a later date. Under such circumstances the original entry is a debit to an account for stock subscriptions receivable, and an offsetting credit to an account for capital stock subscribed. When the cash, or other consideration, is received for the stock the basic entries described above are made to record the issuance of the stock; and a collateral entry is made simultaneously to debit the account for capital stock subscribed and credit the stock subscriptions receivable account.

DETERMINING FAIR VALUE OF STOCK ISSUED

The fair value of the consideration received in exchange for stock should be based on either the fair value of the consideration itself, or on the fair value of the stock issued, whichever is more evident. There is an abundance of official and semiofficial literature on the subject of fair value but, unfortunately, a great deal of such literature is quite inconclusive. Various APB Opinions provide guidelines for the fair value of assets and liabilities in connection with business combinations; [11] set forth conditions to

---

[10] See the section in this chapter captioned "Paid-in Capital."
[11] APB Opinion No. 16, paragraphs 88 and 89.

be considered in arriving at the fair value of property, goods, and services for the purpose of calculating imputed interest rates to be applied to notes for which such consideration is exchanged;[12] offer suggestions for determining the fair value of nonmonetary assets transferred to or from an enterprise in nonmonetary transactions;[13] and propose methods of estimating the fair value of the common stock of closed corporations whose shares are seldom, if ever, traded on the market.[14] The confusion created by such various approaches to determination of fair value renders the respective proposed guidelines almost useless and thus, in many cases, the determination of the fair value to be assigned to consideration, other than cash, which is received in exchange for capital stock, is a matter of personal judgment. However, where stock is freely traded over the counter or on an exchange, the quoted market price of such stock at the time of issuance is perhaps the best evidence of the fair value of the consideration received for it.

EARNINGS PER SHARE

APB Opinion No. 15, "Earnings Per Share," contains intricate, complicated, and highly technical rules for computing and reporting earnings per share. The dilution concept set forth in the Opinion infers that securities other than common stock which are substantially equivalent to common stock, (convertible securities, warrants, etc.) and contingent issuances of common stock, (stock option plans, etc.) should enter into the computation of earnings per share. The principles of the dilution concept provide for specific assumptions to be made for exercise, conversion, and issuance of securities; prices to be applied; and methods to be used in the computation of earnings per share so as to reflect the dilution in earnings per common share that would have resulted had such transactions actually occurred.

The text of this chapter is concerned solely with *changes to be recorded* in stockholders' equity accounts, and provides no guidance whatever for computing or reporting earnings per share. While the computation of earnings per share is based partly on recorded changes in stockholders' equity accounts, nevertheless, this chapter does not, in any way, attempt to develop the relationship between earnings per share and recorded capital changes.[15]

PRESCRIBED ACCOUNTING PROCEDURES FOR RECORDING CHANGES IN COMMON STOCK

The mechanics of recording issuances of common capital stock were discussed in a previous paragraph. The following paragraphs in this section deal with appropriate accounting procedures for recording transactions in common stock which are prescribed by specific official accounting directives.

TRANSACTIONS IN COMMON STOCK

The Accounting Principles Board has reaffirmed the conclusions of a former executive committee of the American Institute of Accountants, formulated in a report dat-

---

[12]APB Opinion No. 21, paragraphs 12–14.
[13]APB Opinion No. 29, paragraph 25.
[14]*Computing Earnings Per Share,* Unofficial Interpretation of APB Opinion No. 15. (New York, NY: Copyright 1970 by the American Institute of Certified Public Accountants. Part II, paragraph 56.)
[15]Refer to Chapter 3 for an explanation of the computation and reporting of earnings per share by corporations having a simple capital structure.

ed April 8, 1938, that adjustments or charges or credits resulting from transactions in the company's own capital stock should be excluded from the determination of net income or results of operations under all circumstances.[16] This directive certainly does not prohibit recording gains and losses that occur from transactions in the company's capital stock. It simply states that such transactions should be excluded from the determination of reported net income. Thus, any transaction in common stock will normally affect only the par or stated value carried in the common stock account for the number of shares involved in the transaction. Any consideration received in excess of, or for less than, the par or stated value of the respective shares will be recorded as a direct credit or charge to some other appropriate stockholders' equity account. The exception to this rule is that the *cost* of capital stock reacquired for the treasury is usually carried in a separate account, and shown as a deduction from aggregate stockholders' equity on the balance sheet.

Many types of transactions result in gains or losses on issuance of capital stock. However, since in all cases the entry for each respective transaction affects the capital stock account only to the extent of the par or stated value of the shares involved, such transactions are not treated in this section, but detailed entries, and appropriate techniques for measurement of gains and losses, are described in the sections that follow. Such transactions include stock dividends, stock purchase warrants, stock option plans, convertible securities, stock split-ups, treasury stock, and stock acquired for redemption.

NONMONETARY TRANSACTIONS IN COMMON STOCK

Common stock is classified as a nonmonetary item[17] and a basic principle set forth by the Accounting Principles Board provides that accounting for nonmonetary transactions should be based on the fair values of the assets or services involved. Thus, the cost of a nonmonetary asset acquired in exchange for another nonmonetary asset is the fair value of the asset surrendered to obtain it, and a gain or loss should be recognized on the exchange.[18] This basic principle does not apply to acquisitions of nonmonetary assets or services on issuance of capital stock of an enterprise, and thus net income is not affected by such issuances.[19]

BUSINESS COMBINATIONS

Business combinations are required to be accounted for either by the purchase method, which is applied where the combination is treated as the acquisition of one company by another, or the pooling of interests method, which is used where the combination results in continuity of ownership by the stockholders of the constituent companies.[20] A business combination accounted for by the purchase method may, or may not, involve issuance of capital stock by the acquiring company. A business combination meeting the criteria to be accounted for as a pooling of interests, of necessity, *must* involve the issuance of stock by the combining company. Accounting for issu-

---

[16] APB Opinion No. 9, paragraph 28.
[17] *Financial Statements Restated for General Price-Level Changes,* Statement of the Accounting Principles Board No. 3. (New York, NY: Copyright 1969 by the American Institute of Certified Public Accountants. Appendix A.)
[18] APB Opinion No. 29, paragraph 18.
[19] APB Opinion No. 29, paragraph 4(c).
[20] APB Opinion No. 16.

ances of common stock under the two methods of accounting for business combinations, respectively, is described in the paragraphs that follow.

Pooling of Interests Method

Under the pooling-of-interests method, the assets, liabilities, and capital accounts of all the constituent companies are combined at their respective carrying values and no cost factors or goodwill are involved. A pooling of interests is effected by one corporation distributing its shares for shares held by stockholders of the other combining companies, and the corporation records the issuance of its shares at par value. Where the shares of the distributing corporation are issued to the stockholders of the other combining companies on a one-for-one basis, the combined corporation has no problem in accounting for its outstanding stock at par value. However, where the shares of the distributing company are issued on other than a one-for-one basis, the amount of outstanding shares of stock of the combined corporation at par or stated value may exceed the total amount of capital stock of the separate combining companies. In such a case the excess should be deducted first from the combined paid-in or other contributed capital, if any, and then from combined retained earnings.[21]

Illustration of Accounting for Changes in Common Stock in a Business Combination Accounted for as a Pooling of Interests

Model Case No. 1 illustrates combining assets, liabilities, and capital accounts of constituent companies in a business combination accounted for by the pooling-of-interests method where the distributing company issues shares to stockholders of the other combining companies on a one-for-one basis. Model Case No. 2 illustrates accounting for a pooling of interests where shares of the distributing company are not exchanged for shares of the other combining companies on a one-for-one basis.

MODEL CASE NO. 1

Hawks, Inc., Jones Company, and Dow Corporation each adopted identical resolutions to effect a pooling of interests of the three companies, and since the fair value

	Hawks	Jones	Dow
Assets	950,000	850,000	700,000
Liabilities	150,000	135,000	110,500
Stockholders' Equity			
Common Stock—Par Value $100			
Issued — 7,200 shares	720,000		
— 6,435 shares		643,500	
— 5,306 shares			530,600
Retained earnings	80,000	71,500	58,900
Total stockholders' equity	800,000	715,000	589,500
	950,000	850,000	700,000

SCHEDULE 1

---

[21]APB Opinion No. 16, paragraph 53.

of each company was approximately equivalent to each of the other two combining companies, the plan required Hawks, Inc. to become the combined company, and issue its shares on a one-for-one basis to the stockholders of Jones and Dow, respectively.

The assets, liabilities, and stockholders' equity accounts for the respective companies at June 30, 19x1, the date of consummation of the combination, are shown in Schedule 1.

The entry made by Hawks to integrate the accounts of the other combining companies into its own accounts was as follows:

	Debit	Credit
Assets	1,550,000	
Liabilities		245,500
Common stock		1,174,100
Retained earnings		130,400

To record issuance of 11,741 shares of common stock to stockholders of Jones Company and Dow Corporation to effect pooling of interests on June 30, 19x1.

The balance sheet of Hawks, Inc. at June 30, 19x1, after consummation of the pooling of interests, is set forth in Schedule 2.

HAWKS, INC.

Balance Sheet — June 30, 19x1

Assets	2,500,000
Liabilities	395,500
Stockholders' Equity	
Common Stock—Par Value $100—Issued: 18,941 shares	1,894,100
Retained earnings	210,400
Total stockholders' equity	2,104,500
	2,500,000

SCHEDULE 2

MODEL CASE NO. 2

Fisher Corporation, Hecht Company, and McNally, Inc. entered into a pooling of interests agreement to be consummated on December 31, 19x2. Fisher was designated as the distributing company and the number of shares to be issued to the combining companies was determined to be on the basis of the ratio of the *net book value* of a single share of stock of each respective combining company to the *net book value* of a single share of Fisher Corporation, applied to the number of shares outstanding at December 31, 19x2.

The assets, liabilities, and stockholders' equity accounts of the respective companies at December 31, 19x2 are reflected in Schedule 3.

	Fisher	Hecht	McNally
Assets	712,500	752,760	608,235
Liabilities	64,500	57,816	82,875
Stockholders' Equity			
Common Stock—Par Value $100			
Issued — 5,400 shares	540,000		
— 4,826 shares		482,600	
— 3,980 shares			398,000
Retained earnings	108,000	212,344	127,360
Total stockholders' equity	648,000	694,944	525,360
	712,500	752,760	608,235

SCHEDULE 3

The net book value of shares of common stock was determined for each company by dividing the stockholders' equity by the number of shares outstanding, as follows:

Fisher Corporation — $648,000 ÷ 5,400 shares = $120
Hecht Company — $694,944 ÷ 4,826 shares = $144
McNally, Inc. — $525,360 ÷ 3,980 shares = $132

The number of shares to be issued by Fisher for each share of stock of the combining companies was computed by dividing the book value of a share of Fisher stock into the book value of a share of stock of Hecht and McNally, respectively, as follows:

Hecht Company — $144 ÷ $120 = 1.20
McNally, Inc. — $132 ÷ $120 = 1.10

Upon completion of the exchange the holdings of Fisher Corporation stock were as follows:

Former Hecht Company stockholders
4,826 shares exchanged at 1.20 for 1 = 5,791 shares at $100 =   579,100
Former McNally, Inc. stockholders
3,980 shares exchanged at 1.10 for 1 = 4,378 shares at $100 =   437,800
Original Fisher Corporation stockholders
5,400 shares retained by stockholders: 5,400 shares at $100 =   540,000
                                                      15,569   1,556,900

The entry made by Fisher at December 31, 19x2 after consummation of the pooling of interests was as follows:

	Debit	Credit
Assets	1,360,995	
Liabilities		140,691
Common stock		880,600
Retained earnings		339,704

To record issuance of 10,169 shares of common stock to stockholders of Hecht Company and McNally, Inc. to effect pooling of interests at December 31, 19x2.

After the above entry was posted, the general ledger accounts of Fisher Corporation reflected a balance of $1,420,600 in the common stock account. Since the total stock outstanding of 15,569 shares at a par value of $100 each amounted to $1,556,900, Fisher had to increase the capital stock account by $136,300. Fisher had no paid-in capital and so an entry was made to reduce combined retained earnings and increase common stock for the difference of $136,300, as follows:

	Debit	Credit
Retained earnings	136,300	
Common stock		136,300

To increase capital stock account by the par value of the excess of the number of shares issued over the number of shares cancelled.

Schedule 4 shows the balance sheet of the combined company after the above entry was posted on December 31, 19x2.

FISHER CORPORATION

Balance Sheet — December 31, 19x2

Assets	2,073,495
Liabilities	205,191
Stockholders' Equity	
Common Stock — Par Value $100	
Issued: 15,569 shares	1,556,900
Retained earnings	311,404
Total stockholders' equity	1,868,304
	2,073,495

SCHEDULE 4

The net book value per share of the combined company is computed by dividing the number of shares outstanding into stockholders' equity, as follows:

$1,868,304 ÷ 15,569$ shares $= 120 per share

The $120 book value per share of the stock of the combined company is the same as the book value per share of the distributing company prior to the consummation of the combination.

Purchase Method

Many business combinations accounted for by the purchase method involve an exchange of stock of the acquiring company for the net assets of the company purchased. Such transactions do not comprehend any changes in the accounting principles that apply to purchases in general. In fact, the same accounting principles apply to determining the cost of assets acquired individually, those acquired in a group, and those acquired in a business combination.[22] Generally, the fair value of the asset received measures its cost and, thus, an asset acquired in a business combination by issuing shares of the acquiring corporation is recorded at the fair value of the asset; that is, shares of stock are recorded at the fair value of the consideration received for the stock.[23]

Recording Issuance of Common Stock for Net Assets Acquired in a Business Combination Accounted for as a Purchase

As stated above, shares of stock issued in a business combination accounted for as a purchase are recorded at the fair value of the consideration received for the stock. However, accounting for the shares actually issued should be on the basis of their par or stated value, and any excess of the value of the asset received over par or stated value of the common stock issued should be credited to a paid-in capital account. Following is an example of recording the issuance of common stock in such a situation:

Wolfe, Inc. issued 1,000 shares of $100 par value common stock to purchase Reedy Company, which had assets fairly valued at $150,000, and actual liabilities of $20,000. Wolfe's entry to record the purchase was as follows:

	Debit	Credit
Assets	150,000	
Liabilities		20,000
Common stock		100,000
Capital in excess of par value of stock		30,000
To record purchase of net assets of Reedy Company for 1,000 shares of $100 par value stock.		

A discussion of paid-in capital, including capital in excess of par value of stock, is set forth in a later section of this chapter.

CAPITAL STOCK ISSUED AT LESS THAN PAR VALUE

If shares of capital stock are issued for less than par value per share, the difference between aggregate par value and the value of the consideration received should be charged to a "Discount on Capital Stock" account, and reported as a reduction of stockholders' equity in the balance sheet. This situation seldom occurs largely because most state laws prohibit issuance of par value stock for cash at a price per share that is less than par value. However, accurate valuation of assets other than cash acquired by issuance of capital stock can conceivably result in the stock being issued for less than par value. Again, this situation seldom occurs because in practically every case where assets are acquired by issuance of stock the managing team of the acquiring company is disposed to place a value on the assets acquired that is at least equivalent to the par value of the shares issued. The courts have permitted management wide discretionary powers in valuing property acquired for capital stock, and thus it is not difficult for a company to inflate the value of assets acquired in order to avoid reporting a negative capitalization account in the stockholders' equity section of its balance sheet.

---

[22]APB Opinion No. 16, paragraph 72.
[23]APB Opinion No. 16, paragraph 67(c).

PREFERRED STOCK

GENERAL ACCOUNTING PROCEDURES FOR PREFERRED STOCK

Preferred stock is that part of stockholders' equity represented by shares that carry stipulated preferences over other shares. There is enormous variety in preferences that are conferred upon holders of preferred stock: some series carry preferences with respect to dividends, and such dividends can be either cumulative or noncumulative as to a fixed rate of return, and either participating or nonparticipating in profits achieved in excess of a specified amount; other issues provide preference as to distribution of net assets in dissolution or liquidation; and certain issues are convertible into common stock, either by election of the shareholder or by call of the issuing corporation. Generally, preferred stock is a nonvoting equity security, but some issues do carry limited voting privileges. However, preferred shareholders seldom have significant control over management of the issuing company.

Preferred stock can be authorized with or without par value, and a stated value per share can be assigned to the authorized no par stock. Preferred stock can be issued for cash, property, and services; and, if stipulated in its terms of issue, can be converted into debt or other equity securities.

While preferred stocks carry certain preferences over other shares, such as those indicated above, nevertheless, the same basic accounting entries for the issuance of common stock described in the previous section of the chapter apply in every respect to the issuance of preferred stock.

PRESCRIBED ACCOUNTING PROCEDURES FOR RECORDING CHANGES IN PREFERRED STOCK

The mechanics of recording the issuance of preferred stock are exactly the same as those previously described for the issuance of common stock. While there are very few official directives that prescribe specific accounting treatment of changes in preferred stock, the following pargraphs set forth the types of such transactions that fall within the scope of existing directives.

TRANSACTIONS IN PREFERRED STOCK

Adjustment or charges or credits resulting from transactions in the company's own preferred stock should be excluded from the determination of net income or results of operations.[24] Thus, any transactions in preferred stock will affect only the par or stated value carried in the preferred stock account for the number of shares involved in the transaction, and any consideration received in excess of, or for less than, the par or stated value of the respective shares will be recorded as a direct credit or charge to some other stockholders' equity account.

NONMONETARY TRANSACTIONS IN PREFERRED STOCK

Preferred stock can be classified as a monetary or as a nonmonetary item, depending upon the terms and conditions surrounding its issue.[25] However, the issu-

---

[24] APB Opinion No. 9, paragraph 28.
[25] *Financial Statements Restated for General Price-Level Changes,* Statement of the Accounting Principles Board No. 3 (New York, N.Y.: American Institute of Certified Public Accountants, 1969) Appendix A.

ance of preferred stock is exempt from the provisions of APB Opinion No. 29 which require that a gain or loss be recognized on an exchange of nonmonetary items.[26]

BUSINESS COMBINATIONS

The accounting treatment of changes in the preferred stock account of companies involved in business combinations depends upon whether the combination is accounted for as a purchase, or as a pooling of interests.

Pooling of Interests Method

Accounting for a business combination as a pooling of interests requires all assets, liabilities, and capital accounts of the constituent companies to be combined at their respective carrying values. However, a new corporation formed to issue its stock to effect the combination may exchange substantially identical securities or voting common stock for outstanding equity and debt securities of the other combining companies. An issuing corporation may also distribute cash to holders of debt and equity securities that either are callable or redeemable, and may retire those securities. However, the issuing corporation may exchange only voting common stock for outstanding equity and debt securities of the other combining companies that have been issued in exchange for voting common stock of those companies during a period beginning two years preceding the date the combination is initiated.[27]

Purchase Method

The fair value of assets acquired and the fair value of liabilities assumed generally measure the cost of the net assets of an acquired company. However, the distinctive attributes of preferred stocks make some issues similar to a debt security, while others possess common stock characteristics, with many gradations between the extremes. Thus, although the principle of recording the fair value of consideration received for stock issued applies to all equity securities, senior as well as common stock, the cost of a company acquired by issuing senior equity securities may be determined, in practice, on the same basis as for debt securities. In such instances the fair value of the company acquired would coincide with the present value of the senior securities exchanged for it. The present value of the senior securities would be calculated on an imputed interest rate, using the specified dividend and redemption terms as factors in the computation.[28]

Model Case No. 3 provides an example of a business combination accounted for as a purchase where the net assets of the acquired company were exchanged for preferred stock. The example demonstrates the method of computing the present value of the preferred stock, and illustrates appropriate accounting procedures to record the transaction.

MODEL CASE NO. 3

On December 31, 19x7 Kessler Corporation exchanged 10,000 shares of $100 par value preferred stock for the net assets of McCann Company. McCann Company had actual liabilities of $80,000 but the fair value of its assets was difficult to determine. Kessler therefore decided to account for the business combination as a purchase and

[26]APB Opinion No. 29, paragraphs 4(c) and 18.
[27]APB Opinion No. 16, paragraph 47.
[28]APB Opinion No. 16, paragraphs 72 and 73.

compute a fair value based on the present value of the preferred stock given in exchange. The preferred stock was nonvoting and nonconvertible, and had no characteristics of common stock. The stock carried an 8.75% cumulative annual dividend rate, payable quarterly, and was redeemable at the 'end of five years. The current interest rate for a loan of $1,000,000 was set at 9.5% at the purchase date, and Kessler decided to use an imputed rate of 9.5%, compounded quarterly, in calculating the present value of the preferred stock. Kessler computed the present value of the payments that would have to be made over the following five years as follows:

Present value of quarterly dividends of $21,875

$$\frac{1 - \left(\frac{1}{1.02375}\right)^{20}}{.02375} = 15.77482473 \times 21,875 = \qquad \$345,074$$

Present value of redemption price of $100,000
preferred stock at end of five years

$$\left(\frac{1}{1.02375}\right)^{20} = .6253479128 \times 1,000,000 = \qquad \frac{625,348}{970,422}$$

Kessler assigned the computed present value of the preferred stock, plus the actual liabilities assumed, to the respective assets acquired, and charged the difference between the fair value and the $1,000,000 par value of the preferred stock to the capital in excess of par account that existed on his books for that particular issue of stock. Accordingly, on December 31, 19x7 Kessler made the following entry to record the acquisition of the net assets of McCann Company:

	Debit	Credit
Assets	1,050,422	
Capital in excess of par—8.75 Preferred	29,578	
Liabilities		80,000
Preferred Stock—8.75 series		1,000,000

To record the fair value of net assets acquired from McCann Company, represented by the present value of 10,000 shares of 8.75% preferred stock, and to charge capital in excess of par with the difference between the present value and par value of the issued stock.

Schedule 5 indicates the series of events that would have occurred had Kessler issued a debt security for $1,000,000 with interest payable quarterly at an annual rate of 8.75%, with the principal amount payable at the end of five years and, simultaneously, had made a cash investment of $970,422 at a 9.5% annual interest rate, compounded quarterly, in order to insure a provision of funds for quarterly interest payments on the debt security, and its ultimate redemption at the end of five years.

It is important to note, however, that Schedule 5 demonstrates only the validity of the present value *measurement*. Had the debt security in fact been issued and a hedging investment of the present value of $970,422 been made by Kessler, the *accounting treatment* would have been quite different from the procedure for recording the issuance of preferred stock. Payments of *dividends* on preferred stock are excluded from determination of net income, while, had a debt security been issued, both interest expense on the debt and the interest income from the covering investment would have been recognized as expense and income, respectively, in the determination of results of operations.

SCHEDULE FOR FUNDING THE PRESENT VALUE OF PREFERRED STOCK TO PROVIDE FOR QUARTERLY DIVIDENDS AND ULTIMATE REDEMPTION

End of Quarter	Dividends to be paid (8.75%)	Balance for computation of interest income	Interest Income (9.5%)	Cumulative balance to redeem stock
—	—	970,422	23,048	993,470
1	21,875	971,595	23,075	994,670
2	21,875	972,795	23,104	995,899
3	21,875	974,024	23,133	997,157
4	21,875	975,282	23,163	998,445
5	21,875	976,570	23,194	999,764
6	21,875	977,889	23,225	1,001,114
7	21,875	979,239	23,256	1,002,495
8	21,875	980,620	23,290	1,003,910
9	21,875	982,035	23,323	1,005,358
10	21,875	983,483	23,358	1,006,841
11	21,875	984,966	23,393	1,008,359
12	21,875	986,484	23,429	1,009,913
13	21,875	988,038	23,466	1,011,504
14	21,875	989,629	23,504	1,013,133
15	21,875	991,258	23,542	1,014,800
16	21,875	992,925	23,582	1,016,507
17	21,875	994,632	23,623	1,018,255
18	21,875	996,380	23,664	1,020,044
19	21,875	998,169	23,706	1,021,875
20	21,875	—	—	1,000,000
	437,500		467,078	

SCHEDULE 5

TREASURY STOCK

GENERAL ACCOUNTING PROCEDURES FOR RECORDING THE ISSUANCE AND DISPOSITION OF TREASURY STOCK

Treasury stock is stock that has been issued and reacquired by a corporation. The reasons for which a company reacquires its own stock vary widely, but the status of the stock, once it has been reacquired, falls into one of two categories: stock held for cancellation, or stock held in the "treasury." Stock reacquired for cancellation is usually cancelled immediately, or accounted for as being *constructively* cancelled, even though the legal process of cancellation may not have been completed. Thus, stock reacquired for cancellation does not normally appear on the balance sheet. On the other hand, stock reacquired and held in the treasury generally *must* be reported on the balance sheet; and, under the historical basis of accounting, it will be reported at *cost.* Where stock is held in the treasury, the cost of the acquired stock may be shown separately as a deduction from the total of capital stock, paid-in capital, and retained earnings, or the shares may be accorded the accounting treatment appropriate for retired stock: in some circumstances treasury stock may be shown as an asset.[29]

The acquisition of treasury stock cannot be treated as an expense[30] and transactions in such stock must be excluded from the determination of net income under all circumstances.[31] Consequently, accounting for treasury stock is restricted to entries to an account representing the stock, and to offsetting credits and charges to accounts representing the consideration paid for its acquisition or received for its reissue; and entries to other stockholders' equity accounts for any gains or losses involved in the transaction. Thus, when treasury stock is acquired, the *cost* of the stock is charged to an account captioned "Treasury stock." If the stock is reissued, the treasury stock account is credited for the cost of the reissued shares, and an account representing the consideration is debited for the fair value of such consideration. The gain or loss on the exchange is credited or charged to another appropriate stockholders' equity account. In cases where the treasury stock is cancelled, constructively cancelled, or treated as being retired, the treasury stock account is credited for its cost; the captial stock account representing the particular issue of the cancelled stock is charged for the par or stated value of the number of shares involved; and any difference between the cost and par or stated value of the treasury stock is charged or credited to some other appropriate stockholders' equity account.

PRESCRIBED ACCOUNTING PROCEDURES FOR RECORDING TRANSACTIONS IN TREASURY STOCK

There is an abundance of official directives which provide guidance in accounting for transactions in treasury stock. These directives generally relate to measurement of the consideration given or received for the stock, and to allocation of the gains and losses resulting from the transactions. However, such directives are scattered haphazardly throughout the whole body of official accounting literature, and this chapter is concerned with presenting the directives in comprehensive continuity, identifying their respective sources, explaining their provisions, and furnishing illustrations of appropriate accounting procedures required in each circumstance.

TRANSACTIONS IN TREASURY STOCK

Transactions in treasury stock generally result in a gain or loss. Gains on such transactions are usually credited to a paid-in capital account set up for the particular series of stock involved. Losses are normally charged to paid-in capital of the same series, if any exists, and any excess of the loss over the balance of the paid-in capital account is charged to retained earnings. Accounting for changes in paid-in capital is the subject of the next section of this chapter, and it should be noted here that the terms

---

[29]APB Opinion No. 6, paragraph 12(b).
[30]APB Statement No. 4, paragraph 154.
[31]APB Opinion No. 9, paragraph 28.

"paid-in capital" and "capital in excess of par or stated value" are used synonymously, both here and in the following sections of the chapter.

The following paragraphs in this section deal with accounting for treasury stock transactions in accordance with existent and pertinent official directives.

TREASURY STOCK REPORTED AS AN ASSET

Normally the cost of treasury stock is reported on the balance sheet as a deduction from aggregate stockholders' equity. However, in some special circumstances a company may elect to carry the cost of reacquired stock as an asset. For example, a certain mineral company reports the cost of treasury stock as a non-current asset on its balance sheet, and discloses in the accompanying notes to the statement that the shares of its own stock are held in the treasury to be available for the purpose of fulfilling awards payable in common stock under the incentive compensation plan of the company. Thus, in cases where companies reacquire their own stock for the purpose of reissuing it in accordance with an obligation that requires payment in common stock, the reporting of such stock by the company as an asset on its balance sheet is not altogether unusual. However, the dividends on stock so held should not be treated as a credit to the income account of the company.[32]

STOCK REACQUIRED FOR THE PURPOSE OF ACTUAL OR CONSTRUCTIVE RETIREMENT

The accounting treatment of stock reacquired for the purpose of actual or constructive retirement depends upon whether the cost of the reacquired stock is in excess of par or stated value, or less than par or stated value.

Purchase Price in Excess of Par or Stated Value

When a corporation reacquires its own stock for the purpose of actual or constructive retirement, the excess of purchase price over par or stated value may be allocated between paid-in capital and retained earnings. However, the portion of the excess allocated to paid-in capital should be limited to the sum of:
(a) all paid-in capital arising from previous retirements and net gains on sale of treasury stock of the same issue; and
(b) the pro rata portion of paid-in capital, voluntary transfers of retained earnings, capitalization of stock dividends, etc. on the same issue.
Alternatively, the excess of purchase price over par or stated value may be charged entirely to retained earnings.

Any remaining balance of paid-in capital applicable to issues fully retired is deemed to be applicable pro rata to common stock.

Par or Stated Value in Excess of Purchase Price

The excess of par or stated value over the purchase price of stock reacquired for actual or constructive retirement should be credited to paid-in capital.[33]

STOCK REACQUIRED FOR PURPOSES OTHER THAN RETIREMENT

When a corporation purchases its own capital stock for purposes other than actu-

---

[32]Accounting Research Bulletin (ARB) No. 43, Chapter 1-A, paragraph 4; and APB Opinion No. 6, paragraph 12(b).
[33]APB Opinion No. 6, paragraph 12(a).

al or constructive retirement, the cost of the acquired stock may be shown separately as a deduction from the total of capital stock, paid-in capital, and retained earnings, or may, in some circumstances, be shown as an asset.

Alternatively, the acquired stock may be accorded the treatment prescribed for stock purchased for retirement, as described in preceding paragraphs. [34]

GAINS AND LOSSES ON SALES OF TREASURY STOCK

Gains on sales of treasury stock not previously accounted for as constructively retired should be credited to paid-in capital; losses may be charged to paid-in capital to the extent that previous net gains from sales or retirement of the same class of stock are included therein, otherwise to retained earnings. [35]

ILLUSTRATION OF ACCOUNTING FOR STOCK REACQUIRED FOR RETIREMENT AND OF STOCK REACQUIRED FOR THE TREASURY

Model Case No. 3A is an example of a corporation recquiring its own shares for the purpose of both retiring reacquired shares and holding reacquired shares in the treasury. The model case illustrates appropriate accounting procedures for each respective circumstance.

MODEL CASE NO. 3A

In 19x2 Shadrow, Inc. entered into an agreement with a stockholder to purchase 2,000 shares of Shadrow common stock on December 31, 19x2 at a price of $120 per share. Shadrow determined to retire 1,000 shares of the reacquired stock, and to hold the other 1,000 shares in the treasury.

The stockholders' equity accounts, at December 31, 19x2 after closing, but prior to the reacquisition of common stock under the agreement, is shown in Schedule 6.

STOCKHOLDERS' EQUITY ACCOUNTS
PRIOR TO REACQUISITION OF COMMON STOCK

Common stock—$100 par value	
Authorized and outstanding—10,000 shares	1,000,000
Paid-in capital	105,000
Retained earnings	80,000
Total stockholders' equity	1,185,000

SCHEDULE 6

In connection with the 1,000 shares to be retired, Shadrow decided to charge paid-in capital with the maximum amount allowable under official accounting directives. Accordingly, he analyzed his paid-in capital account and applied the maximum allocation allowable to each component of the account. Schedule 7 shows the analysis, and the computed charges allowed to be made to paid-in capital.

---

[34]APB Opinion No. 6, paragraph 12(b).
[35]APB Opinion No. 6, paragraph 12(b).

ANALYSIS OF PAID-IN CAPITAL ACCOUNT AND
COMPUTATION OF ALLOWABLE CHARGE TO PAID-IN
CAPITAL ON SHARES OF STOCK RETIRED

	Total Amount	Applicable Rate	Allocable Amount
Premium on issuance of common stock	100,000	10%	10,000
Gains on sale of reacquired and reissued common stock in previous periods	5,000	100%	5,000
	105,000		15,000

SCHEDULE 7

After having computed the maximum charge that could be made to paid-in capital, Shadrow made the following entries to record the reacquisition and retirement of his capital stock:

	Debit	Credit
(1)		
Treasury stock	240,000	
Cash		240,000
To record reacquisition of 2,000 shares of common stock at $120 per share.		
(2)		
Common stock	100,000	
Paid-in capital	15,000	
Retained earnings	5,000	
Treasury stock		120,000
To record retirement of 1,000 shares of treasury stock.		

The stockholders' equity section of Shadrow's balance sheet at December 31, 19x2, prepared after giving effect to the entries outlined above, is reproduced in Schedule 8.

NONMONETARY TRANSACTIONS INVOLVING TREASURY STOCK

The acquisition of treasury stock is a nonreciprocal transfer between the enterprise and its owners.[36] A transfer of a nonmonetary asset to a shareholder or to another entity in a nonreciprocal transfer should be recorded at the fair value of the asset transferred, and a gain or loss should be recognized on the disposition of the asset. The fair value of an entity's own stock reacquired may be a more clearly evident measure of the fair value of the asset distributed in a nonreciprocal transfer, if the transaction involves distribution of a nonmonetary asset to acquire treasury stock for retirement.[37]

---

[36]APB Statement No. 4, paragraph 154.
[37]APB Opinion No. 29, paragraph 18.

STOCKHOLDERS' EQUITY SECTION OF BALANCE SHEET
AFTER REACQUISITION AND RETIREMENT OF COMMON STOCK

Stockholders' Equity	
Common stock—$100 par value	
Authorized: 9,000 shares	
Outstanding: 8,000 shares	900,000
Paid-in capital	90,000
Retained earnings	75,000
	1,065,000
Less: Cost of treasury stock	120,000
Total stockholders' equity	945,000

SCHEDULE 8

Model Case No. 4 is an example of a nonreciprocal transfer of assets to a stockholder to acquire treasury stock for the purpose of retirement.

MODEL CASE NO. 4

Vernon, Inc. entered into an agreement with William Smith, a stockholder, which stipulated that Vernon would transfer a warehouse and land to Smith in exchange for 5,000 shares of Vernon's common stock held by Smith. Vernon's intentions were to eliminate a disproportionate part of owners' interests by reacquiring and retiring the stock held by Smith. Vernon's common stock had a par value of $100, and was selling over the counter at $120 per share. The land and building to be exchanged for treasury stock were carried at a cost of $50,000 and $750,000, respectively, and accumulated depreciation on the building amounted to $500,000. Vernon decided that the market price of the common stock was a more clearly evident measure of the fair value of the asset exchanged in the transfer. Accordingly, when the exchange had been completed, and the stock constructively retired, Vernon made the following entries to record the transactions:

	Debit	Credit
(1)		
Treasury stock	600,000	
Accumulated depreciation	500,000	
Gain on revaluation of assets		300,000
Land		50,000
Building		750,000

To record acquisition of 5,000 shares of $100 par value common stock, valued at $120 per share, in exchange for warehouse and land having a net book value of $300,000, and to recognize a $300,000 gain on revaluation of assets.

(2)

	Debit	Credit
Capital stock	500,000	
Retained earnings	100,000	
Treasury stock		600,000

To record constructive retirement of
5,000 reacquired shares of $100 par val-
ue stock, and charge retained earnings
with the $100,000 difference between the
par value and cost of the shares
reacquired.

ACCOUNTING FOR TREASURY STOCK IN BUSINESS COMBINATIONS

Where a business combination is accounted for as a purchase, the treasury stock
held by the acquired company has no effect whatever. It is simply treated as
unissued, authorized capital stock. However, in a combination accounted for as a
pooling of interests, adjustments must be made to treasury stock in the following two
circumstances.

Distribution of Treasury Stock Held by the Issuing Company

A corporation which effects a combination accounted for as a pooling of interests
by distributing its own treasury stock should first account for those shares as
though retired. The issuance of the shares for the common stock interests of the
combining company is thus accounted for the same way as the issuance of previously unissued shares.[38] An example of this situation follows.

Gramercy, Inc. is the issuing corporation in a business combination accounted
for as a pooling of interests. Gramercy has 10,000 shares of $100 par value common
stock in its treasury, for which it paid $1,200,000. Gramercy decides to charge the
excess of cost of the reacquired stock to retained earnings and, accordingly, makes
the following entry:

	Debit	Credit
Common stock	1,000,000	
Retained earnings	200,000	
Treasury stock		1,200,000

To remove 10,000 shares of treasury
stock from the issued stock account and
charge the excess of cost over par value
to retained earnings.

After the above entry was made, Gramercy had 10,000 additional shares of common stock which could be issued in the combining process.

Stock of the Issuing Company Held by Other Combining Companies

In a business combination accounted for as a pooling of interests, one or more of

---

[38]APB Opinion No. 16, paragraph 54.

the combining companies may hold, as investments, common stock of the issuing corporation. In the combining process such investments are in effect returned to the resulting combined corporation. In such cases the combined corporation should account for the investments as treasury stock.[39]

STOCK ISSUED TO EMPLOYEES

Certain stock option and stock purchase plans permit employees to purchase stock under a variety of conditions. Some plans offer a fixed number of shares at a fixed price, while other plans grant an option for a variable number of shares at a variable option price. Some plans are noncompensatory, while others are considered to be compensatory, and involve an element of compensation to the employee. Noncompensatory plans are essentially simple plans that permit employees to purchase stock on the same basis as other investors. Compensatory plans, on the other hand, offer stock to employees at a discount price, and the measurement of the cost of compensation involved in such plans is measured by the excess of the quoted market price of the stock at the measurement date over the price to be paid by the employee. If a quoted market price is unavailable, the best estimate of the market price of the stock should be used to measure compensation.[40]

Whether treasury stock or unissued shares are used to fulfill the employer's obligation is not material to a determination of value,[41] but measuring compensation of reacquired treasury stock that is distributed through a stock option, purchase, or award plan, by the cost to an employer corporation, is not acceptable practice unless the corporation reacquires the stock during the fiscal period for which it is to be awarded and, in fact, *is* awarded shortly thereafter to employees for services during that period.[42]

An illustration of the entry to be made upon issuance of treasury stock under a compensatory stock option plan is demonstrated in Model Case No. 5.

MODEL CASE NO. 5

Merle Corporation had a stock option plan in which the measurement date had been set at December 31. On December 31, 19x7 Merle was obligated to issue 1,000 shares of $10 par value common stock to its employees at $33.00 per share. Merle decided to issue 1,000 shares of treasury stock on December 31, 19x7 to fulfill its obligation. During the year Merle had reacquired 500 shares of common stock at a price of $34.00 per share. The other shares of treasury stock had been purchased in a prior year at $36.00 per share. The quoted market price of Merle's common stock at December 31, 19x7 was $38.00 per share.

Merle computed the compensation expense involved in the issuance of 1,000 shares of treasury stock as shown in Schedule 9.

---

[39]APB Opinion No. 16, paragraph 55.
[40]APB Opinion No. 25, paragraph 10(a).
[41]ARB No. 43, Chapter 13, paragraph 13, footnote 3.
[42]APB Opinion No. 25, paragraph 11(a).

COMPUTATION OF COMPENSATION EXPENSE

Number of Shares Issued	Valuation Method	Total Value
500	$34 per share—cost of shares reacquired during year	17,000
500	$38 per share—quoted market price at December 31, 19x7 for shares acquired in prior years	19,000
1,000	Total value of shares issued	36,000
	Amount received from employees	
	1,000 shares at $33 per share	33,000
	Compensation expense	3,000

SCHEDULE 9

The entry made at December 31, 19x7 to record the issuance of the 1,000 shares of treasury stock was as follows:

	Debit	Credit
Cash	33,000	
Salary expense	3,000	
Treasury stock		35,000
Paid-in capital		1,000

To record reissue of treasury stock under stock option plan as follows:
500 shares acquired at $36 per share—	18,000	
500 shares acquired at $34 per share—	17,000	
	35,000	

To record cash received and additional salary expense created by exercise of the stock option and to credit paid-in capital with the excess of the sum of cash received and salary expense over cost of the treasury stock.

EARNINGS PER SHARE

As stated in a previous section, this chapter is not concerned with, and provides no guidance for, computing or reporting earnings per share. However, since the dilution concept developed for computing earnings per share calls for application of the "treasury stock" method, and because treasury stock is important in computing the weighted average of shares outstanding during an accounting period, the following explanations are appropriate for this text.

"Treasury Stock" Method

In accordance with the dilution concept the amount of dilution to be reflected in earnings per share data should be computed by application of the "treasury stock" method. Under this method earnings per share data are computed as if options and warrants were exercised at the beginning of the period, and as if the funds obtained thereby were used to purchase common stock at the average market price during the period. Thus, the "treasury stock" method has nothing to do with treasury stock, itself, and applies to only one of many assumptions comprehended in the principles of the dilution concept.[43]

Weighted Average of Number of Shares Outstanding

In computing the weighted average of the number of shares of common stock outstanding during a period, reacquired shares should be excluded from the date of their reacquisition, and thus included in the computation of the weighted average only for the actual time the shares were outstanding.[44]

INCOME TAX TREATMENT OF TRANSACTIONS IN TREASURY STOCK

The fact that certain transactions in treasury stock may give rise to taxable income is no bar to the application of correct accounting procedures to such transactions.[45]

Generally, no taxable gain or loss is recognized to a corporation on the receipt of money or other property in exchange for its own stock, including treasury stock. It is immaterial whether the stock is sold at a premium or at a discount. However, if a corporation uses appreciated property to redeem part or all of a shareholder's stock the corporation must, in most cases, pay tax on any appreciation in value of the property (fair value over adjusted basis) used to complete the redemption.[46]

DISCLOSURE OF RESTRICTION BY STATE LAW ON PAYMENT OF DIVIDENDS DUE TO ACQUISITION OF TREASURY STOCK

When state laws relating to acquisition of stock restrict the availability of retained earnings for payment of dividends, or have other effects of a significant nature, these facts should be disclosed in the financial statements, or notes thereof.[47]

PAID-IN CAPITAL

Paid-in capital represents capital contributed for shares in excess of their par or stated value, or capital contributed other than for shares, whether from stockholders or from others. The paid-in capital representing the excess over par or stated value of shares can arise as a result of original issue of shares in excess of their par or stated value, or from a reduction in par or stated value of shares after issuance, or from

---

[43]APB Opinion No. 15, paragraph 36.
[44]APB Opinion No. 15, paragraph 47.
[45]ARB No. 43, Chapter 1-B, paragraph 8.
[46]IRS Regulation 1.1032-1.
[47]APB Opinion No. 6, paragraph 13.

transactions by the corporation in its own shares.[48] In 1949 the Committee on Terminology of the American Institute of Accountants recommended that the term "surplus," either alone or combined, be discontinued.[49] Even so, Accounting Research Bulletin No. 43, published in 1953 continued to use the term "capital surplus" with reference to contributory capital other than the par or stated value of capital stock. While some companies still cling to the term "capital surplus," there has been a trend away from the use of the term "surplus" to designate paid-in capital in the balance sheet presentation of stockholders' equity. Some of the descriptive captions used by various companies to designate the paid-in capital component of stockholders' equity are as follows:

Additional paid-in capital	Other paid-in capital
Capital in excess of par or stated value	Additional capital
Capital surplus	Other capital
Paid-in capital	Paid-in surplus

All of these terms are synonymous, but the term "paid-in capital" is used almost exclusively in this chapter.

GENERAL ACCOUNTING PROCEDURES FOR RECORDING TRANSACTIONS AFFECTING PAID-IN CAPITAL

Recording the effect on paid-in capital resulting from issuing shares in excess of par value, reducing the par value of shares after issuance, converting preferred stock to common, and paying cash dividends from accumulated paid-in capital are elementary accounting procedures, and there are no specific *official* guidelines that provide for such procedures. The following is a brief outline of the accounting entries required in each of the circumstances previously indicated.

Issuance of Shares in Excess of Par or Stated Value

Capital stock may be issued for cash, property, or services, and the effect on paid-in capital on issuance of stock depends upon the valuation of the consideration received for the shares issued. For example, if stock having a par value of $10,000 is issued in exchange for $12,000 in cash, the entry to record the transaction would be to simply debit cash for $12,000, credit the capital stock account for the par value of $10,000, and credit paid-in capital for the $2,000 received in excess of par value. The same type of entry would be made for stock issued for property or services. However, when stock is issued for property or services, the determination of the fair value of the consideration received for the stock may present a serious problem in valuation.

Reduction of Par or Stated Value After Issuance

A reduction in the par or stated value of a class of capital stock after issuance does not require a complicated entry to record the occurrence. For example, if a company has issued 10,000 shares of common stock at a stated value of $10.00 per share, its common stock account would reflect a credit balance of $100,000. If the Board of Directors adopted a resolution to reduce the stated value of the issued shares to $1.00 per share, it would be necessary to reduce the balance in the common stock account to $10,000. This could be done simply by debiting the common

---

[48]Accounting Terminology Bulletin No. 1, paragraph 69(2)(b).
[49]Accounting Terminology Bulletin No. 1, paragraph 69(1).

stock account for $90,000 and crediting paid-in capital for the same amount. Any paid-in capital that had previously arisen from the sale of the 10,000 shares would remain in the paid-in capital account, and would be combined with the $90,000 resulting from the reduction in stated value.

Conversion of Preferred Stock to Common Stock

The effect on paid-in capital of a conversion of preferred stock to common stock would be simply the difference between the par value of the preferred stock retired and the common stock issued. If, for example, a company had a plan to redeem $10.00 par value preferred stock by issuing five shares of $1.00 common stock for each share of preferred stock converted, and the preferred stockholders surrendered 10,000 shares of preferred stock for conversion, the entry to record the transaction would be as follows:

	Debit	Credit
Preferred stock	100,000	
Common stock		50,000
Paid-in capital		50,000

To record retirement of 10,000—$10.00 par value preferred shares and issuance of 50,000—$1.00 par common shares in exchange therefore, and to record the resulting addition to paid-in capital.

However, the entry becomes more complicated when common stock held in the treasury is used to effect the conversion of preferred stock. In such cases the excess of the cost over par value of the treasury stock reissued must be charged to paid-in capital, if any exists, otherwise to retained earnings. For example, the following entry would be made where a company, having a balance of $30,000 in its paid-in capital account, converted 10,000 shares of preferred stock having a par value of $10.00 per share to 10,000 shares of $10.00 par value common stock held in the treasury, and which cost $115,000.

	Debit	Credit
Preferred stock	100,000	
Paid-in capital	15,000	
Treasury stock		115,000

To record conversion of 1,000 shares of $10.00 preferred stock to 1,000 shares of $10.00 common stock held in the treasury and which cost $115,000.

Payment of Cash Dividends from Paid-in Capital

Where state law permits the payment of cash dividends from paid-in capital, such payment is not in violation of generally accepted accounting principles. In many instances a company having a loss year will pay cash dividends from accumulated paid-in capital. The entry to record the transaction would be to charge paid-in capital and credit cash for the amount of the dividend declared and paid.

A separate paid-in capital account should be maintained for each class of stock issued, so that proper adjustments can be made when transactions occur in a particular series of shares.

PRESCRIBED ACCOUNTING PROCEDURES FOR RECORDING TRANSACTIONS AFFECTING PAID-IN CAPITAL

Most of the official directives that prescribe procedures for accounting for paid-in capital are concerned with the value assigned to the consideration given or received by a corporation in transactions involving issuance or reacquisition of its own capital stock. However, there are other circumstances where particular directives apply, and there are also prohibitions against certain uses of paid-in capital. The following paragraphs in this section explain and illustrate accounting procedures involving paid-in capital which are prescribed by specific official directives.

PROHIBITED TRANSACTIONS IN PAID-IN CAPITAL

The following types of transactions with respect to paid-in capital are prohibited, or restricted in some manner.

Paid-in Capital Cannot Be Used to Relieve Charges Against Income

Paid-in capital, however created, should not be used to relieve net income of charges that otherwise would be made against results of operations, either of the current year, or future years. There is an exception to this rule provided for in quasi-reorganizations, as explained later in the chapter in the section dealing with retained earnings.[50]

Intangible Assets

The cost of an intangible asset, including goodwill acquired in a business combination, may not be written off in a lump sum to paid-in capital or to retained earnings, nor be reduced to nominal amount at or immediately after acquisition.[51] This paragraph is a specific extension of the prohibition outlined in the previous paragraph regarding the use of paid-in capital to relieve the income account of charges that otherwise would be made against it; that is, amortization of goodwill as a charge against current income.

Donated Stock

In some instances capital stock is issued nominally for the acquisition of property when it appears that at or about the same time, and pursuant to a previous agreement or understanding, some portion of the stock is donated back to the corporation. In such cases it is not permissible to treat the par value of the stock nominally issued for the property as the cost of that property. If the stock so donated is subsequently sold, it is not permissible to treat the proceeds as a credit to retained earnings of the corporation.[52] The following example illustrates the appropriate accounting procedures for the type of transaction described.

Springs, Inc. issued 1,000 shares of $100 par value common stock which was selling on the market at $120 per share to James Kelley, in exchange for a die cutting machine, with the understanding that Kelley would return 200 shares to the company at the conclusion of the exchange. The 200 shares were donated to the company, and Springs subsequently sold the 200 shares for $120 per share to

---

[50]ARB No. 43, Chapter 1-A, paragraph 2.
[51]APB Opinion No. 17, paragraph 13.
[52]ARB No. 43, Chapter 1-A, paragraph 6.

a third party. The entries to record the issue, the donation, and the resale of the shares involved in the transaction were as follows:

(1)	Debit	Credit
Machine	96,000	
Excess of cost of stock issued over cost of asset	24,000	
Capital stock		100,000
Paid-in capital		20,000

To record cost of machine based on 800 shares of common stock issued; to record excess of cost of 1,000 shares over cost of machine purchased; to record issuance of 1,000 shares of stock; and to credit paid-in capital with the difference between par and market value of stock issued.

(2)		
Treasury stock	20,000	
Paid-in capital	4,000	
Excess cost of stock issued over cost of asset		24,000

To record donation of 200 shares of common stock from stock from James Kelley at par; to reduce paid-in capital by excess of value of 200 shares of stock over par at time of issue; and to eliminate account for excess of cost of stock over cost of asset acquired.

(3)	Debit	Credit
Cash	24,000	
Treasury stock		20,000
Paid-in capital		4,000

To record sale of 200 shares of $100 par value common stock donated by James Kelley, and record the excess of proceeds over par value of stock issued as paid-in capital.

The above entries would have the net effect of increasing balances in the accounts, and for the amounts, indicated below:

Assets		Stockholders' Equity	
Cash	24,000	Common Stock	100,000
Fixed Assets	96,000	Paid-In Capital	20,000
	120,000		120,000

PAID-IN CAPITAL AFFECTED BY ISSUANCE OF SHARES OTHER THAN IN CONVERSION OF STOCK AND FOR CASH

When stock is issued for cash, or for conversion of another class of stock, the value of the consideration received for the stock issued is easily identifiable, and thus the change to be made in paid-in capital for such transactions is simply the excess, or deficiency, of the value of the consideration over or under the par value of the stock issued in exchange. However, where stock is issued as compensation under an employees' stock option or purchase plan, or for the conversion of debt having stock purchase warrants, serious problems arise as to the value of the consideration received for the stock, and the reciprocally related change to be made in paid-in capital. Prescribed accounting procedures and valuation methods for the two types of transactions indicated arc described in the paragraphs that follow.

Stock Issued Under Employees' Stock Option or Stock Purchase Plan

Compensatory and noncompensatory employee stock option and stock purchase plans are described in the paragraph captioned "Stock Issued to Employees" in the Treasury Stock section of this chapter, and the issuance of *treasury stock* to fulfill the employer's obligation under a stock option plan is illustrated in Model Case No. 5. It is also stated in the discussion about stock option plans that whether treasury stock or unissued shares are used to fulfill the employer's obligation is immaterial to a determination of value, and that the compensation involved in such plans is measured by the excess of the quoted market price at the measurement date, over the price to be paid by the employee, and if a quoted market price is unavailable, the best estimate of the market price of the stock should be used to measure compensation.[53] Thus, where unissued capital stock is issued under an employees' stock option plan, the accounting procedures would be the same as those illustrated in Model Case No. 5, except that the measurement of compensation would depend entirely on the quoted market price of the stock issued, and not on the cost of the treasury stock. The following example illustrates the entries to be made where unissued stock is issued to employees to fulfill the employer's obligation under a stock option plan.

Reppert, Inc. has a stock option plan under which employees may purchase stock at a 10% discount from the quoted market price at the measurement date. The measurement date was set at December 31, 19x3, and Reppert's $100 par value common stock was selling on the market at $120 per share on that date. Reppert was obliged to issue 1,000 shares to his employees at December 31, 19x3; he issued the shares on that date and made the following entry to record the transaction:

	Debit	Credit
Cash	108,000	
Salary expense	12,000	
Paid-in capital		20,000
Capital stock		100,000
To record issuance of 1,000 shares of $100 par value common stock under stock option plan; to record cash received from employees at $108 per share, salary expense at $12 per share, and increase in paid-in capital at $20 per share.		

---

[53]APB Opinion No. 25, paragraph 10(a).

In some cases a principal stockholder arranges to personally finance the cost of an employees' stock option plan. This type of plan should be treated as a contribution of capital by the stockholder with the offsetting charge accounted for in the same manner as compensatory plans adopted by corporations.[54] As an illustration, if a stockholder had agreed to finance the issuance of stock in the foregoing example by purchasing the stock at market value and issuing it to the covered employees personally, compensation would be recognized in the same manner as in the previous example, and the entry to record the transaction would be as follows:

	Debit	Credit
Cash (from stockholder)	120,000	
Salary expense	12,000	
Paid-in capital		32,000
Capital stock		100,000

To record issuance of 1,000 shares of $100 par value stock at $120 per share to stockholder; to recognize compensation cost at 10% of the value of the stock issued; and to credit paid-in capital with the difference between the sum of the cash contributed by stockholder and compensation expense, and the par value of the shares issued.

Tax Benefits Arising from Stock Option Plans

Since the expense of fulfilling a stock option obligation is deductible for tax purposes at the time the stock is issued, an early issue of stock under an option obligation could result in a tax benefit unrelated to the compensation expense that a corporation recognizes. In other words, the tax benefits could be obtained immediately on compensation expense that would be deferred over subsequent periods for accounting purposes.

In such cases an employer should reduce income tax expense (for a period) by no more than the proportion of the tax reduction that is related to compensation recognized for that period. The compensation that would be recognized in subsequent periods would be timing differences, and deferred taxes should be set up based on the reversal of such timing differences. The remainder of the tax reduction, if any, is related to an amount that is deductible for income tax purposes, but does not affect income. This remainder should not be included in income, but should be added to paid-in capital in the period of the tax reduction. Conversely, a tax reduction may be less than it would be if recorded compensation expenses were deductible for income tax purposes. If so, the corporation may deduct the difference from paid-in capital in the period of the tax reduction to the extent that tax reductions under the same or similar stock option plans have been included in paid-in capital.[55]

Convertible Debt and Debt Issued with Stock Purchase Warrants

Current official accounting directives make a significant distinction between convertible debt securities, and debt with detachable warrants to purchase stock, and prescribe different accounting procedures to record the issuance of each type of debt.[56]

---

[54]Accounting Interpretation No. 1 of APB Opinion No. 25.
[55]APB Opinion No. 25, paragraphs 16 to 18.
[56]APB Opinion No. 14.

Convertible Debt

Convertible debt securities are those debt securities which are convertible into common stock of the issuer at a specified price at the option of the holder, which are sold at a price at issuance not significantly in excess of face value.[57] Largely because of the inseparability of the debt and conversion option, no portion of the proceeds from the issuance of convertible debt securities should be accounted for as attributable to the conversion feature.[58] Thus, the issuance of a $100,000 convertible debt security for $100,000 cash would be recorded simply as a credit to long-or short-term debt, and a debit to cash. However, the option price stipulated in the conversion feature of the security would affect paid-in capital upon conversion. The following example illustrates accounting for convertible debt at the time of conversion.

Stovall, Inc. issued a $100,000 convertible debenture for a cash price of $100,000. Since the present value of the debt security coincided with the $100,000 cash proceeds, there was no premium or discount attributable to the security. The debenture stipulated that at the end of five years Stovall would convert the debt security into Stovall's $100 par value common stock at a conversion price of $125 per share. At the end of five years, on December 31, 19x3, Stovall's stock was selling in the market for $110 per share. In accordance with the conversion agreement, at that date Stovall called the debenture and issued 800 shares of $100 par value common stock to the holder of the debenture to effect the conversion and extinguish the convertible debt security. Stovall made the following entry to record the transaction:

	Debit	Credit
Debenture payable	100,000	
Paid-in capital		20,000
Common stock		80,000

To record issuance of 800 shares of $100 par value common stock for conversion of $100,000 convertible debenture, and record resulting increase in paid-in capital.

Debt Issued with Detachable Stock Purchase Warrants

Debt with detachable warrants to purchase stock at a stipulated option price may be treated as separate securities, since the detachable warrants often trade separately from the debt instrument.[59] Thus, the portion of the proceeds allocable to the warrants should be accounted for as paid-in capital. The allocation should be based on the relative fair values of the two securities at time of issuance.[60] Any resulting discount or premium on the securities should be accounted for as such.[61] The following example illustrates the entries required to record the issuance of debt with detachable stock purchase warrants.

Burns Corporation issued a $100,000 debenture bond to which was attached a detachable warrant authorizing the holder to purchase 1,000 shares of Burns' $100 par value common stock at an option purchase price of $110 per share. At the time of the issuance of the debenture, the market price of Burns' common stock was quoted at $120 per share, and Burns received $120,000 for the deben-

[57]APB Opinion No. 14, paragraph 3.
[58]APB Opinion No. 14, paragraph 12.
[59]APB Opinion No. 14, paragraph 13.
[60]APB Opinion No. 14, paragraph 16.
[61]APB Opinion No. 12, paragraphs 16 and 17.

ture. Burns concluded that the fair value of the debenture was $100,000 and coincided with its face value, that the fair value of the detachable warrant was $20,000, and that no premium or discount was inherent in the transaction. Accordingly, Burns made the following entry to record the transaction:

	Debit	Credit
Cash	120,000	
Debenture payable		100,000
Paid-in capital		20,000

To record issuance of $100,000 debenture with detachable stock purchase warrant for $120,000 cash, and to account for the fair value of the warrant as paid-in capital.

Whenever the warrant was exercised, Burns would make the following entry to record the issuance of the stock:

	Debit	Credit
Cash	110,000	
Paid-in capital		10,000
Common stock		100,000

To record issuance of 1,000 shares of $100 par value stock for $110,000 received in cash on exercise of warrant, and to credit paid-in capital with the excess of cash received over par value of stock issued.

The Accounting Principles Board notes that when convertible debt is issued at a substantial premium, there is a presumption that such premium represents paid-in capital, and that the debt should be accounted for in the same manner as that for debt with detachable stock purchase warrants.[62]

BUSINESS COMBINATIONS

Accumulated paid-in capital plays a very minor role in accounting for a business combination. However, there may be some adjustments to paid-in capital that must be made at the time the combination is consummated.

Purchase Method

Paid-in capital of the acquired company has no accounting effect whatever in a business combination accounted for by the purchase method, since it is merely a part of contributory capital, and is eliminated by the purchase. However, the acquiring company may develop paid-in capital if the value of the net assets acquired exceeds the par value of the stock issued to purchase the company. An illustration of this situation was demonstrated in Model Case No. 3.

Pooling of Interests Method

The following adjustments may, or must, be made to paid-in capital in a business combination accounted for as a pooling of interests.

---

[62]APB Opinion No. 14, paragraph 18.

Number of Shares Issued by the Combining Company Exceeds Number of Shares Cancelled

In cases where the distributing company issues shares on other than a one-for-one basis, the total shares issued by the issuing company may exceed the number of shares cancelled and, consequently, the amount of outstanding stock of the combined corporation at par or stated value exceeds the total amount of capital stock of the combining companies. In such cases the excess should be deducted first from the combined paid-in capital, and then from combined retained earnings.[63] Model Case No. 2 illustrated such a situation. However, the combined company in Model Case No. 2 did not have any paid-in capital, and the total excess was charged to combined retained earnings. Had there been any paid-in capital in the combined company, the excess would have been charged to that account to the extent of the balance therein.

Distributing Treasury Stock Held by the Issuing Company

A corporation which effects a combination accounted for as a pooling of interests by distributing its own treasury stock should first account for those shares as though retired.[64] An illustration of this situation was in the "Treasury Stock" section of this chapter. In the cited example the company charged the total cost of the treasury stock to retained earnings. However, if the issuing company in the example had accumulated paid-in capital, the treasury stock would have been accounted for as being retired by charging a part of the cost to paid-in capital in the same manner as that demonstrated in Model Case No. 3.

Stock of Issuing Company Held by Other Combining Companies

As stated in the Treasury Stock section of the chapter, if one or more of the combining companies hold stock in the issuing company, such investments in effect become treasury stock of the combined corporation.[65] In such a situation, it is important to identify any existing paid-in capital that pertains to such "treasury stock" that is acquired from the combining companies, and either record it separately in the accounts of the combined company, or have a collateral record that will permit appropriate accounting for later dispositions of the stock so held.

STOCK DIVIDENDS AND STOCK SPLIT-UPS

The next section of this chapter (captioned "Retained Earnings") contains a comprehensive discussion of stock dividends and stock split-ups. The section also demonstrates methods of measuring the values involved in these occurrences, and describes accounting procedures for recording the resultant changes in stockholders' equity. It is sufficient to say that in some circumstances stock dividends affect paid-in capital, and the next section illustrates examples of such changes.

TRANSACTIONS IN TREASURY STOCK

The preceding section of this chapter sets forth a comprehensive discussion on treasury stock, and explains and illustrates, where applicable, the effect on paid-in capital resulting from cancellation and retirement of reacquired stock, and fulfilling stock option obligations by issuance of reacquired capital stock.

---

[63]APB Opinion No. 16, paragraph 53.
[64]APB Opinion No. 16, paragraph 55.
[65]APB Opinion No. 16, paragraph 55.

CORPORATE READJUSTMENTS (QUASI-REORGANIZATIONS)

Where a corporation elects to restate its assets, capital stock, and retained earnings through a readjustment, the amounts determined to be written off should be charged first against retained earnings to the full extent of such retained earnings; any balance may then be charged against paid-in capital. A company which has subsidiaries should apply the rule in such a way that no consolidated retained earnings survive a readjustment in which any part of the losses has been charged to paid-in capital.[66]

If, in a corporate readjustment, provision is made to cover estimated gains and losses known to have occurred prior to the date of readjustment, and the amounts so provided are subsequently found to be excessive or insufficient, the difference should not be carried to retained earnings, nor used to offset losses or gains originating after the readjustment, but should be carried to paid-in capital.[67]

RETAINED EARNINGS

Retained earnings is defined in official accounting literature as the balance of net profits, income, gains, and losses of a corporation (other than gains from transactions in its own shares, and losses therefrom chargeable to paid-in capital), from the date of incorporation (or from the latest date when a deficit was eliminated in a quasi-reorganization) after deducting distributions therefrom to shareholders and transfers therefrom to capital stock or paid-in capital accounts.[68]

In the earlier years of the accounting profession there was an enormous number of transactions which were not reported in the income statement, but credited or charged directly to retained earnings. However, the development of a "clean surplus" concept initiated a trend away from indiscriminate direct entries to retained earnings and toward using a single entry to that account to represent net income or loss from operations for that period. Thus, today the income statement comprehends practically all revenues and expenses, extraordinary or ordinary, infrequent or recurring, and the bottom line of the statement representing net income or loss is the only entry made to retained earnings to represent results of operations.

The determination of net income or loss involves the whole body of generally accepted accounting principles. Obviously, this chapter cannot attempt to discuss the accounting principles and measurement methods comprehended in the determination of the net income or loss credited or charged to retained earnings. However, it does explain the credits and charges, other than net income or loss, which are required to be made to retained earnings by official accounting directives. This section identifies the specific directives, and illustrates accounting procedures for recording appropriate changes in the retained earnings account.

The major direct charges and credits to retained earnings, other than net income or loss, result from the following:

Cash dividends	Losses on capital stock transactions
Stock dividends	Opening balance adjustments
Cash payment in lieu of fractional shares	Creation, additions to, and restoration of appropriations of retained earnings
Treasury stock transactions	

---

[66]ARB No. 43, Chapter 7-A, paragraph 6.
[67]ARB No. 43, Chapter 7-A, paragraph 5.
[68]Accounting Terminology Bulletin No. 1, paragraph 34.

CASH DIVIDENDS

Recording cash dividends is a simple matter of bookkeeping. Generally, a liability account is set up for dividends payable in accordance with the resolution adopted by the Board of Directors to pay a cash dividend. At the time the dividend payable is recorded it is charged to retained earnings, and when the cash is paid it is charged to the dividend payable account. However, as disclosed in the preceding section of this chapter, cash dividends may also be charged to paid-in capital in some instances.

STOCK DIVIDENDS AND STOCK SPLIT-UPS

A stock dividend is an issuance by a corporation of its own common shares to its common shareholders without consideration, and in contemplation that the number of shares issued will not be sufficient to significantly affect the market value of the stock previously outstanding.[69] On the other hand, a stock split-up is an issuance by a corporation of its own common shares to its common shareholders without consideration, and made for the purpose of increasing the number of outstanding shares to effect a reduction in their unit market price.[70] Thus, by definition, the terms stock dividend and stock split-up are synonymous, and the difference between the two occurrences lies in the intention of the issuer with respect to the effect of the issuance on the market price of the previously outstanding stock. Even so, the point at which the relative size of the additional shares issued becomes large enough to materially affect the unit market price of the stock cannot be absolutely known in advance. Since accounting for stock dividends is quite different from accounting for stock split-ups, a rule of thumb has been established that an issue of 20% to 25% of the number previously outstanding would be a dividend, and any issuance in excess of 25% would be a split-up.[71]

Accounting for Stock Dividends

A stock dividend should be accounted for by the issuing corporation by transferring the fair value of the issued shares from retained earnings to the capital stock account, and to paid-in capital if the fair value exceeds the par value.[72] For example, a company which issues 1,000 shares of $10 par value stock at a time when the market price is $12 per share should make the following entry:

	Debit	Credit
Retained earnings	12,000	
Capital stock		10,000
Paid-in capital		2,000

Accounting for Stock Split-Ups

There is no need to capitalize retained earnings when there is a stock split-up.[73]

Stock Dividends Having the Nature of Stock Split-Ups

Where the number of shares issued in a stock dividend is so great that it has the

---

[69]ARB No. 43, Chapter 7-B, paragraph 1.
[70]ARB No. 43, Chapter 7-B, paragraph 2.
[71]ARB No. 43, Chapter 7-B, paragraph 13.
[72]ARB No. 43, Chapter 7-B, paragraph 10.
[73]ARB No. 43, Chapter 7-B, paragraph 12.

effect of materially reducing the share market value, the dividend clearly partakes of a stock split-up, and under such circumstances there is no need to capitalize retained earnings. In such instances every effort should be made to avoid the use of the word "dividend" in public notices and announcements. Where the word "dividend" cannot be omitted because of legal requirements, such a transaction should be described as a "split-up effected in the form of a dividend."[74]

However, in practice, many companies do issue stock split-ups in the form of *dividends*, and go through the capitalization process prescribed for dividends outlined above. For example, a company may make a 3 for 2 (50%) split in the form of a dividend, retain the same par value for the newly issued shares, and increase the capital stock account for the par value of the dividend shares by charging paid-in capital to the extent it is available for that class of stock, or by capitalizing a portion of retained earnings.

Closely Held Companies

It is not necessary to capitalize retained earnings for a stock dividend declared by a closely held company.[75]

CASH PAYMENTS IN LIEU OF FRACTIONAL SHARES

Retained earnings are usually charged with cash paid shareholders for fractional shares due them as a result of a stock dividend or stock split-up.

TREASURY STOCK TRANSACTIONS

The treatment of gains and losses resulting from transactions in treasury stock were discussed in the "Treasury Stock" section. In general, gains and losses resulting from such transactions are charged or credited first to the portion of paid-in capital that was accumulated in connection with the respective class of stock involved in the transaction, if any exists, and the remainder to retained earnings. However, the corporation has the option of charging all such losses directly to retained earnings.

LOSSES ON CAPITAL STOCK TRANSACTIONS

Losses resulting from transactions in capital stock may be charged to retained earnings. However, if paid-in capital exists in connection with the class of stock on which a loss is sustained, the paid-in capital account may be reduced to the extent of the amount applicable to that class of stock.

POOLING OF INTERESTS

Generally, in a business combination accounted for by the pooling of interests method, the retained earnings of all the constituent companies are transferred to the combined company. However, it was demonstrated in Model Case No. 2 in the "Common Stock" section that where the number of shares issued in a combination exceeds the number of shares cancelled, the resulting deficiency in the capital stock account for the par value of the total shares issued may be charged to combined retained earnings.

---

[74]ARB No. 43, Chapter 7-B, paragraph 11.
[75]ARB No. 43, Chapter 7-B, paragraph 12.

OPENING BALANCE ADJUSTMENTS

Restatements of the opening balance of retained earnings are, in effect, direct charges or credits to retained earnings that circumvent the income statement. Reasons for which the opening balance of retained earnings may be restated include changes in accounting principles, change in the reporting entity, and prior period adjustments.

Changes in Accounting Principles

Changes in the accounting principles described below require that the financial statements of all prior periods presented be restated.[76]
(a) A change from the LIFO method of inventory pricing to another method;
(b) A change in the method of accounting for long-term construction contracts; and
(c) A change to or from the "full cost" method which is used in the extractive industries.

The issuance of an industry audit guide by a committee of the American Institute of Certified Public Accountants also constitutes sufficient support for a change in accounting principles.[77]

Change in the Reporting Entity

Accounting changes which result in financial statements being, in effect, the statements of a different reporting entity, should be reported by restating the financial statements of all prior periods presented in order to show financial information for the new reporting entity for all periods.[78] For this purpose, reporting by a different reporting entity is limited to:
(a) presenting consolidated or combined statements in place of statements of individual companies;
(b) changing specific subsidiaries comprising the group of companies for which consolidated financial statements are presented; and
(c) changing the companies included in combined financial statements.

A business combination accounted for by the pooling-of-interests method also results in a different reporting entity.[79]

Prior Period Adjustments

Items of profit and loss related to the following shall be accounted for and reported as prior period adjustments and excluded from a determination of net income for the current period:
(a) a correction of an error in the financial statements of a prior period; and
(b) adjustments that result from realization of income tax benefits of pre-acquisition operating loss carryforwards of purchased subsidiaries.[80]

APPROPRIATIONS OF RETAINED EARNINGS

Appropriations of retained earnings for various contingencies are permitted, provided the appropriation is shown within the stockholders' equity section of the balance sheet, and is clearly identified as an appropriation. Costs and losses shall not be charged to an appropriation of retained earnings, and no part of the appropriation

---

[76]APB Opinion No. 20, paragraph 27.
[77]APB Opinion No. 20, footnote 5.
[78]APB Opinion No. 20, paragraph 34.
[79] APB Opinion No. 20, paragraph 12.
[80]FASB Statement No. 16, paragraph 11.

shall be transferred to income.[81] Thus, an enterprise may set up an appropriation of retained earnings, such as, a "reserve for foreign business risks created out of retained earnings." Such an appropriation cannot be charged with costs and losses, and subsequently, no part of it can be recognized as income. However, the appropriation can be created and expanded by direct charges to retained earnings, and it can be reduced or eliminated by direct credits to the retained earnings account.

QUASI-REORGANIZATION

Where a corporation elects to restate its assets, capital stock, and retained earnings through a readjustment, when the amounts to be written off have been determined, they should be charged first to retained earnings to the full extent of such retained earnings, and any balance may then be charged against paid-in capital. A company which has subsidiaries should apply this rule in such a way that no consolidated retained earnings survive a readjustment in which part of the losses has been charged to paid-in capital.

After such a readjustment retained earnings previously accumulated cannot be carried forward under that title. A new retained earnings account should be established, dated to show that it runs from the effective date of the readjustment, and this dating should be disclosed in financial statements for not more than ten years. In some exceptional circumstances the discontinuance of the dating of retained earnings could be justified at the conclusion of a period of less than ten years.[82]

DEDUCTIONS FROM STOCKHOLDERS' EQUITY

There are some circumstances where a reduction in stockholders' equity must be reported under a specific caption on the balance sheet. Two such instances are discussed in the following paragraphs.

STOCK ISSUED TO EMPLOYEES

If stock is issued in a compensatory stock option plan before some or all of the services are performed, part of the consideration recorded for the stock issued is unearned compensation, and should be shown as a separate reduction of stockholders' equity. The unearned compensation should be accounted for as an expense of the period or periods in which the employee performs the services.[83]

VALUATION ALLOWANCE FOR MARKETABLE SECURITIES

For enterprises not having specialized accounting practices with respect to marketable securities, the amount by which the aggregate cost of the securities portfolio exceeds its market value shall be accounted for as a valuation allowance. Changes in the valuation allowance for marketable equity securities portfolios included in current assets shall be included in the determination of net income of the period in which they occur. However, *accumulated changes* in the valuation allowance for a marketable equity securities portfolio included in noncurrent assets or in an unclassified balance

---

[81]FASB Statement No. 5, paragraph 15.
[82]ARB No. 43, Chapter 7-A, paragraph 10, as amended by ARB No. 46, paragraph 2.
[83]APB Opinion No. 25, paragraph 14.

sheet shall be included in the stockholders' equity section of the balance sheet, and shown separately.[84]

SPECIAL DISCLOSURES

DISCLOSURE OF CAPITAL CHANGES IN SPECIAL CIRCUMSTANCES

In addition to the general requirement to disclose changes in stockholders' equity accounts, and the number of equity shares issued during a reporting period, the following disclosures concerning stockholders' equity should be made under the circumstances indicated by the paragraph captions.

DEVELOPMENT STAGE ENTERPRISES

Financial statements issued by a development stage enterprise shall present financial position, changes in financial position, and results of operations in conformity with the generally accepted accounting principles that apply to established operating enterprises.[85] However, in issuing the said basic financial statements as an established operating enterprise, a development stage enterprise shall present a balance sheet including any cumulative net losses reported with a descriptive caption, such as, "deficit accumulated during the development stage" in the stockholders' equity section. In addition, the statement of stockholders' equity must show, from the enterprise's inception, the following information:

(1) For each issuance, the date and number of shares of stock, warrants, rights, or other equity securities issued for cash and for other consideration.
(2) For each issuance, the dollar amounts (per share or other equity unit and in total) assigned to the consideration received for shares of stock, warrants, rights, or other equity securities. Dollar amounts shall be assigned to any noncash consideration received.
(3) For each issuance involving noncash consideration, the nature of the noncash consideration and the basis for assigning amounts.[86]

SHORT-TERM OBLIGATIONS EXPECTED TO BE REFINANCED

If a short-term obligation is excluded from current liabilities pursuant to an agreement that permits the enterprise to refinance the short-term obligation on a long-term basis, the notes to the financial statements shall include a general description of the financing agreement and the terms of any new obligation incurred or expected to be incurred or equity securities issued or expected to be issued as a result of a refinancing.[87]

STOCK OPTION PLANS

In connection with the financial statements of enterprises having stock option plans, disclosure should be made as to the status of the option or plan at the end of the period of the report, including the number of shares under option, the option

---

[84]FASB Statement No. 12, paragraph 11.
[85]FASB Statement No. 7, paragraph 10.
[86]FASB Statement No. 7, paragraph 11.
[87]FASB Statement No. 6, paragraph 15.

price, and the number of shares as to which options were exercisable. As to options exercised during the period, disclosure should be made of the number of shares involved and the option price thereof.[88]

STATEMENT OF CHANGES IN FINANCIAL POSITION

In addition to working capital or cash provided from operations, and changes in elements of working capital, the Statement of Changes in Financial Position should clearly disclose the following changes in stockholders' equity:

1. Conversion of long-term debt or preferred stock to common stock.
2. Issuance, redemption, or purchase of capital stock for cash or for assets other than cash.
3. Dividends in cash or in kind or other distributions to shareholders, except stock dividends and stock split-ups.[89]

LIQUIDATING PREFERENCES OF PREFERRED STOCK

Companies at times issue preferred (or other senior) stock which has a preference in involuntary liquidation considerably in excess of the par or stated value of the shares. In these cases, the liquidation preference of the stock should be disclosed in the equity section of the balance sheet in the aggregate, either parenthetically or "in short," rather than on a per share basis or by disclosure in notes.

In addition, the financial statements should disclose, either on the face of the balance sheet or in notes pertaining thereto:

(a) the aggregate or per share amounts at which preferred shares may be called or are subject to redemption through sinking-fund operations or otherwise;
(b) the aggregate and per share amounts of arrearages in cumulative dividends.[90]

COMPLEX CAPITAL STRUCTURES

The use of complex securities complicates earnings per share computations, and makes additional disclosures necessary. In such situations, the financial statements should include a description, in summary form, sufficient to explain the pertinent rights and privileges of the various securities outstanding. Examples of information which should be disclosed are dividend and liquidation preferences, participation rights, call prices and dates, conversion or exercise prices or rates and pertinent dates, sinking fund requirements, unusual voting rights, etc.[91]

ILLUSTRATION OF REPORTING CHANGES IN STOCKHOLDERS' EQUITY

Schedule 10 illustrates a format for reporting changes in stockholders' equity that was used in the annual report of an enterprise having a classified balance sheet. However, in practice there is wide variety in the manner of reporting such changes, and this illustration is simply an example of one method.

---

[88] ARB No. 43, Chapter 13-B, paragraph 15.
[89] APB Opinion No. 19, paragraph 14.
[90] APB Opinion No. 10, paragraphs 10 and 11.
[91] APB Opinion No. 15, paragraph 19.

CONSOLIDATED STATEMENT OF SHAREHOLDERS' EQUITY

	$1.25 Cumulative Preferred Stock	Common Stock	Paid-In Capital	Retained Earnings (Deficit)	Unrealized Loss on Noncurrent Marketable Securities	$1.25 Cumulative Preferred Stock in Treasury	Total
Balance—January 1, 19x6	229,258	243,963	893,993	(534,107)		(2,590)	830,517
Cash distribution paid on $1.25 cumulative preferred stock			(11,173)				(11,173)
16 shares of $1.25 cumulative preferred stock acquired for Treasury						(181)	(181)
Adjustment to carrying value of subsidiary distributed to shareholders			1,122				1,122
Issuance of 681 shares under employment agreement		681	3,712				4,393
Purchase and retirement of 26,377 shares of common stock		(26,337)	(210,699)				(237,036)
Issuance of 111 shares on exercise of stock option		111	403				514
Dividend on common stock			(10,921)				(10,921)
Net income				346,402			346,402
Balance—December 31, 19x6	229,258	218,418	666,437	(187,705)	—	(2,771)	923,637
Cash distribution paid on $1.25 cumulative preferred stock			(8,328)	(2,793)			(11,121)
191 shares of $1.25 cumulative preferred stock acquired for Treasury						(3,245)	(3,245)
Adjustment to carrying value of subsidiary distributed to shareholders			(1,528)				(1,528)
Issuance of 1,111 shares under employment agreement		1,111	7,403				8,514
Issuance of 2,000 shares on exercise of stock options		2,000	7,116				9,116
Dividends on common stock			(33,196)	(16,615)			(49,811)
Write-down of investments in noncurrent marketable equity securities					(7,502)		(7,502)
3% stock dividend paid January 31, 19x8		6,518	40,740	(48,278)			(1,020)
Net income				351,348			351,348
Balance—December 31, 19x7	229,258	228,047	678,644	95,957	(7,502)	(6,016)	1,218,388

SCHEDULE 10

9

Depreciation Accounting—
Depreciable Bases, Allocation Methods, and
Computational Techniques

Accounting Research Bulletin No. 43 states that depreciation accounting is a system of accounting which aims to distribute the cost or other basic value of tangible capital assets, less salvage value (if any), over the estimated useful life of the unit (which may be a group of assets) in a systematic and rational manner; and that it is a process of allocation, not of valuation.[1] In defining depreciation accounting, the Bulletin limits the process to allocation of the cost of depreciable assets, but places no limits whatever on the variety of rational and systematic methods that may be used to allocate such cost. Therefore, since there is no restriction on the choice of alternative methods of allocation, companies choose whatever method they wish, often using different methods under similar circumstances, and sometimes arbitrarily changing methods during the economic life of a particular asset, or group of assets.

For income tax purposes the law permits a deduction of a reasonable allowance for the exhaustion, wear and tear of property used in a trade or business, or of property held for income.[2] However, income tax regulations allow taxpayers to write off 20% of the cost of certain assets in the first taxable year for which a depreciation deduction is allowable, plus the normal depreciation deduction for that year. The regulations also permit a variety of depreciation methods, and provide specific guidelines for the use of straight-line, accelerated, and other consistent methods and, in addition, permit a rapid amortization of certain facilities. This variety in the methods of depreciation permitted by income tax regulations was developed over the years as income tax incentives, for one purpose or another, and the methods have little to do with the stated purpose of allowing a reasonable deduction for exhaustion, wear and tear of the property being depreciated. These tax incentives naturally influence companies in their selection of alternative allocation methods, and result, in many cases, in accounting for depreciation being conducted on the basis of tax considerations rather than on an economic basis, which requires a reasonable estimation of the economic life of the depreciable asset. This situation has caused widespread dissatisfaction with current practice in deprecia-

---

[1] *Restatement and Revision of Accounting Research Bulletins,* Accounting Research Bulletin No. 43 (New York, N.Y.: American Institute of Accountants, 1953) Chapter 9-C, paragraph 5.
[2] Internal Revenue Service Regulations 1.167(a)-1.

tion accounting among accountants and volumes have been written both by critics of the present accounting methods, and by proponents of unrestricted choice.

This chapter is not concerned with the controversy surrounding depreciation accounting, but is directed to a solution of problems encountered in the operation of accounting systems as they exist today, including all the major available allocation alternatives. To that end, it sets forth a general description of the system, explains permissible allocation methods, demonstrates techniques for computing allocation measurements, and describes appropriate accounting procedures to record allocation of the cost of the assets being depreciated.

DEPRECIABLE BASE

Since depreciation accounting is a process of allocation of the cost or other basic value of tangible capital assets, the depreciable base of the asset is the fundamental component of the accounting system. ARB No. 43 states, unequivocally, that depreciation should be on *historic cost*, and not on replacement cost, appraised values, or any other basis.[3] The cost to be allocated is *net cost*, and accordingly, the *original* cost of an asset may be adjusted by cost of acquisition, estimated salvage value, and estimated costs of disposing of, or removing the asset, when applicable.

Acquisition Costs

Most companies record depreciable assets at acquisition cost. Accounting Research Monograph No. 1 lists the following specific elements that are included in acquisition costs by at least some percentage of the companies surveyed in the research study:[4]

Incoming transportation costs	Installation costs
Temporary storage and handling	Cost of removing old assets
Cost of setting up new assets	Import duties
Sales or excise taxes	Purchases discounts
Interest on credit purchases	Gain on assets traded in
Loss on assets traded in	

Salvage Value

Most assets will have some value at the end of their service lives, and this value is required by generally accepted accounting principles to be recognized and deducted from the acquisition cost of the assets to arrive at the value of their depreciable base. However, accurately estimating salvage value is extremely difficult, and most companies simply do not recognize estimated residual values at all.[5] Income tax regulations also require recognition of salvage value in computing deductible depreciation expense.[6] However, as to depreciable personal property, if the estimated salvage value does not exceed 10% of the basis of the property, it may be ignored for tax purposes.[7] Thus, many companies use the 10% exemption as a rule of thumb, and unless the salvage value can be reasonably determined to be in excess of 10% of the acquisition cost, no residual value is recognized.

---

[3] ARB no. 43, Chapter 9-A, paragraph 7.

[4] *Accounting for Depreciable Assets,* Accounting Research Monograph No. 1. (New York, NY: Copyright 1975 by the American Institute of Certified Public Accountants. Chapter 2, Table 5.)

[5] Accounting Research Monograph No. 1 reported that only 25% of the industrial companies surveyed adjusted acquisition cost by estimated salvage value to arrive at a depreciable base. (Chapter 2, page 16.)

[6] Internal Revenue Service Regulations, Section 1.167(a)-1(a).

[7] Internal Revenue Service Regulations, Section 1.167(f)-1.

Cost of Disposal of Assets

Only a small percentage of companies adjust acquisition cost for estimated future costs of disposing of assets acquired, or costs of removing assets replaced.[8]

The following example illustrates a method of computing the depreciable base of a tangible capital asset.

In 19x1 Victor Concrete Corporation purchased a machine for manufacturing concrete blocks from Fairfax Machinery Company. The vendor's invoice from Fairfax was as follows:

1—Model 20 Cement Block Making Machine	108,000
State sales tax @ 5%	5,400
Freight charges	2,500
	115,900

Victor estimated the economic life of the machine to be eight years, and considered that, due to heavy wear and tear, the machine would have no residual value at the end of its service life other than the scrap value of its steel content, which was estimated to be $15,000. Installation costs of the new machine amounted to $8,000, and Victor estimated that the cost of removing the machine at the end of its service life would be approximately one-fourth that amount, or $2,000. Victor decided to capitalize freight and installation costs; to charge sales taxes to current income; and to depreciate the machine to its scrap value, less the cost of removing the machine at the end of its useful life. Accordingly, Victor computed the depreciable base of the machine as follows:

Vendor's price for machine		108,000
Incoming transporation costs		2,500
Installation cost		8,000
		118,500
Less—Residual Value		
Estimated proceeds from sale		
of scrap steel	15,000	
Less—Cost of removing machine	2,000	13,000
Depreciable base		105,500

Victor, of course, did not set the machine up on the books at its depreciable base. The various acquisition costs were set up as the basis of the machine, and the depreciation schedule was computed on the basis of the depreciable base over eight years, so that at the end of eight years the accumulated depreciation would amount to $105,500, resulting in a net book value at that time of $13,000. The sale of scrap metal for $15,000 and the cost of removal of $2,000, would be charged and credited to the asset account, and then, theoretically, the asset account would be equivalent to the accumulated depreciation account. Thus, Victor made the following entry to record the purchase of the machine:

		Credit	Debit
Block-making machine		118,500	
Tax expense		5,400	
Accounts payable			123,900
To record purchase of block-making machine, and set up payable as follows:			
Fairfax Machinery Company	115,900		
Installation charges	8,000		
	123,900		

---

[8] Accounting Research Monograph No. 1, Chapter 2, Table 7.

ESTIMATED USEFUL LIFE

The estimated useful life of a capital asset should be based on its usefulness to the company that depreciates it, and not necessarily on its economic life. For example, a machine may have an economic life of 20 years, but if the company that owns it plans to use it for only ten years, and then dispose of it, depreciation should be based on the cost of the machine, less estimated residual value, over the ten years it will be in service for the owner company. Generally, the depreciable life of an asset is based on the number of years it will be in service for the owner. However, in certain circumstances, the useful life of an asset may be based on the number of units it can produce before it becomes useless for its purpose; in other situations the useful life may be based on the total quantity of units available for production; thus, *time* is not always the only factor in estimating the economic life of an asset.

It is almost impossible to accurately predict useful life with a high degree of confidence and, consequently, conventional guides are generally used. Companies have relied heavily on the guidelines provided by the Internal Revenue Service: originally the old "Bulletin F," later the Class Life System (CLS), and more recently the Class Life Asset Depreciation Range System (ADR).

In any event, management has the responsibility for making estimates of useful lives that correspond as nearly as possible to the economic facts. If in doubt, the Internal Revenue Service guidelines can fairly be relied on, but if management has access to statistical data, empirical evidence, or historical experience in connection with a particular asset or group of assets, that confidently permits a more precise estimate than that indicated in the IRS guidelines, then the guidelines should be ignored and management should use its own estimate. However, the initial estimate of useful life does not terminate management's responsibility in the matter. Capital assets should be reviewed periodically to determine whether they be excess, obsolete, or unsuitable for their intended use and, where warranted, such action as necessary should be taken to reduce particular assets to values that recognize any impaired utility; assign shorter lives to particular assets that are becoming obsolete; and write off assets no longer in use.

RECORDING ACCUMULATED DEPRECIATION

There is almost universal practice in recording allocation of the cost of a depreciable asset in an account separate and distinct from the account representing the asset being depreciated. Such accounts formerly were designated as "Reserves for Depreciation," but at the present time are captioned "Accumulated Depreciation" by a sizeable majority of larger firms. Thus the entry to allocate $1,000, for example, of the depreciable base of an automobile would not reduce the account for the automobile itself, but would be made as follows:

	Debit	Credit
Depreciation expense—automobile	1,000	
Accumulated depreciation—automobile		1,000

The difference between the balance in the asset account and the accumulated depreciation account, of course, represents the net book value of the asset or group of assets, comprehended in both accounts, respectively.

DEFERRED INCOME TAXES RESULTING FROM USING DIFFERENT DEPRECIATION METHODS FOR FINANCIAL AND TAX ACCOUNTING

Where one method of allocating the cost of a depreciable asset is used for financial accounting, and another method used for income tax purposes, timing differences may be originated and reversed over a period of time, and the deferred tax effect of such timing differences should be accounted for in accordance with the provisions of applicable official directives. Accounting for deferred income taxes is comprehensively treated in Chapters 1 and 2.

ALLOCATION METHODS

As stated previously, a variety of allocation methods are used by business enterprises to apportion to current income the cost of capital assets. This diversity of method is found not only in the business community as a whole, but exists within industry groups, and even within single commercial entities. The allocation methods in general use today produce such diverse effects as level, accelerated, and incremental charges to periodic depreciation expense. The most commonly used allocation methods are listed below. (Accounting procedures are described and illustrated, and computational techniques are demonstrated, for each respective method, in the paragraphs that follow.)

Straight-line	Units-of-production	Sinking-fund
Declining-balance	Hours-of-service	Annuity
Sum-of-the-year's digits	Depletion-oriented	Inventory

STRAIGHT-LINE METHOD

The straight-line method is a level charge method that allocates an equal amount of the net cost of an asset to each accounting period during its useful life. The annual depreciation charge can be calculated by dividing the depreciable base of the asset by the number of years of estimated useful life, or an annual percentage depreciation charge can be obtained by dividing 100 by the number of years of the asset's useful life. The percentage thus obtained would be applied to the depreciable base annually to obtain the depreciation charge for the year. Schedule 1 is an example of a depreciation schedule prepared for an asset with a depreciable base of $180,000, having an estimated useful life of ten years and no residual value. The annual charge can be determined by dividing 180,000 by 10, or dividing 100 by 10 and applying the resulting 10% to $180,000. In either case the annual depreciation charge would be $18,000.

Straight-line depreciation is simple to compute, and simple to apply. Also, it is easy to forecast accumulated depreciation or net book value for any year in the future. For example, if at the end of the first year, the owner of the machine being depreciated in accordance with Schedule 1 wished to know what the accumulated depreciation would be at the end of the sixth year without having to prepare a schedule in advance, he need only multiply the annual depreciation of $18,000 by six and he would arrive at $108,000, which is the same amount as that shown on Schedule 1.

It is also important to note that the straight-line depreciation rate is applied to the *depreciable base* (which is cost less salvage value), and not to the carrying value of the asset, if it is being depreciated to a salvage value. For example, if the owner had estimated that the asset being depreciated in Schedule 1 would have a 5% salvage value, or $9,000 at the end of ten years, the depreciation rate of 10% would have been applied to $180,000 less $9,000, or $171,000, and annual allocation would have been as shown in Schedule 2.

DEPRECIATION SCHEDULE—STRAIGHT-LINE METHOD

Depreciable Base: 180,000
Salvage Value: None
Depreciation Rate: 10%

End of Year	Annual Charge	Accumulated Depreciation	Net Book Value
1	18,000	18,000	162,000
2	18,000	36,000	144,000
3	18,000	54,000	126,000
4	18,000	72,000	108,000
5	18,000	90,000	90,000
6	18,000	108,000	72,000
7	18,000	126,000	54,000
8	18,000	.144,000	36,000
9	18,000	162,000	18,000
10	18,000	180,000	-0-
	180,000		

SCHEDULE 1

DEPRECIATION SCHEDULE—STRAIGHT-LINE METHOD

Acquisition Cost: 180,000
Salvage Value: 9,000
Depreciable Base: 171,000
Depreciation Rate: 10%

End of Year	Annual Charge	Accumulated Depreciation	Net Book Value
1	17,100	17,100	162,900
2	17,100	34,200	145,800
3	17,100	51,300	128,700
4	17,100	68,400	111,600
5	17,100	85,500	94,500
6	17,100	102,600	77,400
7	17,100	119,700	60,300
8	17,100	136,800	43,200
9	17,100	153,900	26,100
10	17,100	171,000	9,000
	171,000		

SCHEDULE 2

DECLINING-BALANCE METHOD

The declining-balance method is an accelerated method, and allocation under this method is made by applying a constant rate to the declining balance of the *acquisition* cost of the asset. The rate applied is based on the useful life of the asset, and since it takes a rate somewhat greater than twice that of the straight-line method to depreciate the asset over the same number of years, and because tax regulations permit a "double declining-balance" rate for new tangible personal property, most companies compute the rate to be used by dividing the number of years of estimated life into 100, and then multiplying the resulting percentage by two. Schedule 3 is an illustration of a depreciation schedule prepared under the double declining-balance method of allocation applied to a machine that cost $180,000, having an estimated useful life of ten years and no residual value. The percentage applied annually to the declining balance was computed by dividing 100 by the ten-year estimated life and multiplying the resulting 10% by two to arrive at 20% as the constant rate to be used.

DEPRECIATION SCHEDULE—DOUBLE DECLINING-BALANCE METHOD

Acquisition Cost: 180,000
Salvage Value: None
Depreciation Rate: 20%
Asset Life: 10 Years

End of Year	Annual Charge	Accumulated Depreciation	Net Book Value
1	36,000	36,000	144,000
2	28,800	64,800	115,200
3	23,040	87,840	92,160
4	18,432	106,272	73,728
5	14,746	121,018	58,982
6	11,796	132,814	47,186
7	9,437	142,251	37,749
8	7,550	149,801	30,199
9	6,040	155,841	24,159
10	4,832	160,673	19,327
	160,673		

SCHEDULE 3

Schedule 3 indicates that a net book value of $19,327 remains at the end of ten years. If the asset still has a remaining useful life, the owner could use the straight-line method over the extended years of its revised estimated life to depreciate the balance of $19,327, or if the asset is unsuited for its purpose at the end of the ten-year period, the total balance of $24,159 remaining at the end of the ninth year could be charged off in the tenth year.

COMPUTATION OF DECLINING-BALANCE METHOD MEASUREMENTS

Simple algebraic formulas can be used to calculate various measurements to be made in connection with the declining-balance method. These formulas and resulting measurements are demonstrated in the paragraphs that follow where, for each of the formulas,

C = Cost (or depreciable base where salvage value is not recognized)
S = Salvage value
B = Book value
d = Constant rate
n = Number of years (or accounting periods)

CHANGING FROM DECLINING-BALANCE TO STRAIGHT-LINE TO INSURE FULL DEPRECIATION AT END OF USEFUL LIFE

Without having prepared a depreciation table covering the full life of the asset, the owner of the asset shown being depreciated in Schedule 3 could have computed the net book value at the end of, for example, the sixth year of life of the asset, and then changed to straight-line depreciation for the last four years so that the asset would be fully depreciated at the end of its service life.

The formula for computing the net book value of an asset being depreciated at a constant rate for any specified number of years is:

$$B_n = C (1-d)^n$$

Thus, the net book value of the asset in Schedule 3 at the end of six years would be computed as follows:[9]

$$B_6 = 180,000 (1-.20)^6$$
$$B_6 = 180,000 (.80)^6$$
$$B_6 = 180,000 (.262144)$$
$$B_6 = 47,186$$

The book value of $47,186 could have been divided by four and the resulting $11,796 could have been used for the last four years, and thus the asset would have been fully depreciated at the end of ten years. A depreciation schedule computed in this manner is shown in Schedule 4.

The straight-line method substituted in the seventh year permitted a depreciation charge of $11,796 for tax purposes, whereas continuation of the double declining-balance method would have allowed a deduction of only $9,437 for that year, as indicated in Schedule 3.

---

[9] The same results may be obtained by disregarding the constant rate, and using the following formula, where k represents the number of years the asset will be depreciated:

$$B_k = C \left(1 - \frac{2}{n}\right)^k$$

The computation of book value at the end of six years by this formula would be as follows:

$$B_6 = 180,00 \left(1 - \frac{2}{10}\right)^6 \qquad = B_6 = 180,000 (1 - .2)^6$$
$$B_6 = 180,000 (.8)^6 \qquad\qquad = B_6 = 180,000 (.262144)$$
$$B_6 = 47,186$$

DEPRECIATION SCHEDULE

DOUBLE DECLINING-BALANCE METHOD CHANGED TO STRAIGHT-LINE METHOD
AT THE END OF SIX YEARS

Depreciable Base: 180,000
Salvage Value: None
Life: 10 Years

End of Year		Annual Charge	Accumulated Depreciation	Net Book Value
1	Double Declining-Balance	36,000	36,000	144,000
2	Double Declining-Balance	28,800	64,800	115,200
3	Double Declining-Balance	23,040	87,840	92,160
4	Double Declining-Balance	18,432	106,272	73,728
5	Double Declining-Balance	14,746	121,018	58,982
6	Double Declining-Balance	11,796	132,814	47,186
7	Straight-Line	11,796	144,610	35,390
8	Straight-Line	11,796	156,406	23,594
9	Straight-Line	11,796	168,202	11,798
10	Straight-Line	11,798	180,000	-0-
		180,000		

SCHEDULE 4

DETERMINING A CONSTANT RATE FOR THE DECLINING-BALANCE METHOD

The formula for determining a constant rate for the declining-balance method over a given number of years is as follows:

$$d = 1 - \sqrt[n]{\frac{S}{C}}$$

Use of the above formula will permit computation of a constant rate that will depreciate the asset to any salvage value the owner chooses to estimate. For example, if the owner of the asset being depreciated in Schedule 3 had estimated a salvage value of $5,000 at the end of ten years, the constant rate to be applied to the declining balance could have been computed as follows:[10]

---

[10]Prior to the advent of the four-function electronic calculator, this computation would have been cumbersome, and required the use of logarithms. With an algebraic-entry electronic calculator the solution can be obtained by eleven simple keystrokes, as follows:

Sequence	Key	Display	Sequence	Key	Display
1	5,000	5,000	7	=	.6988271188
2	÷	5,000	8	+/−	−.6988271188
3	180,000	180,000	9	+	−.6988271188
4	=	.0277777777	10	1	1
5	ˣ√y̅	.0277777777	11	=	.3011728812
6	10	10			

$$d = 1 - \sqrt[10]{\frac{5,000}{180,000}}$$
$$d = 1 - \sqrt[10]{.0277777777}$$
$$d = 1 - .6988271188$$
$$d = .3011728812$$

Applying the percentage of 30.11728812 to the declining balance would have resulted in the depreciation shown in Schedule 5.

DEPRECIATION SCHEDULE—DOUBLE DECLINING-BALANCE METHOD

Acquisition Cost:	180,000
Salvage Value:	5,000
Depreciable Base:	175,000
Depreciation Rate:	30.11728812%
Asset Life:	10 Years

End of Year	Annual Charge	Accumulated Depreciation	Net Book Value
1	54,211	54,211	125,789
2	37,884	92,095	87,905
3	26,475	118,570	61,430
4	18,501	137,071	42,929
5	12,929	150,000	30,000
6	9,035	159,035	20,965
7	6,314	165,349	14,651
8	4,413	169,762	10,238
9	3,084	172,846	7,154
10	2,154	175,000	5,000
	175,000		

SCHEDULE 5

For tax purposes, the declining-balance method of depreciation for the asset depreciated in Schedule 5, which uses a constant of 30.11728814%, should be computed in accordance with Schedule 3, which uses a constant of 20%. Thus, if depreciation expense is computed for financial accounting purposes in accordance with Schedule 5, timing differences will be created during the first four years of the life of the asset, which will reverse during the last six years of its life, and deferred income taxes, if significant, should be provided for the timing differences thus created.

LIMITATIONS ON THE USE OF A CONSTANT RATE FOR THE DECLINING-BALANCE METHOD

The formula for determining a constant rate for the declining-balance method,

$$d = 1 - \sqrt[n]{\frac{S}{C}}$$

indicates that S, as a practical value, can never be zero, and accordingly, an asset cannot be fully depreciated by the declining-balance method. Therefore, some nominal value must be used for S, but the reader should be cautioned that an inspection of this formula reveals that as S approaches zero, the constant rate increases exponentially to 100%. Thus, if an insignificant value is used for S, the constant rate computed by the formula may be so large that the computed rate may be unacceptable because it places a disproportionate depreciation charge on the early years of the life of the asset. For example, the following computations disclose the constant rate computed by the formula when the salvage value is estimated at 10%, .1%, and .01% of an asset costing $180,000 and having an estimated life of ten years:

Salvage Value			Constant Rate
10% x 180,000 =	18,000		$r = 1 - \sqrt[10]{.1}$
			$r = 1 - .7943282347$
			$r = 20.56717653\%$
.1% x 180,000 =	180		$r = 1 - \sqrt[10]{.001}$
			$r = 1 - .5011872336$
			$r = 49.88127664\%$
.01% x 180,000 =	18		$r = 1 - \sqrt[10]{.0001}$
			$r = 1 - .3981071706$
			$r = 60.18928294\%$

The disparity in allocation in the early years of the life of the asset where salvage value is estimated at .1% and .01% of cost is displayed graphically in Schedule 6.

DEPRECIATION SCHEDULE

DECLINING-BALANCE METHOD USING CONSTANT RATES FOR SALVAGE VALUES OF $18,000, $180, AND $18

Acquisition Cost: 180,000
Life of Asset: 10 Years

	Rate: 20.56717653%			Rate: 49.88127664%			Rate: 60.18928294%		
End of Year	Annual Charge	Accumulated Depreciation	Net Book Value	Annual Charge	Accumulated Depreciation	Net Book Value	Annual Charge	Accumulated Depreciation	Net Book Value
1	37,021	37,021	142,979	89,786	89,786	90,214	108,341	108,341	71,659
2	29,407	66,428	113,572	45,000	134,786	45,214	43,131	151,472	28,528
3	23,359	89,787	90,213	22,553	157,339	22,661	17,171	168,643	11,357
4	18,554	108,341	71,659	11,303	168,642	11,358	6,836	175,479	4,521
5	14,738	123,079	56,921	5,665	174,307	5,693	2,721	178,200	1,800
6	11,707	134,786	45,214	2,839	177,146	2,854	1,083	179,283	717
7	9,299	144,085	35,915	1,423	178,569	1,431	432	179,715	285
8	7,387	151,472	28,528	714	179,283	717	172	179,887	113
9	5,867	157,339	22,661	358	179,641	359	68	179,955	45
10	4,661	162,000	18,000	179	179,820	180	27	179,982	18
	162,000			179,820			179,982		

SCHEDULE 6

SUM-OF-THE-DIGITS METHOD

The sum-of-the-digits method is an accelerated method that provides for periodic allocation of the cost of capital assets on the basis of a fraction of which the numerator declines by one unit each year. The denominator is an arithmetic progression with a difference of one, and comprised of the number of terms that correspond to the number of years in the life of the asset. For example, where,

> n = the number of terms
> a = the first term
> e = the last term
> S = the sum

the denominator of the fraction can be computed by the formula,

$$S = \frac{n}{2} (a + e)$$

Thus, the denominator of the fraction for an asset having a ten-year life would be computed,

$$S = \frac{10}{2} (1 + 10) = 55$$

The numerator of the fraction used each year is the number of years of estimated life of the asset taken in reverse order, and it corresponds to the number of years remaining in the life of the asset at the *beginning* of the year. For example, a succession of the numerators used in the ten-year life for which the denominator was computed above would be 10/55, 9/55, 8/55, 7/55, 6/55, 5/55, 4/55, 3/55, 2/55, 1/55.

The sum-of-the-digits method reduces to zero the base to which it is applied. Therefore, it should be applied to the *depreciable base* computed by reducing acquisition cost by any estimated residual value.

There are several methods by which the annual allocation under the sum-of-the-digits method can be applied. The annual amount can be calculated by using the proper fraction applicable each year, as described above; it can be calculated by using a series of decimal fractions computed by transposing the proper fractions to decimals; or it can be applied simply by deducting annually the constant decrement between the fractions used each year. For example, the depreciation charge for an asset that costs $275,000, with no estimated salvage value, and having a ten-year life, could be computed by either of the three following methods:

1. $10/55 \times 275,000 = 50,000$
2. $10/55 = .1818181818 \times 275,000 = 50,000$
3. $\dfrac{275,000}{55} = $ (Annual Decrement) $5,000 \times 10 = 50,000$

Schedule 7 sets forth the depreciation schedule prepared for the asset described in the previous paragraph, and it displays the fractional, decimal, and decremental methods of calculating the allocation for each respective year of the life of the asset.[11]

---

[11]Fractions or decimal equivalents also may be computed under the "remaining-life" method, and applied to the net book value at the end of the previous year to arrive at the current depreciation charge. For example, the fraction for the first year would be 10/55, as shown in Schedule 7, but the fraction for the second year would be computed as 9 over the sum of the digits of the remaining 9 years, or 9/45 (20%), and would be applied to the net book value of $225,000 to arrive at a depreciation charge of $45,000 for the second year. Fractions for the following years then would be 8/36, 7/28, 6/21, 5/15, 4/10, 3/6, 2/3, and 1/1.

DEPRECIATION SCHEDULE—SUM-OF-THE-DIGITS METHOD

Depreciable Base: 275,000
Salvage Value: None
Asset Life: 10 Years

End of Year	Method of Computation			Annual Charge	Accumulated Depreciation	Net Book Value
	Fraction	Percent	Decrement			
1	10/55	18.1818	5,000	50,000	50,000	225,000
2	9/55	16.3636	5,000	45,000	95,000	180,000
3	8/55	14.5454	5,000	40,000	135,000	140,000
4	7/55	12.7272	5,000	35,000	170,000	105,000
5	6/55	10.9090	5,000	30,000	200,000	75,000
6	5/55	9.0909	5,000	25,000	225,000	50,000
7	4/55	7.2727	5,000	20,000	245,000	30,000
8	3/55	5.4545	5,000	15,000	260,000	15,000
9	2/55	3.6363	5,000	10,000	270,000	5,000
10	1/55	1.8181	5,000	5,000	275,000	-0-
				275,000		

SCHEDULE 7

DEPRECIATION SCHEDULE—SUM-OF-THE-DIGITS METHOD

Acquisition Cost: 275,000
Salvage Value: 33,000
Depreciable Base: 242,000
Asset Life: 10 Years

End of Year	Method of Computation			Annual Charge	Accumulated Depreciation	Net Book Value
	Fraction	Percent	Decrement			
1	10/55	18.1818	4,400	44,000	44,000	231,000
2	9/55	16.3636	4,400	39,600	83,600	191,400
3	8/55	14.5454	4,400	35,200	118,800	156,200
4	7/55	12.7272	4,400	30,800	149,600	125,400
5	6/55	10.9090	4,400	26,400	176,000	99,000
6	5/55	9.0909	4,400	22,000	198,000	77,000
7	4/55	7.2727	4,400	17,600	215,600	59,400
8	3/55	5.4545	4,400	13,200	228,800	46,200
9	2/55	3.6363	4,400	8,800	237,600	37,400
10	1/55	1.8181	4,400	4,400	242,000	33,000
				242,000		

SCHEDULE 8

If the owner of the asset shown being depreciated in Schedule 7 had estimated a salvage value of $33,000 for the asset, the allocation rate would have been applied to the depreciable base of $275,000 less $33,000, or $242,000, and the depreciation would have been as set forth in Schedule 8.

UNITS-OF-PRODUCTION METHOD

In some exceptional circumstances, it may be appropriate to allocate the cost of an asset on the basis of the total quantity of items it can service or produce. This method recognizes the relationship between usage and physical wear and tear, and anticipates that the service life of the asset will be terminated by such usage in advance of obsolescence or complete deterioration resulting from the passage of time. This method can be used where the operation of the asset can be identified with discrete units or elements of production, and an illustration of its application is shown in the following example:

Bristol Bolt and Nut Company purchased a die stamping machine for $80,000 for the purpose of cutting steel patterns which were drilled and used as nuts for various size bolts. From prior experience with similar machines, Bristol determined that the machine could produce two million dies during its serviceable life. The wear and tear of producing such a quantity of dies would depreciate the machine to an insignificant scrap value. Bristol also determined that the two million production limit of the machine would be reached long before complete deterioration of the machine would occur from passage of time. Accordingly, Bristol decided to allocate the total cost of the machine by the units-of-production method, using each 1,000 units as the basic allocation element. Computation of the cost of each 1,000 units to be allocated was made as follows:

Cost	Production Limit	Cost Per Unit	Production Element	Cost Per Production Element
80,000 ÷	2,000,000 =	.04 ×	1,000 =	$40.00

Schedule 9 sets forth the depreciation charges over the life of the asset.

DEPRECIATION SCHEDULE—UNITS-OF-PRODUCTION METHOD

Depreciable Base: 80,000
Production Limit: 2,000,000 Units
Depreciation per 1,000 Units: $40

End of Year	Units Produced	Production Elements	Depreciation Per Element	Annual Charge	Accumulated Depreciation	Net Book Value
1	600,000	600	$40	24,000	24,000	56,000
2	500,000	500	40	20,000	44,000	36,000
3	200,000	200	40	8,000	52,000	28,000
4	400,000	400	40	16,000	68,000	12,000
5	320,000	320	40	12,000	80,000	-0-
	2,020,000			80,000		

SCHEDULE 9

HOURS-OF-SERVICE METHOD

This method recognizes that excessive use, such as overtime work, etc., will depreciate an asset more rapidly than normal usage, and that such excessive use would exhaust the asset in advance of an estimated lifetime based on reasonable use combined with general deterioration resulting from the passage of time. The hours-of-service method is similar to, and used under similar circumstances as, the units-of-production method described in a preceding paragraph. However, the hours-of-service method is applicable where the operation of the asset cannot be identified with specific units or elements of production. The application of the hours-of-service method is illustrated in the following example:

The Oriole Marble Company was incorporated for the purpose of acquiring a quarry in Cockeysville, Maryland from which it expected to recover 400,000 tons of marble. As a part of the necessary production equipment, Oriole paid $120,000 for twenty saws with which to cut various size blocks and slabs of marble. From available statistical data, the company determined that the saws could be used for a maximum of 500 hours each. The company planned to operate three daily production shifts and thus it was determined that the 500-hour productive limit would be reached for each saw well in advance of total deterioration that would occur from the passage of time combined with normal use of the asset. Oriole therefore decided to depreciate the saws on the basis of the hours-of-service method, and computed the hourly depreciation charge as follows:

Cost of Saws	Number of Hours at 500 Each for 20 Saws		Cost Per Hour
120,000	10,000	=	$12.00

The quarry was totally depleted at the end of five years, and Schedule 10 sets forth the allocation of the cost of the saws for each of the operating years.

DEPRECIATION SCHEDULE—HOURS-OF-SERVICE METHOD

	Depreciable Base:	120,000
	Production Hours Limit:	10,000
	Depreciation Per Hour:	$12

End of Year	Tons Recovered	Operating Hours	Depreciation Per Hour	Annual Charge	Accumulated Depreciation	Net Book Value
1	90,000	2,270	$12	27,240	27,240	92,760
2	85,000	2,150	12	25,800	53,040	66,960
3	87,000	2,200	12	26,400	79,440	40,560
4	70,000	1,760	12	21,120	100,560	19,440
5	65,000	1,650	12	19,440	120,000	-0-
	397,000	10,030		120,000		

SCHEDULE 10

DEPLETION-ORIENTED METHOD

Certain assets, such as mines, timber, oil wells, etc., are subject to depletion for both financial accounting and tax purposes. The theory and practice of depletion accounting is not in the scope of this chapter, but a discussion of the allocation of the cost of tangible capital assets used in connection with a limited quantity of units available for production is deemed appropriate. Where capital assets are acquired for the sole purpose of producing a limited quantity of units, the cost of the asset is, in some cases, allocated on the basis of the assets produced during each accounting period, and thus when the source of the units of production is exhausted, the cost of the assistant assets is fully allocated. An illustration of this method of allocation based on the Oriole Marble Company example in the preceding paragraph is set forth below.

In anticipation of recovering 400,000 tons of marble from a newly acquired quarry, the Oriole Marble Company purchased and installed rails, ties, and railcars at a cost of $1,640,000 for the purpose of removing blocks and slabs of marble from the quarry. The complete rail system would be useless except for insignificant scrap value at the time all the marble had been recovered from the quarry. Oriole therefore decided to allocate the cost of the rail system by applying an appropriate depreciation charge for each ton of marble removed from the quarry, and computed the allocable charge per ton as follows:

Cost of Rail System	Tonnage Expected to be Removed	Depreciation Per Ton
1,640,000	400,000	$4.10

All the marble had been recovered from the quarry at the end of five years, and Schedule 11 shows the allocation of the cost of the rail system to each respective annual accounting period.

DEPRECIATION SCHEDULE—DEPLETION-ORIENTED METHOD

Depreciable Base:	1,640,000
Tons to be Recovered:	400,000
Depreciation per Ton:	$4.10

End of Year	Tons Recovered	Depreciation per Ton	Annual Charge	Accumulated Depreciation	Net Book Value
1	90,000	$4.10	369,000	369,000	1,271,000
2	85,000	4.10	348,500	717,500	922,500
3	87,000	4.10	356,700	1,074,200	565,800
4	70,000	4.10	287,000	1,361,200	278,800
5	65,000	4.10	278,800	1,640,000	-0-
	397,000		1,640,000		

SCHEDULE 11

SINKING-FUND METHOD

The sinking-fund method interpolates an interest factor into the computation of accumulated depreciation and thus, while the depreciation expense is recorded on a straight-line basis, the amount credited to the accumulated depreciation fund increases with each accounting period. The argument for using the sinking-fund method is based on the premise that the depreciation fund contributes to working capital and therefore interest expense as well as depreciation should be credited to the fund. However, allocation methods based on interest or present values are not generally acceptable, and the study reported in Accounting Research Monograph No. 1 found that such methods are seldom used in practice.[12] At any rate, the sinking-fund method *is* acceptable for tax purposes. Therefore, if the sinking-fund method is used for tax accounting and some other and appropriate method used for financial accounting, timing differences may be created.

Under the **sinking-fund** method annual depreciation expense is assumed to be equivalent to an amount that would have to be deposited annually in a fund, over the life of an asset, so that at the end of the economic life of the asset the fund would have accumulated an amount equal to the original cost less salvage value of the asset being depreciated. The sinking-fund concept implies that the process of accumulating and maintaining such a hypothetical fund represents a loss of interest income that would have occurred had the annual deposits actually been made; hence, the loss of interest income represents an interest expense that is distinct from depreciation expense.

Depreciation, interest expense, and the periodic credit to the accumulated depreciation fund may be computed by using the reciprocal of the basic formula for computing the value of an annuity, as follows, where

C = Cost (or depreciable base where salvage value is not recognized)
S = Salvage value
n = number of periods
i = effective interest rate assumed to be earned by the depreciation fund
R = Required annual deposit (depreciation expense)

$$R \left[\frac{(1 + i)^n - 1}{i} \right] = C - S \ or \ R = (C-S) \left[\frac{1}{\frac{(1 + i)^n - 1}{i}} \right]$$

ILLUSTRATION OF THE SINKING-FUND METHOD OF ALLOCATION

The following example is an illustration of application of the sinking-fund method which demonstrates the computation of interest and depreciation expense, and sets forth the entries necessary to record the allocation.

Filbert Foods, Inc. purchased a churning machine for $185,000. Management estimated that the asset would have a serviceable life of ten years, and also determined that at the end of that time it could be sold for $5,000.

Filbert decided to depreciate the machine on a straight-line basis for financial accounting purposes. However, since it appeared that an inflationary trend would continue over the following ten years, management was persuaded that taxable income would increase during that period, and that an increasing tax deduction for interest and depreciation based on the sinking-fund method of allocation would be more beneficial than a level tax deduction based on the straight-line method. Therefore, Filbert decided to use the sinking-fund method for tax accounting and, assuming an interest rate of 8.75%, computed the required annual deposit as follows:

---

[12] *Accounting for Depreciable Assets*, Accounting Research Monograph No. 1. (New York, NY: Copyright 1975 by the American Institute of Certified Public Accountants. Page 97.)

$$R = (185,000 - 5,000) \left[\frac{1}{\frac{(1.0875)^{10} - 1}{.0875}} \right]$$

$$R = 180,000 \left[\frac{1}{\frac{1.313623337}{.0875}} \right]$$

$$R = 180,000 \left[\frac{1}{15.01283814} \right]$$

$$R = 180,000 \quad (.066609657) = 11,990$$

By using $11,990 as the annual level amount required to be contributed to the fund, and annually applying an interest rate of 8.75% to the previous hypothetical balance in the fund, Filbert prepared a depreciation schedule for tax purposes covering the ten years of the estimated life of the machine. Filbert's depreciation schedule is reproduced in Schedule 12.

DEPRECIATION SCHEDULE — SINKING-FUND METHOD

Cost:	185,000
Salvage Value:	5,000
Depreciable Base:	180,000
Asset Life:	10 Years
Imputed Interest Rate:	8.75%

End of Year	Depreciation Expense	Interest on Balance in Fund	Annual Increase In Fund	Cumulative Balance In Fund	Net Book Value of Asset
1	11,990	—	11,990	11,990	173,010
2	11,990	1,049	13,039	25,029	159,971
3	11,990	2,190	14,180	39,209	145,791
4	11,990	3,430	15,420	54,629	130,371
5	11,990	4,780	16,770	71,399	113,601
6	11,990	6,247	18,237	89,636	95,364
7	11,990	7,843	19,833	109,469	75,531
8	11,990	9,578	21,568	131,037	53,963
9	11,990	11,465	23,455	154,492	30,508
10	11,990	13,518	25,508	180,000	5,000
	119,900	60,100	180,000		

SCHEDULE 12

Since Filbert allocated the depreciable base of the asset by the straight-line method for financial accounting purposes, the annual charge to depreciation expense on the books of the company was computed as follows:

Acquisition cost 185,000
Less: Salvage value 5,000
Depreciable base 180,000

Annual depreciation charge - 180,000 ÷ 10 = 18,000

Schedule 13 reflects the annual depreciation expense for financial accounting purposes, and the annual deductible depreciation and "interest" expense for tax purposes over the life of the asset, and sets forth the origination and reversal of income tax timing differences that occurred during that time.

SCHEDULE OF INCOME TAX TIMING DIFFERENCES

End of Year	Financial Accounting Depreciation Expense	Tax Deduction			Timing Difference Book Income Over (Under) Taxable Income
		Depreciation	"Interest"	Total	
1	18,000	11,990	—	11,990	(6,010)
2	18,000	11,990	1,049	13,039	(4,961)
3	18,000	11,990	2,190	14,180	(3,820)
4	18,000	11,990	3,430	15,420	(2,580)
5	18,000	11,990	4,780	16,770	(1,230)
6	18,000	11,990	6,247	18,237	237
7	18,000	11,990	7,843	19,833	1,833
8	18,000	11,990	9,578	21,568	3,568
9	18,000	11,990	11,465	23,455	5,455
10	18,000	11,990	13,518	25,508	7,508
	180,000	119,900	60,100	180,000	-0-

SCHEDULE 13

Assuming an annual effective tax rate of 45%, the entries that would be required to record depreciation expense and the effect on deferred income taxes for the first and tenth years are as follows:

	Debit	Credit
First Year		
Depreciation expense	18,000	
Deferred income tax debits	2,705	
Accumulated depreciation		18,000
Provision for income taxes		2,705
Tenth Year		
Depreciation expense	18,000	
Provision for income taxes	3,379	
Accumulated depreciation		18,000
Deferred income tax debits		3,379

ANNUITY METHOD

The annuity method of allocation is similar to the sinking-fund method in that it introduces an interest factor into the computation of accumulated depreciation. The concept of the annuity method implies that the purchase of a depreciable asset is an investment of capital which otherwise would be earning a given rate of interest. Under the annuity method of allocation annual depreciation expense is computed as the level deposit that would have to be made to a fund, over the life of the asset, so that at the end of the useful life of the asset the fund would be equivalent to the cost less salvage value of the asset being depreciated, *plus* interest earned on such periodic deposits at an imputed interest rate. Interest income is computed annually on the undepreciated cost of the asset, and deducted from annual depreciation expense to arrive at the current increase in the depreciation fund.

Depreciation expense, interest income, and the annual credit to the depreciation fund may be computed by using the basic formula for computing the value of an annuity. Where the mathematical symbols are the same as those used for the sinking-fund method, the formula for the annuity method is as follows:

$$R \left[\frac{1 - \frac{1}{1 + i}^{n}}{i} \right] = (C - S)$$

ILLUSTRATION OF THE ANNUITY METHOD OF ALLOCATION

The following example is an extension of the Filbert Food, Inc. example which illustrated the use of the sinking-fund method. This extended example demonstrates a computational technique for determining depreciation expense, interest income, and the annual credit to the depreciation fund; and describes the entries necessary to record the allocation.

In 19x2 Filbert Foods, Inc. purchased a second churning machine for $185,000, having an estimated life of ten years and a residual value of $5,000. Filbert decided to report depreciation expense for financial accounting by the straight-line method, but, for the same reasons described in the previous example, determined to account for depreciation for tax purposes by a method of increasing charges to the depreciation fund involving an interest factor of 8.75% per annum. However, as a matter of statistical experiment and comparison, Filbert decided to allocate the cost of this second machine by the annuity method instead of the sinking-fund method used for the first churning machine. Accordingly, Filbert computed the level depreciation expense to be used annually, as follows:

$$R \left[\frac{1 - \frac{1}{1.0875}^{10}}{.0875} \right] = (185,000 - 5,000)$$

$$R \left[\frac{.5677775271}{.0875} \right] = 180,000$$

$$R \left[(6.488886024) \right] = 180,000$$

$$R \left[\frac{180,000}{6.488886024} \right] \quad R = 27,740$$

Using 27,740 as level annual depreciation expense, computing assumed annual interest income on the undepreciated balance of the asset at 8.75%, and crediting the depreciation fund with the difference between the income and expense thus computed, Filbert prepared the depreciation table shown in Schedule 14 in order to reflect depreciation for tax purposes over the ten-year life of the asset.

DEPRECIATION SCHEDULE — ANNUITY METHOD

Cost:	105,000	
Salvage Value:	5,000	
Depreciable Base:	180,000	
Asset Life:	10 Years	
Imputed Interest Rate:	8.75%	

End of Year	Depreciation Expense	Interest Income	Net Addition to Accumulated Depreciation	Accumulated Depreciation	Net Book Value
1	27,740	15,750*	11,990	11,990	173,010
2	27,740	14,701	13,039	25,029	159,971
3	27,740	13,560	14,180	39,209	145,791
4	27,740	12,320	15,420	54,629	130,371
5	27,740	10,970	16,770	71,399	113,601
6	27,740	9,503	18,237	89,636	95,364
7	27,740	7,907	19,833	109,469	75,531
8	27,740	6,172	21,568	131,037	53,963
9	27,740	4,285	23,455	154,492	30,508
10	27,740	2,232	25,508	180,000	5,000
	277,400	97,400	180,000		

*Interest income is computed annually on the difference between net book value at the end of the preceding year and $5,000 salvage value

SCHEDULE 14

A comparison of Schedules 12 and 14 reveals that the net increase in accumulated depreciation each year is exactly the same under both the sinking-fund method and the annuity method of cost allocation. Thus, since in both instances the straight-line method was used for financial accounting, income tax timing differences for Filbert's second churning machine will originate and reverse in exactly the same manner as they were created and reversed by use of the sinking-fund method for his first machine, and as set forth in Schedule 13. The entries required to record depreciation expense and the effect on deferred income taxes would be exactly the same under both methods, and would correspond to the entries for the first and tenth year previously illustrated for use of the sinking-fund method for tax purposes.

As stated previously with reference to the sinking-fund method of allocation, the annuity method is seldom used in practice.

INVENTORY METHOD

The inventory method of allocation is not necessarily an acceptable method, but it is used in practice in many instances to allocate the cost of small tools and parts that, individually, do not require a significant capital investment. There are many approaches to this method of allocation but, in any event, materiality and significance should be the primary consideration in electing to use it. It is important that the small tools, etc. be inventoried at their *cost*, less accumulated depreciation, and not at market value, appraisal value, or any other value. In practice, each company has its own plan of computing depreciation by the inventory method. Two widely used plans are described below.

Static Method

Where a company has historical evidence that it purchases relatively the same quantity of small tools, etc. each year, it can set up a reasonably estimated amount on the books to represent the investment, and make no change in the account from year to year, unless some significant change occurs in their normal operating procedures.

Estimated Group Life Method

If fluctuations occur in the quantity of small tools acquired from year to year, a reasonable estimate may be made of the useful life of the major items that make up the *group*, and such estimate may be applied to all items in the group. For example, if it is estimated that the significant items in the group have a life of three years, then, as a practical method, the purchase of such assets could be recorded currently, but the balance existing at the end of the third preceding year should be written off at the end of each accounting period.

MULTIPLE-ASSET ACCOUNTS

Allocation of cost may be made for a single asset, or it may be made for a group of assets combined into one account. The Internal Revenue Service approves the following categories of multiple-asset accounts.

Group Accounts
  Assets similar in kind with approximately the same useful lives.

Classified Accounts
  Assets classified according to use without regard to useful life, such as machinery and equipment, furniture and fixtures, or transportation equipment.

Composite Accounts
  An account composed of assets without regard to their character or useful lives.

Group, classified, or composite accounts may also be set up on the basis of dates of acquisition, cost, character, use, location, or any other basis that provides convenience in allocating the cost of capital assets.

ACCUMULATED DEPRECIATION ON MULTIPLE-ASSET ACCOUNTS

A single account for accumulated depreciation should be set up for a multiple-asset account. If there are more than one multiple-asset accounts, a separate accumulated depreciation account should be set up for each separate multiple-asset account.

COMPUTATION OF DEPRECIATION RATES FOR MULTIPLE-ASSET ACCOUNTS

When a multiple-asset account is initiated, each item comprising the account should be assigned an estimated salvage value and an expected useful life. Depreciation for each individual asset should then be computed on its depreciable base by the straight-line method for a period of one year. The annual depreciation rate to be used for the group account is computed by dividing the aggregate straight-line depreciation for one year by the aggregate *acquisition cost* of the assets; and the average estimated life is determined by dividing the aggregate depreciable base (cost less salvage value) by the aggregate straight-line depreciation for one year. Annual depreciation expense is computed by applying the average rate to the balance in the multiple-asset account at the beginning of the year.

ADDITIONS AND RETIREMENTS—MULTIPLE-ASSET ACCOUNTS

Additions to a multiple-asset account are recorded at cost. Asset retirements are credited to the asset account at cost, and the accumulated depreciation account is debited for cost less any cash proceeds received from the sale of the assets retired. Thus, under this method of accounting, no gain or loss is recognized upon asset retirements. The nonrecognition of gain or loss on retirement of assets from a multiple-asset account is acceptable for both financial accounting and tax accounting purposes as long as the permanent withdrawal of depreciable property from the multiple-asset account follows a pattern contemplated when the depreciation rate was set up. However, when abnormal dispositions of assets in a multiple-asset account occur, the original cost and the amount of depreciation taken on such assets should be determined, and any gain or loss on the retirement should be computed and recognized.

ILLUSTRATION OF ALLOCATING THE COST OF A MULTIPLE-ASSET ACCOUNT

The computational techniques and accounting procedures for determining and recording periodic allocation of the cost of multiple-asset accounts are essentially the same for all three categories of such accounts: group, classified, and composite. Therefore, the following example of maintaining a composite account illustrates simultaneously the procedures required for all three categories.

Scylla Machine Shop, Inc. was organized on January 1, 19x1 to manufacture specialized machine parts. Scylla decided to carry its fixed assets in a composite account, and to depreciate them over the average life of the group. Accordingly, useful lives were estimated for each asset, and the annual rate of depreciation was calculated as shown in Schedule 15.

SCHEDULE OF COMPOSITE GROUP OF FIXED ASSETS
AND COMPUTATION OF ANNUAL DEPRECIATION RATE

	Acquisition Cost	Salvage Value	Depreciable Base	Estimated Life (Years)	Annual Straight-Line Depreciation
Machinery and Equipment					
Lath	5,000	500	4,500	10	450
Drill	4,500	450	4,050	5	810
Milling Machine	8,000	800	7,200	10	720
Cutting Machine	6,000	600	5,400	8	675
Furniture and Fixtures					
Desk	450	45	405	8	51
Chairs	225	24	201	8	25
File Cabinet	400	40	360	10	36
Intercom	3,000	600	2,400	6	400
Transportation Equipment					
Auto	5,000	1,000	4,000	3	1,333
Two-ton truck	10,500	1,500	9,000	5	1,800
Pick-up truck	6,500	400	6,100	5	1,220
	49,575	5,959	43,616		7,520

Composite Depreciation Rate

$7{,}520 \div 49{,}575 = 15.1689\%$

Composite Estimated Life

$43{,}616 \div 7{,}520 = 5.8$ years

SCHEDULE 15

The following transactions involving depreciable assets occurred during the first six years of Scylla's operations.

Assets purchased

	Cost	Estimated Salvage Value
January 1, 19x4 — Automobile	6,500	1,200
January 1, 19x6 — Drill	5,500	550
January 1, 19x6 — Heavy truck	12,000	1,200
January 1, 19x6 — Pick-up truck	7,000	500

Assets sold

	Original Acquisition Cost	Cash Received	Net Charge To Accumulated Depreciation
January 1, 19x4 — Automobile	5,000	900	4,100
January 1, 19x6 — Drill	4,500	400	4,100
January 1, 19x6 — Heavy truck	10,500	1,600	8,900
January 1, 19x6 — Pick-up truck	6,500	500	6,000

Scylla computed depreciation each year on the acquisition cost of the assets held at the beginning of the year, using the average rate of 15.1689%. Accumulated depreciation was credited with the original cost of the assets sold, *less* the amount of cash received in exchange for each respective asset.

Schedule 16 displays the changes that occurred in the multiple asset composite account, and the related accumulated depreciation account from January 1, 19x1 to December 31, 19x6.

SCHEDULE OF FIXED ASSETS AND DEPRECIATION
January 1, 19x1 to December 31, 19x6

	Acquisition Cost	Estimated Salvage Value	Accumulated Depreciation	Net Book Value
January 1, 19x1 Balance	49,575	5,959	—	49,575
December 31, 19x1				
Depreciation Expense	—	—	7,520	(7,520)
Totals	49,575	5,959	7,520	42,055
December 31, 19x2				
Depreciation Expense	—	—	7,520	(7,520)
Totals	49,575	5,959	15,040	34,535
December 31, 19x3				
Depreciation Expense	—	—	7,520	(7,520)
Totals	49,575	5,959	22,560	27,015
January 1, 19x4				
Sale of Automobile	(5,000)	(1,000)	(4,100)	(900)
Purchase of Automobile	6,500	1,200	—	6,500
Totals	51,075	6,159	18,460	32,615
December 31, 19x4				
Depreciation Expense	—	—	7,748	(7,748)
Totals	51,075	6,159	26,208	24,867
December 31, 19x5				
Depreciation Expense	—	—	7,748	(7,748)
Totals	51,075	6,159	33,956	17,119
January 1, 19x6				
Assets Sold				
Drill	(4,500)	(450)	(4,100)	(400)
Two-ton truck	(10,500)	(1,500)	(8,900)	(1,600)
Pick-up truck	(6,500)	(400)	(6,000)	(500)
Assets Purchased				
Drill	5,500	550	—	5,500
Heavy truck	12,000	1,200	—	12,000
Pick-up truck	7,000	500	—	7,000
Totals	54,075	6,059	14,956	39,119
December 31, 19x6				
Depreciation Expense	—	—	8,203	(8,203)
Totals	54,075	6,059	23,159	30,916

SCHEDULE 16

COMPONENT ACCOUNTS

In some cases a unit of depreciable property may be a complex product composed of constituent parts. In such cases the capital asset may be accounted for by treating each component of the property as an individual account. However, accounting for property in this manner requires that accurate costs be allocated to the various components, and that the useful life assigned to each component be estimated on the actual economic life of that particular element, without reference to the capital asset as an entity. For example, where an enterprise purchases or builds a new building, the cost of the components of the building, such as wiring, plumbing, flooring, roofing, etc. generally are easily identifiable, and the components are subject to fairly accurate estimation of separate economic lives. On the other hand, where a company purchases a used building, reasonable allocation of cost and assignment of useful lives to the various components of the building generally is not feasible and, in those circumstances, the building should be accounted for as a single unit.

ACQUISITION AND RETIREMENT OF ASSETS DURING YEAR

The period of depreciation of a capital asset begins when the asset is placed in service and ends when it is retired from service. Thus, where a capital asset is acquired during the year, only a part of the computed annual depreciation should be taken. This procedure presents no particular problems for assets depreciated by the straight-line and declining-balance methods. However, the sum-of-the-digits method requires a special proration procedure when only a part of a year's depreciation is allowed in the first year. As an example, where an asset is held for four months the first year, $4/12$ of the annual depreciation computed for the first year should be allocated to that year. In the second year, $8/12$ of the depreciation computed for the first year, and $4/12$ of the depreciation computed for the second year should be combined and allocated to the second year. This procedure should be continued throughout the entire useful life of the asset.

REVALUATION OF ASSETS AND REVISION OF DEPRECIATION RATES

Generally, the methods of allocation adopted and the estimates of useful life and salvage value made at the time of acquisition of capital assets are valid for the entire economic life of the assets being depreciated. However, changing conditions may, in some instances, impair utility, cause obsolescence, require early abandonment, or shorten service lives of some particular assets; business combinations or corporate reorganizations may have so significant an effect on the carrying value of depreciable assets as to require a revaluation of such assets in the circumstances; and accounting, economic, or tax considerations may indicate the need to change the allocation method for some, or all, of the capital assets being depreciated. The following paragraphs disclose appropriate accounting treatment for specific examples of changes made in asset valuation or in depreciation accounting estimates.

Pooling-of-Interests

In a business combination accounted for by the pooling-of-interests method the recorded assets and liabilities of the separate companies generally become the recorded assets and liabilities of the combined corporation. However, the separate companies may have had capital assets that were being accounted for under differing methods. If so, the methods may be changed to attain uniformity in accounting,

If the change would otherwise have been appropriate for the separate companies. Such changes in accounting methods should be applied retroactively, and financial statements presented for prior periods should be restated.[13]

Quasi-Reorganizations

In some circumstances a corporation may elect to write down, or write off, some of its assets for the purpose of eliminating a deficit in its retained earnings account. Such a readjustment is referred to as a quasi-reorganization, and the problems of what may be permitted in such a readjustment, and what may be permitted thereafter, are dealt with in Accounting Research Bulletin No. 43.[14] If, under the guidelines set forth in ARB No. 43, long-lived assets are *written down* to their market, or realizable values, it constitutes a fresh start for allocating the adjusted basis of the capital assets. Thus, if an asset being depreciated by the straight-line method has a remaining life of eight years at the date of the quasi-reorganization, and its book value is reduced from $100,000 to $80,000 in consequence of the readjustment, the depreciable base becomes $80,000, and this amount should be allocated over the following eight years at the rate of 12-$1/2$%, or $10,000 each year.

Depreciable assets written down in a quasi-reorganization retain their historical-cost basis for tax purposes. Thus, financial accounting depreciation expense will not correspond with the depreciation expense deductible for tax purposes. However, in such a case, the difference between pretax accounting income and taxable income is a permanent difference, and deferral or accrual of income taxes is not required.

Change in Allocation Rate

A change in the service lives or salvage values of capital assets constitutes a change in accounting estimate.[15] Thus, a change in the depreciation rate or salvage values of an asset should be accounted for prospectively from the time of the accounting change. Generally, it will affect the year of change, and the remaining years of the useful life of the asset. For example, an asset purchased at the beginning of 19x1 for $10,000 was assigned an estimated life of ten years and depreciated for two years at the rate of 10%, or a total of $2,000. In 19x3 the estimated life was extended to twelve years, and the $8,000 undepreciated value of the asset was depreciated over the ten years from 19x3 to 19y2 at the rate of $800 each year. Thus, only the year of change and future years were affected by the accounting change. A change in an accounting estimate should not be accounted for by restating amounts reported in prior periods or by reporting pro forma amounts for prior periods.[16]

Change in Allocation Method

A change in depreciation method for previously recorded assets, such as from the double declining-balance method to the straight-line method, is considered a change in accounting principle.[17] Therefore, where there is a change in allocation methods, the procedures set forth in APB Opinion No. 20, and outlined below, should be followed.[18]

1. Financial statements for prior periods should be presented as previously reported.

---

[13] *Business Combinations,* Accounting Principles Board Opinion No. 16. (New York, NY: Copyright 1970 by the American Institute of Certified Public Accountants. Paragraph 52.)
[14] ARB No. 43, Chapter 7-A.
[15] APB No. 20, paragraph 10.
[16] APB Opinion No. 20, paragraph 31.
[17] APB Opinion No. 20, paragraph 9.
[18] APB Opinion No. 20, paragraph 19.

2. The cumulative effect of changing to a new accounting principle on the amount of retained earnings at the beginning of the period in which the change is made should be included in net income of the period of the change.
3. The effect of adopting the new accounting principle on income before extraordinary items and on net income (and on the related per share amounts) of the period of the change should be disclosed.
4. Income before extraordinary items and net income computed on a pro forma basis should be shown on the face of the income statements for all periods presented as if the newly adopted accounting principle had been applied during all periods affected.

However, a change to the straight-line method at a specific point in the service life of an asset may be planned at the time the accelerated depreciation method is adopted to fully depreciate the cost over the estimated life of the asset. Consistent application of such a policy does not constitute a change in accounting principle.[19]

Retirement of Asset Prior to End of Estimated Useful Life

In some instances, an asset is withdrawn prior to the end of its estimated useful life because it has become unsuited for its purpose for one reason or another. In such cases, if there are no proceeds from the sale of the asset, a loss should be recognized in an amount equivalent to its net book value at the time of its disposal.

Assets Continued in Use Beyond Their Estimated Useful Life

Where assets are continued in use after they have been fully depreciated on the books of the company, no further depreciation should be taken during the period of use that extends beyond the original estimated life.

GAINS AND LOSSES ON DISPOSITION OF DEPRECIABLE PROPERTY

As indicated in a previous section, where an asset is withdrawn without compensation, prior to the end of its estimated useful life, a loss equivalent to its net book value should be recognized; and where an asset is continued in use beyond its estimated useful life, no further depreciation should be taken during the period of its extended use, and no loss or gain should be recognized when it is abandoned. It should also be noted that where an asset, having no provision for salvage value, is withdrawn concurrent with the end of its estimated useful life, no gain or loss should be recognized on its retirement. However, under all circumstances other than those outlined above, the disposition of depreciable assets normally will require recognition of gain or loss on their disposition. The paragraphs that follow explain the specific circumstances under which disposal of depreciable assets do or do not require recognition of gains or losses.

Sale of Depreciable Assets

The sale of a depreciable asset results in a gain or loss in the same manner as the sale of any other kind of asset. The special problem involved with the sale of a depreciable asset is that its undepreciated cost must be determined. Where assets are depreciated as separate units, the problem of determining undepreciated cost is usu-

---

[19]APB Opinion No. 20, footnote 3.

ally fairly simple. However, where a sale constituting an abnormal retirement is made of an asset included in a multiple asset account, the process of determining the undepreciated cost is somewhat more involved. At any rate, the gain or loss to be recognized on the sale is the difference between the cash proceeds and the undepreciated cost, or net book value, of the asset sold. Estimated salvage value generally is not a consideration in the determination of gain or loss, unless the asset has been depreciated to its salvage value, and such value coincides with the net book value of the asset. For example, an asset that costs $150,000 and is estimated to have a ten-year life and a $15,000 salvage value, was sold for $75,000 at the end of six years. The gain on the sale would be computed simply as follows:

Proceeds from sale of asset		75,000
Less: Undepreciated Cost of Asset		
Acquisition cost	150,000	
Less: Depreciation — 6 years at $13,500 each	81,000	
Undepreciated cost		69,000
Gain on sale of asset		6,000

In this example, salvage value had no bearing on the computation of gain or loss. However, the estimated salvage value *did* affect the annual depreciation taken during the six-year service life of the asset because depreciation was taken on the depreciable base ($150,000 − $15,000 = $135,000) during that time instead of on the acquisition cost of $150,000.

Exchange of Depreciable Assets

An exchange of depreciable assets for nonmonetary assets constitutes a nonmonetary exchange. The subject of nonmonetary exchanges is comprehensively treated in Chapter 4 of this volume.

Trade-Ins

Accounting for nonmonetary exchanges which include a monetary consideration is fully discussed and illustrated in Chapter 4. In connection with such an exchange the recipient of the monetary consideration generally is required to recognize a portion of any gain on the transaction, while the payer of the monetary consideration is not permitted to recognize any gain at all, but is required to add the monetary consideration to the basis of the asset received. Both the recipient and the payer of monetary consideration in a nonmonetary exchange of depreciable assets are required to immediately recognize any *loss* involved in such transactions.

Casualty Losses

Since depreciable assets are usually covered by hazard insurance, the loss of such capital assets by fire, flood, or some other type of casualty, generally requires accounting treatment similar to that required by a sale. Thus, a gain on the casualty should be recognized for any excess of insurance proceeds over the undepreciated cost of the asset; and a loss in the amount of the deficiency should be recorded, where the insurance proceeds are less than the net book value of the lost asset.

Involuntary Conversion

An involuntary conversion occurs where, for example, cash is received for property which is seized, condemned, or destroyed, and then the cash is reinvested in assets similar to those lost in the conversion. For tax purposes, any gain or loss realized on the conversion is not reported as taxable income, nor allowed as a tax deduction. The gain or loss is deducted from, or added to, the cost of the new asset to arrive at its taxable base. Accounting Principles Board Opinion No. 29 specifically exempts involuntary conversions from the provisions of the Opinion,[20] and thus it appears that, for financial accounting purposes, a company which experiences a casualty loss may either report involuntary conversion gains and losses as such, or use them to adjust the depreciable basis of the newly acquired asset. However, if gains are recognized on an involuntary conversion, the gain should be reduced by the amount of its tax effect, and the resulting deferred income taxes should be amortized over the life of the new asset.

SPECIAL AREAS OF CAPITAL ASSET COST ALLOCATION

Some areas of accounting for depreciation cannot be covered in this chapter because of space limitations. However, the following paragraphs set forth a brief description of these special areas of accounting for depreciable assets.

Regulated Companies

The accounting practices of most regulated companies are, of course, prescribed by regulatory authorities. Generally, the accounting regulations issued by the various supervisory bodies correspond with generally accepted accounting principles. However, supervisory regulations are often so technical and so complex that it is not possible to discuss the details of such regulations in the limited space provided for this chapter.

Cost Accounting

Cost accounting is a highly specialized area in the accounting discipline. All the allocation methods described in the preceding sections and paragraphs of this chapter apply equally to conventional accounting and to cost accounting. However, cost accounting procedures must provide features for reallocating costs to divisions, to departments, and finally to products. These reallocation methods are intricate, and highly technical, and it is not feasible to include a discussion of such methods in the text of this chapter.

Adjustments for General Price Level Changes

Accounting for depreciation adjusted for general price level changes, or for depreciation reported in units of general purchasing power, is accomplished by a method of inflation accounting that requires the use of price indexes and the application of conversion factors for the purpose of reporting prior years' asset acquisitions and depreciation expense in terms of current year dollar values. These accounting procedures are quite complicated and obviously are too involved to be adequately disclosed in the text of this chapter. A comprehensive discussion of financial reporting in units of general purchasing power is included in another accounting procedures book published by the author.[21]

Depreciation of Capitalized Leased Property

Financial Accounting Standards Board Statement No. 13 prescribes strict rules for depreciation of leased property required to be capitalized under the provisions of

---

[20]APB Opinion No. 29, paragraph 4.
[21]Martin F. Towles, *Practical Accounting Systems and Procedures* (Englewood Cliffs, N.J.: Prentice-Hall, Inc., 1978) Chapter 4.

the Statement.[22] Chapters 5 and 6 of this volume comprehend extensive discussions on the directives and guidelines set forth in FASB Statement No. 13.

DISCLOSURE IN FINANCIAL STATEMENTS

The root directive for disclosure of depreciable assets and depreciation is found in Accounting Principles Board Opinion No. 12, published in 1963, which requires the following information to be shown in the financial statements or in the notes thereof:[23]

1. Depreciation expense for the period.
2. Balances of major classes of depreciable assets, by nature or function, at the balance sheet date.
3. Accumulated depreciation, either by major classes of depreciable assets or in total, at the balance sheet date.
4. A general description of the method or methods used in computing depreciation with respect to major classes of depreciable assets.

In 1971 the Accounting Principles Board published Opinion No. 19, "Reporting Changes in Financial Position," which requires that the following specific disclosures in connection with depreciable assets and depreciation be made in the "Statement of Changes in Financial Position":[24]

1. Depreciation expense should be shown under the caption "Expenses not requiring outlay of working capital in current period," and should be added back to net income or loss in order to determine the amount of funds provided by operations.[25]
2. Specific disclosure of the following transactions in depreciable assets should be made in the Statement:
   (a) acquisition of property by issuance of securities or in exchange for other property;[26]
   (b) outlays for purchase of long-term assets (identifying separately such items as investments, property, and intangibles);[27] and
   (c) proceeds from sale (or working capital or cash provided by sale) of long-term assets (identifying separately such items as investments, property and intangibles) not in the normal course of business, less related expenses involving the current use of working capital or cash.[27]

Further elaboration upon depreciable asset disclosure requirements occurred in 1972 with the publication of APB Opinion No. 22, "Disclosure of Accounting Policies," which requires disclosure of information about the accounting policies adopted by a reporting entity. The Opinion states that, in general, the disclosure should encompass important judgments as to appropriateness of principles relating to recognition of revenue and allocation of asset costs to current and future periods; in particular, it should encompass those accounting principles and methods that involve the following:

(a) a selection from existing acceptable alternatives;

---

[22]*Accounting for Leases*—Statement of the Financial Accounting Standards Board No. 13. (Stamford, Connecticut, Financial Accounting Standards Board, 1976. Reprinted with permission. Copies of the complete document are available from the FASB.)
[23]APB Opinion No. 12, paragraphs 4–5.
[24]See Chapter 10.
[25]APB Opinion No. 19, paragraph 9.
[26]APB Opinion No. 19, paragraph 8.
[27]APB Opinion No. 19, paragraphs 14a and 14b.

(b) principles and methods peculiar to the industry in which the reporting entity operates, even if such principles and methods are predominantly followed in that industry; and

(c) unusual or innovative applications of generally accepted accounting principles (and, as applicable, of principles and methods peculiar to the industry in which the reporting entity operates).[28]

It is important to note that duplication of disclosure is not required under any of the directives referred to above. For example, if depreciation expense is disclosed in the statement of changes in financial position, it need not be reported in the notes to the financial statements; if depreciable assets are shown in detail on the balance sheet, they also need not be reported in the notes.

It is also important to bear in mind that where the use of differing methods of depreciation for financial accounting and income tax accounting create timing differences, requiring accrual and deferral of income taxes, the nature of the provision for income taxes must be disclosed in accordance with the provisions of APB Opinion No. 11.[29]

Following is an example of notes to the financial statements made for the purpose of disclosing depreciable assets and depreciation, and accounting policies in connection therewith, modeled after the published annual report of a major business enterprise.

NOTES TO CONSOLIDATED FINANCIAL STATEMENTS

Note 1—Summary of Significant Accounting Policies

The significant accounting policies followed by the company are:

* * * * * * * * * * * *

Property, Plant, and Equipment

Buildings and machinery and equipment are being depreciated over their estimated useful lives using the straight-line method, except for certain assets with an original cost of approximately $21,759 being depreciated using accelerated methods. The principle depreciation rates being used are: Buildings (2.0% to 5.0%) and Machinery and Equipment (4.0% to 33.3%).

Maintenance and repairs are charged to income when incurred and expenditures for renewals and betterments of a permanent nature are capitalized. Upon sale or retirement, the asset and related accumulated depreciation account are eliminated from the accounts and the resulting gain or loss is recognized, except that, in the case of certain equipment for which depreciation is provided on a composite basis, the cost of the asset is charged to the accumulated depreciation account and no gain or loss is recognized. Depreciation expense for the years 19x2 and 19x1 was $11,343 and $7,755, respectively.

Note 2—Property, Plant, and Equipment

Property, plant, and equipment, carried at depreciated cost, include the following at December 31:

---

[28]APB Opinion No. 22, paragraph 12.
[29]See Chapters 1 and 2.

	19x2	19x1
Buildings	32,617	33,185
Machinery and equipment	74,373	70,170
	106,990	103,355
Less accumulated depreciation	51,456	43,597
	55,534	59,758
Land	3,687	4,622
	59,221	64,380

FINANCIAL ACCOUNTING METHODS SHOULD NOT INFLUENCE SELECTION OF ALTERNATIVE INCOME TAX METHODS

Financial accounting systems normally are concerned with aspects of cost allocation which reflect the economic concepts of management. Such systems are designed to accommodate management's accounting policies, and to provide the data necessary for financial reporting in accordance with generally accepted accounting principles. On the other hand, income tax accounting systems should be designed to take advantage of every available income tax benefit, including a judicious selection of alternative tax accounting methods, whether or not such methods be in accordance with proper financial accounting.

This chapter deals with capital asset cost allocation from the standpoint of proper financial accounting and reporting *only*, and does not purport to contend with the enormous ramifications of income tax accounting. Thus, while financial accounting alternatives are available for prudent selection by management for financial accounting purposes, the author recommends that management continuously seek advice from professional tax consultants with reference to specific tax benefits that may be obtained through wise discernment and discrimination in the selection of alternative income tax accounting methods.

10

Reporting Changes in Financial Position—
Concepts, Formats, and Elements of Disclosure

For many years prior to 1963, a number of large firms included in their annual reports a cash flow analysis or a statement of source and application of funds, or a combination of both. During that time the format and component elements of the cash flow analyses varied from company to company, and the concept of "funds" reported in the funds statement was a matter of individual comprehension. Perhaps such statements were informative to the personnel of the respective companies that prepared them, but they were rendered almost totally useless to general users of the statements because of their lack of uniformity in format and concept. In 1963 the American Institute of Certified Public Accountants issued Accounting Principles Board Opinion No. 3, "Statement of Source and Application of Funds," in an effort to standardize such reports. APB Opinion No. 3 encouraged, but did not require, presentation of a funds statement, and also afforded considerable latitude as to form and content of the statement itself. As a consequence, in practice the character of such statements continued to vary widely. Finally, in 1971, APB Opinion No. 3 was superseded by APB Opinion No. 19, which was published for the purpose of establishing guidelines for the preparation of the funds statement,[1] and to designate the circumstances in which presentation of a funds statement would be required.[2]

This chapter sets forth the provisions of APB Opinion No. 19, explains its reporting requirements, and presents examples of worksheets designed to accommodate the computational techniques necessary to calculate the values required to be assigned to the respective elements of the funds statement.

OBJECTIVES OF A FUNDS STATEMENT

The Opinion states succinctly that the objectives of a funds statement are:

(1) to summarize the financing and investing activities of the entity, including the extent to which the enterprise has generated funds from operations during the period; and
(2) to complete the disclosure of changes in financial position during the period.

---

[1] The term "funds statement" used in this chapter is synonymous with "Statement of Changes in Financial Position."

[2] *Reporting Changes in Financial Position,* Opinion of the Accounting Principles Board No. 19. (New York, NY: Copyright 1971 by the American Institute of Certified Public Accountants.)

PURPOSE OF A FUNDS STATEMENT

APB Opinion No. 19 also is succinct in stating that the information shown in a funds statement is useful to a variety of users of financial statements in making economic decisions regarding the enterprise.

BENEFITS OF THE FUNDS STATEMENT

The overriding benefit derived from a funds statement is that it bridges the gap between the balance sheet and income statement by disclosing the effects on elements of the balance sheet that result from operations reported in the income statement. In addition, it accounts for other changes in financial position indicated in comparative balance sheets that result from investing, and other nonrevenue activities of the enterprise.

NONFUNCTIONAL ASPECTS OF THE FUNDS STATEMENT

While the funds statement may be beneficial to independent financial analysts and to management of large companies, generally, individual investors and management of small companies are not capable of comprehending the statistical data contained in such statements. Empirical evidence of this situation has been demonstrated to any accountant who ever had to explain to an entrepreneur, for example, why an *increase* in cash represents an *application* of funds, or why the net book value of assets sold is *added* to net income to represent a *source* of funds. Thus, to the management of many medium and small companies the funds statement is an unnecessary and costly appendage to the basic financial statements.

CONCEPTS OF FUNDS

Prior to the issuance of APB Opinion No. 19, the concept of "funds" varied widely, with resulting variation in the nature of the funds statements presented in annual reports. The major concepts of "funds" that existed at the time were the following:

Cash Concept

In some instances "funds" were defined as cash or its equivalent, and the resulting funds statements represented a summary of cash receipts and disbursements.

Working Capital Concept

Some accountants interpreted "funds" to mean working capital, and funds statements prepared under this concept resulted in a summary of the changes in working capital during the reporting period.

All Financial Resources Concept

This concept of "funds" embraced all the elements in the balance sheet and the funds statement under this concept not only reported changes in cash and working capital, but included the financial aspects of all significant transactions made during the year. For example, the acquisition of property through the issue of securities would be reported even though the transaction did not involve cash or working capital.

ACCOUNTING PRINCIPLES BOARD OPINION NO. 19

It is difficult to paraphrase the elements in APB Opinion No. 19 because each specific provision of the Opinion is prefaced and concluded by editorial comment. Therefore, in order to disclose the philosophical speculations of the Board, as well as the specific provisions of the Opinion, the entire Opinion, excluding footnotes and some parenthetical comments, is set forth verbatim below. The paragraph numbers are the same as those that appeared in the original publication of the Opinion.

OPINION

Applicability

7. The Board concludes that information concerning the financing and investing activities of a business enterprise and the changes in its financial position for a period is essential for financial statement users, particularly owners and creditors, in making economic decisions. When financial statements purporting to present both financial position (balance sheet) and results of operations (statement of income and retained earnings) are issued, a statement summarizing changes in financial position should also be presented as a basic financial statement for each period for which an income statement is presented. These conclusions apply to all profit-oriented business entities, whether or not the reporting entity normally classifies its assets and liabilities as current or noncurrent.

Concept

8. The Board also concludes that the statement summarizing changes in financial position should be based on a broad concept embracing all changes in financial position and that the title of the statement should reflect this broad concept. The Board therefore recommends that the title be Statement of Changes in Financial Position (referred to below as "the Statement"). The Statement of each reporting entity should disclose all important aspects of its financing and investing activities regardless of whether cash or other elements of working capital are directly affected. For example, acquisitions of property by issuance of securities or in exchange for other property, and conversions of long-term debt or preferred stock to common stock, should be appropriately reflected in the Statement.

Format

9. The Board recognizes the need for flexibility in form, content, and terminology of the Statement to meet its objectives in differing circumstances. For example, a working capital format is not relevant to an entity that does not distinguish between current and noncurrent assets and liabilities. Each entity should adopt the presentation that is most informative in its circumstances. The Board believes, however, that the guides set forth in the paragraphs that follow should be applied in preparing and presenting the Statement.

10. The ability of an enterprise to provide working capital or cash from operations is an important factor in considering its financing and investing activities. Accordingly, the Statement should prominently disclose working capital or cash provided from or used in operations for the period, and the Board believes that the disclosure is most informative if the effects of extraordinary items are reported separately from the effects of normal items. The Statement for the period should begin with income or loss before extraordinary items, if any, and add back (or deduct) items recognized in determining that income or loss which did not use (or provide) working capital or cash during the period. Items added and deducted in accordance

with this procedure are not sources or uses of working capital or cash, and the related captions should make this clear, e.g., "Add—Expenses not requiring outlay of working capital in the current period." An acceptable alternative procedure, which gives the same result, is to begin with total revenue that provided working capital or cash during the period and deduct operating costs and expenses that required the outlay of working capital or cash during the period. In either case, the resulting amount of working capital or cash should be appropriately described, e.g., "Working capital provided from (used in) operations for the period, exclusive of extraordinary items." This total should be immediately followed by working capital or cash provided or used by income or loss from extraordinary items, if any; extraordinary income or loss should be similarly adjusted for items recognized that did not provide or use working capital or cash during the period.

11. Provided that these guides are met, the Statement may take whatever form gives the most useful portrayal of the financing and investing activities and the changes in financial position of the reporting entity. The Statement may be in balanced form or in a form expressing the changes in financial position in terms of cash, of cash and temporary investments combined, of all quick assets, or of working capital. The Statement should disclose all important changes in financial position for the period covered; accordingly, types of transactions reported may vary substantially in relative importance from one period to another.

Content

12. Whether or not working capital flow is presented in the Statement, net changes in each element of working capital (as customarily defined) should be appropriately disclosed for at least the current period, either in the Statement or in a related tabulation.

a. If the format shows the flow of cash, changes in other elements of working capital (e.g., in receivables, inventories, and payables) constitute sources and uses of cash and should accordingly be disclosed in appropriate detail in the body of the Statement.

b. If the format shows the flow of working capital and two-year comparative balance sheets are presented, the changes in each element of working capital for the current period (but not for earlier periods) can be computed by the user of the statements. Nevertheless, the Board believes that the objectives of the Statement usually require that the net change in working capital be analyzed in appropriate detail in a tabulation accompanying the Statement, and accordingly this detail should be furnished.

13. The effects of other financing and investing activities should be individually disclosed. For example, both outlays for acquisitions and proceeds from retirements of property should be reported; both long-term borrowings and repayments of long-term debt should be reported; and outlays for purchases of consolidated subsidiaries should be summarized in the consolidated Statement by major categories of assets obtained and obligations assumed. Related items should be shown in proximity when the result contributes to the clarity of the Statement. Individual immaterial items may be combined.

14. In addition to working capital or cash provided from operations and changes in elements of working capital, the Statement should clearly disclose:

a. Outlays for purchase of long-term assets (identifying separately such items as investments, property, and intangibles).

b. Proceeds from sale (or working capital or cash provided by sale) of long-term assets (identifying separately such items as investments, property, and intangibles) not in the normal course of business, less related expenses involving the current use of working capital or cash.

c. Conversion of long-term debt or preferred stock to common stock.

d. Issuance, assumption, redemption, and repayment of long-term debt.

e. Issuance, redemption, or purchase of capital stock for cash or for assets other than cash.

f. Dividends in cash or in kind or other distributions to shareholders, except stock dividends and stock split-ups.

Terminology

15. The amount of working capital or cash provided from operations is not a substitute for or an improvement upon properly determined net income as a measure of results of operations and the consequent effect on financial position. Terms referring to "cash" should not be used to describe amounts provided from operations unless all noncash items have been appropriately adjusted. The adjusted amount should be described accurately, in conformity with the nature of the adjustments, e.g., "Cash provided from operations for the period" or "Working capital provided from operations for the period" as appropriate. The Board strongly recommends that isolated statistics of working capital or cash provided from operations, especially per-share amounts, not be presented in annual reports to shareholders. If any per-share data relating to flow of working capital or cash are presented, they should as a minimum include amounts for inflow from operations, inflow from other sources, and total outflow, and each per-share amount should be clearly identified with the corresponding total amount shown in the Statement.

TECHNIQUES FOR PREPARATION OF FUNDS STATEMENTS

BASIC FORMATS FOR THE STATEMENT OF CHANGES IN FINANCIAL POSITION

There are three basic formats for the Statement of Changes in Financial Position which are in current use. These formats are described below.

Total Financial Resources Format

This type of statement reflects changes in financial position in a balanced format in which the Sources of Funds equals the Application of Funds. If the reporting entity has a classified balance sheet, the change in working capital is entered on one line in the balanced format, and the details of the changes in working capital are set forth in a schedule following the balanced statement.

Working Capital Format

The working capital format starts with a section that reflects all changes in financial position that *provide* working capital; follows with a section showing changes in financial position that *require* working capital; and then sets forth the difference between the two sections as an *increase* or *decrease* in working capital. The increase or decrease in each element of working capital is shown on a separate schedule following the basic statement, and the net increase or decrease in the elements of working capital corresponds to the net increase or decrease shown in the basic statement.

Cash Funds Format

The cash funds format starts with the cash balance at the beginning of the year and reflects all changes in total financial resources in a manner that develops the cash balance at the end of the year. The first section reports cash *provided* by operations, followed by a section that reflects cash *used* in operations. The difference between the total of the two sections represents cash provided by operations or cash applied to operations. The changes in working capital other than cash are used to adjust appropriate income or expense accounts so that they reflect the actual change in cash.

Following the sections that develop the cash provided by, or applied to, operations, is a section that reports the nonrevenue changes in cash during the year. The net increase or decrease in cash provided by, or applied to, operations is added to, or deducted from, the net increase or decrease in cash resulting from nonrevenue changes in cash, and the result is the net change in cash during the year. The net change in cash during the year is added to, or deducted from, the beginning cash balance, to arrive at the cash balance at the end of the year.

DATA USED IN CALCULATING CHANGES IN FINANCIAL POSITION

The basic source of data necessary to compute changes in financial position is the comparative balance sheet. The change in each element of the balance sheet must appear on the funds statement in one manner or another. Additional sources of data must come from the statement of income and retained earnings, and the changes resulting from nonrevenue transactions must come from documentation that supports changes in the related general ledger accounts; for example, issuance of stock for property.

ELEMENTS IN THE INCOME STATEMENT THAT DO NOT AFFECT WORKING CAPITAL

Perhaps the most confusing aspect to users of the funds statement is the addition to, or deduction from, net income of items that do not affect working capital. It is easy to comprehend that depreciation expense does not require an outlay of working capital and that, therefore, it should be added back to net income to reflect funds actually provided by operations. It is much more difficult to comprehend why the net book value of assets sold should be added back to income to increase funds provided by operations. The reason for adding the net book value to net income can be demonstrated as follows.

A company sold a machine for $5,000 which cost $10,000 and to which depreciation amounting to $6,000 had been applied over the years. The book value of the machine, therefore, was $4,000.

The entry to record the sale was as follows:

	Debit	Credit
Cash	5,000	
Accumulated depreciation	6,000	
Machine		10,000
Gain on sale of machine		1,000

From the example we can see that only $1,000 was taken up in net income, while $5,000 was added to the cash fund. Therefore, to reflect correctly the funds provided from operations, the $4,000 net book value of the machine must be added to the net income reflected in the income statement. If no fixed assets were acquired during the year, and no other fixed assets disposed of, the net decrease in fixed assets shown on the funds statement would be $4,000 plus the depreciation taken during the year.

Depreciation and amortization are the most common elements in the income statement that must be added back to net income in order to calculate the working capital provided by operations. However, there are many items of a more or less subtle nature that are required to be added to or deducted from net income in order to determine working capital provided from operations, and it should behoove the accountant to be alert to detect such items in the income statement. Thus, it must always be borne in mind that practically *any* item included in the income statement that increases income, but does not increase cash or working capital, must be deducted from net income to determine working capital provided by operations and, conversely, any item of expense in the income statement that does not use cash or working capital must be added to net income.

ILLUSTRATION OF COMPUTING VALUES OF ELEMENTS IN THE FUNDS STATEMENT FOR ENTITIES HAVING A CLASSIFIED BALANCE SHEET

Model Case No. 1 demonstrates procedures for computing values to be assigned to the individual elements in the Statement of Changes in Financial Position for enterprises having a classified balance sheet. The example includes illustrations of the funds statement presented in the all financial resources, working capital, and cash funds formats, respectively.

MODEL CASE NO. 1

Warrington Research, Inc. is engaged in engineering research, project construction, and the manufacture and marketing of sophisticated utility products.

In 19x7 Warrington requested its accounting department to prepare statements of changes in financial position for the years 19x7 and 19x6 on the total financial resources, working capital, and cash funds formats, respectively. Warrington's purpose was to have the Board of Directors examine the statements prepared by the three different methods, and decide which format was most informative and thus determine which form of statement of changes in financial position should accompany the 19x7 annual report.

Warrington's basic financial statements as of December 31, 19x7 and 19x6, other than the statement of changes in financial position, are shown in Exhibits A, B, and C.

WARRINGTON RESEARCH, INC. CONSOLIDATED BALANCE SHEET

	December 31,	
	19x7	19x6
Assets		
Current		
Cash	20,762	14,836
Accounts receivable	44,094	42,324
Unbilled costs on contracts	38,290	31,806
Inventories	7,472	7,374
Prepaid expenses	1,225	979
Total current assets	111,843	97,319
Property, plant, and equipment—net of depreciation	15,136	15,495
Investment in common stock—at equity	8,489	7,718
Excess of investment cost over underlying equity	2,631	2,729
Other assets	1,341	1,356
	139,440	124,617

EXHIBIT A

Liabilities and Stockholders' Equity

Current Liabilities		
Accounts payable and accrued expenses	38,529	34,997
Advance billings on contracts in progress	2,458	3,775
Estimated additional contract costs	14,416	13,485
Federal and state income taxes payable	343	3,554
Deferred federal income tax	15,711	8,717
Total current liabilities	71,457	64,528
Long-term debt	3,813	3,842
Deferred federal income taxes	670	547
Total liabilities	75,940	68,917
Stockholders' Equity		
Capital stock	4,034	3,999
Paid-in capital	25,931	25,460
Retained earnings	33,535	26,241
Total stockholders' equity	63,500	55,700
	139,440	124,617

EXHIBIT A (continued)

WARRINGTON RESEARCH, INC.

CONSOLIDATED STATEMENT OF INCOME AND RETAINED EARNINGS

	For Year Ended December 31	
	19x7	19x6
Sales	224,052	218,690
Cost of sales	169,358	171,935
	54,694	46,755
Administrative, general, and selling expenses	39,046	34,321
Operating income	15,648	12,434
Other Income (Expense)		
Interest	(307)	(669)
Increase in equity in investments	771	435
Amortization of excess of investment cost over equity	(97)	(97)
Miscellaneous—net	(161)	443
	206	112
Income before income taxes	15,854	12,546

EXHIBIT B

Income Taxes		
Current	1,042	4,298
Deferred	7,117	2,329
	8,159	6,627
Net income	7,695	5,919
Retained earnings—beginning of year	26,241	20,641
	33,936	26,560
Cash dividends paid	401	319
Retained earnings—end of year	33,535	26,241
Earnings per common share	1.82	1.37

EXHIBIT B (continued)

WARRINGTON RESEARCH, INC.

CONSOLIDATED STATEMENT OF CAPITAL STOCK AND PAID-IN CAPITAL

	Capital Stock		
	Shares Out-Standing	Par Value	Paid-In Capital
Balance—December 31, 19x5	3,985	3,985	25,310
Proceeds from exercise of stock option plan	14	14	150
Balance—December 31, 19x6	3,999	3,999	25,460
Proceeds from exercise of stock option plan	35	35	471
Balance—December 31, 19x7	4,034	4,034	25,931

EXHIBIT C

Changes in plant, property, and equipment for the current year, and amortization of the excess of investment cost over equity for the current and three preceding years are shown in Schedules 1 and 2, respectively.

The Statement of Changes in Financial Position for the years 19x6 and 19x5 had been prepared on the all financial resources basis, and the workpapers on the computations provided the accounting department with sufficient data to permit them to prepare the 19x6 funds statement on both the all financial resources, and the working capital bases.

The accountants in the accounting department decided to use the changes in assets, liabilities, and stockholders' equity during 19x7 as the basis for their computation of values to be assigned to elements in the funds statement. In order to simplify the process of preparing the funds statements on three different bases, they used the comparative balance sheet shown in Exhibit A to compute the increases or decreases in in each item in the statement during 19x7. The results of the accountants' computations are shown in Schedule 3.

SCHEDULE OF PLANT, PROPERTY AND EQUIPMENT AND ACCUMULATED DEPRECIATION

	ASSETS				ACCUMULATED DEPRECIATION				
	Balance December 31, 19x6	Addi-tions	Dispos-itions	Balance December 31, 19x7	Balance December 31, 19x6	Current Expense	Dispos-itions	Balance December 31, 19x6	Net Book Value
Land, and land improvements	1,141	140	44	1,237	440	91	35	496	741
Buildings	6,903	1,841	98	8,646	2,671	551	80	3,142	5,504
Machinery and equipment	17,234		1,593	15,641	6,672	1,376	1,298	6,750	8,891
	25,278	1,981	1,735	25,524	9,783	2,018	1,413	10,388	15,136

SCHEDULE 1

EXCESS OF INVESTMENT COST OVER EQUITY

AMORTIZATION SCHEDULE
(Amortized Over 30 Years)

October 15, 19x4

Excess of cost over underlying equity in purchased investment	2,940
19x4	
Amortization	15
December 31, 19x4—Balance	2,925
19x5	
Amortization	98
December 31, 19x5—Balance	2,827
19x6	
Amortization	98
December 31, 19x6—Balance	2,729
19x7	
Amortization	98
December 31, 19x7—Balance	2,631

SCHEDULE 2

SCHEDULE OF INCREASES (DECREASES) IN BALANCE SHEET ELEMENTS

	December 31, 19x7	December 31, 19x6	Increase (Decrease)
Assets			
Current			
Cash	20,762	14,836	5,926
Accounts receivable	44,094	42,324	1,770
Unbilled costs	38,290	31,806	6,484
Inventories	7,472	7,374	98
Prepaid expenses	1,225	979	246
Total current assets	111,843	97,319	14,524
Property	15,136	15,495	(359)
Investment—at equity	8,489	7,718	771
Excess of investment cost over equity	2,631	2,729	(98)
Other assets	1,341	1,356	(15)
	139,440	124,617	14,823
Liabilities and Stockholders' Equity			
Current Liabilities			
Accounts payable	38,529	34,997	3,532
Advance billings	2,458	3,775	(1,317)
Additional contract costs	14,416	13,485	931
Income taxes payable	343	3,554	(3,211)
Deferred federal income taxes	15,711	8,717	6,994
Total current liabilities	71,457	64,528	6,929
Long-term debt	3,813	3,842	(29)
Deferred federal income taxes	670	547	123
Total liabilities	75,940	68,917	7,023
Stockholders' Equity			
Capital stock	4,034	3,999	35
Paid-in capital	25,931	25,460	471
Retained earnings	33,535	26,241	7,294
Total stockholders' equity	63,500	55,700	7,800
	139,440	124,617	14,823

SCHEDULE 3

Using the values in Schedule 3 as a starting point, the accountants prepared a worksheet designed to permit them to distribute the increases and decreases in assets, liabilities, and stockholders' equity to the category in which such changes were required to be reported in the funds statements prepared on both the all financial resources and working capital bases. Exhibit C, and Schedules 1 and 2 were used to determine the detail of amounts required to be classified as capital changes and expenses not involving funds. The accountants' worksheet is shown in Schedule 4.

WORKSHEET FOR CHANGES IN FINANCIAL POSITION
Year Ended December 31, 19x7
(Total Financial Resources Basis and Working Capital Basis)

| | Increase (Decrease) in Balance Sheet Elements | Effect of Change in Current Assets and Current Liabilities on Working Capital | | Effect of Change in Noncurrent Assets and Liabilities and in Stockholders' Equity | | | | Net Income and Income and Expenses Not Involving Funds | |
| | | | | Assets | | Liabilities and Stockholders' Equity | | | |
		Assets	Liabilities	(Decrease) Funds Provided	Increase Funds Applied	Increase Funds Provided	(Decrease) Funds Applied	Increase for Net Income and Expenses	(Decrease) for Net Loss and Income
Current Assets									
Cash	5,926	5,926							
Accounts receivable	1,770	1,770							
Unbilled costs	6,484	6,484							
Inventories	98	98							
Prepaid expenses	246	246							
Total current assets	14,524	14,524							
Current Liabilities									
Accounts payable	3,532		(3,532)						
Advance billing	(1,317)		1,317						
Additional contract costs	931		(931)						
Income taxes payable	(3,211)		3,211						
Deferred income taxes	6,994		(6,994)						
Total current liabilities	6,929	(6,929)	(6,929)						
Increase in working capital		7,595							
Noncurrent Assets									
Property	(359)								
Acquisitions					1,981				
Undepreciated cost of assets sold								322	
Depreciation								2,018	
Investment—at equity	771								771
Excess of investment cost over equity	(98)							98	
Other assets	(15)			15					
Noncurrent Liabilities									
Long-term debt	(29)					29			
Deferred income taxes	123							123	
Stockholders' Equity									
Capital stock	35					35			
Paid—in capital	471					471			
Retained earnings	7,294								
Net income								7,695	
Dividends							401		
	29,646			15	1,981	506	430	10,256	771

SCHEDULE 4

Schedule 4 is a matrix on which the increases and decreases in individual balance sheet items, as developed in Schedule 3, are listed in the left-hand column. The particular changes shown in the left-hand column are distributed in an equivalent *net* amount to columns on the right. The captions over the right-hand columns register the nature of the change and indicate whether the change provides, applies, or has no effect on working capital. For example, the left-hand column reflects a decrease of $359 in property, plant and equipment during 19x7. The net decrease is analyzed from information shown on Schedule 1, and distributed to the right-hand columns of Schedule 4. The distribution on Schedule 4 reveals that the net decrease in property resulted from acquisitions in the amount of $1,981, which represents an application of funds, and which is offset by depreciation of $2,018 and disposition of property having a net book value of $322, both of which do not involve working capital. Similarly, the left-hand column indicates an increase of $7,294 in retained earnings, and the columns on the right disclose that the net increase consists of net income of $7,695 offset by a dividend distribution in the amount of $401. These items represent a source and an application of funds, respectively, and are distributed as such on Schedule 4.

Thus, from the values computed and shown in Schedule 4 the accountants prepared funds statements on both the all financial resources basis and the working capital basis, as set forth in Exhibits D and E, respectively.

Both the statement based on the all financial resources concept, reported on Exhibit D, and the statement based on the working capital concept, reported on Exhibit E, were prepared from the worksheet shown in Schedule 4. However, in order to prepare a statement based on the *cash funds* concept, the accountants had to prepare a second worksheet that would simultaneously accomplish the following two objectives:

(a) Relate *cash flow* involved in the increases and decreases in assets, liabilities, and stockholders' equity, as shown on Schedule 3, to the revenue elements of the statement of income reported in Exhibit B; and

(b) Reflect increases and decreases in *cash* resulting from changes in the nonrevenue components of the balance sheet included in Schedule 3.

Accordingly, the accountants prepared separate worksheets for both 19x6 and 19x7, following the matrix principle used in preparing Schedule 4. However, the accountants analyzed changes in terms of *cash* rather than using the analytical method of Schedule 4, which was based on the effect of changes in working capital. The accountant's worksheet for 19x7 is set forth in Schedule 5.

From the worksheets prepared for 19x7 and 19x6 the accountants prepared the statements of changes in financial position based on the cash funds concept shown in Exhibit F.

In Exhibit F the changes in working capital other than cash and items of income and expense not involving cash are used to adjust appropriate income and expense accounts so that they reflect the actual changes in *cash*. Consequently, the reader may find some elements shown in Exhibit F to be difficult to comprehend on simple inspection. However, in working out the details of each component of the statement, the logicality of the computations becomes evident. For example, the first item under the 19x7 caption "Income Taxes" is labeled "Income taxes—current and deferred—net," in the amount of $8,159. This amount is equivalent to the income tax expense shown on the income statement, and obviously does not represent a pure cash item. However, the purpose of the statement is to show *all* changes in financial position by analyzing *all* elements in the income statement and balance sheet, and showing their relation to

WARRINGTON RESEARCH, INC.
STATEMENT OF CHANGES IN FINANCIAL POSITION

	For Year Ended December 31,	
	19x7	19x6
SOURCE OF FUNDS:		
Funds Provided from Operations		
Net income	7,695	5,919
Expenses (Income) Not Requiring Funds		
Increase in equity in investee	(771)	(435)
Depreciation	2,018	1,854
Amortization	98	98
Undepreciated cost of property sold	322	145
Deferred income taxes—noncurrent	123	(51)
Total funds provided from operations	9,485	7,530
Decrease in other assets	15	19
Provided from long-term debt	—	3,785
Exercise of stock options	506	164
	10,006	11,498
APPLICATION OF FUNDS:		
Additions to property, plant, and equipment	1,981	5,233
Reduction in long-term debt	29	18,069
Cash dividends paid	401	357
Increase (decrease) in working capital	7,595	(12,161)
	10,006	11,498
Increase (Decrease) in Working Capital		
Cash	5,926	9,427
Accounts receivable	1,770	(6,695)
Unbilled costs	6,484	(4,281)
Inventories	98	208
Prepaid expenses	246	354
Accounts payable	(3,532)	(4,766)
Advance billings	1,317	(521)
Additional contract costs	(931)	(663)
Income taxes	3,211	(2,844)
Deferred income taxes	(6,994)	(2,380)
	7,595	(12,161)

EXHIBIT D

WARRINGTON RESEARCH, INC.
STATEMENT OF CHANGES IN FINANCIAL POSITION

	For Year Ended December 31,	
	19x7	19x6
WORKING CAPITAL PROVIDED BY:		
Current Operations		
Net income	7,695	5,919
Expenses (Income) Not Requiring Outlay of Working Capital		
Increase in equity in investment	(771)	(435)
Depreciation	2,018	1,854
Amortization	98	98
Undepreciated cost of property sold	322	145
Deferred federal income taxes—noncurrent	123	(51)
Working capital provided by operations	9,485	7,530
Decrease in other assets	15	19
Proceeds from long-term debt	—	3,785
Exercise of stock options	506	164
Total working capital provided	10,006	11,498
WORKING CAPITAL APPLIED TO:		
Additions to property, plant, and equipment	1,981	5,233
Reduction in long-term debt	29	18,069
Cash dividends paid	401	357
Total working capital applied	2,411	23,659
Increase (decrease) in working capital	7,595	(12,161)
Increase (Decrease) in Working Capital Resulting from Changes in Each Element of Working Capital		
Increase (Decrease) in Current Assets		
Cash	5,926	9,427
Accounts receivable	1,770	(6,695)
Unbilled costs	6,484	(4,281)
Inventories	98	208
Prepaid expenses	246	354
	14,524	(987)
(Increase) Decrease in Current Liabilities		
Accounts payable	(3,532)	(4,766)
Advance billings	1,317	(521)
Additional contract costs	(931)	(663)
Income taxes payable	3,211	(2,844)
Deferred federal income taxes	(6,994)	(2,380)
	(6,929)	(11,174)
Increase (decrease) in working capital	7,595	(12,161)

EXHIBIT E

WORKSHEET FOR CHANGES IN FINANCIAL POSITION
Year Ended December 31, 19x7
(Cash Funds Basis)

	Increase (Decrease) in Balance Sheet Elements	Sales	Cost of Sales	Administrative, Selling, and General Expenses	Other Income (Expense)	Income Taxes	Increase (Decrease) in Cash from Nonrevenue Operations	Net Increase in Cash	Net Income
Components of Net Income— Exhibit B		224,052	(169,358)	(39,046)	206	(8,159)			7,695
Increase (Decrease) in Balance Sheet Elements									
Assets									
Cash	5,926							5,926	
Accounts receivable	1,770	(1,770)							
Unbilled costs	6,484		(6,484)						
Inventories	98		(98)						
Prepaid expenses	246			(246)					
Property	(359)			2,018	322		(1,981)		
Investment—at equity	771				(771)				
Excess of investment cost over equity	(98)				98				
Other assets	(15)						15		
Liabilities and Stockholders' Equity									
Accounts payable	3,532		3,532						
Advance billings	(1,317)		(1,317)						
Additional contract costs	931		931						
Income taxes payable	(3,211)					(3,211)			
Deferred income taxes—current	6,994					6,994			
Long-term debt	(29)						(29)		
Deferred income taxes—noncurrent	123					123			
Capital stock	35						35		
Paid-in capital	471						471		
Retained earnings	7,294						(401)		
	29,646	222,282	(172,794)	(37,274)	(145)	(4,253)	(1,890)	5,926	

SCHEDULE 5

WARRINGTON RESEARCH, INC.

STATEMENT OF CHANGES IN FINANCIAL POSITION

	For Year Ended December 31,	
	19x7	19x6
Cash Balance—Beginning of Year	14,836	5,409
CASH PROVIDED BY OPERATIONS:		
Sales	224,052	204,999
(Increase) decrease in accounts receivable	(1,770)	6,695
Total cash provided by operations	222,282	211,694

EXHIBIT F

CASH USED IN OPERATIONS:

Cost of sales

Cost of sales	169,358	157,423
Increase (decrease) in unbilled costs	6,484	(4,281)
Increase in inventories	98	208
(Increase) decrease in advance billings	1,317	(521)
(Increase) in accounts payable	(3,532)	(4,766)
(Increase) in additional contract costs	(931)	(663)
	172,794	147,400

Administrative, General, and Selling Expenses

Administrative, general, and selling expenses	39,046	35,142
Increase in prepaid expenses	246	354
Depreciation (not involving cash)	(2,018)	(1,854)
	37,274	33,642

Other Expenses (Income)

Other (income)—net	(206)	(112)
Undepreciated cost of property sold (not involving cash)	(322)	(145)
Amortization (not involving cash)	(98)	(98)
Increase in equity in investment—(not involving cash)	771	435
	145	80

Income Taxes

Income taxes—current and deferred—net	8,159	6,627
(Increase) decrease in income taxes payable	3,211	(2,844)
(Increase) in deferred income taxes—current	(6,994)	(2,380)
Deferred income taxes—noncurrent (not involving cash)	(123)	51
	4,253	1,454
Total cash used in operations	214,466	182,576
Net cash received from operations	7,816	29,118

CASH PROVIDED BY NONREVENUE SOURCES:

Decrease in other assets	15	19
Increase in long-term debt	—	3,785
Exercise of stock options	506	164
	521	3,968
	8,337	33,086

CASH USED IN NONREVENUE TRANSACTIONS:

Cash dividends paid	401	357
Additions to property, plant, and equipment	1,981	5,233
Reduction in long-term debt	29	18,069
	2,411	23,659
Net cash received	5,926	9,427
Cash Balance—End of Year	20,762	14,836

EXHIBIT F (continued)

changes in *cash* during the year. Thus, the net decrease in cash related to income taxes is developed by reporting all elements of income taxes, and is computed to be $4,253. The *actual cash expenditures* during the year can be readily analyzed from changes in the income tax payable account, as follows:

Income taxes payable	
Balance—December 31, 19x6—Exhibit A	3,554
Add: Current income taxes due IRS—Exhibit C	1,042
	4,596
Deduct: Balance—December 31, 19x7—Exhibit A	343
Cash expenditures for income taxes in 19x7	4,253

The $4,253 decrease in cash computed above agrees with the *net* decrease in cash on account of income taxes reported on Exhibit F. However, it is necessary to show the development of the decrease in the manner reported on Exhibit F in order to include all the changes in income tax expense that do not involve cash.

REPORTING CHANGES IN FINANCIAL POSITION RESULTING FROM EXTRAORDINARY ITEMS

APB Opinion No. 19 states that the funds statement should prominently disclose working capital or cash provided from or used in operations for the period, and that the disclosure is most informative if the effects of extraordinary items are reported separately from the effects of normal items.

Thus, where an entity reports an extraordinary item in its income statement, the section of the funds statement reporting funds provided from operations should follow the general sequence set forth below.

1. Set forth net income (or loss) before extraordinary items.
2. Add (or deduct) items recognized in determining income (or loss) which do not provide or use cash or working capital, exclusive of items arising from the extraordinary item.
3. Reflect result of (1) and (2) under the caption "Working Capital (or Cash) Provided by (or Used in) Operations During the Period, Exclusive of Extraordinary Items."
4. Set forth the extraordinary item.
5. Follow the routine prescribed in (2) above with reference to items arising from the extraordinary item.
6. Reflect the result of (4) and (5) under the caption "Working Capital (or Cash) Provided by (or Used in) Operations During the Period."

ILLUSTRATION OF REPORTING EFFECTS OF EXTRAORDINARY ITEMS IN STATEMENT OF CHANGES IN FINANCIAL POSITION

The following example provides an illustration of reporting the effects of extraordinary items in the Statement of Changes in Financial Position.

Reynard, Inc. is a manufacturing company that sustained a substantial operating loss in 19x3. The total loss could not be carried back for income tax purposes and, consequently, a loss carryforward was developed. Since Reynard was not assured at any time that the benefits of the loss carryforward would be realized, the estimated benefits were not recognized and set up on the books at the time of the occurrence of the loss. In 19x4 and 19x5 Reynard had operating income on which no taxes were paid due to application of the operating loss carryforward. In accordance with

REYNARD, INC.
STATEMENT OF INCOME

	For Year Ended December 31,	
	19x5	19x4
* * * * * * * * * * *		
Income before income taxes and extraordinary credit	268,000	242,000
Provision for Income Taxes		
Provision in lieu of federal income tax, equivalent to tax benefits derived from net operating loss carryforward	108,708	96,852
State income tax	13,400	12,100
Total provision for income taxes	122,108	108,952
Income before extraordinary credit	145,892	133,048
Extraordinary credit		
Effects of utilizing federal income tax carryforward benefit	108,708	96,852
Net income	254,600	229,900

SCHEDULE 6

REYNARD, INC.
STATEMENT OF CHANGES IN FINANCIAL POSITION

	For Year Ended December 31,	
	19x5	19x4
WORKING CAPITAL PROVIDED BY:		
Operations:		
Net income before extraordinary credit	145,892	133,048
Add: Expenses Not Requiring Outlay of Working Capital in Current Period		
Depreciation	5,643	4,972
Amortization	2,892	2,892
Provision in lieu of federal income tax	108,708	96,852
Working capital provided by operations exclusive of extraordinary credit	263,135	237,764
Extraordinary credit	108,708	96,852
	371,843	334,616
Extraordinary credit not providing working capital	(108,708)	(96,852)
Working capital provided by operations	263,135	237,764

SCHEDULE 7

APB Opinion No. 11, Reynard reported income tax expense based on pretax accounting income at current tax rates, and reported an equivalent amount as an extraordinary credit. The bottom lines of Reynard's 19x5 comparative income statement are shown in Schedule 6.

Reynard's comparative Statement of Changes in Financial Position for the year 19x5 reflected working capital provided by operations both before and after the extraordinary credit. The beginning section of the Statement is shown in Schedule 7.

STATEMENT OF CHANGES IN FINANCIAL POSITION FOR ENTITIES NOT HAVING A CLASSIFIED BALANCE SHEET

APB Opinion No. 19 states that a working capital format for the Statement of Changes in Finanical Position is not relevant to an entity that does not distinguish between current and noncurrent assets and liabilities. Nevertheless, such entities should disclose funds provided from operations by starting the statement with net income (loss) and then adding (deducting) items recognized in determining that income (loss) which did not provide or use funds during the period. For example, a write-down of investments to market value does not involve the use of funds, and should be added back to net income to reflect funds provided from operations. In such a case, the increase in investments reported for the period should be the difference between the beginning and ending investment values, adjusted by the amount of write-down reflected as an addition to net income. In such statements the actual changes in *all* funds are listed in a logical order. Thus, the increase in cash, short-term notes receivable, short-term debt, etc. would be listed individually throughout the statement, and no items would be segregated to reflect a change in cash or working capital, as such.

COMPUTING VALUES OF ELEMENTS IN THE FUNDS STATEMENT FOR ENTITIES NOT HAVING A CLASSIFIED BALANCE SHEET

The computation of values of elements in the funds statement of entities not having a classified balance sheet can be made on a worksheet similar to that shown on Schedule 4. The worksheet should be designed to permit distribution of increases and decreases in the components of the balance sheet to the category in which such changes are required to be reported in the funds statement. Such a worksheet need not separate the effects of changes in current and noncurrent items as provided in Schedule 4, but should follow the format to be reported in the funds statement.

ILLUSTRATION OF A STATEMENT OF CHANGES IN FINANCIAL POSITION FOR AN ENTITY NOT HAVING A CLASSIFIED BALANCE SHEET

Exhibit G is an illustration of a Statement of Changes in Financial Position of an entity that does not have a classified balance sheet. The example is based on the funds statement accompanying the published annual report of a financial corporation engaged in the business of insurance, financial services, and asset management.

CANADAY FINANCIAL CORPORATION

STATEMENT OF CHANGES IN CONSOLIDATED FINANCIAL POSITION

	For Year Ended December 31,	
	19x2	19x1
FUNDS PROVIDED:		
Net income (loss)	(210,142)	15,366
Add or (Deduct):		
Equity in the undistributed net loss of unconsolidated subsidiaries	128,374	19,645
Write-down of investments to market value	21,053	1,951
Write-down of receivables and other assets	2,166	1,945
Depreciation and amortization of investments	7,608	4,869
Decrease in deferred income tax	(1,663)	(7,023)
Amortization of deferred policy acquisition costs	21,433	25,753
Participating policyholders' interest in income (loss)	(4,100)	5,803
Other Changes In:		
Insurance reserves	173,268	297,120
Deferred policy acquisition costs	26,419	(7,234)
Premium deposit funds	15,926	15,843
Net insurance premiums in course of collection	30,325	(68,442)
Additional funds held for policyholders	363	12,764
Taxes payable	13,176	(19,291)
Other items—net	(1,344)	(17,455)
Funds provided from operations	222,862	281,614
Increase in long-term debt	29,708	86,600
Proceeds from issuance of preferred stock	24,317	—
Issuance of common stock under employee purchase plan	2,040	3,869
Decrease in cash	17,514	3,508
Total funds provided	296,441	375,591
FUNDS USED:		
Increase in investments—net	197,305	223,329
Reduction in long-term debt	43,252	81,256
Capitalization of deferred policy acquisition costs	29,985	34,559
Dividends paid to stockholders	18,297	27,283
Acquisition of treasury shares	296	8,847
Net increase in fixed assets and other items	7,306	317
Total funds used	296,441	375,591

EXHIBIT G

11

Subchapter S Corporations—
Accounting for Elections, Operations,
and Terminations

Subchapter S was added to Chapter 1 of the 1954 Internal Revenue Code by the Techinical Amendments Act of 1958. The purpose was to provide shareholders of certain closely held corporations an optional election to have their corporation exempted from federal income tax under the stipulation that exercise of such an option would require the total annual earnings of the corporate entity to be allocated proportionately to the respective shareholders, and to be included in their individual gross taxable income.

The election by a corporation to be taxed under the provisions of Subchapter S immediately creates a hybrid organization in the nature of a quasi-corporation having partnership characteristics, and being subject to complex tax procedures that extend beyond the corporation to produce complicated tax effects on the gross income of its shareholders. While the election does not require any changes whatsoever in the corporation's normal accounting procedures for assets, liabilities, income, and expense, it does create a significant change in the taxable nature of stockholders' equity accounts, and also will require the corporation to annually supply its shareholders with a series of highly technical tax data.

Presumably, because the organizational structure and pretax accounting procedures of a corporation are normally unaffected by its election to be taxed under Subchapter S, neither the American Institute of Certified Public Accountants nor the Financial Accounting Standards Board has published any directive, or offered any guidance, for the application of special accounting procedures to these tax option entities. This lack of attention by the professional supervisory and disciplinary bodies probably has inhibited the authors of accounting textbooks to such an extent that their books generally either do not mention Subchapter S accounting, or dispense with the subject by a casual reference to it. On the other hand, the tax implications of a tax option election are so enormous that there is an abundance of income tax literature on the subject and, of necessity, such literature touches on the subject of the accounting records that the tax regulations require a Subchapter S corporation to maintain. The income tax literature, however, is so preoccupied with tax regulations and tax planning that generally there is little space left to dwell on accounting methods.

This chapter is designed to provide comprehensive procedures for the special accounting requirements of Subchapter S corporations and, accordingly, it outlines a method of appropriately segregating and reclassifying stockholders' equity accounts in accordance with the nature of their income tax implications. The chapter also contains examples, illustrations, and model cases that demonstrate a system of procedures that accurately reflect the tax effects of the Subchapter S corporation's operations as they apply to each respective stockholder's equity account, and thus automatically provide the income tax data necessary to permit the stockholders of the corporation to fulfill their individual income tax reporting obligations.

SUBCHAPTER S CORPORATIONS—AN OVERVIEW

The general purpose of Subchapter S is to permit a qualifying domestic small business corporation to elect to be exempt from federal income tax, and to continue to be exempt until its election is voluntarily revoked by the shareholders or administratively terminated by the Internal Revenue Service. The rules require that taxable income of a Subchapter S corporation for the current year be allocated proportionately to shareholders of the corporation, and be reported on their individual income tax returns as either actual or constructive dividends received from the corporation. The constructive dividends reported by the shareholders, but not actually distributed by the corporation, become previously taxed income that may be distributed tax-free to the shareholders in later years.

Theoretically, the principles of the Subchapter S tax concept are simple and easy to apply. In actual practice, however, tax accounting for Subchapter S corporations is complicated by a vast tangle of complex tax regulations. These regulations are discussed throughout the remaining text of this chapter.

TAX PLANNING FOR SUBCHAPTER S

A corporation's election to be taxed under Subchapter S can result in an enormous ramification of tax consequences to its shareholders, and thus they are confronted by a grave decision when contemplating making such an election. Generally, the tax option offers highly desirable benefits, but their value must be weighed carefully against the serious disadvantages, perplexing problems, and severe dangers that follow from the election. There is no general rule which can be used in making a decision as to whether or not Subchapter S status would be beneficial to shareholders. Each corporation must determine the benefits to be derived from a tax option election by an evaluation of its effects on its own particular organization, and on the tax position of its shareholders.

TAX BENEFITS TO SHAREHOLDERS OF SUBCHAPTER S CORPORATIONS

A Subchapter S corporation, as an entity, derives no special benefits and suffers no particular disadvantages from its tax option election simply because in order to qualify for Subchapter S status it must be, by statutory requirement, a closely held corporation and, consequently, the shareholders (not the corporation) are directly and personally affected by all the tax benefits and tax problems arising from a tax option election. The benefits accruing directly to shareholders of a Subchapter S corporation are the following:

1. *No corporate income tax*

    The corporation does not pay a regular corporate federal income tax. This exemption from double taxation normally assessed on corporate income and, subsequently, on shareholders for dividends received is an overriding benefit of tax option status.

2. *Long-term capital gains passed through to shareholders*

Corporate long-term capital gains are taxed directly to shareholders as capital gains rather than as ordinary income, which would be the case if a conventional corporation distributed such gains as dividends. However, as explained later, the corporation itself in some cases must pay a capital gains tax.

3. *Corporate net operating loss may be taken by shareholders*

Corporate net operating losses may be deducted directly by shareholders instead of being carried backward and forward by the corporation. However, the loss deductible by a shareholder is limited in some circumstances, as described later in the chapter.

4. *Previously taxed income may be left in the corporation*

Shareholders have the option to leave previously taxed income in the corporation and have it removed later as a tax-free distribution.

5. *No tax on unreasonable accumulation of earnings*

The tax on unreasonable accumulation of earnings generally does not apply to Subchapter S corporations.

DISADVANTAGES OF SUBCHAPTER S STATUS

Similar to the situation with regard to tax benefits, the disadvantages, problems, and dangers of Subchapter S status listed below bear directly on the shareholders of the corporation.

Disadvantages

1. *Constructive dividends*

Perhaps the greatest disadvantage of Subchapter S status to a shareholder is the requirement that he include in his gross taxable income his pro rata share of the taxable income of the corporation, whether or not the income was distributed by the corporation.

2. *Limitation on number of shareholders*

Shareholders are restricted in seeking additional participants in the Subchapter S enterprise on a large scale because the Subchapter S corporation can have a maximum of only 15 shareholders at any given time.

3. *Limitation on scope of corporate operations*

A Subchapter S corporation is limited in its expansion into certain areas of operations because excessive passive investment income will automatically terminate its election as a tax option entity.

4. *Foreign tax credit*

A Subchapter S corporation is not allowed a credit for taxes paid to a foreign government.

5. *Tax-exempt income*

Certain income, which ordinarily is tax-exempt to conventional corporations, loses its tax-exempt status when distributed to shareholders of a Subchapter S corporation.

Problems of Subchapter S Corporations

1. *Net operating losses*

Net operating losses in excess of the adjusted basis of a shareholder's stock plus his loans to the corporation are not deductible by the shareholder.

2. *Accrued compensation*

Accrued compensation to a related taxpayer not paid within two and one-half months after the close of the corporation's taxable year is treated as a distribution out of accumulated earnings and profits.

3. *Dividends to family groups*

Dividends received by members of a family group may be allocated to reflect the value of services rendered.

4. *Investment credit recapture*

Investment credit recapture is applicable to the year prior to the election, but can be avoided by shareholders agreeing to assume liability for the tax.

5. *Cash position of corporation*

A Subchapter S corporation may not always have sufficient cash resources to distribute all its taxable income as dividends within the current year and the two and one-half month grace period, resulting in taxable income to the shareholder for constructive dividends.

Dangers Inherent in Subchapter S Status

1. *Involuntary termination of election*

By far the greatest danger to stockholders arising from a tax option election is the possibility that an involuntary, and unexpected, termination of the election may deprive them of the right to nondividend treatment of previously taxed income.

2. *Previously taxed income not transferable*

Nondividend treatment for previously taxed income is personal to shareholders and may not be passed on to another person through sale of stock in the Subchapter S corporation.

3. *Cash distributions during "grace period"*

Nondividend treatment for cash distributions made within two and one-half months after the close of the taxable year cannot be passed on to another person through transfer of the stockholder's stock in the Subchapter S corporation.

MAKING, MAINTAINING, AND TERMINATING THE SUBCHAPTER S ELECTION

MAKING THE ELECTION

An election may be made by a qualifying corporation on Form 2553 at any time during the first 75 days of the tax option year, or at any time during the preceding taxable year. No extension of time for making the election may be granted.

Qualifying corporation

The regulations define a "small business corporation" as one having the following six attributes, and further provide that a small business corporation meeting the six requirements is qualified to make the tax option election under Subchapter S.

1. It must be a domestic corporation.
2. It cannot be a member of an affiliated group except that it can have an inactive subsidiary that does not have taxable income during the parent company's tax year to which the election applies.
3. It must have only one class of stock.
4. It must not have more than 15 stockholders at any given time.

5. It must have only individuals or estates as shareholders except that the following trusts may be shareholders:
   (a) a trust all of which is owned by the grantor;
   (b) a trust created primarily to exercise the voting power transferred to it; and
   (c) a testamentary trust for the 60 days following transfer of tax-option stock to it, or for two years if the entire trust corpus is includible in the estate of the testator.
6. It must not have a nonresident alien as a shareholder.

Consent of shareholders

An election of Subchapter S status by a corporation requires the consent of all shareholders. A shareholder's consent is binding and may not be withdrawn after a valid election is made. Consent to the election is effected by shareholders signing Form 2553 in the space provided, sufficiently early to permit making a timely filing of the form. Generally, the election is not valid if any of the consents are not timely filed but an extension of time may be granted an individual shareholder for reasonable cause if he submits a request for extension of time to the Internal Revenue Center where the Form 2553 is filed.

MAINTAINING THE ELECTION

To maintain Subchapter S status, a corporation must operate under the following conditions:

1. *Small business corporation status*

The corporation must operate so as to retain its small business characteristics, as described in a foregoing paragraph.

2. *Prohibited income*

The nature of a corporation's income is not a condition for its electing Subchapter S status. However, once the election is in effect, the limits indicated below are placed on the types of income described.

Foreign income

The Subchapter S corporation cannot receive more than 80% of its gross receipts from sources outside the United States.

Passive investment income

Passive investment income cannot exceed 20% of the gross receipts of the Subchapter S corporation. Passive investment income includes gross receipts from royalties, rents, dividends, interest, annuities, and gain on sales or exchanges of stock or securities.

TERMINATING THE ELECTION

The Subchapter S election may be voluntarily revoked by the shareholders or involuntarily terminated by administrative action of the Internal Revenue Service.

Voluntary Revocation

A Subchapter S election may be revoked for any tax year after the first year of its election only with the consent of all persons who are shareholders at the time of revocation. The revocation is made by the corporation filing a statement with the Internal Revenue Service specifying that the corporation revokes the election, and attaching thereto a statement of consent signed by all shareholders. If the revocation is made within the first month of the tax year, it will become effective for that year; if it is made after the first month of the tax year, it will become effective for the next tax year, and all succeeding years.

Involuntary Termination

A corporation's tax option election can be administratively terminated in any of the following four situations:

1. a new shareholder affirmatively refuses to consent to the election,
2. the corporation ceases to be a small business corporation;
3. more than 80% of the corporation's gross receipts for the tax year are from sources outside the United States; and
4. more than 20% of the corporation's gross receipts for the tax year are from passive investment income.

The election is terminated as of the beginning of the tax year in which the events causing termination occur.

ELECTION AFTER TERMINATION

When a Subchapter S election is terminated or revoked, the corporation, or its successor, cannot make a new tax option election for a period of five years unless the Commissioner consents to an earlier election. Requests for reelection should be submitted to the Commissioner of Internal Revenue, Washington, D. C.

ACCOUNTING FOR THE OPERATIONS OF SUBCHAPTER S CORPORATIONS

GENERAL ACCOUNTING PROCEDURES OF SUBCHAPTER S CORPORATIONS

An election to be taxed under Subchapter S normally will not change the day-to-day accounting policies and procedures of the electing corporation. All official accounting directives, with the exception of those dealing with federal income taxes, affect Subchapter S corporations in exactly the same manner, and to precisely the same extent as they affect other corporations operating within the same industry. Thus, as stated previously, the only changes necessary for an electing corporation to make in its accounting policies and procedures are those dealing with federal income taxes and stockholders' equity.

SUBCHAPTER S ACCOUNTING FOR INCOME TAXES

A Subchapter S corporation is not subject to federal income taxes and, consequently, if a corporation has deferred federal income tax credits or debits at the time it makes a tax option election, the deferred federal income taxes should be eliminated and charged or credited, as appropriate, to current income. If the election is revoked or terminated before the timing differences otherwise would have fully reversed, the remaining related deferred income taxes should be reinstated and charged or credited, as appropriate, to income of the year of reinstatement.

In some states a Subchapter S corporation is subject to the same state income taxes as an ordinary corporation. In such cases any deferred state income taxes of a corporation should continue to be carried after its election as a Subchapter S entity, even though the deferred federal income taxes are eliminated. However, in many instances, the deferred state taxes, taken alone, are not material in amount, and can be written off at the time the deferred federal income taxes are eliminated.

As indicated previously, and explained later in the text, a Subchapter S corporation may be subject to a capital gains tax under certain special circumstances.

UNIQUE RESPONSIBILITY TO SHAREHOLDERS

Subchapter S corporations have a unique corporate responsibility to shareholders in that the corporation must design its accounting system so as to provide complicated tax information to, and for the benefit of, its individual shareholders. Accounting for stockholders' equity in a Subchapter S corporation is similar to accounting for partners' capital and drawing accounts in a partnership entity. However, the similarity lies solely in the *responsibility* of the two entities to report tax information to participants in the respective enterprises. There is a significant difference between the character of the taxable income alloted to shareholders of a Subchapter S corporation and that allocated to partners of a partnership entity. Unlike a partnership, a Subchapter S corporation is not a conduit for transferring taxable income and loss to its shareholders. Subchapter S corporations pay dividends in the same manner as other corporations, and both actual and constructive dividends to shareholders do not always correspond to the taxable nature of the earnings of the corporation. For example, while municipal bond interest is considered nontaxable to the corporation, it cannot be distributed as nontaxable income to its shareholders. The accounting procedures necessary to permit a Subchapter S corporation to provide its shareholders with appropriate tax information are described in the following sections of the text.

CLASSIFICATION OF SUBCHAPTER S INCOME

Differing combinations of the elements of its income must be arranged by a Subchapter S corporation in order to classify its earnings into three distinct categories: net income (or loss) for reporting under generally accepted accounting principles; and taxable income, and accumulated earnings and profits, respectively, for reporting under income tax regulations.

NET INCOME OR LOSS

Net income or loss corresponds to the amount reported as such by the Subchapter S corporation on its financial statements prepared in accordance with generally accepted accounting principles. The only difference between net income as reported under generally accepted accounting principles by a conventional corporation and a Subchapter S corporation is that a Subchapter S entity does not report a provision for either deferred or current federal income tax expense.

TAXABLE INCOME

The term "taxable income," used in connection with a Subchapter S corporation, is defined in the regulations and corresponds to the income that would be taxable in an ordinary corporation with the exception that the deductions for the dividend credit and net operating losses are not considered in computing the taxable income of the Subchapter S entity.

CURRENT EARNINGS AND PROFITS (CEP)

For income tax purposes the concept of current earnings and profits is of vital importance in accounting for the operations of a Subchapter S corporation. However, neither the Code nor regulations offer a precise definition of the term "current earnings and profits," but inference as to its meaning can be drawn from the provision in the regulations which declares that all income, whether taxable or not, enters into the calculation of earnings and profits. The logical extension of that meaning of "current earnings and profits" would indicate that CEP are earnings and profits of the current taxable period. However, the regulations *do* provide that earnings and profits of a specific tax year cannot be reduced by nonallowable deductions to compute CEP for that particular year.

In general, CEP represents accounting net income plus expenses that are not allowable as tax deductions, and corresponds to taxable income plus tax exempt income. A classical example of the computation of CEP is shown in the following allocation of the components of income of a Subchapter S corporation for a particular tax year.

Statement of Income

Operating income	100,000
Add: Interest on municipal bonds	30,000
	130,000
Deduct: Premiums on officers' life insurance	15,000
Income before income taxes	115,000
Provision for state income taxes	5,000
Net income	110,000

In this example the adjustments to net income necessary to compute taxable income correspond to the Schedule M-1 adjustments reported on the federal income tax return, which are as follows:

Net income	110,000
Less: Nontaxable interest	30,000
	80,000
Add: Nonallowable premiums	15,000
Taxable income	95,000

In this case, the computation of CEP could be made by either of the two following methods:

Net income	110,000		Taxable income	95,000
Add: Nonallowable premiums	15,000	or	Add: Nontaxable interest	30,000
Current earnings and profits	125,000		Current earnings and profits	125,000

The concept of CEP was developed solely as a measurement device to be used to determine the annual amount to be reported as taxable income by shareholders of a Subchapter S corporation. Since CEP is simply a measurement to be applied once a year to the income of that particular year, CEP itself has no cumulative attribute and, consequently, it is not amenable to being set up as a separate account on the books of the company.

NATURE OF SUBCHAPTER S RETAINED EARNINGS ACCOUNTS

In order to accommodate accounting for the required combinations and classifications of the elements of its income, a Subchapter S corporation must maintain at least four separate retained earnings accounts. Income tax regulations require and define three of such accounts: undistributed taxable income, previously taxed income, and accumulated earnings and profits. The fourth retained earnings account, which may conveniently be termed "Paid-in capital for tax purposes," is an overflow account for amounts viewed as retained earnings under generally accepted accounting principles, but which do not meet the criteria for inclusion in the three retained earnings accounts defined in the tax regulations and referred to above.

UNDISTRIBUTED TAXABLE INCOME (UTI)

Undistributed taxable income is the amount of taxable income earned and allocated to shareholders in the current year and not paid to them in cash dividends either during the year, or within the two and one-half month grace period following the end of the taxable year. UTI is reduced by any capital gains tax paid by the corporation. Any UTI remaining at the end of the two and one-half month grace period automatically becomes previously taxed income, and should be transferred to the Previously Taxed Income (PTI) account at that time. Thus, the account for UTI will always have a zero balance at the end of the grace period.

PREVIOUSLY TAXED INCOME (PTI)

The previously taxed income account represents the accumulated taxable income of prior years that was not paid in cash dividends during the year it was earned or within the two and one-half month grace period for each respective prior tax year. PTI is personal to individual shareholders and cannot be transferred to anyone else. Thus, a shareholder loses his PTI when he sells, or otherwise disposes of his stock. PTI may be reduced by cash dividends paid to shareholders after the earnings and profits of the current year have been distributed. Also, taxable losses transferred to individual stockholders reduce PTI.

ACCUMULATED EARNINGS AND PROFITS (AEP)

Accumulated earnings and profits represents preelection accumulations, increased by tax exempt income, and reduced by nondeductible expenses over the election period. AEP may be reduced by cash dividends paid shareholders after PTI has been distributed. Dividends distributed in property other than cash are charged to AEP.

PAID-IN CAPITAL (FOR TAX PURPOSES ONLY)

This account represents amounts which are retained earnings for generally accepted accounting principles purposes, but which are not UTI, PTI, or AEP for tax purposes. This account is used primarily to accumulate the PTI which is forfeited by shareholders who dispose of their stock at a time when they have accumulated PTI in the Subchapter S corporation.

ALLOCATING INCOME AND LOSSES TO INDIVIDUAL SHAREHOLDERS

At the end of each year taxable income increases UTI, and is allocated pro rata to each individual shareholder. Nontaxable income and nondeductible expenses increase or decrease AEP, but are not specifically allocated to individuals. Taxable losses first decrease PTI, and any amount of loss in excess of PTI generally is used to decrease AEP. Taxable losses are allocated pro rata to individual shareholders, and reduce their personal PTI. However, the allocation of a taxable loss to a shareholder cannot exceed the basis of his stock in the Subchapter S corporation, plus any indebtedness of the corporation to him.

It is important to remember, however, that while earnings for the full year are allocated pro rata to shareholders of record at the end of the year, losses are allocated to new shareholders on the basis of the number of days they were shareholders. Thus, the loss deductible by a taxpayer who became a shareholder during the year would be computed by multiplying his pro rata share of the loss by the number of days he was a shareholder, and dividing the result by 365.

ALLOCATION OF CASH DISTRIBUTIONS TO STOCKHOLDERS' EQUITY ACCOUNTS

Cash distributions to shareholders of a Subchapter S corporation should be charged to stockholders' equity accounts in accordance with a specific sequence of allocations, as outlined below.

1. *Undistributed Taxable Income of Prior Years*
   Cash distributions made during the first two one and one-half months following the taxable year should be charged to Undistributed Taxable Income (UTI) of the prior year to the extent of such UTI, if any exists.
2. *Undistributed Taxable Income of Current Year*
   After charging UTI, if any, during the grace period, the remaining cash distributions should then be charged to UTI of the current year to the extent of such UTI.
3. *Current Earnings and Profits*
   If cash dividends are in excess of the amounts required to be charged to UTI, as indicated above, the remaining distribution should be charged to Accumulated Earnings and Profits (AEP) to the extent of the excess of Current Earnings and Profits (CEP) over taxable income.
4. *Previously Taxed Income*
   Where cash dividends exceed the amounts required to be charged to UTI and AEP, as outlined above, the remaining cash distribution should be charged to Previously Taxed Income (PTI) to the extent of the amount carried on the books of the corporation.
5. *Accumulated Earnings and Profits*
   When the cash distribution is in excess of the amounts required to be charged to UTI, AEP, and PTI described in the foregoing order of allocation, then the remaining distribution should be charged to Accumulated Earnings and Profits (AEP) to reduce the AEP brought forward from previous years.
6. *Paid-in Capital for Tax Purposes*
   In some rare circumstances where the cash distribution is so large that an excess remains after the allocations described above have exhausted the balances in the UTI, AEP, and PTI accounts, the remaining portion of the dividend should be charged to Paid-in Capital for Tax Purposes.

DIVIDENDS DISTRIBUTED IN PROPERTY OTHER THAN CASH

Dividends distributed in property other than cash are charged to Accumulated Earnings and Profits (AEP), and cannot be used to reduce Undistributed Taxable Income (UTI) or Previously Taxed Income (PTI). The distribution must be reported at fair market value in the shareholders' gross taxable income. However, if the corporation's AEP is *less* than the fair market value of the property distributed, the shareholder can report a portion of the dividend as nontaxable return of capital by applying a ratio to the fair market value of the property. The ratio is computed by dividing the fair market value by the sum of CEP and the fair market value of the distribution. The remaining portion of the fair market value of the property constitutes a taxable dividend.

ILLUSTRATION OF ACCOUNTING FOR SUBCHAPTER S OPERATIONS

Model Case No. 1 illustrates generally normal operations of a Subchapter S corporation over a four-year period from the date of its election. The example is designed to provide solutions to accounting problems encountered in the special situations outlined below, and to demonstrate appropriate procedures to account for the required changes in the particular stockholders' equity accounts affected in each respective situation.

1. *Transfer of Retained Earnings to AEP*
   (a) transfer of retained earnings at beginning of first election year to AEP.
2. *Current Earnings in Excess of Cash Dividends*
   (a) dividends charged to UTI,
   (b) transfer of remaining UTI to PTI,
   (c) constructive dividends reported to shareholders.
3. *Current Dividends in Excess of Current Earnings*
   (a) computation of CEP,
   (b) dividends charged to stockholders' equity accounts as follows:
       1. dividends equivalent to taxable income charged to UTI,
       2. dividends equivalent to the excess of CEP over taxable income charged to AEP,
       3. remaining dividends charged to PTI,
       4. taxable dividends and nontaxable PTI reported to shareholders.
4. *Sale of Stock by Stockholder*
   (a) loss of UTI by stockholder,
   (b) transfer of lost UTI to Paid-in Capital for Tax Purposes account.
5. *Corporation Has Net Operating Loss*
   (a) decrease in PTI,
   (b) debit balance in PTI account of new stockholder,
   (c) proportionate share of loss reported to new and former stockholders, respectively.
6. *Noncash Dividends Paid*
   (a) dividend charged to AEP,
   (b) taxable dividend, based on fair market value of distribution, reported to stockholder.

MODEL CASE NO. 1

Wagner & Company, located in the State of Maryland, is a small business corporation engaged in publishing books for children. In 19x0 the corporation resolved to seek tax option status and, accordingly, in December of that year it filed Form 2553 making an election to be taxed under Subchapter S for the following year, and for all subsequent years. At the time of the election the company had issued 10,000 shares of $100 par value common stock, and Henry Womack and Charles Allman each owned

5,000 shares of the outstanding stock. The company maintained a portfolio of State of Maryland bonds,[1] and also paid premiums on officers' life insurance. For both state and federal tax purposes, the bond interest income was tax exempt and the life insurance expense was nondeductible. The State of Maryland recognizes federal Subchapter S status and consequently Wagner & Company is not subject to either federal or state corporation income taxes.

On January 2, 19x1, in preparation for accounting for stockholder equity accounts in accordance with income tax regulations, Wagner & Company set up a series of such accounts as follows:

> Accumulated Earnings and Profits (AEP)
> Undistributed Taxable Income (UTI)
> Previously Taxed Income (PTI)
> Paid-in Capital for Tax Purposes

At December 31, 19x0, the company had retained earnings of $500,000, and on January 2, 19x1 this balance in the retained earnings account was closed and transferred to the Accumulated Earnings and Profits account by the following entry:

	Debit	Credit
Retained Earnings	500,000	
Accumulated Earnings and Profits		500,000
To transfer retained earnings to AEP.		

The other newly established accounts, of course, carried zero balances until the end of the first election year.

19x1 OPERATIONS

During the year 19x1 the company paid cash dividends in the amount of $50,000, and charged the payments to an account captioned "Dividends Paid."

After closing income and expenses into a Profit and Loss account at the end of 19x1, the account reflected a credit balance of $250,000, representing net income for the year. An analysis of net income made for the purpose of determining taxable income is shown below:

Net income	250,000
Less: Nontaxable bond interest income	20,000
	230,000
Add: Nondeductible insurance expense	10,000
Taxable income	240,000

Since cash dividends paid in the amount of $50,000 were less than taxable income, a computation of current earnings and profits was not relevant in the circumstances. Therefore, the company made the following entries to clear the Profit and Loss and Dividends Paid accounts:

---

[1]Generally, municipal bonds are not a beneficial investment for Subchapter S corporations. Such securities usually bear a very low interest rate, and the tax exempt nature of interest income to the corporation cannot be passed on to its shareholders, but becomes fully taxable to them when distributed as dividends. Municipal bond interest is used in this example solely to illustrate a method of accounting for tax exempt income by a Subchapter S corporation.

	Debit	Credit
1. Profit and Loss	240,000	
Undistributed Taxable Income		240,000
To transfer taxable income to UTI.		
2. Profit and Loss	10,000	
Accumulated Earnings and Profits		10,000
To transfer to AEP the difference		
between net income and taxable income.		
3. Undistributed Taxable Income	50,000	
Dividends Paid		50,000
To charge UTI with cash dividends paid		
during 19x1.		

Wagner did not pay any cash dividends during the grace period from January 1, 19x2 to March 15, 19x2, and therefore at the latter date, the company made the following entry:

	Debit	Credit
Undistributed Taxable Income	190,000	
Previously Tax Income		190,000
To transfer remaining 19x1 UTI to PTI.		

At the same time Wagner credited each shareholder with his pro rata share of UTI in the shareholders' personal accounts in the UTI subsidiary ledger.

At March 15, 19x2, the balances in the shareholders' equity accounts were as follows:

Capital Stock		1,000,000
Retained Earnings		
Accumulated Earnings and Profits	510,000	
Previously Taxed Income	190,000	700,000
		1,700,000

19x2 OPERATIONS

Between March 16, 19x2 and December 31, 19x2, Wagner paid cash dividends amounting to $220,000, and charged the payments to Dividends Paid.

After income and expenses were closed into Profit and Loss, the account had a credit balance of $200,000, representing net income for the year. Wagner computed the corporate taxable income in the following manner:

Net income	200,000
Less: Nontaxable bond interest income	5,000
Taxable income	195,000

The amount of cash dividends paid subsequent to March 15, 19x2 exceeded the taxable income for the year and it was therefore necessary for Wagner to compute current earnings and profits for the year 19x2 in order to charge an appropriate portion of the dividends to AEP. Wagner made the computation as follows:

Taxable income	195,000
Add: Nontaxable bond interest income	5,000
Current earnings and profits	200,000

Dividends of $195,000 had to be charged first to UTI, which represented taxable income for the year. Then dividends amounting to $5,000 were required to be charged to AEP so that all current earnings and profits (CEP) would be recorded as being distributed in the current year. The remaining dividends of $20,000 were then charged to UTI, and recorded pro rata in the respective stockholders' accounts in the UTI subsidiary ledger.

Wagner made the following entries at December 31, 19x2:

		Debit	Credit
1.	Profit and Loss	200,000	
	Undistributed Taxable Income		195,000
	Accumulated Earnings and Profits		5,000
	To transfer net income to UTI and AEP.		
2.	Undistributed Taxable Income	195,000	
	Accumulated Earnings and Profits	5,000	
	Previously Taxed Income	20,000	
	Dividends Paid		220,000
	To distribute cash dividends to appropriate stockholders' equity accounts.		

At December 31, 19x2 the balances in the stockholders' equity accounts were as follows:

Capital Stock		1,000,000
Retained Earnings		
Accumulated Earnings and Profits	510,000	
Previously Taxed Income	170,000	680,000
		1,680,000

19x3 OPERATIONS

On June 30, 19x3 Charles Allman sold his stock in Wagner & Company to Ralph Zink. At the time of sale Allman had accumulated $85,000 in his personal PTI account. Since ownership of PTI is personal and cannot be transferred to another person, Wagner & Company made the following entry to decrease UTI and credit it to Paid-in Capital for Tax Purposes:

	Debit	Credit
Previously Taxed Income	85,000	
Paid-in Capital for Tax Purposes		85,000
To transfer forfeited PTI of Charles Allman to Paid-in Capital for Tax Purposes.		

Simultaneously, Wagner made an entry in Allman's personal account in the PTI subsidiary ledger to eliminate the balance therein.

Wagner sustained a net loss of $50,000 in 19x3 and consequently did not pay any cash dividends during the year. The $50,000 loss was reflected as a debit balance in the Profit and Loss account after the income and expense accounts had been closed. Wagner computed the taxable loss as follows:

Net (loss)	(50,000)
Less: Nontaxable bond interest income	(20,000)
	(70,000)
Add: Nondeductible insurance expense	10,000
Taxable (loss)	(60,000)

Since no dividends were paid during the year, a computation of current earnings and profits for 19x3 was not relevant in the circumstances. Wagner was required, however, to determine the effect of the loss on the various stockholders' equity accounts. The distribution of the loss was computed to be as follows:

Charged to PTI		
Womack's pro rata share of one half of the taxable loss for the year	(30,000)	
Zink's pro rata share of one half of the taxable loss for one half of the year	(15,000)	(45,000)
Charged to Paid in Capital for Tax Purposes		
Allman's pro rata share of one half of the taxable loss for one half of the year		(15,000)
Total taxable loss charged to shareholders' equity accounts		(60,000)
Credited to Accumulated Earnings and Profits		
Difference between $60,000 taxable loss and $50,000 accounting loss		10,000
Net loss distributed		(50,000)

Therefore, Wagner made the following entries to close the Profit and Loss account at December 31, 19x3:

	Debit	Credit
Previously Taxed Income	45,000	
Paid-in Capital for Tax Purposes	15,000	
Accumulated Earnings and Profits		10,000
Profit and Loss		50,000
To close profit and loss into appropriate stockholders' equity accounts.		

At December 31, 19x3 the balances reflected in the stockholders' equity accounts were as follows:

Capital Stock		1,000,000
Retained Earnings		
Accumulated Earnings and Profits	520,000	
Previously Taxed Income	40,000	
Paid-in Capital for Tax Purposes	70,000	630,000
		1,630,000

19x4 OPERATIONS

Wagner had net income of $100,000 for the year 19x4, and that amount was reflected as a credit balance in the Profit and Loss account before allocation to the appropriate stockholders' equity accounts was made. Wagner computed taxable income of the corporation as follows:

Net income	100,000
Less: Nontaxable bond interest income	10,000
	90,000
Add: Nondeductible insurance expense	5,000
Taxable income	95,000

During the year Wagner distributed cash dividends in the amount of $145,000, and distributed marketable securities having a basis of $15,000, which was equivalent to their fair market value. Both types of dividends were charged to the Dividends Paid account. Since the cash dividends were in excess of taxable income, Wagner computed current earnings and profits (CEP) to determine the appropriate portion of the cash dividends to be charged to AEP. The computation was made as follows:

Taxable income	95,000
Add: Nontaxable bond interest income	10,000
Current earnings and profits	105,000

Cash dividends equivalent to taxable income of $95,000 were charged to UTI. Cash dividends amounting to $10,000 were charged to AEP in order to record distribution of the total CEP for the year. The remaining cash dividends of $40,000 were charged as follows:

Henry Womack	
This amount was a tax-free distribution and was charged to PTI, with an appropriate entry in Womack's personal account in the PTI subsidiary ledger.	20,000
Ralph Zink	
This amount was not a tax-free distribution because Zink had a debit balance in his personal PTI account. The distribution was a taxable dividend to Zink and was charged to AEP.	20,000
	40,000

The noncash dividend consisting of marketable securities was charged to Accumulated Earnings and Profits.

At December 31, 19x4 Wagner made the following entries to distribute income and charge dividends to the appropriate stockholders' equity accounts.

		Debit	Credit
1.	Profit and Loss	100,000	
	Accumulated Earnings and Profits		5,000
	Undistributed Taxable Income		95,000
	To transfer net income to UTI and AEP.		
2.	Accumulated Earnings and Profits	45,000	
	Undistributed Taxable Income	95,000	
	Previously Taxed Income	20,000	
	Dividends Paid		160,000
	To charge dividends paid to appropriate stockholders' equity accounts.		

At December 31, 19x4 the balances in the stockholders' equity accounts were as follows:

Capital Stock		1,000,000
Retained Earnings		
Accumulated Earnings and Profits	480,000	
Previously Taxed Income	20,000	
Paid-in Capital for Tax Purposes	70,000	570,000
		1,570,000

The personal accounts in the PTI subsidiary ledger for the respective stockholders at that date reflected the following balances:

	(Debit) Credit
Henry Womack	35,000
Ralph Zink	(15,000)
Net credit balance	20,000

Schedule 1 is a summary of the operations of Wagner & Company for its first four election years, and shows the effect on each stockholder's equity account resulting from allocation of income and losses, and charges for dividend distributions.

WAGNER & COMPANY
(A Subchapter S Corporation)
Summary of Income, Dividends Paid, and Changes in Stockholders' Equity Accounts
For Years 19x1, 19x2, 19x3 and 19x4

| TRANSACTIONS | INCOME TAX DATA | | GAAP | SUBCHAPTER S STOCKHOLDERS' EQUITY | | | | SUBCHAPTER S PTI SUBSIDIARY LEDGER | | |
	Computa-tion of Taxable Income	Current Earnings and Profits (CEP)	Total Retained Earnings	Accum-ulated Earnings and Profits (AEP)	Undis-tributed Taxable Income (UTI)	Pre-viously Taxed Income (PTI)	Paid-In Capital For Tax Purpose Only	Allman	Womack	Zink
1/2/x1—Balance			500,000	500,000						
Year 19x1										
Net income	250,000		250,000							
Nontaxable interest	(20,000)	20,000		20,000						
Nondeductible expense	10,000			(10,000)						
Taxable income	240,000	240,000			240,000					
CEP		260,000								
			750,000	510,000	240,000	—	—			
Cash dividends paid			(50,000)	—	(50,000)	—	—			
12/31/x1—Balance			700,00	510,000	190,000					
Year 19x2										
3/15/x2										
Transfer UTI to PTI					(190,000)	190,000		95,000	95,000	
3/15/x2—Balance			700,000	510,000	—	190,000		95,000	95,000	
Net income	200,000		200,000							
Nontaxable interest	(5,000)	5,000		5,000						
Taxable income	195,000	195,000			195,000					
CEP		200,000								
			900,000	515,000	195,000	190,000	—	95,000	95,000	
Cash dividends paid			(220,000)	(5,000)	(195,000)	(20,000)	—	(10,000)	(10,000)	
12/31/x2—Balance			680,000	510,000	—	170,000	—	85,000	85,000	

SCHEDULE 1—Page 1 of 2

SPECIAL ACCOUNTING PROBLEMS OF SUBCHAPTER S CORPORATIONS

Accounting procedures for generally normal operations of Subchapter S corporations were described in the foregoing sections of this chapter and illustrated in Model Case No. 1. However, there are many special accounting problems peculiar to Subchapter S operations that arise in particular circumstances. This section of the chapter describes these particular situations and illustrates accounting procedures and demonstrates computational techniques for the solution of the problems attendant to each respective accounting event.

CAPITAL GAINS TAX ON SUBCHAPTER S CORPORATIONS

Prior to 1966, many corporations deliberately timed their transactions to build up enormous capital gains potential. They then elected Subchapter S status, realized the gains in the election year, and passed them on as capital gains to the corporation's shareholders. In many cases the corporations revoked their tax option election the fol-

TRANSACTIONS	INCOME TAX DATA		GAAP	SUBCHAPTER S STOCKHOLDERS' EQUITY					SUBCHAPTER S PTI SUBSIDIARY LEDGER		
	Computation of Taxable Income	Current Earnings and Profits (CEP)	Total Retained Earnings	Accumulated Earnings and Profits (AEP)	Undistributed Taxable Income (UTI)	Previously Taxed Income (PTI)	Paid-In Capital For Tax Purpose Only	Allman	Womack	Zink
12/31/x2 — Balance			680,000	510,000	—	170,000	—	85,000	85,000	
Year 19x3										
6/30/x3										
Sale of Allman stock						(85,000)	85,000	(85,000)		
6/30/x3 — Balance			680,000	510,000	—	85,000	85,000	—	85,000	
Net (loss)	(50,000)		(50,000)							
Nontaxable interest	(20,000)			20,000						
Nondeductible expense	10,000			(10,000)						
Taxable (loss)	(60,000)					(45,000)	(15,000)		(30,000)	(15,000)
12/31/x3 — Balance			630,000	520,000	—	40,000	70,000		55,000	(15,000)
Year 19x4										
Net income	100,000		100,000							
Nontaxable interest	(10,000)	10,000		10,000						
Nondeductible expense	5,000			(5,000)						
Taxable income	95,000	95,000			95,000					
CEP		105,000								
			730,000	525,000	95,000	40,000	70,000		55,000	(15,000)
Dividends Distributed										
Cash			(145,000)	(30,000)	(95,000)	(20,000)			(20,000)	
Marketable securities			(15,000)	(15,000)						
12/31x4 — Balance			570,000	480,000	—	20,000	70,000		35,000	(15,000)

SCHEDULE 1—Page 2 of 2

lowing year. To eliminate this tax loophole, Congress enacted Public Law 89-389 in 1966 which, under certain conditions, levys a capital gains tax on Subchapter S corporations at the corporate level.

Conditions Under Which Capital Gains Tax Is Levied

A capital gains tax will apply to a Subchapter S corporation if *all three* of the following conditions exist:
1. Its long-term capital gain exceeds its net short-term capital loss for the year by *more* than $25,000.
2. The excess of its net long-term capital gains over its net short-term capital losses for the year is more than 50% of its taxable income.
3. Its taxable income for the year exceeds $25,000.

Exceptions to Applicability of Capital Gains Tax

The capital gains tax will not apply in the following circumstances:
1. The corporation has been a Subchapter S corporation for at least the three preceding years.
2. The corporation has been a Subchapter S corporation for the entire period of its existence if the corporation has existed for less than four years.

Dispositions of Property to Which the Exceptions Do Not Apply

If the three conditions for taxing capital gains exist, the foregoing exceptions will not apply to gains and losses from disposition of certain property under the following circumstances:

1. The property was acquired in the tax year, or within a period beginning 36 months prior to the first day of the tax year.
2. The property was acquired from a corporation that was not itself a Subchapter S corporation during the period described in the foregoing sentence, and up to the time of acquisition.
3. The property has a basis to the Subchapter S corporation determined by reference to its base in the hands of the transferor (a "substituted basis").

Amount of Capital Gains Tax

The tax on capital gains is the *lower* of:
1. 30% of the amount by which the excess of the net long-term capital gains over the net short-term capital losses exceeds $25,000;

or

2. the tax that would have been imposed on *the taxable income* had the corporation not been a Subchapter S corporation.

Limitation of Tax for Certain Property

If the tax applies because of gain on property with a substituted basis, the tax may not exceed 30% of the excess of the net long-term capital gain over the net short-term capital loss attributable to that property.

No credit may be taken against the capital gains tax other than for certain uses of gasoline and oil.

MINIMUM TAX ON PREFERENCE ITEMS

A Subchapter S corporation normally is not subject to the minimum tax. The items of tax preference are computed at the corporate level and apportioned pro rata among the shareholders in the same way the corporation's net losses are apportioned.

EXCEPTION TO PASS THROUGH OF MINIMUM TAX PREFERENCE ITEMS

Capital gains that are subject to the capital gains tax imposed on the corporation, as outlined in preceding paragraphs, are not passed through to the shareholders as tax preference items. Instead, the corporation pays the minimum tax on such capital gains, and the shareholder reports his pro rata share of the capital gains *net* of his applicable share of the minimum tax paid by the corporation.

DETERMINING THE CORPORATE TAX PREFERENCE

Determination of the capital gains items of tax preference on which the corporation must pay the minimum tax requires a complicated computation. This computation is described in the following five steps, and is in accordance with the procedure outlined in IRS Publication 589.

Note, however, that item (b) of Step 2 is necessary only if all or a portion of the capital gain is attributable to property with a substituted basis.

Step 1. Compute the amount of tax that would be imposed on the corporation if it were an ordinary corporation.
Step 2. Compute the tax on Step 1 except *exclude the lesser* of:
    (a) the portion of the excess of net long-term capital gain over net short-term capital loss that exceeds $25,000;

or

    (b) the portion of the excess of net long-term capital gain over net short-term capital loss that is attributable to property with a substituted basis, but only if the limitation for certain property, described previously, is applicable to all or a portion of the capital gain.

Step 3. The amount computed in Step 2 is subtracted from the amount computed in Step 1.

Step 4. Subtract the amount of tax actually imposed on the capital gain from the amount computed in Step 3.

Step 5. The result in Step 4 is divided by the sum of the normal tax and surtax rates applicable to ordinary corporations. The result is the amount of the tax preference.

COMPUTATION OF MINIMUM TAX

The minimum tax is 15% of the tax preference that exceeds the greater of $10,000 or one-half of the capital gains tax liability reduced by the sum of the foreign tax credit, investment credit, work incentive program credit, and the new jobs credit.

ILLUSTRATION OF ACCOUNTING FOR TAX ON CAPITAL GAINS AND TAX PREFERENCE ITEMS PAID BY SUBCHAPTER S CORPORATIONS

Model Case No. 2 illustrates accounting procedures for recording and allocating the taxes paid by a Subchapter S corporation on capital gains and tax preference items, and demonstrates techniques for computing the amounts of such taxes.

MODEL CASE NO. 2

D & L Enterprises was incorporated in Maryland in 19x1, and operated as a conventional corporation until 19x7. In December, 19x7 the corporation filed Form 2553 making an election to be taxed under Subchapter S for 19x8 and all subsequent years. At December 31, 19x7 the company had issued 5,000 shares of $100 par value stock and Ted Lewis and George Davis each owned 2,500 shares of the outstanding stock.

On January 2, 19x8 the company set up accounts to classify its stockholders' equity accounts into Accumulated Earnings and Profits, Undistributed Taxable Income, and Previously Taxed Income, then transferred the balance of $200,000 in its retained earnings account to Accumulated Earnings and Profits. The State of Maryland generally bases its income tax law on the Internal Revenue Code and thus recognizes federal Subchapter S status. Consequently, D & L Enterprises is not subject to either state or federal income taxes on *ordinary* income, and is subject to *federal income tax only,* on capital gains as set forth in the federal regulations.

In 19x8 the company had net income of $80,000 and taxable income of $78,000. The taxable income was computed as follows:

Net income	80,000
Less: Nontaxable bond interest income	5,000
	75,000
Add: Nondeductible premiums on officers' life insurance	3,000
Taxable income	78,000

During the year the company paid cash dividends in the amount of $28,000, and charged them to Dividends Paid. Since taxable income of $78,000 exceeded the amount of cash dividends paid, it was not necessary to compute CEP for the year.

At December 31, 19x8 D & L made the following entries to close out its Profit and Loss and Dividends Paid accounts:

		Debit	Credit
1.	Profit and Loss	80,000	
	Accumulated earnings and profits		2,000
	Undistributed taxable income		78,000
	To transfer taxable income to UTI and the difference between net income and taxable income to AEP.		
2.	Undistributed Taxable Income	28,000	
	Dividends paid		28,000
	To charge UTI with cash dividends paid during the year.		

At December 31, 19x8 the balances in the stockholders' equity accounts were as follows:

Capital stock		500,000
Retained Earnings		
Accumulated earnings and profits	202,000	
Undistributed taxable income	50,000	252,000
		752,000

D & L did not pay any cash dividends between January 1, 19x9 and March 15, 19x9, and therefore on that latter date it made the following entry to close its UTI account, together with appropriate entries in the individual accounts in the PTI subsidary ledger:

	Debit	Credit
Undistributed taxable income	50,000	
Previously taxed income		50,000
To transfer balance of 19x8 UTI to PTI.		

19x9 OPERATIONS

In 19x9 D & L had pretax accounting income of $95,000 consisting of $20,000 in ordinary income and $75,000 capital gains. D&L computed its taxable income as follows:

Pretax Accounting Income		
Ordinary income	20,000	
Capital gains	75,000	95,000
Less: Nontaxable bond interest income		5,000
		90,000
Add: Nondeductible insurance expense		2,000
Taxable income		92,000

D & L was subject to capital gains tax because it had been in existence for eight years prior to the current tax year, but the current year was only its second election year; and also because all three of the following conditions existed:

1. Its capital gains were more than $25,000.
2. Its capital gains exceeded 50% of its taxable income.
3. Its taxable income exceeded $25,000.

To ascertain the amount of capital gains tax to be paid at the corporate level, D & L made the following two computations:

1. Tax on Capital Gains in Excess of $25,000 at a 30% Rate

Total capital gains	75,000	
Less: Exemption	25,000	
Taxable capital gains	50,000	
Tentative tax on capital gains: 50,000 × 30% =		15,000

2. Tax on Taxable Income of D & L Had It Been an Ordinary Corporation

Taxable income	92,000	
Tax Computation		
25,000 at 20%	5,000	
25,000 at 22%	5,500	
42,000 at 48%	20,160	
Total		30,660

D & L therefore determined that the lower amount of $15,000 was the appropriate capital gains tax to be paid by the corporation.

Upon finding that the corporation was, in fact, subject to a capital gains tax in 19x9, it was necessary then for D & L to resolve whether or not the company would have to pay a minimum tax on tax preference items and, if so, how much. D & L made the following computation, following the five steps outlined in a previous paragraph:

Step 1.	Tax on income of D & L if it had been an ordinary corporation, as computed above			30,660
Step 2.	Ordinary corporate tax on taxable income of D & L less the excess of capital gains over $25,000:			
	D & L taxable income	92,000		
	Excess of capital gains over $25,000	50,000		
		42,000		
	Tax on $42,000			
	25,000 at 20%	5,000		
	17,000 at 22%	3,740	8,740	
Step 3.	Subtract Step 1 from Step 2		21,920	
Step 4.	Subtract actual amount of capital gains tax to be paid by corporation		15,000	
			6,920	

Step 5.   Divide the amount arrived at in Step 4 by
the sum of the normal and surtax rates
applicable to ordinary corporations to
compute the amount of tax preference:
Amount of tax preference: 6,920 ÷ .48 =   14,416

D & L then computed the amount of minimum tax preferences as follows:
Amount of tax preference, above   14,416
Less: Greater of 10,000 or one-half the capital gains tax of
15,000   10,000
                                                                         4,416

Tax on tax preference items: 4,416 × 15% =   662

Between March 16, 19x9 and December 31, 19x9 D & L had paid cash dividends in the amount of $100,000. Since cash dividends exceeded taxable income it was necessary for D & L to compute CEP in order to charge an appropriate amount of the dividends to AEP, and also provide a basis for allocating the taxable portion of the dividend between ordinary income and taxable gains for purposes of reporting income to shareholders. D & L computed CEP for 19x9 as follows:

Taxable income   92,000
Add: Nontaxable bond interest income   5,000
Current earnings and profits   97,000

After computing CEP and determining the amount the company had to pay in capital gains tax and tax on tax preference items, D & L made the following entries to close its books. Prior to the closing, the balances in the income summary account and dividends paid account were as follows:

Profit and loss   Credit   95,000
Dividends paid   Debit   100,000

                                       Debit   Credit

1. Profit and Loss   15,662
   Income taxes payable   15,622
   To make provision for income taxes to be paid
   by the corporation.
2. Profit and Loss   79,338
   Accumulated earnings and profits   3,000
   Undistributed taxable income   76,338
   To allocate net income to appropriate stock-
   holders' equity accounts.
3. Accumulated Earnings and Profits   5,000
   Undistributed taxable income   76,338
   Previously taxed income   18,662
   Dividends paid   100,000
   To charge dividends to appropriate stock-
   holders' equity accounts.

At December 31, 19x9 the balance in D & L's stockholders's equity accounts were as follows:

Capital stock		500,000
Retained Earnings		
Accumulated earnings and profits	200,000	
Previously taxed income	31,338	231,338
		731,338

Schedule 2 is a summary of the operations of D & L Enterprises for the first two election years, and shows the effects on each shareholder's equity account resulting from income, income taxes paid by the corporation, and charges for cash dividend distributions.

D & L Enterprises
(A Subchapter S Corportation)
Summary of Income, Dividends Paid, and Changes in Stockholders' Equity Accounts
For Years 19x8 and 19x9

TRANSACTIONS	INCOME TAX DATA Computation of Taxable Income	Current Earnings and Profits (CEP)	GAAP Total Retained Earnings	SUBCHAPTER S STOCKHOLDERS' EQUITY Accumulated Earnings and Profits (AEP)	Undistributed Taxable Income (UTI)	Previously Taxed Income (PTI)	SUBCHAPTER S PTI SUBSIDIARY LEDGER Lewis	Davis
1/2/x8—Balance			200,000	200,000				
Year 19x8								
Net income	80,000		80,000					
Nontaxable interest	(5,000)	5,000		5,000				
Nondeductible expense	3,000			(3,000)				
Taxable income	78,000	78,000			78,000			
CEP		83,000						
			280,000	202,000	78,000	—		
Cash dividend paid			(28,000)		(28,000)			
12/31/x8—Balance			252,000	202,000	50,000	—		
Year 19x9								
3/15/x9								
Transfer UTI to PTI					(50,000)	50,000	25,000	25,000
			252,000	202,000	—	50,000	25,000	25,000
Net Income	79,338		79,338					
Nontaxable interest	(5,000)	5,000		5,000				
Nondeductible expense	2,000			(2,000)				
Tax on capital gains and preference items	15,662				(15,662)			
Taxable income	92,000	92,000			92,000			
CEP		97,000						
			331,338	205,000	76,338	50,000	25,000	25,000
Cash dividend paid			(100,000)	(5,000)	(76,338)	(18,662)	(9,331)	(9,331)
12/31/x9—Balance			231,338	200,000	—	31,338	15,669	15,669

SCHEDULE 2

ACCELERATED DEPRECIATION

The earnings and profits of a Subchapter S corporation in the tax year of a distribution are reduced for depreciation claimed on its tax return which is in excess of straight-line depreciation solely for the purpose of determining whether the distribution constitutes a distribution of PTI. Thus, where CEP exceeds taxable income due to this excess depreciation in a year in which the corporation makes a distribution in excess of taxable income, that excess will be considered a distribution of PTI to the extent that PTI exists on the books of the corporation. Consequently, the amount charged to PTI will not be taxable to the shareholders and will not reduce AEP.

If the distribution exceeds the sum of the PTI and taxable income in the year of distribution the excess will be considered a taxable dividend and charged to AEP.

ILLUSTRATION OF ACCOUNTING FOR THE EFFECTS OF EXCESS DEPRECIATION CLAIMED ON A SUBCHAPTER S TAX RETURN

Model Case No. 3 illustrates accounting for the allocation of income to stockholders' equity accounts in a situation where a Subchapter S corporation uses straight-line depreciation for accounting purposes and claims sum-of-the-digit depreciation for tax purposes.

MODEL CASE NO. 3

Whist & Company, Inc. is a Subchapter S corporation located near Deep Creek Lake in Maryland, and is engaged in the manufacture of sail boats. The State of Maryland recognizes federal Subchapter S status and consequently Whist & Company, Inc. is not subject to either state or federal income taxes at the corporate level. At December 31, 19x0 Whist had issued 3,000 shares of $100 par value common stock and William Coulter and J. A. Jameson each owned 1,500 shares, respectively. At that date the company had retained earnings of $240,000, classified for tax purposes as follows:

Accumulated earnings and profits		200,000
Previously Taxed Income		
Coulter	20,000	
Jameson	20,000	40,000
Total retained earnings		240,000

In 19x1 Whist purchased a planing machine, having an estimated useful life of three years, at a cost of $75,000. Whist decided to depreciate the machine over three years by the straight-line method for accounting purposes, and to claim tax depreciation over three years computed by the sum-of-the-digits method. Accordingly, Whist prepared a table of depreciation, computed under both methods, to be used as a guide for reporting depreciation for accounting and tax purposes, respectively, in each of the three years. Whist's computations are shown in Schedule 3.

19x1 OPERATIONS

In 19x1 Whist had net income of $100,000, but because of the accelerated depreciation for tax purposes, its taxable income was only $87,000. During the year Whist distributed $100,000 in cash dividends, which was $12,500 in excess of taxable income. Had the $12,500 difference between taxable income and net income not resulted from accelerated depreciation the CEP for the year would have been $100,000, and the total cash distribution would have constituted a taxable dividend: $12,500 charged to AEP and $87,500 charged to UTI. However, since Whist had a balance in its PTI at December 31, 19x1 the CEP is considered to be only $87,500 solely for the purpose of determining whether the corporation had distributed PTI in its cash distribution. In this case it is considered to have done so, and therefore $87,500 of the dividend was charged to UTI and $12,500 charged to PTI. The $12,500 charge to PTI constituted a tax-free distribution to the shareholders.

WHIST & COMPANY, INC.
Schedule of Depreciation—Planing Machine
Cost—$75,000—Useful Life—3 Years

| | For Accounting Purposes | | | For Income Tax Purposes | | | |
| | Straight-Line Method | | | Sum-of-the-Digits Method | | | |
Year	Depre-ciation Expense	Accum-ulated Depre-ciation	Net Book Value	Depre-ciation Expense	Accum-ulated Depre-ciation	Net Book Value	Pretax Income Over (Under) Taxable Income
19x1	25,000	25,000	50,000	37,500	37,500	37,500	12,500
19x2	25,000	50,000	25,000	25,000	62,500	12,500	—
19x3	25,000	75,000	—	12,500	75,000	—	(12,500)

SCHEDULE 3

19x2 OPERATIONS

In 19x2 Whist had net income of $120,000 and taxable income in the same amount since, in that year, the amount of financial accounting depreciation computed on a straight-line basis coincided with the amount computed by the sum-of-the-digits method for tax purposes. During the year Whist paid cash dividends of $150,000, which was $30,000 in excess of taxable income. The cash distribution was allocated as follows:

Undistributed taxable income	120,000
Previously taxed income	27,500
Accumulated earnings and profits	2,500
	150,000

The distributions charged to both UTI and AEP were fully taxable to the shareholders, while the amount charged to PTI constituted a tax-free distribution of income previously taxed to the recipients.

19x3 OPERATIONS

The net income of Whist in 19x3 amounted to $150,000, while the taxable income was $162,500. The difference of $12,500 was due to nondeductible depreciation reported on the statements that had already been taken for tax purposes. During the year Whist paid cash dividends in the amount of $175,000 and since PTI had been fully distributed in 19x2, the total cash dividend of $175,000 was taxable to the shareholders, and was charged on the books of the company as follows:

Undistributed taxable income	162,500
Accumulated earnings and profits	12,500
	175,000

A summary of the operations of Whist & Company, Inc. is shown on Schedule 4. The entries necessary to record the allocton of income, and charge distributions of dividends, as shown in the Schedule, are of the same type as those described in Model Cases 1 and 2, and therefore a description of such entries is not repeated in the present example.

WHIST & COMPANY, INC.

(A Subchapter S Corporation)

Summary of Income, Dividends Paid, Accelerated Depreciation, and Changes in Stockholders' Equity Accounts

For Years 19x1, 19x2, and 19x3

	INCOME TAX DATA		GAAP	SUBCHAPTER S STOCKHOLDERS' EQUITY					
TRANSACTIONS	Computation of Taxable Income	Current Earnings and Profits (CEP)	Total Retained Earnings	Accumulated Earnings and Profits (AEP)	Undistributed Taxable Income (UTI)	Previously Taxed Income (PTI)	SUBCHAPTER S PTI SUSIDIARY LEDGER	
							Coulter	Jameson
12/31/x0 — Balance			240,000	200,000	—	40,000	20,000	20,000
Year 19x1								
Net income	100,000	100,000	100,000					
Accelerated depreciation	(12,500)	(12,500)		12,500				
Taxable income	87,500				87,000			
CEP		87,500						
			340,000	212,500	87,500	40,000	20,000	20,000
Cash dividends paid			(100,000)		(87,500)	(12,500)	(6,250)	(6,250)
12/31x1 — Balance			240,000	212,500	—	27,500	13,750	13,750
Year 19x2								
Net income	120,000		120,000					
Taxable income	120,000				120,000			
CEP		120,000						
			360,000	212,500	120,000	27,500	13,750	13,750
Cash dividends paid			(150,000)	(2,500)	(120,000)	(27,500)	(13,750)	(13,750)
12/31/x2 — Balance			210,000	210,000	—	—	—	—
Year 19x3								
Net income	150,000	150,000	150,000					
Nonallowable depreciation	12,500	12,500		(12,500)				
Taxable income	162,500				162,500			
CEP		162,500						
			360,000	197,500	162,500	—	—	—
Cash dividends paid			(175,000)	(12,500)	(162,500)			
12/31/x3 — Balance			185,000	185,000	—	—	—	—

SCHEDULE 4

DISALLOWED BONUSES

An accrual method Subchapter S corporation is allowed a deduction for an accrued bonus payable to a cash-basis related taxpayer[2] only if the bonus is actually paid within two and one-half months after the close of the tax year. If the accrued bonus is not paid within that time it is disallowed as a tax deduction. This disallowance requires that UTI and CEP of the corporation for the preceding year be increased by the amount of the unpaid bonus, and the shareholder would have to include an equivalent amount in his gross income as a constructive dividend from the corporation for the year in which the disallowed bonus was accrued. However, since UTI of the preceding year is increased by the amount of the disallowed bonus but the amount of the increase is not distributed during the grace period, the actual effect of the disallowance is to increase PTI of the shareholder by the amount of the disallowed bonus and decrease AEP by the same amount. Payment of the accrued bonus after the two and one-half months following the close of the tax year would be a reduction in the corporation's cash and a reduction in its accrued bonus account. For the cash-basis shareholder, the bonus would have to be reported as income in the year in which it was received, but the equivalent amount in the taxpayer's UTI account would be a tax-free distribution whenever it was paid to him.

Model Case No. 4 illustrates the accounting procedures required to record the disallowance and subsequent payment of an accrued bonus to a cash-basis related shareholder.

REVERSAL OF THE ORDER OF CHARGING DIVIDENDS TO PREVIOUSLY TAXED INCOME ACCOUNTS

Regulations 1.1375-4(c) provides for an election, with the consent of all shareholders, to reverse the order of distribution of previously taxed income and accumulated earnings and profits. Thus, in any year where cash dividends exceed CEP, and the company has PTI on its books, the shareholders can elect to have the distribution charged to AEP that normally would be charged to PTI.

For any taxable year for which such election is made, a statement of election should be attached to a timely tax return on Form 1120S filed for such year. Such election applies to all distributions during the year which otherwise would be distributions of previously taxed income. An election applies only for the year for which it is made, but a new election may be made in any subsequent year.

Model Case No. 4 illustrates appropriate accounting procedures for allocating cash dividends under the special election provided in Regulations 1.1575-4(c), as outlined above.

MODEL CASE NO. 4

Latka Company is a Subchapter S corporation that has two shareholders and outstanding common stock in the amount of $1,000,000. Saul Riga owns 75% of the issued stock, and the remaining 25% is owned by David King. The company is located in a state that recognizes federal Subchapter S status, and therefore it is not subject to either state or federal income taxes. At December 31, 19x0 the company had total retained earnings of $500,000, which were carried in the following accounts:

---

[2] In general, a "related taxpayer" is an individual who owns more than 50% of the outstanding stock of the Subchapter S corporation.

Accumulated earnings and profits		400,00
Previously Taxed Income		
Saul Riga	75,000	
David King	25,000	100,000
		500,000

Results of operations, and allocation of earnings and dividends among the stockholders' equity accounts for the years 19x1 to 19x4 are outlined below. The company had no tax exempt income and no nondeductible expenses. Consequently, net income constituted taxable income for each year covered by the example.

19x1 OPERATIONS

In 19x1 the company had taxable income of $100,000. Included in tax deductible expenses for the year were accrued bonuses of $10,000 and $5,000 to Riga and King, respectively, both of whom were cash-basis taxpayers. During the year the company paid cash dividends of $100,000 and charged the payments to Dividends Paid. At December 31, 19x1 Latka made appropriate entries to allocate the $100,000 taxable income to UTI, and to charge that account with the $100,000 balance in the Dividends Paid account.

In March, 19x2, Latka paid the $5,000 accrued bonus to King but did not have sufficient cash to pay the $10,000 bonus to Riga prior to the 15th of the month. Therefore the deduction for Riga's bonus was disallowed, and an additional $10,000 was required to be reported by him as a constructive dividend. Latka then made the following entry:

	Debit	Credit
Accumulated earnings and profits	10,000	
Previously taxed income		10,000
To increase PTI of Saul Riga for		
19x1 UTI not distributed by March		
15, 19x2.		

On June 30, 19x2 the company paid Saul Riga the $10,000 bonus, and made the following entry:

	Debit	Credit
Accrued bonus payable	10,000	
Cash		10,000
To record payment of accrued bonus		
to Saul Riga.		

19x2 OPERATIONS

In 19x2 the company had taxable income of $160,000 for the year and paid cash dividends of $280,000 between March 16 and December 31 of that year. On December 31, 19x2 Latka made the following entries to allocate income and charge dividends to the appropriate stockholders' equity accounts:

		Debit	Credit
1.	Profit and Loss	160,000	
	Undistributed taxable income		160,000
	To transfer 19x2 taxable income to UTI.		
2.	Accumulated Earnings and Profits	10,000	
	Undistributed taxable income	160,000	
	Previously taxed income	110,000	
	Dividends paid		280,000
	To charge cash dividends to appropriate stockholders' equity accounts.		

After the above entries were posted, Latka had retained earnings of $380,000 which were reflected as a credit balance in the Accumulated Earnings and Profits account.

Saul Riga was required to report the following in his gross income for the calendar year 19x2:

Cash bonus paid in June (salary)	10,000
75% of distribution from Undistributed Taxable Income (75% × 160,000)	120,000
75% of distribution from Accumulated Earnings and Profits (75% × 10,000)	7,500
	137,500

Riga was not required to include any portion of PTI distribution of $85,000 in taxable income for 19x2.

19x3 OPERATIONS

Latka had taxable income of $200,000 in 19x3, and did not pay any dividends, either during the year 19x3 or in the grace period ending on March 15, 19x4. At December 31, 19x3 Latka made an entry transferring net income to UTI, and then on March 16, 19x4 it made another entry transferring the UTI to PTI.

At March 16, 19x4 the stockholders' equity accounts of Latka were as follows:

Capital stock			1,000,000
Retained Earnings			
Accumulated earnings and profits		380,000	
Previously Taxed Income			
Riga	150,000		
King	50,000	200,000	580,000
			1,580,000

19x4 OPERATIONS

In 19x4 Latka had taxable income of $180,000 and during the period from March 16 to December 31 of that year it paid cash dividends in the amount of $300,000 which were charged to the Dividends Paid account. Since taxable income and accounting income were equivalent in amount, CEP also coincided with taxable income. Thus, the normal distribution of the $300,000 dividend would have been to charge UTI with $180,000 to close out the amount of taxable income that had been transferred to that account, and to charge the remaining $120,000 against the $200,000 balance contained in the PTI account.

However, the shareholders of Latka resolved to make an election in accordance with Regulation 1.1375-4(c) to reverse the order of charging dividends to PTI. Accordingly, Latka filed an election statement with its tax return on Form 1120S, and at December 31, 19x4 made the following closing entries:

		Debit	Credit
1.	Profit and Loss	180,000	
	Undistributed taxable income		180,000
	To close taxable income into UTI.		
2.	Undistributed Taxable Income	180,000	
	Accumulated earnings and profits	120,000	
	Dividends paid		300,000
	To charge dividends to appropriate stockholders' equity accounts under Regulation 1.1375-4(c) election.		

At December 31, 19x4 Latka's stockholders' equity accounts were as follows:

Capital stock				1,000,000
Retained Earnings				
Accumulated earnings and profits		260,000		
Previously Taxed Income				
Riga	150,000			
King	50,000	200,000		460,000
				1,460,000

Schedule 5 is a summary of the operations of Latka Company for the years 19x1 through 19x4, and discloses the effect on stockholders' equity accounts of a disallowed bonus, and an election to reverse the order of distributing previously taxed income under Regulation 1.1375-4(c).

ACCOUNTING FOR TERMINATION OF ELECTION

It should behoove shareholders of a Subchapter S corporation to adopt a comprehensive tax plan prior to voluntarily revoking the tax option election. Generally, it is advisable to seek the advice of an attorney or CPA to insure that a minimum, if any, of the undistributed taxable income or previously taxed income existing at the date of termination will be lost as future nontaxable dividends to the shareholders. Aside from formulating a definite plan in contemplation of a deliberate revocation of the Subchapter S election, the officers of such corporations, as a matter of policy, should continually be alert to the possibility of an administrative termination by the IRS, and should retain professional guidance on an ongoing basis, either to avert such a contingency, or to be prepared if it occurs. For example, it should constantly be borne in mind that a termination by the IRS is effective as of the first day of the year in which occurs the event that generates the termination. Thus, any UTI on the books at the end of the prior year which was not distributed during the grace period has lost its potential as a future tax-free distribution.

LATKA COMPANY
(A Subchapter S Corporation)
Summary of Income, Dividends Paid, and Changes in Stockholders' Equity Accounts
For Years 19x1, 19x2, 19x3, and 19x4

	INCOME TAX DATA		GAAP	SUBCHAPTER S STOCKHOLDERS' EQUITY			SUBCHAPTER S PTI SUBSIDIARY LEDGER	
TRANSACTIONS	Computation of Taxable Income	Current Earnings and Profits (CEP)	Total Retained Earnings	Accumulated Earnings and Profits (AEP)	Undistributed Taxable Income (UTI)	Previously Taxed Income (PTI)	Riga	King
12/31/x0—Balance			500,000	400,000		100,000	75,000	25,000
Year 19x1								
Net income	100,000		100,000					
Taxable income		100,000			100,000			
			600,000	400,000	100,000	100,000	75,000	25,000
Cash dividends paid			(100,000)		(100,000)			
12/31/x1—Balance			500,000	400,000	—	100,000	75,000	25,000
Year 19x2								
3/16/x2								
Adjustment for bonus				(10,000)		10,000	10,000	
3/16/x2—Balance			500,000	390,000	—	110,000	85,000	25,000
Net income	160,000		160,000					
Taxable income		160,000			160,000			
			660,000	390,000	160,000	110,000	85,000	25,000
Cash dividend paid			(280,000)	(10,000)	(160,000)	(110,000)	(85,000)	(25,000)
12/31/x2—Balance			380,000	380,000	—	—	—	—
Year 19x3								
Net income	200,000		200,000					
Taxable income		200,000			200,000			
12/31/x3—Balance			580,000	380,000	200,000	—	—	—
Year 19x4								
3/16/x4								
Transfer UTI to PTI					(200,000)	200,000	150,000	50,000
3/16/x4—Balance			580,000	380,000	—	200,000	150,000	50,000
Net income	180,000		180,000					
Taxable income		180,000			180,000			
			760,000	380,000	180,000	200,000	150,000	50,000
Cash dividends paid*			(300,000)	(120,000)	(180,000)			
12/31/x4—Balance			460,000	260,000	—	200,000	150,000	50,000

*Regs. 1.1375-4(c) election.

SCHEDULE 5

The accounting procedures following termination of an election are not at all complicated. However, whether the termination is deliberate or involuntary, the accounting treatment of shareholders' equity accounts will depend entirely on the tax plan adopted and pursued.

At the end of the final election year, accumulated earnings and profits, and previously taxed income existing on the books should be transferred to a conventional retained earnings account. The undistributed taxable income at that date should remain in that account. Cash distributions made from UTI during the grace period of two and one-half months following the close of the final election year should be charged to the UTI account, since such distributions are nontaxable to shareholders. At the end of the grace period, any balance remaining in the UTI account should be transferred to the retained earnings account to which AEP and PTI had been transferred at the end of the prior tax year.

If a terminating Subchapter S corporation eliminated deferred income taxes from its books in its first election year, any significant portion of such deferred taxes should be reinstated if the timing differences which created the deferral have not completely reversed at the time of termination. The reinstatement should be made in the year following the termination, and should be charged or credited, as appropriate, to income for that year.

ILLUSTRATION OF ACCOUNTING FOR TERMINATION OF AN ELECTION

Model Case No. 5 illustrates accounting for accumulated earnings and profits and previously taxed income at the date of termination, and accounting procedures to record events following termination with respect to undistributed taxable income and deferred income taxes.

MODEL CASE NO. 5

Grayson & Company is a small business corporation that has two shareholders, James Jones and Robert Rose, each of whom owns 2,500 shares of $100 par value capital stock of the Corporation.

In December, 19x2 the company filed Form 2553 with the IRS, electing to be taxed under Subchapter S for the following year. At December 31, 19x2 the company had retained earnings of $50,000, and its books reflected a credit balance of $7,273 in a Deferred Income Tax Credits account. The deferred income tax credits had developed from accelerated depreciation taken for tax purposes on a $100,000 machine purchased in January, 19x1. Schedule 6 sets forth the timing differences, and their tax effect, over the life of the machine, resulting from computing depreciation expense by the straight-line method for accounting purposes, and using the sum-of-the-digits method for tax purposes.

On January 1, 19x3 Grayson made the following entry to transfer retained earnings to Accumulated Earnings and Profits, and to eliminate deferred income tax credits:

	Debit	Credit
Retained earnings	50,000	
Deferred income tax credits	7,273	
Accumulated earnings and profits		50,000
Income from elimination of deferred income		
tax credits		7,273
To set up AEP account to take deferred income tax credits into current income.		

19x3 OPERATIONS

In 19x3 the company had an operating profit of $100,000 and the Profit and Loss account reflected net income of $107,273 after crediting the deferred income taxes of $7,273 to current income. During the year the company paid cash dividends

GRAYSON & COMPANY
DEPRECIATION SCHEDULE AND DEFERRED INCOME TAX CREDITS

	Straight-Line Depreciation Schedule for Financial Accounting		Sum-of-the-Digits Depreciation Schedule for Tax Purposes		Timing Difference		Deferred Income Tax Credits	
	Expense	Book Value	Expense	Book Value	Current	Cumu-lative	Current	Cumu-lative
Cost		100,000		100,000				
19x1	10,000	90,000	18,182	81,818	8,182	8,182	4,091	4,091
19x2	10,000	80,000	16,364	65,454	6,364	14,546	3,182	7,273
19x3	10,000	70,000	14,545	50,909	4,545	19,091	2,272	9,545
19x4	10,000	60,000	12,727	38,182	2,727	21,818	1,364	10,909
19x5	10,000	50,000	10,909	27,273	909	22,727	454	11,363
19x6	10,000	40,000	9,091	18,182	(909)	21,818	(454)	10,909
19x7	10,000	30,000	7,273	10,909	(2,727)	19,091	(1,364)	9,545
19x8	10,000	20,000	5,455	5,454	(4,545)	14,546	(2,272)	7,273
19x9	10,000	10,000	3,636	1,818	(6,364)	8,182	(3,182)	4,091
19y0	10,000	—	1,818	—	(8,182)	—	(4,091)	—
	100,000		100,000		—		—	

SCHEDULE 6

amounting to $50,000, which it charged to a Dividends Paid account. Taxable income was computed as follows:

Net income, per book		107,273
Less: Accelerated depreciation (Schedule 6)	4,545	
Income from elimination of deferred income tax	7,273	11,818
Taxable income		95,455

Grayson made the following entries to close Profit and Loss Dividends Paid at December 31, 19x3:

	Debit	Credit
1. Profit and Loss	107,273	
Accumulated earnings and profits		11,818
Undistributed taxable income		95,455
To transfer net income to stockholders' equity accounts.		
2. Undistributed Taxable Income	50,000	
Dividends paid		50,000
To reduce UTI by amount of cash dividends paid during year.		

At December 31, 19x3 Grayson's stockholders' equity accounts were as follows:

Capital stock		500,000
Retained Earnings		
Accumulated earnings and profits	61,818	
Undistributed taxable income	45,455	107,273
		607,273

19x4 OPERATIONS

The cash position of the company during the first two and one-half months of 19x4 did not provide funds to make cash distribution of the UTI on the books at December 31, 19x3. Accordingly, on March 16, 19x4 Grayson made the following entry:

	Debit	Credit
Undistributed taxable income	45,455	
Previously taxed income		45,455
To transfer remaining 19x3 UTI to PTI.		

During the year 19x4 the company discerned enormous sales potential in its product and it resolved to seek additional shareholders and capital in order to expand its operations. Accordingly, in June, 19x4, Grayson filed a statement with the IRS revoking its tax option election effective the first of the following year.

Grayson's net income for 19x4 was $150,000, and during the period from March 16 to December 31 it paid cash dividends amounting to $100,000. Grayson computed its taxable income as follows:

Net income	150,000
Less: Accelerated depreciation	2,727
Taxable income	147,273

The company made the following entries to transfer the results of operations and cash dividends paid to its stockholders' equity accounts:

	Debit	Credit
1. Profit and Loss	150,000	
Accumulated earnings and profits		2,727
Undistributed taxable income		147,273
To transfer net income to stockholders' equity accounts.		
2. Undistributed Taxable Income	100,000	
Dividends paid		100,000
To charge cash dividends to UTI.		

After the books were closed on December 31, 19x4 the stockholders' equity accounts were as follows:

Capital stock		500,000
Retained Earnings		
Accumulated earnings and profits	64,545	
Undistributed taxable income	47,273	
Previously taxed income	45,455	157,273
		657,273

19x5 ADJUSTING ENTRIES

The company made the following entries on January 2, 19x5 to record the change in status at that date in the stockholders' equity accounts, and to reinstate unamortized deferred income tax credits:

	Debit	Credit
1. Accumulated Earnings and Profits	64,545	
Previously taxed income	45,455	
Retained earnings		110,000
To transfer AEP and PTI to retained earnings.		
2. Loss on Reinstating Deferred Income		
Tax Credits	10,909	
Deferred income tax credits		10,909
To reinstate unamortized deferred income tax credits (Schedule 6).		

The company could pay only $30,000 in cash dividends on March 15, 19x5, and accordingly, it made the following entry on that date:

	Debit	Credit
Undistributed taxable income	47,273	
Cash		30,000
Retained earnings		17,273
To charge cash dividends to UTI, and transfer remaining balance of UTI to retained earnings.		

Schedule 7 outlines the entries made to record the tax option election, the allocation of results of operations and dividends paid during 19x3 and 19x4, and the entries made in 19x5 to adjust the stockholders' equity accounts to accommodate the effects of the tax option revocation effective January 1, 19x5. (See page 342.)

ACCOUNTING FOR STOCK REDEMPTION AND LIQUIDATION

The Internal Revenue Code provides for a number of stock redemption procedures and full or partial liquidation plans, each with a specific proviso as to the taxable nature of the transaction. Generally, the same rules apply to Subchapter S corporations as to other corporations, but in some instances certain Subchapter S regulations may take precedence over the liquidation rules. In any event, the internal Revenue Service rules and regulations for stock redemptions and liquidations are complex and highly technical, and fraught with grave tax consequences to shareholders of Subchapter S corporations. Thus, redemptions and liquidations both require comprehensive tax planning, and such planning should be done with professional guidance from a tax attorney or CPA.

In the space alloted to this chapter it is not feasible to discuss the various tax alternatives available to Subchapter S corporations for redemptions and liquidations. However, once a redemption or liquidation plan has been organized, and its taxable nature fully determined, accounting for the redemption or liquidation transactions is relatively simple. Under such circumstances the procedures for accounting for Subchapter S special stockholders' equity accounts, as set forth in preceding sections of this chapter, should be adapted to the specific tax treatment of each phase of the redemption or liquidation process.

GRAYSON & COMPANY
(A Subchapter S Corporation)
Summary of Entries for Election, Operations, and Termination of Subchapter S Corporation
For Years 19x3 and 19x4

TRANSACTIONS	GENERAL LEDGER-ORDINARY CORPORATION		INCOME TAX DATA		SUBCHAPTER S STOCKHOLDERS' EQUITY			SUBCHAPTER S PTI SUBSIDIARY LEDGER	
	Retained Earnings	Deferred Income Taxed	Computation of Taxable Income	Current Earnings and Profits (CEP)	Accumulated Earnings and Profits (AEP)	Undistributed Taxable Income (UTI)	Previously Taxed Income (PTI)	Jones	Rose
12/31x2 — Balance	50,000	7,273							
Year 19x3									
1/1/x3									
Transfer of retained earnings to AEP	(50,000)				50,000				
Elimination of deferred taxes		(7,273)		7,273	7,273				
12/31/x3									
Operating income			100,000	100,000					
Excess depreciation			(4,545)		4,545				
Taxable income			95,455			95,455			
Net income (CEP)				107,273					
					61,818	95,455	—		
Cash dividends paid						(50,000)			
12/31/x3 — Balance	-0-	-0-			61,818	45,455	—		
Year 19x4									
3/16/x4									
Transfer UTI to PTI						(45,455)	45,455	22,728	22,727
3/16/x4 — Balance					61,818	—	45,455	22,728	22,727
Net income			150,000	150,000					
Excess depreciation			(2,727)		2,727				
Taxable income			147,273			147,273			
CEP				150,000					
					64,545	147,273	45,455	22,728	22,727
Cash dividends paid						(100,000)			
12/31/x4 — Balance					64,545	47,273	45,455	22,728	22,727
19x5 Adjustments									
Cash dividends paid						(30,000)			
Termination entries	127,273	10,909			(64,545)	(17,273)	(45,455)	(22,728)	(22,727)
3/15/x5 — Balance	127,273	10,909			-0-	-0-	-0-	-0-	-0-

SCHEDULE 7

FINANCIAL REPORTING FOR SUBCHAPTER S CORPORATIONS

There are no official accounting directives specifically designed to provide guidance for Subchapter S corporation operations. Thus, it must be assumed that reporting requirements under generally accepted accounting principles are precisely the same for Subchapter S as for other corporations. The elements of full disclosure required under generally accepted accounting principles that are peculiar to Subchapter S corporations are discussed in the following paragraphs.

GENERAL DISCLOSURE

It appears to the author that in order to avoid the possibility of misleading the users of Subchapter S corporation financial statements, all such statements, including the Notes, should show the tax option status of the corporation directly under the caption indicating the name of the company; for example,

JONES, HAMMERMAN & COMPANY, INC.
(A Subchapter S Corporation)

BALANCE SHEET

It is not necessary to classify retained earnings on the balance sheet in accordance with the taxable nature of the elements contained therein; it may be shown in total amount on one line in the statement, and captioned simply Retained Earnings. However, such classification is not prohibited as long as the caption for the total amount indicates that the classified accounts constitute *retained earnings,* as defined under generally accepted accounting principles.

INCOME STATEMENT

Subchapter S corporations operating in states that recognize federal Subchapter S status will not show a provision for income taxes on the income statement. The lack of such provision does not have to be explained on the statements, but an explanation thereon of the circumstances is not prohibited.

NOTES TO FINANCIAL STATEMENTS

Generally, notes to financial statements are the most important source of disclosure for Subchapter S corporations. The following information should be set forth fully in the Notes.

1. The company's election to be taxed under Subchapter S.
2. Detailed classification of the tax elements in the retained earnings account.
3. Income taxes that would have been paid had the tax option not been in effect.
4. The amount of deferred income taxes that would be reinstated on termination of the tax option election.
5. The amount of carryback and carryover of the following tax elements, as appropriate, should the election be terminated;
   > Net operating loss,
   > Investment credits,
   > Capital losses.

Since the shareholders are directly involved in the tax status of all elements in a Subchapter S corporation's financial statements, it is important that the Notes disclose to them certain information that would not necessarily be significant to other users of the statements.

The balance sheet, income statement, and statement of changes in financial position are presented for Subchapter S corporations in the same manner as for conventional corporations. Therefore, it is not necessary to display a format for such statements in this chapter.

However, the special disclosures required of Subchapter S corporations are illustrated in the following example, which consists of extracts from the Notes to Financial Statements of Suffolk Automotive Equipment Company at December 31, 19x6.

SUFFOLK AUTOMOTIVE EQUIPMENT COMPANY

(A Subchapter S Corporation)

NOTES TO FINANCIAL STATEMENTS

December 31, 19x6

SUMMARY OF SIGNIFICANT ACCOUNTING POLICIES

In 19x1 the company made an election not to be taxed as a corporation, as provided in IRC Chapter 1, Subchapter S, Sec. 1372(a), for the year 19x2, and all subsequent years. As a result the company is not subject to federal income tax at the corporate level, but the income and losses of the company are includable in the gross income of its shareholders. However, the State does not recognize federal Subchapter S status and, consequently, the company is not exempt from state income taxes.

* * * * * * * * * * *

Note 6—RETAINED EARNINGS

For federal income tax purposes, retained earnings consist of the following federal income tax elements:

	19x6	19x5
Accumulated Earnings and Profits	90,000	95,000
Previously Taxed Income	50,000	50,000
Undistributed Taxable Income	50,000	—
	190,000	145,000

The Undistributed Taxable Income of $50,000 existing at December 31, 19x6 was distributed in cash to shareholders on March 10, 19x7.

* * * * * * * * * * *

Note 8—INCOME TAXES

The company paid no federal income taxes for the years 19x6 and 19x5 because of its tax option status. Had the tax option not been in effect, federal income taxes would have been $12,000 and $10,000 for 19x6 and 19x5, respectively.

* * * * * * * * * * *

Note 10—TAX EFFECTS CONTINGENT UPON TERMINATION OF ELECTION

The company has no plans to voluntarily revoke its tax option election. However, the following tax effects would follow if the election were administratively terminated by the IRS effective January 1, 19x6.

1. Deferred income tax credits amounting to $85,000 would be reinstated and charged to income for the current year.
2. A net operating loss carryover of $74,000, representing losses sustained in the pre-election year 19x0, would be reinstated and would operate to reduce taxable income for 19x6.

* * * * * * * * * *

Index